Berlin
Culture and Metropolis

Berlin
Culture and Metropolis

Charles W. Haxthausen
and
Heidrun Suhr
Editors

University of Minnesota Press
Minncapolis and Oxford

The University of Minnesota Press gratefully
acknowledges assistance in the publication of this
book through the grant provided by the German
Academic Exchange Service, New York.

Published by the University of Minnesota Press
2037 University Avenue Southeast, Minneapolis, MN 55414.
Printed in the United States of America.

Library of Congress Cataloging-in-Publication Data

Berlin : culture and metropolis / Charles W. Haxthausen and Heidrun
    Suhr, editors.
        p.   cm.
    Includes index.
    ISBN 0-8166-1860-7 (alk. paper)
        1. Berlin (Germany) — Civilization.   I. Haxthausen, Charles
    Werner.   II. Suhr, Heidrun.
    DD866.B425   1991
    943.1'55 — dc20   90-49453
                                                                      CIP

A CIP catalog record for this book is available from the British
Library

The University of Minnesota
is an equal-opportunity
educator and employer.

Contents

v

Illustrations

Preface

In 1987, the city of Berlin, then still divided by a wall, celebrated the 750th anniversary of its founding. While both halves of the city remembered the event in their own fashions, emphasizing their particular ideologies and philosophies and in some ways competing with each other, this 750th anniversary became a cultural event of the first order. There were dozens of exhibitions, many citywide and others focusing on districts and neighborhoods; there were symposia, literary evenings, concerts, restoration projects — all designed to revive public consciousness of Berlin's history and culture. It was a major event of urban self-reflection.

The Berlin anniversary also was the impetus for two international, interdisciplinary conferences in North America: at the Université de Montréal and the University of Minnesota, Minneapolis, both in October 1987. The organizers of the Minneapolis conference, Charles W. Haxthausen, Heidrun Suhr, and myself, selected as the conference theme (and title) "Culture and Metropolis: Production and Reception of Culture and the Arts in Berlin, 1900 to the Present." The participants found that the interdisciplinary perspectives offered through the fifty-five papers presented by speakers representing a variety of disciplines greatly enriched their own understanding of Berlin and stimulated new approaches to questions about urban culture in general. Encouraged by the success of this undertaking, we, the conference organizers, have put together this volume of essays on twentieth-century cultural responses to Berlin, in the hope that it will be of interest to a broader readership.

Charles Haxthausen and Heidrun Suhr have edited the twelve essays in the present collection, and have shaped it, not as the usual "conference proceedings," but as a coherent compilation of contributions to the study of metropolitan culture, using Berlin in a paradigmatic sense. These essays have in most cases been substantially revised and significantly expanded beyond the papers presented at the conference.

The essay by Peter Jelavich is an expanded version of a paper presented in Montreal but not in Minneapolis, included here because of its appropriateness. We are grateful to the Woodrow Wilson International Center for Scholars, Washington, D. C., which holds the copyright on the essay, for permission to include it here.

While there was considerable enthusiasm for this publication, there were no funds to translate concept into reality until the German Academic Exchange Service (DAAD) generously offered its support. We are deeply grateful for their generosity, not only because it made the book's publication financially feasible, but also because it reflects a basic interest in a part of German studies that centers on the urban scene, one that is particularly conducive to interdisciplinary inquiry.

Thanks are also due to the Max Kade Foundation of New York for its financial assistance. The foundation is well known in the United States for its support of research and scholarship with a German focus.

We hope that the present volume will further the goal to which the Max Kade Foundation, the German Academic Exchange Service, and the contributors to this volume all subscribe: a critical and, therefore, better understanding of German culture, politics, and society in this century.

Gerhard Weiss

Introduction

Charles W. Haxthausen and Heidrun Suhr

> *There are cities that one can describe only insofar as one proceeds from
> what is common and typical in their origins, then there are others for
> which their peculiar determinants are more important. The former are
> almost always true capitals and centers of a country, are rich and beautiful
> cities, harmoniously developed organisms of history; the latter are, on the
> other hand, as a rule cities that had to develop artificially, under all kinds
> of difficulties, and had to adapt to unfavorable circumstances. If those of
> the first type resemble happy persons with nobly developed talents, the
> others resemble characters who let themselves be soured by life and,
> because of the hardships of existence they have endured, become surly and
> problematic.*
>
> *Berlin belongs to the cities of this latter type.*
>
> Karl Scheffler, Berlin: Ein Stadtschicksal

The purpose of this volume is not to document yet again Berlin's contribution to modern German and international culture. The theme "Culture and
Metropolis" is not intended as a celebration of Berlin as a cultural capital,
according to the *Wunschbild* of an "Athens on the Spree," or as the German
equivalent of Paris, London, or New York. Nor is this book intended as a
representative survey of Berlin's cultural history, although its twelve essays
touch nearly every decade of this century. Some of the cultural phenomena
treated here are little known outside the German-speaking world, and, conversely, this volume has little to say about some of Berlin's most celebrated
cultural personalities. These studies have another focus: the often uneasy relationship between twentieth-century Berlin and the culture produced
there—in literature, poetry, film, cabaret, and the visual arts. In short, they
explore the cultural mediation of a city in which such mediation has always
been problematic.

The novelist Georg Hermann once remarked that the relationship of
most Berliners to their city is an ambivalent one, "neither fish nor fowl:
they cannot do without it, but neither can they come to terms with it. And
least of all can they comprehend Berlin. Between the old and the new there
is no harmony, as there is in Paris. And no art knows how to span a bridge

across this gaping crevice." This statement vividly evokes the experience of living in Berlin today. It clearly applies to the city that was divided by a wall for twenty-eight years, and despite the rapid, dramatic, and unexpected changes set in motion on November 9, 1989, it is arguably still as hard to come to terms with Berlin as ever. Yes, the flow of traffic between the eastern and western halves of the city has been restored, and the *Zusammenwachsen*, or growing together, of the divided city has occurred at a pace exceeding the boldest predictions, but these historic developments have if anything only dramatized the disharmony, the abnormality, the incomprehensibility of Berlin.

The idiosyncratic character of this city might seem to be merely the most enduring, most palpable consequence of a war that ended nearly half a century ago, leaving a "gaping crevice" between past and present. Gazing at the ruins of the Anhalt Railway Station, or standing on the once hectic Potsdamer Platz, where the restored stream of traffic only exacerbates the emptiness of the surrounding grassy spaces, it is tempting to sentimentalize "lost Berlin," the rupture with the past is so painfully apparent here.[1] Blaming Hitler and the cold war for Berlin's present condition is of course partly justified, but the experience of discontinuity is not peculiar to postwar Berlin—Georg Hermann's observation on Berlin was not inspired by the city of today, but by the Berlin of 1912, and it could have been written at almost any time during the past two centuries.[2]

To idealize Berlin as if it had once been a German Paris or Vienna is profoundly to misunderstand its history and its unique ethos. The year before the *Machtergreifung* and more than a decade before the first Allied bombs rained down on the city, Siegfried Kracauer was already writing of Berlin's streets "without memory." This city, he wrote, seemed to have "a magical means of eradicating all memories. . . . Only in Berlin are the transformations of the past so radically stripped from memory."[3] In a book published the same year, Wilhelm Hausenstein described Berlin as seemingly a city without history, without origins, without foundation. "It is as if Berlin were built on nothing. . . . One feels no ground, and precisely this is the location of the city."[4] In Berlin the present overwhelmed the past, unrelenting change assaulted the sense of continuity and stability. For Carl Einstein, Berlin was a place "destined to dissolve and to overcome every tradition . . . and daily prepared for any change."[5] This characterization, dating from the Weimar era, has been resoundingly confirmed since November 9, 1989, but even before World War I, Karl Scheffler was saying the same thing: it was the tragic fate of Berlin "always to be in the process of becoming and never to be."[6]

Even before Berlin was transformed by Germany's political unification and late industrialization into a modern metropolis, there was considerable testimony concerning its otherness, its anomalous character among European cities. Early in the nineteenth century, when Berlin was still essentially a *Hof- und Residenzstadt*, Madame de Staël described it as a "quite modern city" seemingly without a past, in which one had "no sense of the history of the land or the character of its inhabitants." This might be fine for an American city, she conceded, "but in our ancient part of the world one has need of the past."[7]

In characterizations of the city, this trait of a relentlessly self-renewing modernity, unchecked by any ballast of tradition, is complemented by other qualities that seem to be equally part of the Berlin ethos. It has long been decried as an *artificial city*, configured by pecuniary or political ambition rather than by an urbane architectural vision, a city without organic relationship to the surrounding land. It has, at least since the immigration of 6,000 Huguenots in the seventeenth century, had an ethnically heterogeneous population—it has been a melting pot somewhat in the American fashion, and yet a capital whose population did not constitute a cross-section of the German nation. Berlin has also been noted for its hard-nosed practical-minded materialism and a caustic skepticism toward the lyrical and metaphysical.

Such observations have constituted a recurrent litany for over two centuries. From today's perspective, however, what earlier critics saw as anomalous about Berlin has made it, uniquely among European cities, a paradigm of modernity. If one accepts Marshall Berman's broad definition of modernism "as a struggle to make ourselves at home in a constantly changing world,"[8] then Berlin is and has been for more than a century the European capital of modernism.

Moreover, Berlin's history in the last hundred years is uniquely a microcosm of the major upheavals of the modern era. It has been successively an imperial capital, the site of violent political revolution, and the capital city of a fragile, ill-fated democracy and subsequently of the fascist Third Reich, after which it was reduced to rubble. Following the war it became a divided city, reflecting the major geopolitical division of the world. And even now, as the once rigid political blocs of the Cold War are breaking up, Berlin has been by far the European city most profoundly affected by this dramatic development. It appears that in the foreseeable future it will be uniquely a microcosm of a Europe in which "east" and "west" have again become primarily geographical designations. All of this makes the cultural response to Berlin a matter of more than parochial significance, and an issue that transcends the agenda of German studies.

Through all these changes Berlin has experienced another significant genesis. While it has retained its most characteristic traits through two centuries of continual transformation, the city's raison d'être has changed. First it evolved from a royal residence and garrison city to an industrial center whose primary business, to borrow Calvin Coolidge's famous phrase, was business. "Noisy, matter-of-fact Berlin," Walter Benjamin called it, "the city of work and the metropolis of business."[9] Then Hitler dreamed of re-making the city into a latter-day imperial Rome. After 1949 the eastern half of the city insistently presented itself as "Berlin, capital of the GDR," thereby seeking to underline its legitimacy and its continuity with the historical Berlin; but the western half of Berlin, geographically and demographically the larger of the two, developed into a city whose business was culture, not only through the creative activity that flourished there, but also through its festivals, theaters, and orchestras and its rapidly proliferating museums. At the end of the 1980s, the annual culture budget of West Berlin was over 550 million marks, well more than half the federal outlays for culture in the entire United States.[10] This statistic, however, must be interpreted in light of another: over half of West Berlin's income budget came from federal subsidies.[11] These two figures are intimately connected, for during the era of the wall, West Berlin's vibrant cultural life was no spontaneous flowering of the human spirit. However authentic its individual components, in its totality this was a cultural program that served political ends. As the wall became a seemingly permanent and accepted feature of Berlin life, culture became indispensable to the successful functioning of the city's life-support system. Otherwise, as Jane Kramer wrote, nothing was asked of West Berlin "beyond its own complicity in surviving." Hence, it could be said that for the western half of the city, "the real business of Berlin [was] Berlin."[12]

After the opening of the borders, however, West Berlin suddenly rediscovered business of a more conventional kind: it became a marketplace for the GDR. This glittering enclave of Western consumer culture soon proved to exacerbate the impatience of East Germans with the dream of a "third way" between capitalism and communism, a radical democratic socialism that would be a viable alternative to the social market economy of the Federal Republic. Those GDR citizens who remained sober in the face of West Berlin's seductions proved, by the beginning of 1990, to be in the minority. But whatever happens, Berlin has clearly entered a new era whose shape remains as yet uncertain, but which seems likely to restore the city's former status as a major European metropolis. It is today, perhaps more dramatically than ever, in that "process of becoming" that Scheffler saw as its fate among cities.

The abruptness of the drastic changes Berlin has undergone over the past century and a half has meant that the relationship between the city and its inhabitants has not evolved gradually, but has had to be repeatedly renegotiated with each generation. Culture has been both an agent and a product of these negotiations, and it is this function of culture that the present collection addresses.

The first four essays in this volume deal with early twentieth-century attempts to come to terms with the reality of a city that had undergone a rapid metamorphosis. In 1871 Berlin had become the capital of a united Germany, but prior to this it had begun a period of rapid growth as a consequence of industrialization, which had begun in the 1830s and subsequently attracted an ever-increasing flow of immigrants, mostly from the east. Between 1800 and 1900, Berlin's population increased from 170,000 to nearly 2 million; at the peak of the city's growth, between 1871 and 1919, the population of Greater Berlin quadrupled, from 915,000 to 3.7 million.[13] This phenomenal tempo of development and the surge of construction it generated made Berlin the most modern city in Europe—a decidedly mixed blessing.

John Czaplicka's essay, "Pictures of a City at Work, circa 1890–1933," examines selected images of Berlin as reflections of "how the city functioned, how precisely it was reconstituting itself" during this period of runaway growth, intense social flux, and industrial expansion. Central within this process was the subdivision of the city according to functions and social classes, and it is this phenomenon that is the primary focus of Czaplicka's essay. Drawing on specific works by Hans Baluschek, Franz Skarbina, Heinrich Zille, George Grosz, and Karl Hubbuch, Czaplicka examines how the visual signification of the functioning city in specific images both reflected and reinforced class consciousness. He sees the visual arts not as a passive mirror of the city as it was configured by other discourses, but as an active contributor to the conceptualization and interpretation of urban experience.

Lothar Müller's essay, "The Beauty of the Metropolis: Toward an Aesthetic Urbanism in Turn-of-the-Century Berlin," examines the critique of modern Berlin as the "Capital of all modern ugliness," the "Chicago on the Spree," and the attempt to develop an aestheticized relationship to this urban reality, so offensive to the cultivated eye. In 1908 August Endell, the Jugendstil designer and architect,[14] published a book, *Die Schönheit der großen Stadt* (The beauty of the metropolis), which constituted a pioneering effort to redeem the uncongenial urban landscape of Berlin as a domain conducive to aesthetic experience. Endell's book introduced into German discourse on the city the Parisian concept of the *flâneur*.[15] For Endell, however, the aesthetic experience of Berlin did not arise from a discovery of aesthetic virtue in the architecture, alternately drearily prosaic and eclectically pompous, which made any comparison to the more established European capitals an embarrassment. Rather, the beauty Endell discovered in Berlin could, Müller explains, "peacefully co-exist with the architectural ugliness and shapelessness" of the city, for it was a beauty centered not in the object but in the *mode of seeing*, in a cultivated responsiveness to the fugitive charms of accidental tableaux. These were born of the interaction of the artificial and the natural, by the transfiguration of the ugly, graceless cityscape by the intervention of nature, by light, and by atmosphere—creating a beauty that took form in the eyes of the aesthetically sensitized *flâneur*.

In this manner, Endell approached the city with the emergent formalist aesthetic articulated by the Munich sculptor Adolf von Hildebrand in his highly influential book *Das Problem der Form in der bildenden Kunst.* There Hildebrand wrote that in the visual arts the "true poetic effect" arises from "the manner of seeing," from how the object is transfigured by representation, not in any significance that it may have in itself.[16] However, Endell's manner of seeing, of representing the city to himself and to his readers, was shaped by French impressionism, a late import to Germany, a movement that had itself discovered modern, Haussmannized Paris as subject matter in the 1860s and 1870s. There is irony in the fact that Endell offered an impressionistic verbal painting of Berlin that found no equivalent among the city's best impressionist artists—Liebermann, Corinth, and Slevogt. At the peak of their careers in these years, they shunned the urban landscape of the city in which they lived and worked.

It was left to the expressionist generation, in both literature and art, to embrace the city passionately, if no less ambivalently, and to exalt its very artificiality. Georg Hermann, no expressionist himself, spoke for this new sensibility when he declared that "this strange phenomenon the metropolis stands outside of all laws known to the earth. . . . All the laws of space, the laws of light of the countryside—of the plain as well as the mountains, of the forest and even of the villages—are violated here."[17]

In general, for the Berlin expressionist artists and writers, their relationship to the city was a tortured love-hate affair. There was an intensification of feeling toward the city; that "blasé indifference" that Georg Simmel thought necessary for the mental balance of the urbanite was shed as a stultifying bourgeois defense. Now the extremes of Berlin were celebrated in a liberation of feeling and instinct. For the avant-garde the city, widely viewed from the provinces as the "Whore Babylon," became an ally in the attack on bourgeois values.[18] Yet, for the first time there also appeared an overtly apocalyptic tone in the verbal and visual images of Berlin: verses such as Georg Heym's "Umbra vitae" and Jakob van Hoddis's "Weltende" are classic poetic examples, as are the painter Ludwig Meidner's frenzied apocalyptic cityscapes of 1913. This foreboding aspect, however, has perhaps been overemphasized, leading many commentators to caricature and oversimplify the relationship of the expressionist generation to Berlin as a wholly negative one.

In his essay, Charles W. Haxthausen reexamines the Berlin imagery of Ernst Ludwig Kirchner, who during the Weimar era came to be viewed as *the* painter of prewar Berlin, as the artist who more than any other found an effective plastic expression for the daily life of the capital. Since World War II, however, Kirchner's images of the city have increasingly come to be viewed as images of urban alienation and anxiety. Haxthausen, returning to the source material, reaffirms the original critical view of Kirchner as a celebrant of the city, who discovered within its hectic flux and saturation of the senses a manifestation of vitalist energies and the basis of a new aesthetic.

The largest component of Kirchner's Berlin imagery consists of subjects drawn from popular culture—the circus, revues, and variety shows—subject matter that was largely new to German art. For this reason, Peter Jelavich's essay on vaudeville, cabaret, and revue in Berlin forms an interesting complement to Haxthausen's, for Jelavich shows that these modern, popular art forms were themselves important to Berliners as representations, as mediations, of the modern city they inhabited. Such entertainments, he argues, contributed to the molding of an urban identity for an expanding immigrant population. "In the face of a large body of literature (and not merely 'provincial' literature) condemning the 'German Chicago,' " writes Jelavich, these shows exhorted Berliners "to be proud of their modernity." The very form of the revue, with its short acts and abrupt contrasts, was seen as especially suited to the altered urban psyche: "The fragmentation and intensification of sense experience in everyday metropolitan life transformed the perceptual apparatus of modern urbanites to such an extent that they were no longer capable of the type of continuous reflection demanded by conventional drama. Stage presentations thus had to become as multiform and disjunct as the presentation of everyday life in the streets, the shops and the offices of the modern metropolis."

After Germany's defeat in the war, the tone of these entertainments changed: instead of celebrating Berlin's modernity, the shows were now permeated with nostalgia for prewar Berlin, when they dealt with the city at all. And where modernity was celebrated, the United States rather than contemporary Berlin was its paradigm.

Beth Lewis's essay examines the artistic appropriation of a darker side of popular culture, the theme of sexual violence, which had enjoyed enormous popularity in the dime novels of the Wilhelmine era and which during the war and its aftermath became, for the first time, a common subject in the visual arts. If Holofernes and John the Baptist were the victims of sexual violence in the symbolist art of the *fin de siècle*, the tables were now turned: artists such as George Grosz and Otto Dix seemed to exact revenge; the theme of the femme fatale, Lewis writes, gave way to the *Lustmord* or sex murder. George Grosz, a native Berliner and an avid reader of this literary *colportage*, was the first German visual artist to focus on this type of urban theme. Here, Grosz offers an interesting contrast with prewar attempts to view the city aesthetically. Adopting the posture that the very concept of art was an invention of the hated bourgeoisie, Grosz made no attempt to aestheticize the city as had Kirchner and Endell. For him its ugliness was not merely visual, but above all moral. Although Kirchner's eroticism bordered on the kinky, it manifested an innocent, quasi-religious belief in sexual instinct as inherently good—a kind of redemption would ostensibly come from its liberation and fulfillment. For Grosz, sexuality again became linked with vice and with brutality, with the darkest, most sordid human impulses. And if Kirchner celebrated the public Berlin—the streets and popular entertainments—Grosz, in his *Lustmord* images, at least, presented a brutal exposé of the horrors that went on behind closed doors in the metropolis. One of the ironies of this is that, in spite of his radical political position of those years, Grosz's vision of urban depravity coincided with the view of the reactionary "völkisch" elements that would triumph in 1933.

The essays by Harald Jähner and David Frisby are concerned with the literary responses to Berlin by two of the major German writers of the Weimar Republic—Alfred Döblin and Siegfried Kracauer. Döblin's *Berlin Alexanderplatz* (1929) is the most celebrated *Großstadtroman*, or big city novel, in German literature. Because of its formal innovation and its subject matter—it traces the odyssey of its protagonist, Franz Biberkopf, through contemporary Berlin—it has been compared to Joyce's *Ulysses*, published seven years earlier. In Harald Jähner's essay, "The City as Megaphone in Alfred Döblin's *Berlin Alexanderplatz*," we encounter once more a brutal and alienating Berlin—the city functions as the antagonist of Franz Biberkopf, just released from prison in the northern suburb of Tegel. But the root of this antagonism is here not presented as a flaw of the "dehumanizing" city but of Biberkopf himself, who persists in clinging to a mode of subjectivity, to an illusion of personal autonomy that the city has rendered anachronistic. Similarly, as Jähner formulates it, Döblin felt that "the city had so profoundly altered the relationship of individuals to their environment and to the apparatus of their own consciousness that it was no longer possible to write about its inhabitants in classical narrative forms." Accordingly, Döblin mixed conventional narrative with montage. Line (narration, or the movements and actions of Biberkopf) penetrates plane (a montage of disparate depersonalized texts out of which the city is constructed, making it, as Jähner evocatively characterizes it, "a speaking fabric of texts"). These two devices represent the mutually antagonistic principles of textual construction in the novel.

Siegfried Kracauer, the subject of David Frisby's essay, belongs in an altogether different category from Döblin. Best known in this country for his classic study of early German film, *From Caligari to Hitler*, Kracauer served as Berlin review editor of the *Frankfurter Zeitung* from 1930 to 1933, and much of his writing on the city was originally published on its *Feuilleton* page. He approached his task as a critical one: to decipher the deeper social reality behind the city's epiphenomena, to deconstruct urban experience—or, as Frisby puts it, "to reveal what lies beneath the surface of the world taken for granted." There is much in this enterprise that is reminiscent of

Benjamin's writings on Paris. Yet, if Kracauer's characterization of the fugitive character of Berlin's modernity continues a tradition of urban discourse, the nature of his view of the city is a product of Weimar Berlin. There is here a greater concern with the inner workings of the city; this is an attempt to *understand* Berlin rather than merely to represent or aestheticize its distinctive brand of urban experience.

During the New York fiscal crisis of the 1970s Ronald Reagan, not yet president, reportedly expressed his opposition to federal bail-out proposals with the remark that "true Americans *don't* love New York." This opposition between patriotism and *gesundes Volksempfinden* (wholesome popular sentiment) on the one hand and the "decadent" cosmopolitan culture of the metropolis on the other was a favorite theme of the Nazis. In her essay, Linda Schulte-Sasse explores the fascinating subject of the treatment of Berlin in Nazi films. Initially, the city was often dealt with retrospectively, serving as a metaphor for the negative memories of the Weimar Republic—communism, capitalism, fragmentation, moral decadence, the subversion of national identity and German tradition through internationalism. The importance of Berlin in early Nazi films, Schulte-Sasse explains, lay in its function as a corrupted *Heimat* of the past, which needed to be retrieved, restored to its proper status as the heart of "Germany"—a redemption that could be achieved only by forces that had remained incorruptibly German. If the films made before 1940 tended to deal with Berlin retrospectively, culminating in the triumph of National Socialism, those made after 1940 usually presented the city as a locus of German *Gemeinschaft*, or community, thus illustrating a boast made by Joseph Goebbels: "In barely ten years we have succeeded in making of this, the reddest city in the world after Moscow, a *truly German city*."[19]

After 1945, Berlin remained a uniquely German city, although hardly in the way that Goebbels meant. Berlin became a conspicuous scar of German history. Far from being a city that eradicated memories, as Kracauer described it in the last days of the Weimar Republic, the Berlin of the postwar era compelled remembrance. Harald Hartung's essay, "Lyric Poetry in Berlin since 1961," addresses the evolving but always tense relationship between lyric poetry and this obtrusive political reality. The year 1961 marked, of course, the erection of the wall, which consolidated, with concrete and barbed wire, the political division of the city. "To be sure," Hartung states, "the erection of the wall . . . has nothing to do with lyric poetry, yet in a special way it brought to a head the problem of writing poems, of writing poems in this city. . . . Lyric poetry in Berlin is different from lyric poetry in Munich, Cologne, Heidelberg, or in the Bavarian Forest." Now it was no longer Berlin's modernity and urban complexity that challenged the poet's powers of representation, but its unique political status. It was a reality that colored the simplest experiences, altered one's sense of space and, at times, called into question the value, the legitimacy even, of the lyric enterprise. Completed shortly before the opening of the wall, Hartung's essay can be valued as a survey of lyric poetry in a period that has since come to an end.

Dorothy Rosenberg's essay also addresses literature in Berlin during the era of the wall, not the insular city in the west, but the one that remained a capital, "Berlin, capital of the German Democratic Republic." Rosenberg argues that for Westerners, "the cultural history of the city tends to follow a relatively straight line of development and then suddenly shifts to a cultural history of its western half," reflecting an assumption "that there is no postwar cultural history in its eastern half." Her essay is an antidote to this cultural myopia: she surveys the representation of the city in recent East German fiction, in the works of Christa Wolf, Günter Kunert, Ulrich Plenzdorf, Helga Schubert, and others. Rosenberg is concerned both with the experience of East Berlin as reflected in that literature and with the perception of the city on "the other side," which from the perspective of the East was not an island but, in Helga Schubert's inspired conceit, "the forbidden room."

As was pointed out earlier, Berlin has for centuries attracted large numbers of *Fremde*, outsiders either from the provinces or from foreign countries, who have immigrated there and settled, or have stayed for shorter periods. Most have come in search of economic well-being, but significant numbers have come for political freedom, for artistic and intellectual stimulation, or in quest of a freer and more adventurous style of living. This pattern has not changed. By the mid-1980s, approximately 250,000 of West Berlin's 2 million inhabitants were foreigners, not to mention the large numbers who have moved there from West Germany. If this sounds American, the analogy was not lost on commentators on Berlin: Suhr quotes Herwarth Walden's remark, "Berlin is America as microcosm," and she also takes a critical look at this metaphor, which concealed important differences. After briefly surveying the patterns of immigration to Berlin, Suhr examines two current genres of writing relating to the experience of *Fremde* in Berlin: literature by foreign nationals, mostly Turkish writers, about their experience and that of the *Gastarbeiter* ("guest workers"); and literature — the often trendy so-called *Szeneliteratur* — which deals with West Germans who forsake the provinces to partake of the "Berlin scene." Although these two categories of literature are written from vastly different sociological perspectives and present radically different experiences of the city, to a striking degree both revolve around a single district of Berlin — Kreuzberg. This district, where the first neighborhoods designed to house the urban poor were built, is today the site of a "Turkish ghetto," a "little Istanbul," and is also the center of Berlin's "alternative culture" — an alternative culture that is nurtured in part by the city's generous federal subsidies.

Our volume concludes with an essay by Gerhard Weiss on yet another form of urban representation, the festivals commemorating Berlin's anniversaries. Cultural festivals have themselves become a contemporary art form, a form of mediation and representation. As Weiss observes: "Anniversary celebrations tend to have their own agendas, for which history simply offers a convenient forum. They become happenings that reflect, amplify, and popularize the ideologies dominant in a society at a given time." Although Berlin has existed for 750 years, it has only twice marked the anniversary of its founding: in 1937, when the celebration became a "Nazi festival"; and in 1987, when it was celebrated on both sides of the wall, with two discrete festivals. Weiss's account of the 1937 celebration is interesting to read in relation to Linda Schulte-Sasse's essay on the image of Berlin in Nazi film, in which the city had been the focus of most of the evils Nazism was supposed to cure. The message of the 1937 celebration was that Berlin had become Nazified: It was the "capital of the Third Reich, . . . aware of its German-Aryan heritage and of its Prussian military tradition. Its history had been reinterpreted to fit the National Socialist mold."

For the 1987 celebration, early efforts at cooperation between the two halves of the city broke down. Each half had its own agenda: for East Berlin, the festival became a means by which the German Democratic Republic could assert its legitimacy by stressing East Berlin's role as a capital, and therefore as the locus of historical continuity, a message to which the massive architectural restorations of recent years lent support. In West Berlin, on the other hand, the stress was on such issues as the city's internationalism, the Jewish contribution to Berlin's history and culture, and of course, the continuity of West Berlin's culture with that of the city's past.

In the divided festival that marked its 750th anniversary, Berlin, without intending to, remained true to the origins that it celebrated. "From the beginning," Karl Scheffler wrote in 1910, "Berlin has been a victim of its dualism."[20] However, the dualism Scheffler was referring to was the dualism of the medieval nuclei of the present city, Berlin and Cölln. Despite their proximity, for most of their history until 1709, there had been two cities and two administrations. "The cities were at once divided and bound together in all things."[21] Now, what was unthinkable in 1987 appears, less than three years later, to be imminent: Berlin will again become a single city, under a single administration. But it is likely to remain as problematic, as much the insistent, intrusive protagonist in the cultural artifacts produced there as ever.

February 1990

NOTES

1. The phrase served as the title of a book that exemplifies this cliché: *Lost Berlin*, by Susanne Everett (Chicago, 1979). Even had there been no World War II, Hitler's plans for Berlin would have left little of the central city's physiognomy intact. With the blackest irony he commented to Albert Speer, as they surveyed the damage inflicted by British bombers in 1944, "For our new building plans you would have had to demolish 80,000 houses in Berlin alone. Sadly the British have not carried it out exactly according to your plans. But nevertheless it's a beginning!" Quoted from *Mythos Berlin — Wahrnehmungsgeschichte einer industriellen Metropole*, ed. Ulrich Baer (Berlin, 1984), 92.

2. Georg Hermann, "Um Berlin," *Pan* 2 (22 August 1912): 1101–2.

3. Siegfried Kracauer, "Wiederholung," *Frankfurter Zeitung*, 29 May 1932, quoted from David Frisby's essay in this volume, 157.

4. Wilhelm Hausenstein, *Europäische Hauptstädte* (Erlenbach-Zurich, 1932), 372–73.

5. Quoted from Eckhart Gillen, "Provinz/Metropole," in *Die Metropole: Industriekultur in Berlin im 20. Jahrhundert*, ed. Jochen Boberg, Tilman Fichter, and Eckhart Gillen (Munich, 1986), 6.

6. Scheffler, *Berlin: Ein Stadtschicksal*, 2d ed. (Berlin, 1910), 267.

7. Germaine de Staël, *Über Deutschland* (1810), quoted from Baer, *Mythos Berlin*, 74.

8. Marshall Berman, *All That Is Solid Melts into Air: The Experience of Modernity* (London, 1988), 6.

9. Walter Benjamin, "Berlin Chronicle," in *Reflections: Essays, Aphorisms, Autobiographical Writings*, ed. Peter Demetz (New York, 1979), 28.

10. See Jane Kramer, "Letter from Europe," *The New Yorker*, 28 November 1988, 70.

11. In 1983, subsidies from Bonn totaled 10.5 billion marks, 53 percent of the city's income budget for the year. (Figures taken from a publication of the Informationszentrum Berlin: *Berlin im Überblick*, text by Udo Wetzlaugk and Christian Koziol [Berlin, 1985], 75.)

12. Kramer, "Letter from Europe," 69–70.

13. In 1800 Berlin had a population of 172,122, including 25,221 military personnel. By 1849, in its second decade of industrialization, the population had reached 412,154. This figure had exactly doubled twenty-two years later, when Berlin became the capital city of the new German Reich, with 825,937 inhabitants. By 1895 — twenty-five years later — its population had more than doubled again, to 1.7 million. A decade later, the population was 2,040,148. After that, because of an exhausted housing supply, the population of the city proper began to level off, and the expansion shifted to the *Vororte*, the surrounding communities. Between 1871 and 1919, the total population of Greater Berlin grew by a rate of 402 percent. See Wolfgang Ribbe, ed., *Geschichte Berlins* (Munich, 1987) 1:413; 2:661, 693–99.

14. Although he was prolific as a designer, Endell is best known for a single work, his ornamental frieze for the facade of the Elvira Photographic Studio in Munich (1897–98), one of the most extravagant and imaginative products of the Jugendstil aesthetic. For an illustration, see Robert Schmutzler, *Art Nouveau* (New York, 1962), fig. 199.

15. Jules Laforgue had commented in 1887: "The German, even the Berliner, is no flâneur." See Laforgue, *Berlin: Der Hof und die Stadt*, 2d ed. (Frankfurt/Main, 1981), 70. Laforgue's book was first published in French in 1887.

16. Adolf von Hildebrand, *Kunsttheoretische Schriften: Das Problem der Form in der bildenden Kunst*, 10th ed. (Baden-Baden, 1961), quoted from foreword to the 3d ed. (1903), 6–7.

17. Hermann, "Um Berlin" (see note 2), 1103.

18. See Hanne Bergius, "Berlin als Hure Babylon," in Boberg, Fichter, and Gillen, *Die Metropole* (see note 5), 102–19.

19. From Goebbels's speech at the 700th anniversary celebration of 1937, quoted from Baer, *Mythos Berlin* (see note 1), 92.

20. Scheffler, *Berlin, Ein Stadtschicksal* (see note 6), 52.
21. Ibid., 53.

Berlin
Culture and Metropolis

CHAPTER 1

Pictures of a City at Work, Berlin, circa 1890–1930: Visual Reflections on Social Structures and Technology in the Modern Urban Construct

John Czaplicka

In the discourse on the constitution of the modern *Großstadt*, or big city, that took place in late nineteenth- and early twentieth-century Germany, critics usually praised or reviled the city, viewing it as an agent of change that would either destroy German culture and debase the German people or promote the social and technological advance of civilization. Though sociologists, philosophers, and historians such as Ferdinand Tönnies, Max Weber, Georg Simmel, and Oswald Spengler described Berlin with quite different emphases and biases, each of them drew a picture of how the city functioned, how precisely it was reconstituting itself, and each took a political or moral stance toward the effects of this functioning and reconstitution. These discussants of urban transformation recognized new patterns emerging in the social, economic, and political relationships, and they saw that as a result of these changes the city was taking on a new gestalt. Accordingly, they tended to view the city as a system contingent on the modernizing forces of social, economic, and technological change.

  To a degree, one can propose that recognition of the city as a functioning system generated a discourse that extended to its pictorial imagery as well. This recognition led certain artists to configure Berlin not only in terms of its appearance, but also in terms of its workings, while it led others to devise ways to obscure the workings of the city. In the following analyses of selected Berlin images from the late Wilhelmine and early Weimar periods, my main concern is the pictorial configuration of this city as a functioning system with regard to its social and technological components. I also suggest the artists' active engagement in the contemporary discourse about the constitution of the modern city, and at least cursorily delineate their posi-

For Tadashi and Reiko

3

tions in regard to major issues such as social and technological progress. I discuss only those Berlin artists who subscribed to a naturalistic portrayal of those urban workings, but delved beneath the naturalistic surfaces to the concepts and abstractions that seemed to govern the particular imaging of the modern big city.

I begin by discussing an allegorical and anecdotal work by Hans Baluschek, to demonstrate the concepts underlying his "staging" of an urban scene. I concentrate then on paintings by Franz Skarbina, raising questions about how the image of the functioning city was determined by social class and by attitudes toward social and technological progress. In a third section, "The Rhythm of Man's Work," I look at several artists who represent the compulsive patterns of modern urban functioning. Finally, I examine a work by *Neue Sachlichkeit* artist Karl Hubbuch: a view of Berlin that reveals the contradictions and effects of that modern city at work.

1. Staging an Urban Allegory circa 1900:
The Functional Signs in Place

Circa 1900 Hans Baluschek (1870–1935), an artist who had earned the titles of "proletarian painter" and "painter of poor people" for his "naturalistic" representation of urban life,[1] composed an allegory of modern working-class life entitled *Berlin Landscape* (figure 1). In this unassuming cityscape Baluschek arranges some telling if still standard city props around a lone urban denizen making her way through the streets of Berlin. Using a montagelike method similar to one employed by several other late Wilhelmine and early Weimar artists,[2] Baluschek constructs an urban environment from a few set pieces that, in their arrangement and relationships, manifest the artist's broader understanding of the functioning city and its operative signs and signals. This understanding enables the artist effectively to combine those signs with a more conventional iconography drawn from landscape painting in order to compose a compelling picture of proletarian existence in Berlin. It is an image that goes beyond the merely anecdotal.

To characterize the appropriate milieu for his working-class figure, Baluschek sets the mood with subdued color and light, blue undertones—visible where the artist has scratched away the surface—earth colors, and the reflections from wet pavement. The dark, dank, enclosed space of the city contrasts with a clearing sky after a downpour. Color, light, and the atmospheric conditions temper the setting, suggesting the emotional disposition of its sole occupant. This mood and the signal props that Baluschek employs characterize and configure the generic image of a big, modern, industrial city while typifying certain highly industrialized working-class districts

Figure 1. Hans Baluschek. Berlin Landscape, c. 1900. Mixed media on cardboard, 96 x 63 cm. Bröhan Museum, Berlin.

of Berlin such as Wedding, Neukölln, Kreuzberg, Moabit, or parts of
Schöneberg, where Baluschek himself lived. For as is often the case with the
artist's Berlin imagery, while the specific location is left indeterminate, the
character of a specific type of district in Berlin is evoked.

Taking careful inventory of the scenic elements selected by the artist, the
attentive beholder notes an exemplary "one of each" in the composition. In
the left foreground a wooden barrier hung with a red warning sign closes
off a street under construction; sand lies on the ground beside it. These temporary props convey the constant transformation within Berlin during this
period, suggesting a *process* of modernization.[3] A gas lantern on the curb
next to the street, no longer modern in a city lighted in part by electricity
(but maintained for its economy of operation), was a fixture of the less prosperous areas of the German capital. The arched red-brick viaducts together
with the iron-and-glass station of the Berliner Municipal Railway (*Stadtbahn*) landmarked certain areas of the central city. The more immediate
proximity of such stations to tenements (*Mietskasernen*) forms an iconographic constellation of mass housing and mass transportation that typified
the modern metropolis. By inserting a proportionally smaller figure into
this urban staging, Baluschek projects a human story that appears contingent upon a particular urban milieu. But, before interpreting this relationship that allegorizes the fate and purpose of an individual who stands as em-
blematic for a class, a structural reading of the artist's urban construct can
offer insight into how he conceived the city in terms of its larger functioning.

Baluschek's image evinces a typical state for most big and modern cities:
every square meter of the urban surface is shown fenced-in and parceled-
off—i. e., taken possession of. This partitioned surface is further subdivided
by the arteries of road and rail and by the walkways of pedestrians. With an
eye to these divisions and away from any of the symbolic or allegorical
meanings, reference need be made to a central aspect of cities in general,
their compartmentalization. For the compartmentalization of the city estab-
lishes frames of reference for the interpretation of its various signs. Exemplified lucidly in Baluschek's painting are the multifarious urban enclosures
demarcated along functional and property lines. The street separated from
the sidewalk by a curb conducts wagons; the sidewalk, pedestrians; trains
run along the elevated tracks supported by a viaduct that allows for under-
passage. The firewall that closes off the background thoroughly hinders the
spread of fires, and the fence dividing the lot not only demarcates property,
it also reserves and protects this parcel of remnant nature. The signature of
laws, ordinances, and deeds is evident in this setting. This is a view of the
city often given in *Heimatbücher*[4] of the nineteenth century, a view meant to
inform the German burgher about the modern and highly systematized
functioning of the city.[5]

Each of the functional compartments demarcated in the cityscape has a set of distinct signs related to a relatively closed system of communications. A red lantern warns vehicular traffic of danger. The sign on the fence may prohibit the entry of pedestrians; the movable signal high on the tracks directs commuter trains. By pairing such artificial signs with those found in nature, Baluschek seems to draw an analogy between reading the cityscape and reading the landscape. The flowers on the tree signify spring, and the clouds in the sky warn of rain or tell of its passing. The signs of the city, of course, belong specifically to its nature, which is maintained in a systematic and smooth functioning. From a broader perspective Baluschek appears to have conceived his urban construct as a system of such signs operative in their distinct functional contexts. One reads this city of functions. One heeds its signs. *semiotics*

Beginning with the woman, the tree, and the *Mietskasernen* aligned in the center of the image, a second, more speculative and allegorical reading of the image presents little difficulty. In an enclave between the viaduct, the sidewalk, and the tenement, a remnant of nature in this landscape remains inaccessible to the urban denizen whose movements are guided by fence and railing. Clothed modestly in a blue apron over her plain dark dress, with a peaked hat adorned by a single red blossom, this working-class woman blends into her environment socially and chromatically (i.e., through corresponding blue undertones in her apron, in the back court of the tenement, and in various other places throughout the image). Only the red of the flowers in the wreath she holds sets her apart and has a symbolic function.

The red blossoms arranged in a wreath to honor the dead have a vital counterpart in the blossoming of a chestnut tree in the spring. Correlating the colors of the wreath and the warning lantern, one might surmise that the woman is on the way to a demonstration. Given the season, the reds of a working woman free from work, and taking into account Baluschek's Social Democratic inclinations, one might suppose this landscape represents a first of May, and that the season and the raised semaphore signaling free passage are meant to imply progress. The season and the urban condition are meant to be understood in a state of transition, one motivated by political and technological change. Whether or not one agrees with this particular reading, Baluschek's urban composite does cross signs to suggest a relationship between the working class, the modern structure of the city, and technological and political progress while implying the artist's own commitment to them.

In modern fashion, this image conceives the city as a pattern of operative signs, as a heterogeneous field of communication. Traditionally, it appropriates the modern signs from the more strictly functional urban gestalt to construct an allegory and to tell an anecdote. Within this complex construct, Baluschek correlates the social situation with the forces of technological and political progress. These forces of modernization were thematized in an urban imagery that had a part in the larger discourse about the city at the turn of the century in Germany.

2. Perspectives on the Forces of Change in a City at Work

> Kaum will das erste, matte Tageslicht
> Mit seinem Strahl die Gegend rings erhellen,
> Da stehn sie schon bereit zu ihrer Pflicht,
> Der harten Arbeit rüstige Gesellen;
> Es gilt in Reih', geordnet Schicht auf Schicht,
> Heut' schwere Felsenquadern aufzustellen
> Am hohen Damm, wo unten auf den Schienen
> Die Dampfkraft keucht, dem Menschengeist zu dienen.
>
> Jakob Audorf[6]

Jacob Audorf's poetic image of dawn in a modern urban environment at the end of the nineteenth century admits two contrary perspectives on the industrial city current in Wilhelmine Germany. Reinforced by the rhyme and rhythm of the verse, the transition from night to day coincides with the beginning of a new shift to imply a temporal consonance between the movements of nature and those of the laborers. First light finds dutiful workers well-ordered and ready to execute their tasks high above a backdrop colored by the "panting power of steam." The workers, though integrated rhythmically into the modern urban pattern, are set off dramatically against a modern and animate technology. Seen together these phenomena offer a syncretic image of a city working, one whose near and far serve to frame an important aporia in the contemporary discourse about the city in turn-of-the-century Germany.

For though the power of advanced technology appears here to serve the spirit of humanity, masses of people are yet pictured engaged in a routine of hard physical labor. The instrument of humanity, modern technology, figures against humanity's own instrumentalization in the urban construct.[7] Humans act mechanically[8] and the machines appear animate; this configures an image that evaluates those two phenomena most responsible for restructuring the nineteenth-century city. It was this evaluation of new technology and mass labor in an industrial situation that was central to contemporary debates about modernity and progress in Germany.[9] In such debates during the late nineteenth and early twentieth centuries, these constitutive elements were sometimes pitted one against the other and sometimes coordinated as two complementary aspects of progress (as in the Berlin cityscape by Balus-chek described earlier).

Liberal bourgeois praise engendered by pride in the advance of civiliza-tion through modern technology was countered by a reproach conditioned by a view of people massed, caught, and debased in the compulsions of an urban-industrial system;[10] or, depending on whether reform or revolution was on the agenda, a socialist might have bet either on those volatile masses gathered in the industrial city, seeing them as means to social and political progress, or on the new technologies, viewing them as a means to better the worker's material condition. Suspicious of both the technological and social formulations of progress,[11] conservative critics such as Wilhelm Heinrich Riehl and Oswald Spengler would oppose progress by any means, associ-ating it with the decline of traditional cultural and moral values and the eventual debasement of humankind. For these critics the locus of such de-cline and debasement was the modern industrial city,[12] where the effects of the forces of progress were most apparent. In the context of these debates about progress and decline, one reconfigured the image of the city.

In painting and graphic art of Berlin in the second half of the nineteenth century such refiguration began to supplant the traditional *vedute* and the simple urban genre scene. These conventional modes of urban representa-tion composed an image of the city either in grand and beautiful vistas dis-playing historical and monumental-representative edifices,[13] or in quaint domestic interiors and street scenes populated by artisans and street callers.[14] One pictorial tradition projected a city in grandiloquent facades and vast public spaces, giving expression to civic pride and projecting the presence of great beauty, wealth, and power as well as a long history. This form of pictorial praise often served to affirm the urban status quo. The other pictorial tradition, the urban genre image, tended to reduce the city to an aggregate of private spaces or city interiors that espoused a myth of eter-nal return to a preindustrial state, in which the city had offered refuge to the "community" of its inhabitants. By the end of the nineteenth century this retrospective image was simply one of nostalgic longing and an implicit protest against modernity.

In contrast to these conventions of pictorial praise and nostalgia, the more modern images of the city began to attend to patterns of its current constitution and functioning. This was perhaps most clearly—if partially and tendentiously—expressed with the metaphors of the giant capitalist, the Herculean proletarian, and the steaming locomotive,[15] those modern icons of exploitation or social and technological progress found in the political caricatures and illustrations scattered through German magazines and news-papers of the late nineteenth and early twentieth centuries. The proletarian, the capitalist, and the locomotive embodied the modern forces with a role in the city's functioning and in the establishment of a modern urban-industrial system.

Formally, that which corresponded to these more symbolic figurations of modern urban workings was the nonfigurative projection of a new urban gestalt. This type of imagery tended toward abstraction as it responded to the larger patterns of the functioning city and dealt less with its individual monumental-representative structures, with anecdotal views of its human population, or even with the particular signs and signals indigenous to the modern, functioning city. One might understand this imagery as one corresponding more closely to a changing conceptualization of the city that is no longer simply an object, no longer merely a collection of buildings and people, but an integral system whose functioning is governed by abstract laws and abstracting forces such as money and commercialization.[16] The new and more abstract image of the city shines through the allegorical and topical aspects of Baluschek's cityscape to reveal functional divisions of the urban surface or, in the poem by Audorf, a rhythmic and temporal pattern of work apparently underlies the pictures of men at work and trains passing. And these images already begin to reconfigure the city as a system and to frame questions about the nature of men at work in that system, about its social composition, and about the city's modern reconstitution as a system under the banners of technological and social progress.

Through an exacting interpretation of the urban-industrial nocturne, *Railways in the North of Berlin* (figure 2), by Berlin Secessionist and academy professor Franz Skarbina (1895), one may relate traditional pictorial genres and contemporary artistic styles to propositions concerning the role of social class in the functioning of a modern city. The style of the painting evinces the influence of both the contemporary German *Naturalismus*[17] and an impressionistic tonalism that may be attributed to various international influences. In its eclectic style and its choice of subject, it is an uncertain and, for the artist, peculiar picture, which relates two perspectives of the industrial city: the city near at hand as the milieu of the worker and the city distant and "landscaped" by the formative powers of industry and new technology.[18] Interpreted with regard to contemporary discussions about the constitution of the modern city, this dichotomy would seem to respond to divergent ideological positions taken toward the processes of modernization in turn-of-the-century Germany and even seems to suggest partial views of the city as experienced by different classes.

Somewhere in the industrial north of Berlin on the elevation of a bridge or platform of the *Ringbahn*,[19] a proletarian couple makes its way above an extensive industrial plain of rail lines and passing trains.[20] This cityscape, blanketed in a murky monochrome of blue-black tones, is illuminated by artificial lights that cluster in the distance like stars to delineate the horizon. Darkness, vacuity in the homogeneity of color and tones, the vastness of the

Figure 2. Franz Skarbina. Railways in the North of Berlin, *1895. Tempera on paper, 72 x 91 cm. Berlin Museum.*

industrial plain, and the solitude of the foreground couple crossing high above that expanse render the setting sublime.[21] In a manner reminiscent of Whistler,[22] the painterly effects of artificial light and atmospheric veils of smoke and steam articulate that setting in a way that lends it color and drama, making it into a spectacle.

Beyond the sober ironwork railing that abruptly separates near and far, a gasometer and smokestacks—the conventional icons of industry—loom large, pitch black, but barely discernible; before them freight and commuter trains trace their routes in light while emitting smoke and steam that unify the surface of the painting and signify a city technologically advanced and at work. In the glow of artificial illumination and behind the veils of active industry, the physical presence of the city almost dissolves in a guise meant to evoke mood and perhaps to connote "naturalness." This dissolution in the painterly effects, which suggests energy being expended and gives the time of day, transforms the city from a disparate sum of structural details into a moody, atmospheric scene that simulates landscape.[23] It was in Wilhelmine Germany that the modern city first became *bildwürdig*, worthy of representation; it was viewed as a landscape and seen for the spectacle it presents.[24] And it is in this pictorial guise, a *Stimmungsbild*[25] consistent with a turn-of-the-century aesthetic, that the technologically and industrially modern city is first projected as an object of artistic appreciation and contemplation.

In Skarbina's painting, what transgresses the simply appreciative gaze and intrudes on the contemplative point of view are two figures crossing from right to left. They are proletarian types drawn from districts of Berlin that were seldom visited, rarely represented, and only vaguely charted in the illustrated newspapers and magazines or other popular media; for the life in such districts existed only on the margins of the larger public consciousness.[26] To those curious about and foreign to this "other" Berlin, contemporary guidebooks recommended a tour on the *Ringbahn*, the commuter railway that girded the inner city.[27] For from that elevated train one had a view that allowed the visitor to keep one's distance while taking in the sights. Essentially, Skarbina offers us the same perspective, except that by introducing those who work this landscape he shifts the focus from the distant object, from an aesthetically pleasing and auratic city, to the workaday experience of those whose motions were inscribed into the surface of the city and who were a part of its functioning. The manners and motions of this proletarian couple define the subliminal and evocative cityscape, objectify it in a way that makes it less an indefinite space open to subjective projection.

The drably clothed railroad yardman and his well-bundled wife tread their way to or from work. Sullied snow lines their route, adding a seasonal note to a routine dramatized by atmospheric effects of smoke and steam, the conventional pictorial signs of an active industrial city. Trudging bent-shouldered down an asphalt path and along an iron railing that runs strictly parallel to the picture plane, the couple ignores the urban panorama and does not see the available spectacle of the cityscape below. In passing across the picture plane they appear very much the urban nomads later decried by Oswald Spengler as the rootless denizens of the big city.[28] The movement of these modern urban types is calibrated by the intervals in the railing beside them and channeled between the edge of the walkway and line of the horizon. They are profiled against and contained within an industrial setting that is their place of work. Their execution in broken contours, loose brush strokes, and earth colors blend them into that workscape and make them appear indigenous to it, inseparable from it. Only a sideward glance by the woman suggests any other awareness and separation from the routines of urban and industrial time and place.

Her look askance catches the beholder's eye and is reinforced by the orthogonals of the railway marking the cityscape beyond, which, though leading into the distance, almost seem to converge in the working woman's head. Thus the viewer's gaze, though open to the distant cityscape, is at once engaged and refocused on the proximate. From this composition cleaved into near and far, a tension arises between proletarian genre — or naturalism, as it is sometimes called — and the contemporary tendency to aestheticize the city, to dramatize its work, and effectively to propagate its modernity. At the point of intersection between these two disparate perspectives lies humankind at work and the workings of the city.

Skarbina's pendant painting of 1901, *View of the Seine and Paris at Night* (figure 3), shows a well-heeled holiday couple viewing the illumination of Paris and provides a telling contrast to his depiction of proletarian gyrations in the north of Berlin. The couple in the Paris painting lean at ease against a sturdy marble balustrade, looking from a building near the Eiffel Tower on the Quai Branly and toward the Trocadéro and the World Exposition of 1900. They engage themselves with things distant and appreciate the spectacle of the Parisian night. They fix their gaze and span their attention in seeing. Thoroughly aware of their surroundings and detached from the city in their position and pose, fascination marks their regard, directed toward an aestheticized and landscaped city.[29] There is a cleft of consciousness between this holiday pair and Skarbina's proletarians, one evident in their different bearing, in their affectations. The presence of proletarians following their workaday routine and subsumed instrumentally in the city opposes that disinterested and disengaged appreciation of the nocturnal beauty of the metropolis. Each distinct type of urban experience results from predispositions of the beholders.

For that disinvolved and appreciative gaze there are prerequisites. First, there is the factor of time, a question of whether one is or is not subject to the temporal patterns of the functioning city. For an aesthetic perspective presupposes disengagement from the uniform and measured flow of public time in the urban system.[30] Second, to gain a perspective from which to fix and observe that environment demands a distancing that cannot be achieved by one engaged instrumentally in its functioning. Disengagement and distancing are prerogatives of the privileged gaze, a gaze contingent largely on social class. Subject to the functioning city, the workers appear part of it and remain indigenous in and subject to it. Theirs is not the gaze that surveys the city out of time and removed, leisurely and disinterestedly partaking of its beauty as if it were a natural and subliminal landscape.[31] Referring to such parameters of time and distance, one can simply map out those experiential paradigms proposed by Skarbina's paintings. One paradigm, seen in the relationship of the workers to the city, suggests a practical and realistic viewpoint, which is set against the experience of the beholder whose view of the city is more aesthetic and romantic. Both viewpoints suggest a degree of alienation conditioned by, on one hand, a more purely functional relationship to the city and, on the other, a more purely aesthetic one.

Figure 3. Franz Skarbina. View of the Seine and Paris at Night, *1901. Oil on canvas, 92 x 62.5 cm. Berlin Museum.*

In granting the beholder distance and evoking a mood, Skarbina invites him or her to project subjectively. That distance, which is separation and absence, composes an image perhaps of yearning, and certainly one meant to cause reverie or stir the imagination. Distant and separated from the viewer, the object of contemplation assumes an aura, the aura of that of which one cannot avail oneself. This auratic city is one of the imagination and for the imagination. For such visible indistinction in the imaging of the city invites not so much reason as the imagination to configure the city in the mind.

Such evocative views are called *Stimmungsbilder* in German; they are images of mood or paintings of disposition. They call forth the subjective disposition of the beholder and activate the imagination. The city pictured in this manner suggests a strategy for subjectively overcoming objective circumstance; it also suggests a comprehension of the modern urban complex in its great expanse, complexity, and heterogeneity through an empathetic seeing. The experience of place—and experience is the key concept here—is more emotional than rational. One might say it is as if *ratio* had not yet learned to comprehend the city or accept it when it is represented only as mood evoking. The totally subjective premise suggests that the city can in its complexity, heterogeneity, and expanse be reduced to a mood of the beholder.

Such reduction is to impermanence. The constancy and concreteness of the object are denied both in the transitory condition of the atmosphere and in the subjective response of the beholder; the city-object is literally dematerialized in its effects. In *Stimmungsbilder* the identity of the particular place is secondary. There is a loss of topicality and a lack of emphasis on the monumental facades and the relationship of the city to its setting, which had been the focus of urban view painting. Those traditional paintings (*vedute*) were souvenirs that also indicated and reminded the beholder of the actual hierarchy of power within the city, and they generally transcribed place to lend it a certain significance. In the *Stimmungsbild*, signification of place is decidedly subordinate to evocation of atmosphere. Pictorial effect takes precedence over material, objective, or historical presence. The historical, bound to particular place and time, is subsumed in the painterly representation of changing seasons, weather, and time of day, so that the history of human accomplishment and picture of human labor and its products is subverted by the immutable cycles of natural history and by the daily transitions in the quality of light and conditions of the atmosphere. The effects of artificial light and of energy, smoke, and steam (i.e., of the city's functioning) are pictured blended into this *natural* spectacle, or as a simulation of it, so as to appear indistinct in nature. There is a subtle denial of the city as artifice, a making natural of the city's functioning, and a subtle relinquishing of humanity's responsibility for having made this environment.

In such projections of the urban spectacle and landscape, the subjective predominates in a way that reminds us of those landscaped vistas the German romantics veiled in fog or rain, or colored in the changing hues of dawn or dusk. And in their composition these two Skarbina urban views seem to refer particularly to the *Söllerbilder* of the German romantics, which presented the city or a landscape from an elevated viewpoint, a promontory, balcony, bridge, or tower. Such paintings by Carl Gustav Carus or Caspar David Friedrich[32] composed a similar view of near and far without abridging middle ground; they were also paintings of mood, depending on what Carus called *Luftschleier*[33] for their effect. Given this, it is not surprising to find Skarbina's contemporary, the architect August Endell, referring exactly to these "atmospheric veils," or *Luftschleier*, in his book, *Die Schönheit der großen Stadt* (1908); he even proposed such pictorial means as a way to redeem the city from ugliness.[34] In his book Endell recommends specific times of the day and especially dawn, dusk, or the night for seeing the city.

> If the day produces a thousand colorful veils, the night does more. If the star-filled sky and the moon hardly ever shine fully in the city, artificial light still compensates in its endless play of hues. Twilight already brings this light into play. One is delighted by the glimmering blue street under the fading rose sky in the chiaroscuro that mutes color as the long rows of greenish gaslights emerge. At first these are hardly visible, they form colored points, and finally with a life of their own they emerge brightly in sinking darkness.[35]

He proposed the effects of *artificial* illumination on the surface of the city not merely as a simulation of natural light, but as an extension of it.

Referring to this play of light elsewhere in the text, Endell writes: "[It is] a picture of the most delicate charm, completely 'unnatural,' but still Nature, and above all beauty."[36] "But still Nature" is the relevant phrase; for Endell sees the big city as Nature, and furthermore as landscape. This nature lies, as he writes, in the power of the artist's imagination to naturalize and to beautify the city by seeing it as one sees nature—the forest, the mountains, and the sea. The solution to the seeming paradox of "unnatural" Nature lies then in the *seeing*, in the willed assumption of the point of view and an empathetic projection of self into the object perceived. This strategy for redeeming the urban-industrial complex for aesthetic appreciation managed to coalesce its disjunct "fragments of modernity"[37] into a single picture that could serve as an image of praise as well as one of fascination. Considering that until this time the "city beautiful" had been largely one of grand and impressive monuments or one situated advantageously *in* the landscape, Endell's aesthetic of effects, which proposed no hierarchy of subject matter, had the advantage of including all aspects of the city's modernity in the canon of painting.

There are many questions to ask about this strategy of aestheticizing and naturalizing the modern urban construct. What did this reconstitution of the modern city in the language of romantic landscape painting mean? Why did it coincide with a revival of the fortunes of the *Großbürgertum* after a longer recession in the 1890s? Was it merely the adaptation of fashionable stylistic elements taken from the vocabularies of impressionist and tonalist painting? Certain intent can be seen simply in the project of making the modern city worthy of depiction and finding a pictorial manner to appraise its modernity. Another reason lies in the attempt to be contemporary in subject as well as style. Still, it seems one is always seeing the city as an "other" place in such paintings. There is a will not to be taken up in but to see oneself apart from the city and to hold it distant in the fixed and intent gaze. Although a certain avoidance of the new physical and material structure of the city is indicated, which suggests a discrepancy between style and motif, still in this style—which might be called a new romanticism—the modern city was for the first time consistently represented in German painting. And with this style the dissolution of the urban surface and the kinetic involved in the play of forces across that surface was first vividly suggested.[38]

There is, of course, the purely painterly aspect affecting this choice of style, in that the homogeneity of tones and color lends unity to the surface of a variegated motif. And the facile employment of color to suggest the new hues of gas and electric lights (preferably on wet pavement) became the urban artist's touchstone for a demonstration of skill in the representation of the modern, artificial environment; critic after critic would, for example, praise Skarbina and his contemporaries for their skills in rendering the hues called forth by artificial illumination.[39]

Finally, this type of urban imagery provided a vehicle for the expression of the psychological. Its emphasis on sense impressions, emotional states, and radically personal viewpoint subordinated the subject of the city more and more to what one might call an "urban state of mind." Thus in this style the image of the city seemed to become increasingly dependent on the personal urban experience of the artist, a turn of mind that prefigures the expressionist city. There was an opposite side to this more subjective vision of the city that is also evident in Skarbina's painting of the north of Berlin.

3. The Rhythm of Man's Work

Skarbina foregrounds the landscaped and naturalized city presented in his *Railways* (figure 2) with a "going to work" that typified the modern metropolis in its separation of place of work from place of habitation. This pictorial referent points toward the rationalized work process geared to mass production, industrial work schedules, and the division of labor that had begun to condition such daily peregrinations of the working population in the nineteenth century. The surface of the modern city was structured more and more to accommodate this process and those ordered motions until the city took on the aspect of an urban system.[40] And the rhythmic movements of energy, people, and goods within this structured superficies (the so-called tides of the city[41]) were recognized and well described by observers of the urban phenomena such as Skarbina's contemporary Karl Buecher.[42] This evident organization of the urban-industrial complex had its pictorial precedent in representations of factory interiors early in the nineteenth century; but only in the mid-1890s did modern patterning in the structure and workings of the city affect the urban imagery of German artists, photographers, and illustrators.

Similar patterning of structure and movement is, for instance, evident in a photograph taken by the artist Heinrich Zille, circa 1902 (figure 4).[43] Three workers are shown proceeding with a measured stride on the sidewalk along a wooden fence and before a row of tenements. "On the way to work," that everyday urban motion, would even seem the subject of this photograph, for though viewed from a pedestrian perspective and up close, the photograph does not suggest the workers' individuality. On the contrary, with their backs turned, clothed uniformly, and coordinated in their motion they more closely resemble that modern and anonymous genre type, "the worker" or "the proletarian," who bore individuality neither in person nor in profession. This modern urban-industrial type, whose image in Berlin derives from certain *Volkstypen*[44] associated with the city, appeared without the attributes of a particular trade, uniformed in simple clothing, and often grouped in masses. His appearance is impersonal and interchangeable. As the working- and lower-class inhabitant of cities, this more generic type succeeded the collections of individual types—of artisans and street vendors[45]—who had represented the big city populace in pictorial and literary compendiums during the first half of the nineteenth century. According to political persuasion, this contemporary type was rendered to embody the debilitating circumstance of people in the modern and industrial city (social Darwinism) or, conversely, the prospective vanguard of social progress (socialism and Marxism). Either the agent of change or its victim, this worker was identified as the "native" of the city.

In reviewing the painting and the photograph one notes that neither Skarbina nor Zille chose to cast the worker in the potential revolutionary role.[46] The heroic gesture that other contemporary artists like Steinlen or Meunier lent their workers is absent, as is the potent massing.[47] Their naturalistic figures have little relation to the classic proletarian Hercules or banner carriers set against and dominating an industrial-urban skyline in the socialist iconography of progress. Their workers conform to the ebb and flow of the modern industrial city and appear caught at a moment of transience between home and place of work. It is exactly this elemental transience, called rootlessness by some, that would pose an apparent threat

Figure 4. Heinrich Zille. Workers on the Way Home, Charlottenburg, Sophie-Charlotten-Straße, *ca. 1902. Photograph, 9 x 12 cm. Landesbildstille Berlin.*

to the conservative critics of the city; and this transience coupled with the massing of the working classes that would also inspire Marx and Engels to coin the metaphors of the "giant proletariat" and "grand machinery" to suggest the potential of this unbound social force.[48] That metaphor of the machine, however, was ambivalent in its connotations, for it suggests both organization and control.

Hans Baluschek, George Grosz, Karl Holtz, Hugo Krayn, Franz M. Jansen, Ludwig Meidner, Otto Nagel, Karl Völker, and other artists who worked in Berlin during the period 1890–1920 would variously configure this machinery of the modern city. They described either the disciplined coming and going to work or the uprisings of those masses and the many shades of meaning in between. Hans Baluschek, influenced by literary naturalism and the politics of the Social Democratic Party, would confront the viewer with the working-class types pouring out of factories and mass transportation into the city and out of the picture frame. However, this confrontation would, for the most part, be mitigated by the exhausted faces of the *types* or even *stereotypes* composing a working-class crowd. The worn and weary faces and a child here or there were meant to elicit the beholder's sympathy for the condition of the working classes.[49] These pitiable proletarian crowds took no strident pose and exhibited little unity. They were unified only in their common channeling and containment by the evident structures of the urban surface. Baluschek did not lend his working-class crowds the motive force of the masses that was so evident in graphic series such as Käthe Kollwitz's *Bauernkrieg* (1903–8) or her graphic cycle *Ein Weber Aufstand* (1893). Baluschek's configuration appeared more conformative than formative in its gestalt. Their conformity was with the functioning city.[50]

Contrasting with this imagery of the well-disciplined urban masses and their consummate integration into the urban system was the imagery of the unruly and revolutionary masses whose motions through the city were pictured as disruptive of the reigning authority and the urban system itself. At least since Alfred Rethel's presentation of the Revolution of 1848, showing an unruly citizenship behind the barricade confronting an advancing phalanx of soldiers, such images were conventional for representing violent social and political confrontation within the city.[51] Order and disorder in the city is projected with regard to social classes, for besides having their distinct ways of experiencing the city, each class would be pictured with a distinct gestalt and manner of moving through the city. Caricatures appearing in satirical magazines such as *Simplicissimus* and *Kladderadatsch* provide a rudimentary guide to these forms of movement. "Der—Die—Das," a caricature by Bruno Paul that appeared in 1898 in *Simplicissimus* (figure 5), draws satirical distinctions between the mob (politically active, but disordered rioting workers), the crowd (observant bystanders of various classes behind a police cordon), and the people (a representative view of the urban oligarchy in Berlin), thereby delimiting the radius of activities allotted to various social groups within Wilhelmine society. In each of the three

Der Pöbel

Die Menge

Das Volk

Figure 5. Bruno Paul. "Der—Die—Das" (subscript: Der Pöbel/ Die Menge/ Das Volk). Caricature from Simplicissimus, *8 May 1897.*

Suum cuique

Der Kaiser hat angeordnet, daß an schönen Tagen am Hippodrom im Berliner Tiergarten frühmorgens eine Militärkapelle spielen soll, um die zahlreichen Tiergartenreiter bei ihrem Morgenritt zu unterhalten.

Wie verlautet, soll der Gedanke, auch die zahlreichen Arbeiter auf ihrem Morgenspaziergang zur Arbeit durch Militärkonzerte zu unterhalten, vorderhand nicht zur Ausführung gelangen.

Figure 6. Erich Schilling. "Suum cuique" (subscript: The Kaiser has decreed that on beautiful days a military band should play early in the morning at the Hippodrome in the Berlin Tiergarten, so as to entertain the numerous horseback riders in the Tiergarten during their morning ride./ As stated, the proposal to accompany the numerous workers on their morning walk to work with military concerts will not be implemented). Caricature in Simplicissimus, *22 May 1911.*

Figure 7. Karl Holtz. Workers' Demonstration, *ca. 1930. Lithograph, 31.5 x 48.3 cm. Museum der bildenden Künste, Leipzig.*

vignettes, figures of authority are present to guide the unruly populace, which is denied access to the street, that conduit of and access to the urban system.

Posing an alternative view, another caricature by Erich Schilling taken from the 1911 *Simplicissimus* (figure 6) sets the free play of an equestrian bourgeois in the Tiergarten against the movements of the working masses being funneled through the city by mass transit. The atomistic and individ-ualistic configuration of a leisure class contrasts the mass configuration of the other. The proposed removal of one class from the compulsions of the city, as well as the supposed complete subjection of another to them, is of course illusory. The exaggeration on both counts here points to the artist's recognition of stereotypical class configurations as well as to his negative conceptualization of the city as a place to escape and a locus of control. An otherwise politically engaged artist like Karl Holtz might turn his percep-tion around by showing the proletarians as actors in the city, while design-ing the bourgeoisie (white-collar workers and businesspeople) as those driven by their engagement in the city (figures 7 and 8). Important in the contrast is the concern of both artists with the inherent compulsions of the urban environment.

Figure 8. Karl Holtz. Berlin Street Scene, *ca. 1932. Gouache on cardboard, 29.5 x 49 cm. Märkisches Museum, Berlin.*

Considering the expressionists generally within this framework of the urban gestalt and patterning of the working city, one notes their related viewpoint. However, with the exception of painter Ludwig Meidner and a very limited number of paintings by other artists, their city view reverted to the monumental vista (albeit in a new style) and tended to concentrate on certain street types and scenes restricted to the more familiar fashionable outlying districts in the west and the southwest of Berlin, where they lived. Kirchner positioned his consuming and consumed urban types—the gentlemen and ladies of fashion—in the pedestrian traffic on the *Bürgersteig*, the sidewalk, between the traffic in goods in the shop windows and vehicular traffic on the street. The manner of their presence in this circulation of the city was in attitude and dress more akin to the *flâneurs* and promenaders of the nineteenth century. Their positioning and fashionable clothing signified their active participation in the flow of people, money, and goods on the urban surface, and their representation in broken contours and through an emphatic repetition of forms (a futurist device) suggestive of speed integrated them into the larger rhythms of the city. Still, and despite all speculations about alienation and the subjective experience of the metropolis, this choice of subject did not vary greatly from the standard impressionist renderings of the nineteenth century, nor can it be considered an innovative configuration of the city.

In examining the imagery of urban movement and compulsion in the work of George Grosz, one notes how this politically engaged artist retains the conventional figure of the weary worker in profile, and how he configures such workers in dissolute crowds rather than resolute masses, so that although the social circumstance is evident, the political potential is not. In the division of such scenes as "Early Morning at 5" in his graphic series *Das Gesicht der herrschenden Klasse* (The face of the ruling class) of 1921 (figure 9), the social configuration of the city is represented through the bipartite division of the picture into a scene satirizing the debauchery of the bourgeoisie in the early morning hours while the workers march to work.[52] The pictorial device of composite scenes is a conventional nineteenth-century device to represent the social divisions within a city, and the pictorially implied confrontation and apparent discrepancy between those classes has a history going back at least to the 1820s in Berlin. What is important in this configuration of the city is the emphasis on the temporal aspect that points out the coincidence of distinct "occupations" for each social class at a certain time of day.[53]

These contrasting schedules of the urban classes are well described in "The Armies of Work," which appeared in the *Berliner Illustrierte Zeitung* in 1912.

> Whoever wants to get to know Berlin as an industrial and a worker's city must get up early. As the last night owls are being driven home to the west, the new day begins in the northern, eastern, and southern districts of the city. Day has hardly dawned, when the legions of workers from the outlying districts begin their march to the shops and factories. At Gesundbrunnen, in Wedding, along the Frankfurter Allee . . . the masses make their way to the commuter stations. People, people and more people as far as the eye can see . . . wander to the train stations. At the most crowded stations . . . it is always the same routine. In no time at all the special trains for the workers, which only have a third class, are overfilled. . . . Though the trains follow one another in short intervals, the crowding does not let up until seven in the morning. Then the huge army of white-collar workers marches out. They only have different faces and are better dressed, but en masse they have the same effect.[54]

The military terminology used to describe this regimented mass migration reverberates in Heinrich Kley's drawings, which accompany the article. The point of reference in such description is less the individual worker (although certain aspects of that type of urban resident are described) than a more abstract concept, the idea of traffic. Time, flow, volume, mass, and capacity are the underlying parameters in this discussion of the urban tides. Management of the masses, not individual fates, is the concern. The individual urban denizen, whether blue-collar or white-collar worker, is subsumed into a larger motion of the city. This image of the tact and tempo in urban life in Berlin differs greatly from the imagery of the fashionable urban promenad-

Figure 9. George Grosz. "Early Morning at 5" from Das Gesicht der herrschenden Klasse, *1921. Courtesy of the Fogg Art Museum, Harvard University, Cambridge, Massachusetts, Friends of the Fogg Fund.*

ers or *flâneurs* on Unter den Linden and from the peaceful genre scenes of artisans at work that pervaded much of Berlin's nineteenth-century imagery. The visible patterning of the human component that had begun to change in the Berlin scenes by artists such as Lesser Ury and Franz Skarbina came to resemble more what Siegfried Kracauer would call the "ornament

Figure 10. Karl Hubbuch. By the Old Savings Bank in Berlin, *1922. Drypoint, 24.9 x 30.7 cm. Galerie Michael Hasenclever, Munich.*

of the masses." The visualization of this regimented ornamentation would find its most potent expression in the cinematic representation of the city; images of the city in Fritz Lang's *Metropolis* (1927) coordinated the movements of machine with the movement of the masses, and the camera eye in Walter Ruttmann's *Berlin, Symphonie einer Großstadt* (1927) would follow the cycle of motions through the urban day to suggest a timed animation of each social grouping by the city.

4. Composite Analysis

Less anecdotal and more analytic is a composite urban image constructed by Karl Hubbuch from fragments of the cityscape gathered at the historical center of Berlin. His drypoint, *By the Old Savings Bank*, 1922 (figure 10), can be understood as one in a long series of such representations by other artists, who also sought to represent the modern metropolis Berlin in relation to its

Figure 11. Karl Hubbuch. Scene at the Mühlendamm in Berlin, *ca. 1922. Pencil on paper, 92 x ca. 126 cm. Staatliche Kunsthalle, Karlsruhe, Hams-Thoma-Str. 2-6, 7500 Karlsruhe 1, Federal Republic of Germany.*

landscape and, perhaps, consciously chose this river crossing where the original settlement of Berlin had taken place. In a preparatory sketch of the same location (figure 11), Hubbuch presents the view from across the river toward an incomplete city silhouette. Workboats and barges line up before monumental structures to form the center of the city. Read from left to right, the silhouette includes: the savings bank, and, rising behind it, the palace dome; the old Stadtvogtei (the city prison); the cathedral dome; and the oldest church in Berlin, the Nicolaikirche. These buildings and monuments compose a representative historical view of the city seen in relation to the river that flows through its center. In the change from the drawing to the drypoint Hubbuch eliminates both the landscape and the monumental-representative aspect of the scene to concentrate on a few elements, to concentrate meaning in a way that goes beyond Baluschek and Skarbina. To gain some impression of the extreme point of view assumed by Hubbuch in this scenic reduction, one need only compare the same site represented panoramically by the view painter Julius Jacob in 1885 (figure 12).

Hubbuch's disowning of the view's scenic potential can be attributed to his keen awareness of the social-political contradictions inherent in the modern urban construct and its workings. His representation of that construct is analytical and revelatory; or, to paraphrase Carl Einstein in reference to

Figure 12. Julius Jacob. View across the Spree toward Old Berlin, *1885. Oil on canvas [measurements unavailable]. Private collection.*

Otto Dix: for Hubbuch, painting equals critical ascertainment. Through a careful selection and recombination of signs easily understood by an informed viewer, Hubbuch is able to define the city through its evident contradictions. This process of evidential deposition characterizes many of the Berlin etchings he executed between 1920 and 1922. Their drawing is finely transcriptive, almost academic, but in the selection and recombination of those finely drawn elements, Hubbuch analyzes and is not given to artistic speculation or stylistic experimentation. His mode is satirical. To understand this pictorial analysis and its satirical bent, however, one must examine and be able to interpret these prints in all their meaningful detail. Yet any attempt at detailed interpretation is necessarily limited by the personal symbolism and inherent topicality of this imagery.

By the Old Savings Bank presents the viewer at first with the simple configuration of large curvilinear tugboats set slightly askew against the strict rectilinearity of the edifice behind them, a bank whose lower floors in so-called Normanic style date from 1838. Crowded at the center by this juxtaposition, the print has been left incomplete at its edges. Furthermore, as a comparison with photographs of the same location shows, the horizontal extension of the bank has been compressed by reducing the number of bays in its facade, and the riverbank on the left has been foreshortened and made to bend more sharply than in reality.

Tugboats are moored in the foreground to wooden piles and next to a wooden rail, the last vestiges of the Fischerbrücke and Old Berlin, which once occupied a bridge over the water. They wait for barges to come through the new locks that were built between 1888 and 1893 on this site to handle the increased river traffic. The river itself, widest at this point within the city, is not allowed naturally to mitigate the urban artifice, but instead is reduced to patches of water between the boats and its banks.

The tugboats dominating the setting bear names, Minna and Anna, that were typical for maids in Berlin.[55] These "service" vessels jut diagonally, contraposed, smokestack against tower, against the castlelike bank whose historicized architecture appears part Palazzo Vecchio and part Tower of London. The bridge before this castellated structure is abutted by a minia-ture Loire castle that masks the modern machinery used to operate the locks located at this busiest river intersection in Berlin. This complex of juxtapositions poses contemporary questions about work and capital, about history and technology, and about the more general functioning of the city. Pseudohistorical facades and modern mechanized work meet significantly.

The urban signs composing this setting provide a nexus of meaning in which a small human drama literally takes place. Examining the scene in more detail, one notes aboard the tugboat "Minna" a boatsman, looking to-ward the riverbank. Hands in pockets, unshaven, unkempt, and idle, he may be based on one of Hubbuch's frequent studies of the unemployed. He looks away from the locks, his source of work, and toward an incident on the shore. There a helpless man with the dark recessed eyes of the artist is being supported and cared for. Before him is a scavenger goat, behind him, an aristocrat in a carriage; further in the background one sees a truck loaded with workers.

If one resituates this small human drama and the larger signifiers in the economic crisis of Germany in 1922, all the elements fall into logical place. The boatsman's unemployment, the drunk or attempted suicide on the shore, the capitalist in a carriage and his bank, contrasted with the workers in the truck and the moored work vessel, all are understood with topical reference to the Berlin of the early Weimar period. Hubbuch, selectively using modern and extant urban signs, presents a real distillate of the socio-economic and political relationships of this historical moment. He activates historical contradictions in a coalescence of meanings that gives exacting clue to the contemporary constitution of the modern metropolis. His con-figuration of the city, as well as those by Baluschek, Skarbina, Zille, and Grosz, can be understood to pose questions about and evince the constitu-tion of that city with regard to a historical sociopolitical process.

NOTES

1. See Friedrich Naumann, "Ein proletarischer Maler" (A proletarian painter, 1902), in Friedrich Naumann, *Werke*, ed. Heinz Ladendorf (Cologne, 1964), 119.

2. E.g., Max Klinger, Hugo Krayn, George Grosz, and Karl Hubbuch.

3. Berlin was known as a *Buddelstadt*, a sandbox city, at this time. With the construction of its subway and the constant technical improvement in its sewage, water, and communications systems, it was a city marked by excavation and construction sites. In 1910, partly in reaction to the situation, the art critic Karl Scheffler coined a much-quoted phrase about this constant transformation: "Berlin (ist) dazu verdammt: immerfort zu werden und niemals zu sein." (Berlin is damned always to become and never to be.) *Berlin: Ein Stadtschicksal*, 2d ed. (Berlin, 1910), 267.

4. These were local histories with a didactic and patriotic aspect.

5. See, e.g., "Das unterirdische Berlin," a text illustration in Ernst Friedel's *Die Deutsche Kaiserstadt* (Berlin, 1882), 103.

6. "At the first dull shimmer of dawn,/ whose rays light the region all round,/ there they stand ready to fulfill their task,/ hard work's hale and hearty companions./ Today theirs is to set up, orderly,/ row on row of heavy stone blocks/ along an embankment, while on tracks below,/ steampower pants to serve the human spirit." Jakob Audorf, "Vom Schlachtfeld der Arbeit" (From the battlefield of work), in *Deutsche Arbeiter Dichtung. Eine Auswahl Lieder und Gedichte deutscher Proletarier* 2 (Stuttgart, 1893): 25; quoted in *Arbeit als Thema in der deutschen Literatur vom Mittelalter bis zur Gegenwart*, ed. Reinhold Grimm and Jost Hermand (Koenigstein/Taunus, 1979), 107.

7. This was of course the dilemma of the reform wing of the Social Democrats. The party was critical of alienation of the workers and yet took pride in the worker's role as a conveyer of technical-industrial progress.

8. E.g., in a pamphlet distributed by workers in Berlin in 1846 one already reads the following: "Man stahl (dem Arbeiter) seinen Menschenwerth und benützte ihn als todter Werkzeug, als Maschine" (One stole the worker's human dignity and used him as an inanimate instrument, as a machine), quoted by Wolfgang Dreßen, "Maschinenbauer und Erdarbeiter." in *Exerzierfeld der Moderne, Industriekultur in Berlin im 19. Jahrhundert*, ed. Jochen Boberg et al. (Munich, 1984), 71.

9. The most complete survey of these attitudes in English is Andrew Lees, *Cities Perceived: Urban Society in European and American Thought, 1820–1940* (New York, 1985).

10. By *compulsions* two things are meant. One is the compulsion to consume, to display, and to accrue wealth that was characteristic of the ascendant bourgeoisie. The other is a being compelled by the economic system that had begun to instantiate itself upon the city in new patterns of circulation and production. For the first of these see T. J. Clark, *The Painting of Modern Life; Paris in the Art of Manet and His Followers* (New York, 1985); for the second see Hubert Treiber and Heinz Steinert, *Die Fabrikation des zuverlässigen Menschen. Über die "Wahlverwandtschaft" von Kloster-und Fabrikdisziplin* (Munich, 1980), particularly 23–52.

11. One is social and linked either to the united and politically conscious masses or to the civic consciousness of an ascendant and enlightened urban bourgeoisie; the other is technological and trusting in the invention and ingenuity of humankind.

12. If the operative elements of the new urban classes and technological change were rejected from an antiprogressive stance, such as that taken by conservative cultural philosophers in Germany from Justus Moser to Wilhelm Heinrich Riehl to Oswald Spengler, the point of view was necessarily antiurban as well. If one accepted the quite simple and yet many-faceted dichotomies of civilization against culture and *Gesellschaft* versus *Gemeinschaft* (Ferdinand Tönnies) and their implicit valuations, then one was either pro- or antiurban. And from an antiurban and conservative point of view, the view of the cultural pessimists who decried the loss of

community, the modern city was simply ugly in appearance and detrimental in its effect, and therefore not worth representing (*nicht bildwürdig*). For those civic boosters who positioned themselves in support of the advance of civilization in the form of economic and technological progress there was a need for an iconography and a style that could repicture the traditional city beautiful in accordance with a new aesthetic. The somewhat belated and initial configuration of the modern city in the pictorial reception of Wilhelmine Germany in the 1880s can be best understood in relationship to these various and contrary interests and perspectives. The antiurbanism and antimodernism of the conservative critics did not spawn a new pictorial representation of the city except perhaps in caricature. The modern metropolis functioned as a field of debate for various discourses—about technological development, the massive accumulation of wealth and capital, mass exploitation, the establishment of a new social and political order with the rise of an urban-industrial bourgeoisie and an urban working class, and the supposed threat of revolutionary change or anarchy with the disintegration of the old political order. Compare Lees, *Cities Perceived* (see note 9) and Klaus Bergmann, *Agrarromantik und Großstadtfeindschaft* (Meisenheim am Glan, FRG, 1970).

13. From the late eighteenth century until the mid-nineteenth century the *vedute* by artists including Johann Gottfried Wilhelm Barth, Wilhelm Brücke, Eduard Gärtner, Johann Georg Rosenberg, and Johann Erdmann Hummel, among others, dominate the imagery of Berlin. Their urban vistas were popularized in guidebooks or as decorative motifs on porcelain. After 1850, perhaps in part due to the introduction of photography, these city views went out of fashion.

14. More so than in painting there is an encyclopedic inventory of everyday Berlin in illustrations, caricatures, and broadsheets of the period. Compare Karl Riha, *Die Beschreibung der "großen Stadt": Zur Entstehung des Großstadtmotivs in der deutschen Literatur (ca.1750-ca. 1850)* (Bad Homburg, FRG, 1970); Gotthard Brandler, "Frühe Stadtgänge. Die Entdeckung der werdenden Großstadt Berlin (1760 bis um 1850)," in *Studien zur Berliner Kunstgeschichte*, ed. Karl-Heinz Klingenburg (Leipzig, 1986), 193–220; and Ursula Cosmann, "Die Realimus-Tradition und die Darstellung des Volkslebens in der Berliner Grafik des 18. und 19. Jahrhunderts," in *Heinrich Zille*, exhibition catalog, Märkisches Museum (Berlin, 1981).

15. These modern iconographic formulations of the city were posterlike in their political message. In many socialist posters and illustrations a proletarian Hercules or giant dominated the skyline of an industrialized city, and in the symbolization of technological progress a steaming locomotive was often shown cutting diagonally and powerfully through the picture planes and the urban surface. In these iconographic configurations, the worker and the machine embodied two distinct projections of progress that determined views of a city working and constituting itself. Both are images of the city that attribute it to one force of progress or another. Compare Richard Hiepe, "Riese Proletariat und Große Maschinerie, Revolutionäre Bildvorstellungen in der Kunst des 19. Jahrhunderts," in *Die Taube in der Hand: Aufsätze zu Kunst und Kulturpolitik, 1955–1975*, ed. Richard Hiepe (Munich, 1976), 156–67; and Knut Hickethier, "Karikatur, Allegorie und Bilderfolge: Zur Bildpublizistik im Dienste der Arbeiterbewegung," in *Beiträge zur Kulturgeschichte der deutschen Arbeiterbewegung, 1848–1918*, ed. Peter von Rüden (Frankfurt/Main, 1981), 81–165.

16. For an interesting discussion of this new city and the difficulty in "reading" it, let alone representing it, compare William Sharpe and Leonard Wallock, "From 'Great Town' to 'Nonplace Urban Realm': Reading the Modern City," in *Visions of the Modern City*, ed. Sharpe and Wallock (New York, 1983), 7–46.

17. On *Naturalismus*, see Richard Hamann and Jost Hermand, *Naturalismus* (Frankfurt/Main, 1977). And for a perceptive discussion of the painting, see Rolf Bothe, "Franz Skarbina, Gleisanlagen im Norden Berlins," in *Berlinische Notizen, Festgabe für Irmgard Wirth* (1981), 137–38.

18. These distinct but not exclusive positions as to what the city represented might be said to correspond with a disparateness in the styles or the content of the styles Skarbina employed. Contemporaries of Skarbina located his style between the tradition of Berlin "realism" exemplified in the work of Adolf von Menzel and the more "modern" and "foreign" influences such as the impressionist painters di Nittis and Caillebotte. Skarbina was noted and sometimes derided for such experiments in the representation of artificial light and atmospheric effects during this period, and for some critics he had ventured too far from the solid realism of Menzel by the early 1890s. The painting frames a pictorial question about how to view the modern metropolis. Compare Rolf Bothe, "Stadtbilder zwischen Menzel und Liebermann," in *Stadtbilder*, exhibition catalog, Berlin Museum (Berlin, 1987).

19. The commuter railway system girding the inner districts of Berlin was built in 1877 and expanded in the following years.

20. Written on the back of the painting is the notation "in the north of Berlin," and according to Rolf Bothe (*Stadtbilder*, 227) it may be the commuter railway at the Weißensee station with a view toward the highly industrialized and working-class district of Wedding.

21. By subliminal is meant here the vastness of solid form, its transformation into vapor and light, the diminutive scale of the human presence, and the lack of spatial delimitation within the image.

22. It is worth noting that Whistler was exhibited in Berlin in 1886 at the *Jubiläum* Exhibition for the Academy of the Arts and was accorded a mixed reception from contemporary art critics (see, e.g., Herman Helferich, *Neue Kunst* [Berlin, 1887], 18). One might compare Whistler's painting, *Falling Rocket Nocturne: Study in Black and Gold* (1875, Detroit Institute of Arts), and note a similar if more dramatic use of artificial illumination. I thank Reinhold Heller for the reference to Whistler.

23. By *landscape* I mean approximately what Georg Simmel described as a delimited and unified space that nonetheless seems woven into the endless expanse and process of nature. See Georg Simmel, "Philosophie der Landschaft," in *Das Individuum und die Freiheit* (Berlin, 1984), 130. (This essay first appeared in 1913 in *Die Güldenkammer*, vol. 3).

24. Of course this is premised on the idea of excluding the ugly and common from the realm of art and suggests an elevated aesthetic based in part on the choice of subject matter.

25. Literally, a painting of mood. Indication of emphasis on the conveyance of mood or atmosphere can be read from the titles appearing in catalogs of the Royal Academy in Berlin or in the Berlin Secession catalogs from the turn of the century. Titles such as *Abenddämmerung: Motive aus dem Norden von Berlin* ([Evening twilight, motifs from the north of Berlin], by Erich Sturtevant, in *Große Berliner Kunstausstellung*, exhibition catalog [Berlin, 1893], no. 2064) suggested both a working class motif and a tonal style. However, a painting by Lesser Ury in the same catalog (no. 927), listed as *Frühlingsstimmung*, without an accompanying illustration, left one uncertain whether the "Mood of Spring" was located in the country or in the city. Circa 1900 the sporadic double titles specifying the time of day, condition of the atmosphere, or season suggest a certain naturalizing tendency in the representation of the city. E.g., the *Katalog der dritten Kunst-Ausstellung der Berliner Secession* (Berlin, 1901) lists works by Charles Fromuth (*Im Hafen, Abendstimmung* [In the harbor: Evening mood] no. 60), by Max Giesecke (*Regenstimmung im Hamburger Hafen* [Rainy mood in Hamburg Harbor], no. 62), and by Ulrich Hübner (*Dezemberstimmung* [December mood], no.101) that all follow this pattern.

26. The "other" industrial metropolis was thought to stretch northward from the monumental-representative core of the German capital in an undifferentiated system of *Mietskasernen* (literally, rent barracks). Actually, the districts of Berlin populated largely by workers extended to the north, to the east, and to the south and southeast of the city. Nonetheless, together they were popularly known as *Der Norden Berlins*, the northern reaches of Berlin, perhaps because the initial and largest working-class districts developed in this direction. Compare, for example, the descriptions by Julius Rodenberg, "Der Norden Berlins," in *Bilder aus dem Berliner*

Leben (Berlin, 1984), originally published 1887. Rodenberg notes, "Unter allen Weltgegenden unserer Stadt ist es diese von welcher man in den übrigen am wenigstens weiß; woraus indessen nicht folgt, daß die Bewohner derselben Recht haben, wenn sie den Norden als das 'Stiefkind' Berlins darzustellen lieben. Ein Blick auf den Plan genügt, um zu zeigen, daß das Areale dieses Stadttheils umfangreicher ist, als das irgend eines anderen Berlin." (Of all the quarters of the city, this is the one denizens from other parts of the city know the least about; still this doesn't give these people the right to refer to this northern district as a stepchild of Berlin. One look at a map suffices to show us that this is actually the largest area of Berlin [134].) Appropriately, *Ein Bärenführer*, a guidebook published in 1912, reminded its readers: "Auch das ist Berlin!" (That is also Berlin!) (in *Die Berliner Moderne, 1885–1914*, ed. Jürgen Schutte and Peter Sprengel [Stuttgart, 1987], 97–98). Alfred Döblin refers to this "invisible" and contemporary city in his introduction to Mario von Bucovich's *Berlin*, a photographic portrait of Berlin published in 1928 (viii–xii). He notes that only this city unseen by the tourist evinces the essential character of the modern mass settlement that is Berlin. Compare also Christine Wolf, "Das Berliner Leben. Dargestellt in der Druckgraphik 1871–1914," master's thesis, Institut für Kunstwissenschaft, Technische Universität, Berlin, 1984.

27. Completed in 1877, the *Ringbahn* together with the *Stadtbahn* (or S-Bahn), built in 1882, constituted the major means of commuter transport by rail. To some it was the introduction of this transportation system that put Berlin on a par with other "world cities." See, e.g., Georg Brandes, "Die Stadtbahn im Februar des Jahres 1882," in *Die Berliner S-Bahn*, exhibition catalog Nationalgalerie (East) (Berlin, 1982), 50. Also note Paul Lindenberg, *Berlin in Wort und Bild* (Berlin, 1895), who recommended the *Ringbahn* for a quick sight-seeing tour that would take you to all the districts of the metropolis, and among the scenes he describes are those of the north of Berlin.

28. See Oswald Spengler, *Der Untergang des Abendlandes: Umrisse einer Morphologie der Weltgeschichte* (Munich, 1972), 673–87. Baluschek gave the idea of "urban nomads" a more actual representation in a caricature that appeared in the satirical magazine *Das Narrenschiff* 1 (1898): 208. Entitled "Nomaden der Großstadt," the cartoon shows a proletarian family moving from one tenement to the next, as was the quarterly custom for renters in Berlin at that time ("Der Quartals-Umzug").

29. To experience the city as "nature" or at least "like nature" was a typical trope in the travel literature of the period. In his essay "Auf dem Eiffelturm," Friedrich Naumann (*Ausstellungsbriefe* [Berlin, 1909], 103–9) described the "spectacle of a cosmopolis in a panorama of indescribable sublimity (Erhabenheit) seen from an edifice that is among the architectural wonders of the world. . . . " This is an excellent example of this particular *manner* of seeing. Reminiscing on the Eiffel Tower, he begins: "Ich saß einmal früher einen Abend ganz allein auf dem Stanser Horn am Vierwaldstättersee und blickte in die Schneekette der Berner Hochalpen. Je länger ich die Berge ansah, desto ernster wurden sie. Der Abend löschte die kleinen Lichter auf den Firmen und ließ nichts übrig als die Wand des weißen Gebirges und den dämmernden Untergrund . . . eine beseelte Masse, die nur das eine fragt: wer bist aber du? An solchen Abend im dämmernden Gebirge erinnert der Abend, der jetzt über der Rundfläche von Paris sich niedersenkt. . . . Vor kurzem noch war ganz Paris geradezu verklärt, purpurn begossen, unerhört bunt in aller seiner Größe, Farben des glühenden Herbstwaldes auf allen grauen Kalkgeländen. . . . Man kann es nicht erzählen, was solche Augenblicke alles bieten. Das Unerzählbare ist die Unendlichkeit der Flächen. . . . Was weiß ich, was in diesen Minuten das Schönste war? Vielleicht *gefällt es dem Auge*, eine beliebige beleuchtete Kaserne für goldener zu halten als alles andere. Das war das Alpenglühen der Riesenstadt" (emphasis added). The saccharine description makes the city pleasing to the eye and relates the subjective and emotive experience of a sublime city, which cannot be narrated or told about and is therefore experienced as a subliminal, aestheticized, and naturalized expanse.

30. Compare Stephen Kern, *The Culture of Time and Space, 1880–1918* (Cambridge, Mass., 1983), 10–35.

31. Compare Joachim Ritter, *Landschaft: Zur Funktion des Ästhetischen in der modernen Gesellschaft* (Münster, 1963), 12.

32. See, e.g., the painting by Caspar David Friedrich, *Die Schwestern auf dem Söller*, Leningrad, Hermitage.

33. The urban images entitled *December Atmosphere, An Evening Mood,* or *The Mood of Spring,* collectively known as *Stimmungsbilder* (see note 25), were typified by the use of atmospheric filters, called *Luftschleier* (i.e., atmospheric veils) by the romantic painter and landscape theorist Carl Gustav Carus (*Briefe und Aufsätze über Landschaftsmalerei* [Leipzig, 1982], 124).

34. August Endell, *Die Schönheit der großen Stadt* (Stuttgart, 1908). Two segments of his book are entitled "Veils of the Night" and "Veils of the Day." These *Luftschleier*—subtle gradations of tones, colors, and light—served to unify, to aestheticize, and to naturalize the otherwise disparate urban surface in painting. They could transform an urban scene into a subliminal expanse, or, in a less skillful rendering, cause it to degenerate into a rehashing of effects. In this type of rendering, the atmospheric condition might be considered more the subject matter than any aspect of the city, for what the artist often sought was primarily to convey an "impression to the senses" (*Sinneseindruck*).

35. Ibid., 60–61.

36. Ibid., 30–31.

37. See Simmel, "Landschaft" (see note 23).

38. Lesser Ury (1862–1931), a member of the Berlin Secession like Skarbina, was one of the earliest and most persistent Berlin painters to employ style in this manner. The effect of that application was well described by a critic in 1922: "So wird dort die Weltstadt in der Umnebelung zur Landschaft, die sich bis zu einer beinahe transcendentalen Unrealität vergeistigt. (So there the cosmopolis becomes, through its veiling in mist, a landscape, one that gains an almost transcendental and ethereal unreality.) Paul Friedrich, in *Lesser Ury*, exhibition catalog, Kunstkammer Berlin (Berlin, 1922), 14.

39. Consult Endell. On artificial illumination see Wolfgang Schivelbusch, *Disenchanted Night: The Industrialization of Light in the Nineteenth Century,* trans. Angela Davies (Berkeley, 1988).

40. As has been noted by Oscar Handlin in his essay "The Modern City as a Field of Historical Study": "The altered situation of the city called also for a new conception of time. In the rural past, years, months, days, and hours had been less meaningful than seasons, than the related succession of religious occasions, than the rising and setting of the sun. Each household had large margins within which to set its own pace, for the tempo of all activities was leisurely. The complex life of the modern city, however, called for an unprecedented precision. . . . There was no natural span; . . . arbitrary beginnings and ends had to be set, made uniform and adhered to. The dictatorship of the clock and schedule became absolute." In *The Historian and the City,* ed. John Burchard and Oscar Handlin (Cambridge, Mass., 1963), 13.

41. Compare Volker Klotz, Die erzählte Stadt (München, 1969), especially 317ff.

42. Karl Buecher, *Arbeit und Rhythmus,* Abhandlungen der königlichen sächsischen Gesellschaft der Wissenschaft (Leipzig, 1896), 39.

43. See Winfried Ranke, *Heinrich Zille, Photographien: Berlin 1890–1910* (München, 1975), catalog 90.

44. Cosmann, "Die Realismus-Tradition" (see note 14), 19–36.

45. Brandler, "Frühe Stadtgänge" (see note 14), 197–202.

46. For this type of idealization, see Hiepe, "Riese Proletariat und Große Maschinerie" (see note 15), 156-57. For a thorough discussion of the heroic aspect with relation to monuments to labor, see J. A. Schmoll gen. Eisenwerth, "Denkmäler der Arbeit—Entwürfe und Planungen,"

in *Denkmäler im 19. Jahrhundert: Deutung und Kritik*, ed. Hans-Ernst Mittig und Volker Plage-mann (München, 1972), 253–81.

47. On Meunier, see *Arbeit und Alltag: Soziale Wirklichkeit in der belgischen Kunst, 1830–1914*, exhibit catalog, Nationalgalerie (East Berlin) (Berlin, 1979).

48. Hiepe (see note 15).

49. See Margrit Bröhan, *Hans Baluschek, 1870– 1935, Maler—Zeichner—Illustrator* (Berlin, 1985), and Günter Meißner, *Hans Baluschek* (Dresden, 1985).

50. Compare Kollwitz's *Heimkehrende Arbeiter am Lehrter Bahnhof*, illustrated in *Pan* 5 (1899): 177; also Edvard Munch, *Workers Returning Home*, 1913, Munch-Museet, Oslo.

51. Alfred Rethel's wood engraving series, *Auch ein Totentanz* (1849), created in response to the failed bourgeois revolution of 1848, presents one of the earliest and perhaps the most in-fluential pictorial representations of urban revolution.

52. See Beth Irwin Lewis, *George Grosz: Art and Politics in the Weimar Republic* (Madison, Wis., 1971), for a thorough study of Grosz's politics.

53. Thematizing this in a German context are, e.g., Adolf Muenzer's design for a mural, *Luxus und Arbeit* (1900), which confronts the celebrating urban bourgeoisie with a scene of "on the way to work" (*Die Kunst*, 1900, 530–31); and Hugo Krayn's *Großstadt* (1914), which pic-tures exhausted workers confronting fashionably dressed promenaders before the Jannowitz-brücke in Berlin (Berlin, Deutsches Historisches Museum). This pictorial trope, which ap-peared early in the nineteenth century as an index of social conflict, also appears in the Hubbuch drypoint discussed below.

54. *Berliner Illustrierte Zeitung*, 1912, no. 39: 897–99.

55. I thank Bettina Götz for this information.

CHAPTER 2

The Beauty of the Metropolis:
Toward an Aesthetic Urbanism in
Turn-of-the-Century Berlin

Lothar Müller

Ever since Baudelaire anticipated the discovery of the fugitive beauty of
modernity through cultivation of an art of seeing, an art that would reveal
in the ephemeral of the present the unlikely equivalent of the classical beauty
of the past, there has been a continuing reflection on a possible aesthetic of
the metropolis—an aesthetic grounded in the disposition of the viewing
subject, rather than in the object of perception.[1] Artifacts whose formal
logic was determined purely by functional considerations, yet which were
nonetheless sources of aesthetic experience—the Crystal Palace of the London Great Exhibition of 1851 is a celebrated example—attracted attention
precisely because they challenged the traditional concepts of beauty. Technology and industry—ostensibly the mortal enemies of art and of natural
beauty—had here, in the glass-and-iron architecture of a functional building
that was dismantled with the exhibition, created a monument both fugitive
and functional, and therefore of a specifically modern beauty. The theoretical response to this challenge ensued mainly under the rubric of *l'art industriel*, whose genesis in the nineteenth century scholars have only recently
begun to examine systematically.[2] In this process, the development that encompassed the Crystal Palace, the iron architecture of the Second Empire in
Paris, and the Eiffel Tower constitutes the basis for an aesthetics of the inorganic and technical-artificial. In this recounting, the metropolis, which in
all pathographies of modernity was considered the monstrously ugly antithesis of nature, now appeared as a locus of beauty. The city's status as an
object of aesthetic fascination was no less real for its being simultaneously a
locus of alienation.[3]

   In the following essay I will examine historiographically the impassioned
discursive and perceptual models that governed the discussion of the
"beauty of the metropolis," focusing on a single city—turn-of-the-century
Berlin. In the first section, I shall demonstrate how the Berlin of this era, in
contrast to Paris, the capital of *aesthetic* modernity in the nineteenth century,

✓ was perceived as a center of a *technological*, civilizing modernity. And it was there, in the cultural criticism of the day, that the equation of industrialization with ugliness seems to have been born. In the second section I shall sketch, against the background of the German reception of French impressionism, how the concept of impressionism, accepted as a diagnostic formula for analyzing all cultural phenomena of the period, became central to the debate on urban life. Finally, I will clearly show, through analysis of a text by the architect August Endell on "The Beauty of the Metropolis," how the perceptual model of an "impressionistic seeing" entered into the program of an aestheticized urbanism in Berlin at the beginning of the century.

1. "The Capital of all Modern Ugliness"

Berlin in 1900: that was not only the world of spiked helmets and a pompously ceremonious empire, of a social hierarchy on the defensive, of a flourishing cult of monuments and architectural historicism. The facades of houses and of public buildings may have invoked the past, but only the perfunctory glance could be deceived: Wilhelmine Berlin, like its Kaiser, was in love not only with costumes and uniforms but with technology, and was a capital of industrial modernity in Europe. In the last third of the nineteenth century, no other European city had grown so rapidly, had changed its outer physiognomy so drastically. In few cities had the acceleration of industrial expansion so exacerbated the tensions between traditional and modern rhythms of life; in few cities did urban misery exceed that in the tenements of Berlin's northern and eastern districts.[4] Berlin, with its factories, its dense traffic, its advanced technology, its expansive dynamism, and its exemplary sewage system was regarded as the quintessence of a modern industrial metropolis. In newspapers, journals, and popular novels people followed, with a mixture of horror and fascination, Berlin's resolute farewell to the "good old days" and its rise to the status of a metropolis.[5] In 1899, an essay on Berlin "The Most Beautiful City in the World," appeared in Maximilian Harden's *Zukunft* (Future). Its author, who had used an easily decipherable pseudonym, was the young Walther Rathenau; its title was to be understood not literally, but ironically. For in this text Rathenau portrayed Berlin as an ugly bastard among cities, an impure mixture of the old, with its showy parvenu facades, and the new, mindless and formless in its relentless triumphal march. The city's only authentic culture—the Prussian culture of Frederick the Great and Karl Friedrich Schinkel—had been lost, supplanted by the bogus nouveau riche splendor of the Wilhelmine era; culture had not yet found a new form that could counterbalance the city's rash growth. Berlin had, without reflection, broken with its past, yet had not grasped its modernity.[6]

Rathenau's critique of his native city as the hideous monster of modernity is doubly determined. First, Berlin appears as a "parvenupolis," a locus of architectural tastelessness and semiofficial kitsch. The demolition of the old cathedral, designed by Schinkel, and its replacement by Raschdorff's colossal "cathedral in World-Exposition style" becomes, in this topical polemic against the dominance of historicism and eclecticism in the buildings of the Wilhelmine era, a symbol for the alliance of bold parvenu gestures and the thoughtless destruction of tradition. At the center of this argument, whose aesthetic standard is a classicism that anticipates modern functionalism, is the critique of the hypertrophic facades of the capital.[7] The second argument is considerably wider in scope than this ironic architectural critique of an "art-historical Babel of facades." It concerns the configuration of the city and its streets, and proceeds from the thesis that, in comparison with Paris, London, and even an internally consistent New York, Berlin could offer nothing to compete with the characteristic urban prospects of other major cities. What Rathenau defined as the "overall image" (Gesamtbild) of a metropolis was intended as a formulation of something Berlin lacked, and it was a defect more serious than the offensive style of the city's architecture.

> A city does not necessarily need beautiful buildings. But when it must also do without scenic beauty, without a liberating view of the sea, without broad, flowing rivers, without even the picturesque charm of sky and atmosphere, then it has the duty to create a significant and well-planned arrangement of its streets. . . . I prefer to say "streetscape" (Straßenlandschaft), or cityscape, as that which is of utmost importance is the actual scenic view in general; this is created through the organizing and arranging of masses in the same manner as a natural landscape proceeds out of the grouping of masses of mountains and vegetation. Whoever has once set foot on Trafalgar Square or the Place de la Concorde, Piccadilly or the Piazza della Signoria can appreciate what a stirring impression urban scenery—purely as a general picture, not as an effect of single works—is called upon to make.[8]

Rathenau's longing for a distinguished "overall image" of Berlin is easily recognizable as the longing for a German Baron Haussmann, even if Napoleon III's prefect of the Seine is not mentioned in the text. For the "play of thoughts" with which Rathenau concludes his reflections, in which he envisions the rebuilding of the formless conglomerate Berlin after the model of Paris, as a metropolis structured around grand boulevards, is born of the spirit of Haussmann's démolitions. Only through a "work of planned destruction" could the German monstrosity of modernity become a worthy pendant of Paris, which was unrivaled in the "art of creating a grand parade of streets."[9] Were he mayor of Berlin, Rathenau declared, he would appropriate billions in credit and grant himself the "right of pitiless expropriation" in order to build, from the conjoining Potsdam and Leipzig Squares, a "South Boulevard," which should end at a proposed central railway station, and a "West Boulevard," extending from the Potsdam Bridge to the Memorial Church, so as to encircle the center of the growing metropolis by a *corso*, a ring of boulevards. "It is not a matter of construction," he wrote. "Razing and destruction, opening up space: that is the important thing."

Rathenau's concept here is an echo of the urban ideals of Haussmann: "Air, open prospects, perspective."[10] Many of Haussmann's contemporaries had seen in the modernization of Paris a Babylon of the future, the demise of the city of Balzac, the erasure of the past from memory. Yet, lamentations on the "American" character of the newly developing physiognomy of Paris had persisted only superficially. Despite the demolitions, Paris conveyed the sense of a successful melding of tradition and modernity. It was most often regarded, particularly by outside admirers, as the product of organic growth—Hugo von Hofmannsthal characterized it as "a landscape built out of life itself."[11] In Berlin speculation and recklessness were not, as in Paris, merely the means through which an overall planning concept was realized; on the contrary, during Berlin's most explosive growth, speculation determined the very form of the city. Accordingly, at the turn of the century Berlin established itself in the popular consciousness as an "American" metropolis, profoundly hostile to tradition. Rathenau's essay neatly articulates this viewpoint.

> Berlin has not grown; rather, it has undergone a transformation. The culture of the Kingdom of Prussia no longer has a place in Imperial Berlin. Athens on the Spree is dead and Chicago on the Spree is emerging.[12]

A failed slice of America on the sands of the March of Brandenburg: after Rathenau's essay this became a standard image for twentieth-century Berlin.

Karl Scheffler, editor of the leading art journal *Kunst und Künstler* (Art and artist) developed Rathenau's critique in a book of 1910, *Berlin: Ein Stadtschicksal* (Berlin: A city's destiny), an unflattering portrait of "the capital of all modern ugliness."[13] "For the concept of the modern metropolis," declared Scheffler, "what is decisive is not the number of inhabitants, but the spirit of the city."[14] Moreover, his concept of "primary urban culture"—which Berlin lacked—was juxtaposed to a critique of the city's physiognomy, which he formulated (following Rathenau) as a polemic against the clandestine provincialism of the Wilhelmine period, a critique of Berlin's dearth of urban traditions. Scheffler varied his diagnosis of this lack of cultured urbanity, citing the history of the visual arts as well as literature, table manners as well as the forms of political and social life, the character of places of amusement as well as the caste spirit of the social classes. Paris,

London, and Vienna and their significance within their respective nations functioned as a foil, against which "the utilitarian city on the Spree" was contrasted negatively. There thus appeared, and not only in the works of Scheffler and Rathenau, definitions of Berlin built on comparisons with other European capitals: measured against London, a classic industrial metropolis with a sense of tradition, Berlin seemed an economic-industrial center brutal and uncultivated in the American style. Measured against Paris, the organically beautiful city, Berlin appeared as artificial and ugly. The contrast was between an urban culture of poetry and one of prose—Paris, even as a modern metropolis, was capable of poetry; Berlin was hopelessly prosaic.[15] The comparison of Berlin with Vienna offered, in the eyes of Berlin sociologist Werner Sombart, the contrast between "civilization" determined by industry and technology and "culture" founded on tradition. Vienna could thus be stylized into an Old European bulwark against the onslaught of "Americanism," which, as an alarming glimpse of a possible future, had already established itself in Berlin.[16]

One could summarize all of these contrasts as follows: nowhere is the abyss between the "modernity" and the "beauty" of a metropolis as wide as in Berlin; nowhere is the ground for the formation of a specifically metropolitan art and culture more sterile; nowhere is the prose of modern conditions more prosaic than in Berlin.

2. Impressionism as the Art of the Metropolis

> No one would think any longer of having the iron supports in a hall appear as columns; we have progressed too far in forming wholly new conceptions of proportion and of the organization of space. The greenhouse has produced the Crystal Palace, the engine house the railway station hall. The modern office building has arisen. The iron bridge swings, as if incorporeal, above the abyss with a poetic enchantment from which even the most obdurate soul of a Greek or Gothic romanticist will not be able to escape.[17]

What Julius Lessing, in his essay of 1898 on "the modern in art," suggested through the image of the iron bridge has recently been thoroughly investigated by Karlheinz Stierle in a fascinating study on the central role of iron-and-glass architecture in the aesthetic of industrial modernity. In a general topographic investigation focusing on Paris of the Second Empire, Stierle demonstrates the importance of iron for the discovery of industrial modernity's capacity for poetry—in the seemingly weightless structures of the giant urban market halls, the railway stations, the Bibliothèque Nationale, the arcades, and the department stores. He also shows how iron architecture, from which greenhouses and the public winter gardens of the Champs-Elysées also originated, was present as the experiential background in the "artificial paradises" of poetry from Baudelaire to Rimbaud, and how Émile Zola, beyond what one generally designates as his "naturalism," became the "Homer of iron architecture."[18]

One would be justified in relating the revolutionary transformation of pictorial space in modern painting to the new dimensions of experience opened up by iron architecture. Hans Sedlmayr, for one, has made this connection: "The new plein-air painting, with its cult of the brightest, most scintillating, most natural light, is related in spirit to the new open-air architecture of steel and glass."[19] To this way of thinking, light is a means of dissolving the heaviness of matter and therefore a factor in the modernist undermining of architectural tradition, which until then had understood the monumental only in terms of the massive, the enduring, of that which was, as it were, rooted in the ground. Opposed to this is the modern aesthetic of lightness, of the suspended, which attains its culmination in the transparent skin of, for example, a glass roof. This is the vision of a tentlike architecture, intimately united with movement, an architecture that had allowed itself to be infiltrated by the subversive quality of the fugitive. That such iron structures primarily served "transitory purposes" strengthened their tendency to forsake the static experience of space.[20] Sedlmayr's analogy is not merely capricious: Klaus Herding, in his discussion of the representation of space in Monet's series of the *Gare St. Lazare* (1877), makes a similar point.

> The glass and iron construction of the railway station (in the first version) forms the upper and the right borders, the "nouveau Paris" of Haussmann fills the background. Three locomotives, at various distances, belch forth steam. Gas lanterns are no more absent than the "metropolitan factor," the crowd. In the second version the side halls of the train station have disappeared; instead of the crowds upon the platforms there are empty tracks. The transparency and lightness of the construction of the station, i.e., its specifically industrial quality, have come to the fore; because the roof has virtually disappeared in the steam, it appears totally weightless. In the final version the machines and tracks, formerly heavy and dark, have been drawn into the atmospheric effect: their size, their weight within the picture have been diminished.[21]

Painting thus develops, in the motif of iron architecture, a language of forms corresponding to its constructive logic, so that both can be recognized as complementary variations of an aesthetic of *Entschwerung*, an elimination of weight.[22] The thesis that impressionist painting owes its specifically modern character not only to the discovery of the present, in particular, of the modern metropolis, but, more profoundly, to the sensitive energy with which it accounts for the new experiential dimension on a formal level, was put forward as early as 1910 by Max Weber in a discussion at the First German Sociologists' Conference. He responded affirmatively to the question concerning a connection between modern technology and "formal aesthetic values," arguing that:

> the distinctive formal values of our modern artistic culture could only have come to be through the existence of the modern metropolis, the modern metropolis with its tramways, underground railways, its electric . . . lamps, display windows, concert halls, and restaurants, cafés, smokestacks, masses of stone, and the wild dance of impressions of sound and color, impressions and experiences which have an effect on sexual fantasy, all variants of a spiritual constitution, which brood voraciously over the seemingly inexhaustible possibilities of means to life and happiness.[23]

Weber specifically mentioned "the restless masses, nocturnal lights, and reflexes of the modern metropolis with its means of transportation" as the experiential background for the formal development of modern painting.[24]

The initial reception of French impressionism in Germany, between 1890 and the beginning of the First World War, is simultaneously a history of the reflexive processing of the technological and industrial in the vision of aesthetic modernity. What authors such as Julius Meier-Graefe, patrons such as Harry Count Kessler, museum directors like Hugo von Tschudi, art dealers like Paul Cassirer, and journal editors such as those of the exclusive *Pan* or the influential *Kunst und Künstler* did to bring to attention—through exhibitions or critical commentary—the works of the French impressionists, postimpressionists, and Matisse was not only a process of aesthetic importation, of interest chiefly for the art-historical investigation of influences. Certainly this became the aesthetic foundation, complete with journalistic-organizational infrastructure, without which the German breakthrough to modernity, leading to the explosive development of expressionism, would have been inconceivable. The "old" Secessionists had prepared the ground for the "new."[25] However, bound up with this reception of *pictures* from the capital of modern art—and hardly to be sharply distinguished from it—was the discursive elaboration of the *concept* of impressionism beyond the medium of painting. Impressionism was transformed into a diagnostic category of reflection on the period as a whole, a category in which ultimately the artistic style was only an epiphenomenon, a symptom of the underlying style of life.

The highpoint of this process of the discursive universalization of "impressionist culture," or of the "impressionistic world view" as a formula for the self-interpretation of industrial modernity at the turn of the century, was achieved in Richard Hamann's 1907 book, *Impressionismus in Leben und Kunst* (Impressionism in life and art).[26] The money economy, modern commerce and trade, and above all the metropolis as the locus of an intensifying condensation of these first two factors are here seen as the fertile soil of a style of life whose characteristics are acceleration and transitoriness, hectic activity and mobility, as well as the erosion of all established norms and values. In the book's diagnosis of impressionism, the "impressionist" life-style, as manifested in all social and cultural phenomena, becomes synonymous with the fugitive, with the dissolution of form, with the antiarchitectonic. In philosophy impressionism is evident in the aestheticization of thinking; in ethics it is manifest in the tendency to reject any moral imperative; in drama it is the development of the undramatic; in music, the sublime cultivation of sonority and atmosphere.[27]

I shall not trace the life of this concept of impressionism in the flourishing journalism of the turn of the century; but I do intend to indicate those points where the debate concerning impressionism in painting crossed over into the discourse on modern urban culture. To this end it will be necessary to analyze the concept of *impression*, which, with Monet's painting of Le Havre from 1872, becomes the name, suggestive of unity, for Manet's challenge to both public and critics. In so doing I shall examine how the *physiological* and *temporal* dimensions of meaning in this concept are correlated with its *aesthetic* one.

What is regarded as impression in the *physiological* sense is the immediate contact between the retina and the visible world. To see landscape and objects, people and space, the organic as well as the inorganic elements in nature and civilization as they appear in the moment of perception, without correcting the sensuous impression through knowledge of the objects: this is one of the most frequent descriptions of impressionist seeing. In this Rousseauistic train of thought, wherein the eye is liberated from the conventions that had dominated it, the retina becomes the metaphor for a perception of the world prior to all reflection, independent of the intellect. In place of the unsophisticated savage whose ingenuous glance, free of the compulsions of convention, discovers the beautiful that remains hidden to the knowing eye, there is the figure of the child. Thus writes Hermann Bahr, the noted Viennese commentator on the *Zeitgeist* and popularizer of everything modern, in making his case for impressionism.

> A child on the beach sees a woman walking in the sun and says, "Look, Papa, the shadow is blue!" The Papa says, "No, the shadow is black; it only looks that way." The child is actually more clever; she clings to the immediate truth, about which she is certain. She believes her eyes; she sees in a way which is as yet unspoiled.[28]

This praise of the child's retina is a symbol for the immediacy of perception, which corresponds to the emphatic plea for the "natural" light of plein-air painting in contrast to the regulated, cold light of the studio.

This admittedly is only one side of the physiology of the impression. The other results from the investigation into the highly artificial and reflexive character of the isolation of the "retinal image." Impressionistic seeing is a medium, an immaterial apparatus as well as a fiction of the "naturally pure" glance. The figure who thus appears as the complement to the child is the experienced artist of perception, whose retina is not an organ of a naïveté, but a refined virtuoso of sensitivity to light. The photographic plate finds a place in this manner in the metaphorical context of the retina, and the physiological argumentation, in its systematized variants, seeks above all else the proximity to nature through radically modern means, in alliance with science and technology. In Germany around 1900 it becomes a part of the public consciousness that, in Seurat's pointillism, the theory of spectral colors becomes the perceptual and physiological foundation of "chromoluminarism" in painting. This is largely the result of the translation of the theoretical works of Paul Signac.[29] "Apparently the physiological theorems of the impressionists were compatible with their experience, partly enraptured, partly socially critical, of big cities as well as with the dynamism of their pictures," writes Adorno.[30] The bridge between the physiologically understood impression and the experience of the metropolis was, in the late nineteenth and early twentieth centuries, primarily constructed through the concept of "stimulation" (Reiz). The historian Karl Lamprecht, for example, regarded the culture of the *fin de siècle* as the epoch of *Reizsamkeit*, of sensitivity to stimulation. For both him and his student, the social psychologist Willy Hellpach, this concept served to mediate between the spheres of art and reality, in that it assigned impressionism as an art of calculated sensory stimulation to the modes of expression of nervousness. Its career as a specifically modern sickness dates its beginnings from about 1890, so that by 1900 the discursive equation of impressionism and nervousness can draw upon a rich reservoir of motifs.[31]

The aesthetician Broder Christiansen conceived of pointillism as the "perfection of modern impressionism," and defined the construction of the picture out of dots of color as the dissolution and disintegration of spatial forms through a "radical decomposition of the continuum." In its preference for the "depiction of the agitated," its tendency toward the hasty, the precipitate, and the abruptly interrupted, the impressionist privileging of the discontinuous was comparable to the "impressions of the cinematograph," in which the organic sequence of movement is transformed into a mechanical, sporadic advance of images. In placing the human retina's physiological capacity to preserve a momentary optical stimulus in the service of a systematic dissolution of the experience of continuity, modern impressionism could be seen to produce images permeated by the spirit of agitation according to the principle of "intermittent stimulation."

To this formal "adaptation of the era's craving for stimulation" there corresponds, in the material realm, the preference for the "crass, the shrill, the caustic, the repulsive and the common" on the part of artists such as Manet and Degas, Rops and Toulouse-Lautrec, Slevogt, Corinth, Thomas

Theodor Heine, Beardsley, Rodin and Heinrich Zille: "The miserable people of Berlin in Heinrich Zille's paintings do not want to move," wrote Christiansen; "they are not there as a social indictment, but rather as a means of producing intense nervous stimulation. Their putrescence gives a stimulant to art, and in Zille's paintings the latrine is seldom missing."[32] Here, as elsewhere, the emphasis on the physiological dimension of the "impression" is in the service of a polemical pathography of modernity: the decadence of the nervous inhabitant of the metropolis and the "aesthetic sensualism" of an art determined by the retina, so it was argued, reflected each other.

The *temporal* aspect of impressionism becomes palpable in the optical metaphor for the extremely short time span, the "fleeting glance of an eye" (*flüchtigen Augenblick*). It is intimately linked with the physiological dimension and emphasizes the ennobling of the momentary and the transient as a cultural basis as well as an effect of the reception of impressionism. Christiansen's *Philosophie der Kunst* discusses impressionism's dissolution of that traditional alliance between the pictorial image and time as duration, the sense of time arrested, as an attack on one of the basic tenets of painting. The inner structure of the image had been invaded by the disquiet of the momentary. What was permissible in a graphic sketch on paper seemed, on the framed canvas, an impermissible neglect of the plastic depth of space in favor of the suggestion of the moment's immediate intensity.

> And as the impressionist method badly harmonizes with the substances of painting, so the impressionist depiction of motion in particular is in opposition to that quiet flowing of spiritual life which the portrait demands. . . . For an impressionist treatment always produces . . . a devaluation of what is represented. This technique has something of the mood of a fleeting glance and as such gives the motif a nuance that suggests that it is only for fleeting observation. In the case of a portrait, this is sensed as a lack of respect, and in its extreme form, as with certain moderns, it has the effect of an insult. As a consequence, Liebermann's portrait of Berger in the Hamburg Kunsthalle has the character of a zoological study.[33]

That a person ought not to be painted as if one had seen him/her only quickly, en passant, challenges the right of the metropolitan passerby, as a figure of contingency, to a portrait that transcends the hasty sketch. Such verdicts lead one to suspect, *ex negativo*, what has been achieved in paintings like Degas's *Vicomte Lepic on the Place de la Concorde* (ca. 1875): a formal equivalent to the transitory and the contingent in the everyday life of the metropolis.[34] Out of a world of dynamism, movement, and sudden encounters, there emerges the impression in a temporal sense. Its historical locus is the eye of the city dweller. This is not only the case in the polemical interpretation of Broder Christiansen, but also holds true for neutral writers, from Richard Hamann via Max Weber and Walter Benjamin to Arnold Hauser.[35] From the physiological and temporal determinations of the impression there emerges, as its aesthetic formula, the radicalism of the visual: to declare the visibility of the world to be the proper and sole object of painting.

In his study on the entry of the specifically Japanese into French painting, Yujiro Shinoda has described this as a development from "tactile values to optical values."[36] Painting had always been an art for the eye, but never before had anyone so wanted to emancipate this eye; never before had anyone so disregarded the fact that the things of the world are something other than visible; never before had anyone conceived of the play of color and light as so autonomous, as a source of images transcending all considerations of theme or motif; nor had anyone experimented so boldly with the two-dimensionality of the picture surface. Astounded or horrified, contemporaries reacted to the banishment of the allegorical, the rhetorical, and the historical from painting in favor of the visibility of the moment. The retreat of the plastic and the architectonic in the conception of space gradually came to be perceived ambivalently: as the collapse of all perspective order and solidarity of the represented, or as painting's finally having come to itself through the autonomous eye, the organ of perception liberated from all material constraints.[37] In the next section I will show how the eye of impressionist vision became the model for the discovery of the beauty of Berlin, the capital of all ugliness.

3. Aesthetic Excursions through Berlin

Like *life*, *beauty* also belongs to the magic words with whose emphatic auraticization Jugendstil evoked the utopia of a liberation from the restraints of mechanization, industrialization, and the disfiguration of the world. We are accustomed to emphasizing the regressive, illusory, and mawkish aspects of this program of eliminating the ugliness of industrial modernity, a program carried out in the spirit of an art that approached "life" and that beautified and ennobled all of its forms, down to the most quotidian details. We regard the exuberant intertwining lines with which the Jugendstil embraced everything within its reach—from the facades of houses to the endpapers of its books and journals—as the symptoms of an attempt to insulate itself against those spheres of technology and industry that eluded its decorative intentions. In the cult of the organic and especially of the vegetative ornament we see the constructive imperative of modern materials—iron, for example—betrayed and twisted in favor of a masking and stylizing of technology as nature. In revolt against the *Gründerzeit* (the culture of the early years of the empire) and the pompous stylistic masquerades of historicism, we recognize above all else the propaganda generated by and for this "new" style.[38] In this speculation on Jugendstil as a last evasive maneuver away from technology, we easily overlook its functional and practical qualities— qualities that locate it within the prehistory of the Bauhaus. One correctly recognizes the reconciliation claimed between the realms of the beautiful and the technical as a seeming transfiguration of a tension that continues to exist; we unjustly neglect, however, because of our general suspicion of escapism, those motifs of Jugendstil in which its ornaments and lines signal the birth of a modern aesthetic of the industrial-inorganic. It is significant that Harry Count Kessler, in defining the English Arts and Crafts Movement, which was based upon premodern forms and materials, contrasted it with the modern lines of van de Velde, which he found analagous to contemporary technology: "the affinity of its character with the long, elegant movement of lines which is now, remarkably, bursting forth everywhere: not simply in iron constructions, in the mighty suspension bridges, in machines, racing yachts, automobiles, but also in private life, in skirts, in the cut of dress-coats, in tailor-made women's clothing. This curve of modern strength is the tuning fork for van de Velde's lines."[39]

August Endell, whose programmatic text of 1908, *Die Schönheit der großen Stadt* (The beauty of the metropolis), will be analyzed presently, lived from 1871 until 1925. His most productive period was prior to the First World War. He studied psychology and philosophy in Munich, then became, as an autodidact, an architect and a decorative artist. He was a master of vegetatively inspired ornamentation and, especially in his earlier works, a radical of the Jugendstil. His famous Elvira photo studio in Munich, its facade adorned with an exotic dragon and with a no less bizarre bannister in its interior, soon became notorious far beyond Munich as a modern monstrosity. In 1901 he came to Berlin, where he designed Wolzogen's Buntes Theater. It is distinguished by an interior inspired by pointillism, a "roaring symphony" of ornamental lines and surfaces. From 1904 until 1914 Endell directed a school for applied design in Berlin, where students were instructed in the decorative layout of magazines, furniture, and carpet design, and the creation of thoroughly harmonious interiors. He designed shoe stores and villas, hotels and dining cars. According to Karl Scheffler's assessment of Endell, the matter-of-fact engineer successfully emancipated himself from the decorative ornamental artist in his few buildings in Berlin—for example, in an apartment house on the Steinplatz or the festival hall of a factory in the Rosenthaler Straße. Above all, Scheffler singled out Endell's design for a trotting racecourse in Mariendorf as "a light, representative summer architecture, at once both austere and gay."

The iron and wood supports of the grandstands, normally hideous, have become the witty, austerely gracious edifices of an engineer; he has made of the obligatory restaurants a free and elegant pavilion. . . . The engineering component of his fantasy reveals itself above all in the finely delineated webbing of the iron support structures.[40]

Endell's contribution to an aesthetics of the metropolis, *Die Schönheit der großen Stadt*, has as its chief stage the ugly city of Berlin. It refers with polemic élan to the then current consensus, summarized by Sabine Lepsius as follows: "For the person seeking beauty it is impossible to feel at home in Berlin — unless he possesses the strength to set himself apart, determined to work alone, and retires to an island in the Spree where he will not notice the surrounding insipidity."[41] It is precisely this idea, that in Berlin beauty is at best an extraterritorial island in a sea of the prosaic, that Endell challenges. He asserts that any concept of *Heimat*, or home, that is bound up with the village, the soil, Gothic marketplaces, and Baroque squares is anachronistic. In a plea for the "passionate love of the here and now," he defines the metropolis as the only authentic *Heimat* of the present. He quickly disposes of the three forms most often taken by the "renunciation of the present": the sentimental idyllizing of nature, the theatrically pompous presentation of past art, and the historicist empathy for an idealized past. Then Endell turns to his own topic. As an alternative to the pathographic characterization of the metropolis "as the symbol of present-day decay" he offers a view equally one-sided: "that the metropolis, despite all the offensive buildings, despite the noise, despite everything for which one can reproach it, is, to one who wishes to see, a miracle of beauty and poetry, a fairy tale brighter, more colorful, more variegated than anything related by a poet."[42] It is noteworthy that Endell expressly concedes that diagnosis of the formlessness of the modern metropolis with which we are familiar through Rathenau and Scheffler. "The streets have no essence, no pattern or character peculiar to them. The squares are empty spaces without dimension or form; the houses do not blend with the streets, are loud, conspicuous, and yet without effect. Between house and street there is no interrelationship."[43]

It is not the vistas offered by the city, nor what Rathenau called its "overall picture" that is Endell's focus. The beauty of which he writes can peacefully coexist with the architectural ugliness and shapelessness of Berlin. It is a beauty not of planning but of seeing; its locus is not the buildings and avenues of the city but the eye of the *flâneur*. Endell's "poetry" of the city is a product of the accidental, if always aesthetically sensitive, perception.

First, Endell reveals the eye of the engineer, who observes the rhythmic play of "forces and inner movement" with an almost naive enthusiasm and to whom, as he surveys bolts, vents, and cylinders, the seemingly confused noise of a factory becomes a clearly articulated language.

An iron bridge, assembled out of hundreds of functioning members, all
stressed in accordance with their strength, lightly expanding in response to
each pressure and thereafter contracting with the same elasticity, the main
elements moving against each other, the whole playing in steel joints and
shifting . . . under the influence of weight, the sun, the cold, in a gentle
and hardly visible swinging, expanding, and contracting.[44]

This focus, at the very beginning of his text, on factories, machines, and
iron structures, signals Endell's conscious disregard of everything that even
the despisers of the city could accept as islands of beauty: inner-city parks,
"nice old houses," and "squares from time past." Endell seeks beauty precisely in what is considered ugly: "I wish to speak only of the modern city,"
he insists.

For this purpose he develops a propaedeutic of aesthetic perception that
would instruct "one to regard a city as one regards a forest, mountains, and
the sea."[45] In this school of seeing, the artificial, inorganic world of the metropolis becomes the equivalent of the beauty of nature; it is, however,
rather misleading when Endell explains his plea for the perception of the
metropolis as a landscape with a view of the sea. For *landscape* does not refer
to a panoramic prospect of the city, but describes exclusively the mode of
aesthetic experience that should be tested by walking through the streets—
the glance freed from all pragmatic considerations. Just as nature appears as
landscape to this glance purged of troubling secondary concerns, so it
should ensure that the still-undiscovered beauty of modern civilization be
properly valued. Endell's key passage "On Seeing and the Visible World"
traces, through the history of painting, a long trend toward the liberation of
seeing from all subordinate functions and finally celebrates—with themes
borrowed from a Kantian theory of the autonomy of art—the realization
"that seeing as such is pleasurable" as a splendid moment for humanity. The
historical locus of this realization is French impressionism, which Endell
suggestively apostrophizes not as the mere discovery of a new pictorial
technique, but as a Columbus-like discovery of a new world, the "world of
the visible." Here, in polemical contrast to the abandoned metaphysical
transcendental world "behind" phenomena, it is a dimension of pure surface, the sensuously perceptible skin of the empirical world, which becomes
the domain of "wonder" and of "poetry." What unlocks this beauty from
its everyday invisibility is the autonomous eye; and it was French impressionism that refined it into a virtuoso organ for registering even the most
subtle of nuances.

The French discovered the veil of air which can transform things into
wholly other configurations with new laws and new kinds of beauty. They
no longer painted people, bridges, towers, but the strange apparitions that
air, light, dust, and glare make of them. . . . It is not that Manet painted

asparagus with a wonderfully perfected technique that is significant, but that he discovered that a bundle of asparagus — which until then had been regarded solely as an edible object — is an enchanted realm of the most delicate, glorious colors, that it is as beautiful and fascinating as the most fragrant flower, as the most beautiful woman. He discovered that, alongside and within a known something, there is a quite different something, accessible only to the eye, and therefore he attempted to paint it.[46]

Endell's theory of pure visibility, which allows him to equate the beauty of Manet's asparagus with that of orchids and lilies, indicates the path by which prosaic Berlin could compete with poetic Paris. For his summation of impressionism's achievement is that it accomplished "the separation of the visible from the object."

In the world of pure surface that thus comes into being, the architectural recedes in importance for the perception of the city; the objects of vision are not plastic but optical, detached from their material foundations. Consequently Endell can now view positively even such paragons of historicism and monstrous monumentality of Wilhelmine Berlin as Raschdorff's Cathedral or the Kaiser-Wilhelm-Memorial Church. To be sure, as an architect he sees in them "the most hideous thing imaginable"; but as a painter with words he describes the fascinating, ever-fluctuant play of light and shadow, of color and contour that transfigures such structures according to the weather and time of day. Thus does architecture become a canvas on which the autonomous eye, sensitized to the reading of surfaces, experiences the metropolis as a play of light.

Endell's text becomes a peculiarly hallucinative and phantasmagoric literary document of aesthetic urbanism in that he does not just propose that one walk through Berlin with the eyes of an impressionist painter, but actually does so himself. Whistler's London, perhaps Lesser Ury's images of Berlin, and, of course, Paris — which, by his own admission, Endell knew only through French paintings — seem to have served as models for his inventory of the beauties of the urban landscape. The fog, the atmosphere, the rain, the twilight, the artificial luminosity of the city at night assist Endell in finding, amid the apparently uniform gray sea of stone and houses, the images from which he is able to assemble a kaleidoscope of aesthetic fascination, Berlin. Moving through the streets, he traverses a spectrum of light and of colors; he makes his own plein-air studies within the urban space. There is no hierarchy of objects in his kaleidoscope of form, color, movement, of chiaroscuro; there are only differences of viewpoint, of distance and of proximity, of framing. The dark monster of a railroad bridge at night stands juxtaposed to the crescendo of colors of an advertising pillar; the gable wall made of bad brick rises alongside a reflecting streetcar rail in the asphalt; the "glass ships" of the trams pass next to the arches of the elevated train tracks at a triangular intersection; the garish colors of posters in the

evening light glow next to the modern monumentality of industrial buildings. In the main streets, side streets, and streets along the river bank Endell
tests his art of impressionist seeing. It is above all the great halls of the factories and the railway stations that for him become fantastic palaces: "glint-
ing, almost playful, and yet overwhelming." Such is the Silesian Railway
Station, for example, "when a fine fog fills the hall, making the iron vaulting
appear as an endlessly gleaming spider's web"; or the Friedrichstraße Station,
"when one stands on the entrance steps over the Spree, where one sees nothing
of the 'architecture,' but has only the gigantic surface of the glass apron before
one's eyes and the contrast to the paltry tangle of houses all around."[47]

Endell dedicates one section to the "street as a living being." Here two
traditional ingredients of metropolitan life are recommended to the attentive
viewer: the crowd and fashion. Fashion as the advocate for a "culture of the
eye" is here defended against the charge of foolish superficiality. Similarly,
the crowd does not appear as a threatening mass, but is seen from the perspective of a positive theory of anonymity. Precisely because the people in
the metropolis glide past each other hastily, without greeting, they become
mute elements of the landscape; they fill the architecturally "dead" streets
"with the music of rhythmically changing spatial life," and within the image of the street they give the times of day their unmistakable physiognomy.
Through the example of a view from the terrace of the Romanisches Café
onto the square "as a field with people distributed across it," Endell describes the charm of the moving crowd.

> All of the people are free from each other; now they move toward each
> other in dense groupings; now there are gaps; the articulation of the space
> is always changing. Pedestrians interpenetrate, conceal each other, detach
> themselves again and walk freely, each emphasizing, articulating, his share
> of space. The space between them thus becomes a palpable, vast living
> entity, which becomes all the more remarkable when the sun bestows upon
> each pedestrian an accompanying shadow or the rain spreads a glistening,
> unstable reflection at his feet.[48]

It is as if Endell already had the photographic experiments of the twenties
before his eyes—that series of pictures taken from atop the Berlin Funkturm
(radio tower) of the patterns inadvertently formed by people on the ground
below. He thus touches upon the conception of the crowd as a moving trel-
lis of points upon an empty, more or less "white" background, but he returns immediately to the impressionistically inspired, atmospheric conception of the subject.

> These things have, to all intents and purposes, never been painted; in
> paintings, crowds of people almost always fuse to become formless lumps;
> some space remains between them toward the foreground, but there is no
> living space between them. The atmospheric tones would have to be seen

with more delicacy and perspicacity than is the norm. I remember a painting by Monet that reproduced the peculiarity of appearances. On the bank of a river there is a large barge to which several parallel planks are extended from the shore; workers carrying coal walk over them. This overlapping, the perspective displacement, the diminution of the figures and their loose grouping—all of this is wonderfully conspicuous. I once saw something very similar in a great hall that was under construction. Its walls were unfinished and there were iron supporting beams overhead; the windows were boarded up against the cold so that inside, across the floor, which also consisted only of rhythmically arranged iron beams, a semidarkness filled the space. Then there came, over a walkway built of planks, a column of workers moving slowly and ponderously, each carrying a sack of cement on his back.[49]

Monet's painting, to which Endell juxtaposes a Berlin version painted in words, is easily identifiable as *Unloading Coal* (1875).[50] This juxtaposition not only accentuates to what extent the "discovering" vision of the German author is a rediscovery of his French models, but simultaneously gives the key to the understanding of the stylistic peculiarities of this prose so steeped in images: these peculiarities result from Endell's attempt to write of the metropolis as Monet paints it. Hence the chromatic scale of color adjectives; the unceasing effort to preserve within the text the indistinct elements of an impression, floating in the mists or barely recognizable; hence the cult of verbal nuance and with it the propensity for renewed descriptions of what is seen; hence the consistent presence of metaphors drawn from the sea and the landscape; hence the persistent quest for verbs of motion and for variations of the representation of perspective, light, and shadow. That Endell, without being committed to a narrative structure, can string his rhetorical images of the metropolis like pearls along the chain of his line of thought increases the impression that someone, here, in the midst of sober Berlin, has fallen victim to the intoxicating power of the streets.

This hypertrophic study in perception by this Jugendstil *flâneur* addicted to beauty departs from narrative not simply because the author is essentially concerned with the development of an aesthetic program rather than with the recounting of a walk through Berlin. This manner of viewing the city is, by its very nature, disinterested in the narrative, the anecdotal, and the dramatic. The city is not a diorama, whose equivalent in painting would be a genre scene; nor is it the site of events generating raw material for modern novels and novellas. With impressive consistency, the city is purged of drama; it becomes a landscape. It is a reservoir of sketches, not of developed scenes; a world of motifs, not of events. The section titles of Endell's text read like the titles of paintings: "Before the Cafe," "Workers at the Construction Site," "The Drill Ground," "Unter den Linden," "Potsdamer Platz," "Before the Brandenburg Gate."

Sitting at the death bed of his wife, Claude Monet noticed with horror how he began to observe the nuances of color and the reflections of light upon the face of the dying woman. This anecdote relating the painter's horror at the realization that he was a prisoner of his own virtuosic eye is included in every history of impressionism. That the cultivation of the autonomous eye may be accompanied by cynicism and moral indifference becomes clear in the case of Endell when he describes the victims of Berlin's tenements. "How exquisite the sickly colors of the city's children often are; how their features have, sometimes precisely because of need and privation, an austere beauty. Even depravity, insolence can possess beauty, power, even greatness."[51] It is easy, in the face of such delicately sensitive detachment, to interpret Endell's discovery of the beauty of the metropolis as a document of aestheticism and its twin, immoralism. It is all too apparent that the social privilege of the flâneur is the implicit precondition for his confining himself to the domain of the visible. The success of this seeker after beauty sounds all too contrived. This judgment may be tempered, however, if one recognizes in Endell's extreme aestheticism and moral anesthesia the polemical reversal of that other extreme, the pathography of the metropolis, which saw the city only as the locus of moral decay. It then becomes clear that the attempt to discover in the modern "landscape" of the city an equivalent of natural beauty does not necessarily have as its consequence the rejection of all nonaesthetic reflection. On the contrary, Endell formulates in an exemplary way a type of perception that, even apart from its emphatic exaggeration, is effective and significant: as an expression of the ambivalent experience of the metropolis. Only in part is it the soulless machinery, the barbaric modern Moloch, the world of total mechanization and monotony; on the other it is the fascinating aesthetic object of modernity par excellence, center of a positive mythology of modernity.[52]

Siegfried Kracauer, to whom Endell's confessed yearning for beauty would certainly have been an abomination, participated nonetheless in the cultivation of the urban sense of sight that Endell carries under the banner of impressionism. Even when the "surface" can only be discussed under Kracauer's engaged, sociologically analytical glance as a socially determined surface, it is nevertheless equally and simultaneously a sphere of aesthetic perception. Kracauer's introduction to the text "Berliner Landschaft" (A Berlin landscape, 1931) can be read in this sense as a theoretical commentary upon Endell's manner of proceeding.

> One can distinguish between two types of images of the city: those that are consciously formed and others that reveal themselves unintentionally. The former have their origin in the artificial intention that is realized in squares, vistas, groups of buildings and perspectival effects that Baedeker illuminates with a small star. In contrast, the latter emerge without having been previously planned. They are not compositions . . . but rather

fortuitous creations that do not allow themselves to be called to account. Wherever masses of stone and lines of streets are to be found together, whose elements emerge out of quite diversely oriented interests, there such an image of the city comes into existence that is itself never the object of some interest or other. It is no more constructed than is nature and is similar to a landscape in that it unconsciously asserts itself. Unconcerned with how it looks, it continues to glow through time. Before my window, the city is condensing to an image, one as delightful as any comedy of nature. . . . [53]

One can thus conclude: the metropolis as a landscape is the sphere of its nonintentional, accidental, and unpredictable beauty. Endell, who with an eye schooled in impressionism took his sketches from this sphere, was satisfied with the aesthetic yield as such. Kracauer, for whom the art of seeing was only one element of his engagement with the metropolis, understood the images of the "unordered" Berlin as material in need of interpretation, material that wants to be understood as the unconscious gesture of a person. "The knowledge of cities is a decoding of their images, ones uttered thoughtlessly, as if in a dream."[54]

Translated by Charles W. Haxthausen,
with the assistance of Joe Brown

NOTES

1. See Charles Baudelaire, "The Painter of Modern Life," in *The Painter of Modern Life and Other Essays*, trans. and ed. Jonathan Mayne (London, 1965), 1–40.

2. Helmut Pfeiffer, Hans Robert Jauss, and Françoise Gaillard, eds., *Art social und art industriel. Funktionen der Kunst Im Zeitalter des Industrialismus* (Munich, 1987).

3. Compare Hans Robert Jauss's critique of Walter Benjamin's reading of Baudelaire as a melancholy allegorist of alienation in *Literaturgeschichte als Provokation* (Frankfurt, 1970), 57–66.

4. Compare Gottfried Korff, "Mentalität und Kommunikation in der Großstadt. Berliner Notizen zur 'inneren' Urbanisierung," in *Großstadt. Aspekte empirischer Kulturforschung*, ed. Theodor Kohlman and Hermann Bausinger (Berlin, 1985); see also Jürgen Reulecke, *Geschichte der Urbanisierung in Deutschland* (Frankfurt/Main, 1985).

5. Compare Lothar Müller, "Modernität, Nervosität und Sachlichkeit. Das Berlin der Jahrhundertwende als Hauptstadt der 'neuen Zeit'," in *Mythos Berlin*, exhibition catalog (Berlin, 1987).

6. Walter Rathenau, "Die schönste Stadt der Welt," in *Impressionen* (Leipzig, 1902), 137–63.

7. On the "classical roots" of modern architecture, see Tilmann Buddensieg and Henning Rogge, eds., *Industriekultur. Peter Behrens und die AEG (1907–1924)* (Berlin, 1978), especially 63ff.

8. Rathenau, "Die schönste Stadt der Welt," 148ff.

9. Ibid. Rathenau presented his program euphemistically as a "play of thoughts" (*Gedankenspiel*); it was, however, intended as a serious provocation and demand for a consistent modernity.

10. The interpretation of this "Haussmannization" should not be based solely upon Walter Benjamin and Siegfried Kracauer, who saw in the appearance of the boulevards a means of prohibiting barricades and a strategic rebuilding of the city in the interests of the ruling classes. In opposition to them, but without reactionary intentions, are other authors who portray Haussmann as the principal agent of a historically legitimate and functionally necessary modernization without which Paris, in the late nineteenth and early twentieth centuries, would have been threatened by the collapse of its urban infrastructure. Compare Siegfried Giedion, *Space, Time and Architecture* (Cambridge, Mass., 1964), as well as David J. Olson, *The City as a Work of Art. London-Paris-Vienna* (New Haven, 1986), 44ff.

11. Quoted from Walter Benjamin, *Gesammelte Schriften*, 4 (Frankfurt am Main, 1982): 134.

12. Rathenau, "Die schönste Stadt der Welt," 144.

13. Karl Scheffler, *Berlin. Ein Stadtschicksal*, 2d ed. (Berlin, 1910), 200.

14. Karl Scheffler, "Die Großstadt," *Die neue Rundschau* 21 (1910):881.

15. In one long passage also following this pattern of comparison, Scheffler argued that Berlin, this prosaic city, had never had a writer who could effectively capture it in literary prose, including the city's greatest novelist of that era, Theodor Fontane. Scheffler argued that "a thoroughly modern chronicler of Berlin such as Theodor Fontane utterly lacks the mental capacity to portray the incredible chaos of a metropolis. He is a conversationalist where what one needs is rather someone with a creative temperament. . . . Fontane is a feuilletonist who has become a novelist, not a poet of a capital city." The basis of comparison is apparently Balzac. See Scheffler, *Berlin*, 102ff.

16. Werner Sombart, "Wien," *Der Morgen*, 1907, No. 6: 172–75.

17. Julius Lessing, *Das Moderne in der Kunst* (Berlin, 1898), 23.

18. Karlheinz Stierle, "Imaginäre Räume. Eisenarchitektur in der Literatur des 19. Jahrhunderts," in Pfeiffer, Jauss, and Gaillard, *Art Social*, 39–47.

19. Hans Sedlmayr, *Verlust der Mitte* (Salzburg, 1976), 23.

20. Compare Benjamin, *Gesammelte Schriften* 5.2 (Frankfurt, 1982):216. "The first buildings of iron served transitory purposes: market halls, train stations, exhibition halls. Iron thus became immediately bound up in economic life. But what at that time was functional and transitory is today beginning to be formal and stable in a different tempo." See also Stierle, "Imaginäre Räume."

21. Klaus Herding, "Industriebild und Moderne. Zur künstlerischen Bewältigung der Technik im Überbergang zur Grossmachinerie (1830–1890)," in Pfeiffer, Jauss, and Gaillard, *Art social*, 456–57.

22. Ibid.

23. Compare *Verhandlungen des Ersten Deutschen Soziologentags. Reden, Vorträge und Debatten* (Frankfurt, 1969), 98ff. In the debate Weber spoke in response to Werner Sombart's lecture on "Technology and Culture."

24. Ibid.

25. Compare Peter Paret, *The Berlin Secession: Modernism and Its Enemies in Imperial Germany* (Cambridge, Mass., 1980).

26. Evelyn Gutbrod, *Die Rezeption des Impressionismus in Deutschland 1880–1910* (Stuttgart, 1980); see also Hartmut Marhold, *Impressionismus in der deutschen Dichtung* (Frankfurt, 1985), 66ff.

27. Richard Hamann, *Der Impressionismus in Leben und Kunst* (Cologne, 1907).

28. Hermann Bahr, "Impressionismus," in *Essays* (Leipzig, 1912), 165.

29. Specifically, a German translation of his text *D'Eugène Delacroix au Neoimpressionisme* (Paris, 1899) appeared at the beginning of the century in *Kunst und Künstler*.

30. Theodor W. Adorno, *Aesthetic Theory*, ed. Gretel Adorno and Rolf Tiedemann, trans. C. Lenhardt (London, 1985), 463 (slightly altered translation). Compare also one of Walter Benjamin's rare remarks on Impressionism. "Perhaps the daily spectacle of an agitated mass of

people had once presented itself as a play, one to which the eye had to adapt. . . . The technique of impressionist painting, to draw the image into the tumult of flecks of color, would then have been a reflex from experiences which had become common to the inhabitants of the metropolis." Benjamin, *Gesammelte Schriften* 1 (Frankfurt/Main, 1972): 628.

31. Compare Willy Hellpach, *Nervosität und Kultur* (Berlin, 1902).

32. Broder Christiansen, *Philosophie der Kunst* (Hanau, FRG, 1909), 311.

33. Ibid., 331.

34. Max Imdahl, "Die Momentphotographie und 'le Comte Lepic' von Edgar Degas," in *Wege zu Degas*, ed. Wilhelm Schmidt (Munich, 1988), 298–309.

35. "Impressionism is an urban art par excellence not simply because it discovers the city as a landscape and transports the painting of the countryside back to the city, but also because it views the world with the eyes of the city dweller and reacts to external impressions with the overexcited nerves of the modern technical man. It is an urban style because it portrays the changeability, the nervous rhythm, the impressions of city life—sudden, sharp, but always immediately effaced." Arnold Hauser, *Sozialgeschichte der Kunst und Literatur* (Munich, 1967), 929.

36. In Schmidt, *Wege zu Degas*, 292.

37. Mallarmé belonged to the admirers of the "antiplastic" implications of modern painting: "I leave the massive and tangible solidity to its fitter exponent, sculpture. I content myself with reflecting on the clear and durable mirror of painting, that which perpetually lives, yet dies every moment, which only exists by the will of Idea, yet constitutes in my domain the only authentic and certain merit of nature—the Aspect." Stephane Mallarmé, "The Impressionists and M. Manet," *The Art Monthly Review*, 1876, here quoted from Penny Florence, *Mallarmé, Manet and Redon* (Cambridge, 1986), 18.

38. Compare Dolf Sternberger, *Über Jugendstil* (Frankfurt, 1977), who reviews the critical objections against Jugendstil as meaningfully as he relativizes overly harsh judgments.

39. Harry Graf Kessler, "Van de Veldes Tafelsilber" (1904), in *Künstler und Nationen. Aufsätze und Reden, 1899 bis 1933* (Frankfurt, 1988), 91.

40. Karl Scheffler, "Neue Arbeiten von August Endell," *Kunst und Künstler* 11 (1913): 359.

41. Cited in Sternberger, *Über Jugendstil*, 41.

42. August Endell, *Die Schönheit der großen Stadt* (Stuttgart, 1908), here quoted from *August Endell. Der Architekt des Photoateliers Elvira 1871–1925*, exhibition catalog (Munich, 1975), 94ff. All further references are to the latter publication.

43. Ibid., 95.

44. Ibid., 96.

45. Ibid., 98.

46. Ibid., 101. Max Liebermann acquired Manet's *Asparagus* in 1907; Endell may have seen it in Liebermann's home.

47. Ibid., 108ff.

48. Ibid., 115ff

49. Ibid., 116.

50. On the relatively isolated position of *Unloading Coal* (Les dechargeurs du charbon) in the oeuvre of Monet, see T. J. Clark, *The Painting of Modern Life. Paris in the Art of Manet and His Followers* (Princeton, 1984), 190ff.

51. Endell, 112.

52. In the history of the perception of the city, this orientation on the model of landscape plays a role of critical importance, one that cannot be exhaustively treated under the catchword *aestheticism*.

53. Siegfried Kracauer, *Straßen in Berlin und anderswo* (Berlin, 1987), 40. The text "Berliner Landschaft" is here printed as "Aus dem Fenster gesehen."

54. Ibid., 41.

CHAPTER 3

"A New Beauty":
Ernst Ludwig Kirchner's Images of Berlin

Charles W. Haxthausen

> *The life of our city is rich in poetic and marvelous subjects. We are*
> *enveloped and steeped as though in an atmosphere of the marvelous; but*
> *we do not notice it.*
>
> Charles Baudelaire

"I don't know why it is," wrote the Berlin novelist Georg Hermann in
1912, "the Berliner is truly ashamed of his city, and the art is especially so."[1]
Although Berlin, after the unification of Germany in 1871, had quickly
emerged as the cultural and artistic capital of Germany and its only true metropolis, there was at first little reflection of this new urban reality in the art
and literature produced there. The contrast with Paris during the same period is striking, for there the 1870s—the years immediately following the
Prussian victory over the French—were marked by the ascendancy of impressionism, the first artistic movement of the nineteenth century to embrace contemporary urban reality as subject matter. The works of Manet,
Degas, and Monet, to name only the most illustrious, present the recreational life of modern Paris; they offer an affirmative image of this modern
urban spectacle, documenting the distinctive pleasures offered by the city.[2]
Of Berlin during this same period we see comparatively little in the visual
arts. The Berlin impressionists, led by Max Liebermann, Lovis Corinth,
and Max Slevogt, largely ignored the city in which they lived and worked.
Although Liebermann's studio was housed in the family residence on
Pariser Platz, where Unter den Linden, the city's most celebrated avenue,
emerged from the Brandenburg Gate, we see neither this Berlin landmark
nor any other in his art. Yet, Liebermann was not disinterested in urban
motifs—only in those of Berlin. Instead, he preferred pleasurable recreational scenes from Amsterdam or Hamburg.[3]

Why was this so? Why should Berlin, during this period of dynamic economic and political ascendancy, have been *imago non grata* in the visual arts?

For one, although the German capital may have been the political counterpart of Paris, it was hardly its equal in other ways. Charles Huard, the
French travel writer and illustrator, offered a Parisian perspective on this
question in a book, *Berlin comme je l'ai vu*, published in 1907. His first chapter, on the capital's most famous street, set the general tone for his sober
view of the city.

> What sort of enthusiastic Berliner was it, who, on my departure from
> Paris, could sing to me the praises of the beauties of the Linden? . . . You
> cannot imagine its charm, he said: it is more discreet, more elegant, more
> aristocratic than your Parisian boulevards, than Piccadilly, the Corso, than
> every other vaunted street in the world. I anticipated an admirable avenue
> decorated with magnificent trees, bounded by the palace and frequented by
> princely carriages. To be sure, I found a large avenue, but it was planted
> with ordinary trees, unwelcome chestnuts and linden trees, topped and
> stunted; unsightly hired carriages drawn by emaciated, decrepit horses and
> driven by coarse coachmen rolled along the pavement. Dense, inelegant
> crowds of people halted at the intersections, and, docile and superbly
> trained, stomped along again at the order of the vigilant policemen. My
> disillusionment was complete.[4]

Such observations abound in Huard's travelogue, and these impressions
cannot be dismissed merely as manifestations of French chauvinism or of
lingering resentments over the Franco–Prussian War — there were too many
similarly negative characterizations of the city by thoughtful Berliners,
many of whom considered it second-rate as a European capital. Even an ar-
dent nationalist like Heinrich von Treitschke once remarked that the Germans alone among the peoples of the earth had attained the rank of great
power without having a great city, although he meant this as a boast.[5]

Karl Scheffler, one of the most influential art critics of the period and
author of a book-length historical critique, *Berlin: Ein Stadtschicksal* (1910),
claimed for the city the distinction of being not only the ugliest in Germany,
but "the capital of all modern ugliness."[6] Like Huard, he measured Berlin
against Paris, with depressing conclusions. Architecturally, Scheffler found
the city devoid of any properly urban physiognomy. In contrast to the
French capital, with its grand design of boulevards, parks, and public monuments, its ordered but dramatic vistas, Berlin was shapeless, confused, and
arbitrary. It had grown piece by piece, without any sense of the whole,
without any larger urbane vision of what a city should be. Most of its radial
arteries, according to Scheffler, tended to "disappear into a tangle of streets
on the periphery of the old city, before they have reached its center." There
was but one axis of orientation — Unter den Linden. It alone led to the core
of the city, and yet ended drearily in the New Market like a dead-end street.[7]
And like Huard, Scheffler found Berlin's population graceless and uncul-
tured: "Nine-tenths of the urban population makes an impression of hope-

less inferiority," he lamented. "Not a trace of the born gentleman does one find in the modern Berliner. At times it seems as if the entire male population consisted of building contractors and their assistants."[8] This was a colonial population, "dull and dreary, which . . . had streamed into the city from the eastern plains, lured by the promise of Americanism."[9]

What made Berlin so ugly in the eyes of cultivated observers was above all its flagrant modernity. Even a contemporary Baedeker guide to the city commented that in its visual aspect Berlin suffered from this condition, since "three-quarters of its buildings are quite modern," resulting in "a certain lack of historical interest."[10] This condition was due to Berlin's extraordinary growth: it had burgeoned from a relatively sleepy town of 170,000 inhabitants in 1800 to a city of nearly 2 million only a century later. In the views of most observers, according to Georg Hermann, Berlin was "in a state of becoming, in constant transformation, and for that reason has as yet no physiognomy."[11] Huard described it as "new, clean and devoid of character, completely new, too new, newer than any American city, newer than Chicago, the only city in the world with which one can compare it in terms of the incredible rapidity of its growth."[12]

Karl Scheffler also found Berlin distressingly American in other ways: in its diverse migrant population, its robust materialism, its lack of culture, and, for better or worse, its pioneer spirit. It had, he declared, "literally become like a colonial city, like . . . the American and Australian cities that arose deep in the bush."[13] Completing this unappealing urban picture was Berlin's failure to accommodate its expanding population: the city's growth had brought with it scandalous housing conditions—the worst in Europe after Budapest—a situation that led the architectural critic Werner Hegemann to dub it the "largest tenement city in the world."[14]

Even as Georg Hermann was lamenting the evident shame the Berlin artist felt toward his city, this condition of neglect had already begun to change. The avant-garde, the so-called expressionists, had taken up the life of the city as a major theme. Indeed, as Jost Hermand has recently written, expressionism—in literature as in the visual arts—was "the first real urban art in Germany, and for that reason found its logical center in Berlin."[15] In this regard, at least, expressionism performed a role in German art comparable to that of impressionism in French art nearly half a century earlier. But while the French impressionists' image of Paris was basically celebratory, discovering a new aesthetic in the modern city, the image of Berlin in avant-garde art of 1910–1914 has traditionally been seen as harsh and alienating, even apocalyptic—as anything but an art of affirmation and celebration. In 1917 Emil Waldmann observed, in a newspaper article entitled "The Artistic Discovery of the Metropolis," that in contrast to the French impressionists, who had aestheticized the modern city, the new generation of German artists had unflinchingly embraced its essential reality: "What the artists of today seek in the city is not to obscure its ugliness with light and color; rather, they have elevated precisely this ugliness to its characteristic feature."[16]

This essentially negative view of the expressionist representation of the city, above all of Berlin, has become the dominant one in the art-historical literature since World War II. Art historians, like their colleagues in German literary studies of this period, have tended to see in the artistic treatment of Berlin symptoms of "ein Leiden an der Stadt," a chronic state of suffering and alienation brought on by urban experience.[17] This is especially true of much of the literature on Ernst Ludwig Kirchner, the prewar expressionist who is widely regarded as the master of this urban genre, to which other artists — Ludwig Meidner, Max Beckmann, Erich Heckel, and the early George Grosz — also made notable contributions. Kirchner's images of Berlin, nearly all of which date from between 1911 and 1915, have most typically been read as virtual psychograms of urban anguish.[18] For the late Donald Gordon, the leading American scholar of Kirchner's art, his images of Berlin revealed "better than . . . the vision of any other twentieth-century artist . . . insight into a desperately diseased European society whose . . . days are numbered."[19] This dark interpretation of Kirchner's Berlin paintings as symptoms of a profound alienation from urban life, as products of an intensely critical, even apocalyptic view of the metropolis, has gained increasing acceptance in the recent literature.

In the present essay I shall propose a different reading: that on the whole Kirchner's images of Berlin were born of an essentially affirmative attitude toward the metropolis, as were the French impressionists' images of Paris; that, indeed, within German art these works manifested the belated discovery of what Baudelaire, in reference to mid-nineteenth-century Paris, called "a new and special beauty," the beauty of the modern city.[20] I shall argue that Kirchner saw his art not as an expression of urban alienation and anxiety, but as a contribution to an aestheticization of urban life, a visual reality that most of the German art world still viewed negatively.

I am hardly the first to make this claim for Kirchner; it was the dominant view in the literature before 1933. "No other artist experienced the metropolis Berlin, as it was in the last years before the War, so intensely, with every fiber of his being, as did Kirchner," wrote Curt Glaser in the 1920s. "Beyond the ephemeral charm of the bizarre lines of modish elegance he sensed plastic form in the life of the metropolitan street."[21] In 1920 Karl Scheffler, like others before him, stressed Kirchner's affinity with the French impressionists, comparing him to Manet.[22] Paul Westheim characterized Kirchner's city images as a "Symphonie der Großstadt," a symphony of the metropolis.[23] To be sure, this view still occasionally appears in the Kirchner literature after 1945. One finds it in Will Grohmann's monograph of 1958.[24] Annemarie Dube-Heynig, in her 1961 study of Kirchner's graphic art, echoed Glaser in portraying the artist as the "chronicler of Berlin and its people" in the years before the Great War; Kirchner, she declared, was "the first to give form to lived experience of the large modern city."[25] Yet, by this time a very different Kirchner had begun to emerge in the critical and scholarly literature: a deeply alienated artist who viewed the city with anxiety and foreboding.[26] Since the publication of Donald Gordon's monograph of 1968 this reading seems to have become the dominant one, even if there remain significant voices in the German-speaking world who do not share it. It is beyond the scope of this essay to explore the complex reasons for this historiographic phenomenon, but this much can be said: this new interpretation was based neither on new evidence nor on a more exacting reading of the source material, which to a large extent has evidently been ignored or dismissed as irrelevant. In the case of Kirchner, it appears, historical distance has blurred distinctions that were very evident to his contemporaries. Today, his vision of Berlin appears to many viewers as akin to Meidner's apocalyptic nightmares, Beckmann's *Hell*, or the frenzied insanity of Grosz's urban pandemonium.[27] To those who lived and wrote about art in the Berlin of that time, however, the distinctions were clearly apparent.

Berlin's abrupt genesis into a modern metropolis is undoubtedly a central factor in the history of its representation—and, for long periods, its neglect—in the visual arts.[28] The charm of the preindustrial city had attracted architectural painters such as Eduard Gärtner (1801–77), best known for his gracious views of the official face of Berlin. But as Berlin's character changed, as it grew into a modern, industrial city, it seemingly became, in the eyes of its major artists, a subject unworthy of representation. Adolph Menzel (1815–1905), the greatest Berlin painter of the nineteenth century, produced several strikingly modern images of the city in the 1840s, but he rarely chose it as a motif thereafter, except for events of an official nature.[29] Significantly, the Menzel paintings that best capture the texture of everyday urban life are scenes of Paris, a city in which modernity presented a more aesthetically pleasing aspect.[30]

The acknowledged dreariness and gracelessness of Berlin, this parvenu among European capitals, did not, however, mean that its artists found it entirely unworthy of their attentions. Beginning in the 1880s, Hans Baluschek drew and painted the everyday life of the proletarian outer city and factories, and unaestheticized images of such industrial motifs as railroad yards. One contemporary critic described him as "the painter of that Berlin which became a metropolis overnight, but which, like a lucky speculator, lacks the breeding and culture to play the new role with decorum, without meanness."[31] But Baluschek's quotidian, proletarian subject matter was unpalatable to official taste, and his social engagement made him a marginal figure within the Berlin Secession, dominated as it was by the formalist values of impressionism.

Certain Berlin impressionists, like Lesser Ury, Franz Skarbina, and Ulrich Hübner, also painted Berlin, but it was a different city from Baluschek's: they usually chose their motifs either from Berlin-Mitte — Unter den Linden, Leipziger Straße, and Friedrichstraße — or from the western districts of the city. Moreover, the impressionistic style of such paintings, emphasizing transient effects of light and atmosphere, functioned, in John Czaplicka's phrase, as a "natural veil," transfiguring and thereby concealing the sober urban reality.[32] Light and atmosphere redeemed the city. Although "the dreary desolation and abomination of our streets are beyond despair," wrote August Endell in 1905, "all of these awful facades and streets are continuously enveloped by light and atmosphere which unceasingly transform their appearance. . . . And whoever observes these things finds in the midst of all of the unspeakable hideousness exquisite things."[33] In the evening, when the street lamps were lit, continued Endell, the city became like the setting for a fairy tale "more colorful and charming than any we were told as children."[34] Scheffler, too, found consolation in such impressionistic transfigurations. Berlin's very ugliness intensified those rare aesthetic pleasures to be found in it. "The less pleasure one derives from the architectural aspect, the more one feels repulsed by the pervasive artificiality," he wrote, "all the more passionately does one grasp toward the cosmic beauty of light and air."[35]

Four years after the appearance of Scheffler's book, a young Berlin artist published an essay in Scheffler's magazine, Kunst und Künstler, that articulated a radically new attitude toward the metropolis. The text, Ludwig Meidner's "Anleitung zum Malen von Großstadtbildern" (Directions for painting images of the metropolis), began: "We must finally begin to paint our Heimat, the metropolis, for which we have an infinite love."[36] To call the city "Heimat" — August Endell had already done so in 1908[37] — was to suggest that it had become humanized, that its inhabitants had put down roots and were establishing traditions, that Berlin was moving beyond the status of Scheffler's cultureless "Kolonialstadt" of the uprooted. More significantly, the beauty of the metropolis for Meidner was, in contrast to the impressionist vision of Scheffler or Endell, not to be found in the transfiguring effects of light and atmosphere, but in the unnatural, fabricated enviroment of the city — the "tumultuous streets, the elegance of iron suspension bridges, the gasometers . . . the howling colors of the Autobuses and express locomotives, the rolling telephone wires, the harlequinade of the advertisement pillars . . . "[38] Meidner condemned the Paris scenes of Monet and Pissarro; they had painted urban architecture like brooks, and boulevards like flower beds. "A street," Meidner continued, "is composed not of tonal values, but is a bombardment of whizzing rows of windows, of rushing beams of light between vehicles of many kinds, of a thousand leaping spheres, tatters of people, advertisements, and droning, formless masses of color."[39] This urban environment was a product of mathematics, the creation of the engineer. Light remained a major concern; however, it did not soften objects, but was itself transformed by the movement of the city. Meidner's rhetoric is clearly indebted to the texts of the Italian futurists, which had been published in German translation by 1912; but he looked not to *their* paintings but to Robert Delaunay's cubistic images of the the Eiffel Tower as a model of a truly urban art grounded in a new perceptual experience of the modern city.[40]

Yet, for all his rapturous exhortations, Meidner was, in the words of one scholar, a "terrified enthusiast."[41] Although many of his drawings of 1913–14 seem virtual illustrations of his text, his paintings of these same fertile years are most often feverish apocalyptic visions of a city with the unmistakable features of Berlin—his *Burning City* (1913, The St. Louis Art Museum) is a typical example.[42] As Reinhold Heller has written, in spite of Meidner's verbal dithyrambs to the metropolis, his "urban imagery, like Jakob van Hoddis's epochal poem 'Weltende,' predicts—or yearns for— urban destruction, a violent termination of the dehumanizing, materialistic cities that contain within themselves the explosive, doom-filled powers invented by modern man."[43]

As I have already noted, Kirchner's images of Berlin have been widely interpreted in this same spirit. For Wolf-Dieter Dube the underlying theme of Kirchner's Berlin scenes is "the hectic and unnatural condition of the modern metropolis," revealing "the helpless compulsion, the desolation of the alienated man, which he was himself."[44] Rosalyn Deutsche, in an article on Kirchner's street scenes entitled "Alienation in Berlin," declares these works "immediately recognizable as pictures of an unnatural, thoroughly dehumanized world."[45] And the late Donald Gordon, in his posthumously published study of expressionism, reaffirmed his earlier dark reading of Kirchner's city pictures, calling them images of "a lonely wasteland."[46] Although these and other authors do not discuss Kirchner's urban imagery in relation to the earlier impressionist treatment of Berlin, they suggest by implication that his pictures, like those of other urban expressionists, are symptomatic of a dramatic exacerbation of that uneasy relationship with the city manifested in the "natural veils" of impressionism.

Central to these dark interpretations of Kirchner's urban imagery has been the distinctive style of his Berlin period. Compared to the fluid, curvilinear, fauve-inspired manner that dominated the Dresden period, Kirchner's Berlin painting style is decidedly angular and more tautly schematic in composition: forms and spaces are subject to often extreme distortions—pulled and stretched by compositional forces, bodies are drastically attenuated, horizontal planes are tilted up at steep angles. Yet, for all the carefully calculated, often geometric rigor of their compositions, these pictures convey an effect of excited spontaneity through their rapidly brushed liquid pigment, set down with a nervous, energized graphic facture evocative of pastel. In the best of Kirchner's Berlin compositions, such as *Two Women on the Street* (figure 13), this contrast, this sense of raw, animal energy harnessed by uncompromising pressures of pictorial design, produces a tension that is explosive. It is precisely this style that has been widely interpreted as the sign of an aggressively negative attitude toward the city. "Tottering ground planes, crooked houses, fugitive, distorted perspectives draw an apocalyptic vision of doom and the end of the world," one commentator has written.[47] "Grotesque caricature, garish color, entrapping spatial distortion and harshly angular line function as agents of protest against an alienating, impenetrable city," declares another.[48]

This reading of an antinaturalistic style as an expression of urban alienation has a parallel in the scholarly writing on Berlin expressionist poetry. Jakob van Hoddis, Alfred Lichtenstein, Georg Heym (whose *Umbra Vitae* Kirchner illustrated in the 1920s), and others of their generation adopted a so-called *Reihungsstil*, displacing narrative or descriptive continuity with abrupt, jarring sequences of fragmented, seemingly disconnected images. Traditionally, literary scholars—like commentators on expressionist art—have offered existential explanations for this style: it was interpreted as a negation of literary form and linguistic coherence, symptomatic of the alienation brought about by the *Verlust der Sinnmitte*, the loss of metaphysical coherence, in the metropolis. In a study published in 1974, however, Silvio Vietta reexamined the question and proposed another explanation for the *Reihungsstil*.[49] He argued that a *positive* stylistic principle was at work here—the product of a historically determined change in the structure of perception itself within the metropolis, a phenomenon described in Georg Simmel's classic essay of 1903, "The Metropolis and Mental Life." According to Simmel, the city dweller experienced an "intensification of emotional life due to the swift and continuous shift of external and internal stimuli." This urban environment was characterized by "the rapid telescoping of changing images, harsh differentiation in the perceptions of a single glance, and the unexpectedness of intrusive impressions."[50] On this basis Vietta argued that the *Reihungsstil* of the early expressionist poets should be understood not primarily as a negatively motivated symptom of alienation, but as the "literary mimesis of a new, historically mediated collective norm of perception and consciousness."[51]

There are firm grounds for accepting Kirchner's Berlin style as a parallel phenomenon. He wrote that he developed his style of the years 1913–14 out of "the perception of movement."[52] And turning to one of his most lucid statements on the novel character of urban perception, we find a description of the complex, ever fluctuant tissue of visual reality in the modern city that is reminiscent of Simmel.

Figure 13. Ernst Ludwig Kirchner. Two Women on the Street, *1914. Oil on canvas, 91 x 120.5 cm. Kunstsammlung Nordrhein-Westfallen, Düsseldorf. Reproduced by permission of Dr. Wolfgang und Ingeborg Henze, Campiono d'Italia, Switzerland.*

If we see a modern metropolitan street at night with its thousands of light sources, some of them colored, then we must realize that any objective [pictorial] construction is futile, since a passing taxi, a bright or dark evening dress transforms the entire laboriously achieved construction. If we consider the stimulating impact that is produced in us through the sight of unfamiliar effects and that is really the origin of the artist's impression, something quite different comes into being than an exact reconstruction.[53]

At the same time this statement makes a point that parallels Vietta's argument about the style of urban expressionist poetry: *that the altered nature of modern perceptual experience renders traditional modes of representation inadequate.* Accordingly, like the poets, Kirchner sought new means to render his experience in its fullness. The abstract nature of this pictorial sign is evident from the following Kirchner text, in which he refers to himself in the third person.

> He discovered that the feeling that pervades a city presented itself in the qualities of lines of force (*Kraftlinien*). In the way in which groups of persons configured themselves in the rush, in the trams, how they moved, this is how he found the means to capture what he had experienced. There are pictures and prints in which a purely linear scaffolding with almost schematic figures nevertheless represents the life of the streets in the most vital way.[54]

In his stress on the qualitative difference of modern urban perception and on the impossibility of rendering that experience by traditional naturalistic means, Kirchner recalls the Italian futurists. As already noted, their manifestos were published in German (in *Der Sturm*) and their first exhibition, after opening in Paris, was shown in Berlin in March and April 1912, half a year after Kirchner had settled there. In the catalog of that exhibition, they declared "that there can be no modern painting without the starting point of an absolutely modern sensation."[55] Fundamental to this sensation for both the futurists and Kirchner is the experience of movement. Kirchner's formulation is a retrospective one, but it nevertheless is strikingly close to the futurist language of that time. They wrote of translating the fluctuant object according to "the force lines (*Linienkräften*) which distinguish them," creating a picture that was "a synthesis of the various abstract rhythms of every object, from which there springs a font of pictorial lyricism hitherto unknown."[56]

But what of the psychological effects of this new urban sensory experience? According to Simmel, the metropolitan type must create "a protective organ for itself against the profound disruption with which the fluctuations and discontinuities of the external milieu threaten it." Reaction to these stimuli is therefore "moved to a sphere of mental activity which is least sensitive and which is furthest removed from the depths of the personality."[57] Consequently there is for Simmel "perhaps no psychic phenomenon which is so unconditionally reserved to the city as the blasé outlook," because the perception of the city tears "the nerves about so brutally that they exhaust their last reserves of strength, and are unable to react to new stimulations."[58] There is a faint echo of Simmel in the discourse on urban alienation that has dominated commentary on Kirchner's Berlin imagery since World War II. Both the Berlin sociologist and certain present-day art historians see urban reality as essentially brutal and dehumanizing, except that the expressionists would appear to have shed the "protective organ" earlier described by Simmel, recklessly embracing those threatening "fluctations and discontinuities" of the metropolis, conveying that raw, psychologically corrosive experience in the formal dislocations of their art.

Yet, if there was indeed a correspondence between Simmel's characterization of urban perception and Kirchner's, their respective responses to that sensory experience were strikingly antithetical. For Kirchner the city was, to be sure, a place of intense sensations, but, in marked contrast to Simmel and to Kirchner's typical commentators, he consistently described those sensations in positive, aesthetic terms. "The sensuous delight in what is seen (die sinnliche Lust am Gesehenen) is the origin of all plastic art from the beginning," he wrote in 1913, near the peak of his Berlin period.[59] Indeed, his accounts of the artistic process are often overtly Dionysian; the "so-called distortions," he wrote, "are generated instinctively by the ecstasy of what is seen."[60] And there are paeans to the beauty of the modern city, as in a text of 1930.

> The modern light of cities, in combination with the movement of the streets, continually gives me new stimuli. It spreads a new beauty out across the world, one which does not lie in details of the object.[61]

Simmel found no source of pleasure in these perceptions; they threatened the equilibrium of the psyche; it had to defend itself against these sensory shocks with a "protective organ." Kirchner approached these same stimuli not as a threat but as a source of sensuous and emotional exaltation, a response that was the antithesis of that blasé indifference that for Simmel was the inevitable and necessary defense of the overloaded, overstimulated city dweller. Finally, Kirchner claimed to represent through his urban art "the emotional values" (Gefühlswerte) of things, a disposition that Simmel associated with the gentler tempo of small-town life.[62]

If Kirchner differed from Simmel in his psychological reaction to the city, he also differed from his contemporaries, the expressionist poets, in his approach to the representation of urban perceptual experience. He did not, as did the poets, attempt mimetically to structure the picture to reflect those dislocations. According to Vietta, in the verse of the early expressionist poets the overloaded stimuli of the object world dissociate the subject, while the dissociations within the perceiving subject lead in turn to a breakdown of the perceived reality. He cites the closing verse from Alfred Lichtenstein's poem "Punkt": "Die Welt fällt um. Die Augen stürzen ein" (The world collapses; the eyes cave in). "When the perceiving subject can no longer sustain its perceptual activity," Vietta argues, "the object world mediated by the subject collapses. Subject and object cave in like a house gutted by fire."[63]

It is here that Kirchner parted company with the expressionist poets. If both he and they developed styles intended to reflect the accelerated tempo and disjunctive quality of modern urban perceptual experience, the artistic results were markedly different in character. For Kirchner, in contrast to the expressionist poets, what was externally dissociated was internally fused.

> From (movement) comes the intensified feeling for life that is the origin of the work of art. A body in movement shows me many different aspects, these fuse within me to a *unified* form, to an inner image. (Emphasis added.)[64]

It was this unified "inner image (*Innenbild*)," not "the fluctuations and discontinuities of the external milieu," that became for Kirchner the signified of the work of art. It was the psyche's ecstatic response to the optical image (*Augenbild*), the perceptual referent, and it found sensuous form in the artistic image (*Kunstbild*), or signifier. This artistic image was for Kirchner conditioned only partly by mimetic aims. Its "distortions" of natural form were determined by two factors. The first was a nonmimetic compositional logic through which the configurations of individual forms were radically simplified and altered to conform to an overall compositional schema: "The forms emerge and are transformed through working on the surface as a whole," Kirchner wrote in 1920. "It is this that also explains the so-called distortions of the individual forms; the small must subordinate itself to the large."[65] The second factor in these distortions was affective purpose, directed toward what Umberto Eco has called "programmed stimulation" of the viewer.[66] According to Kirchner, the goal of the artistic image (*Kunstbild*) was to produce in the viewer the interior image (*Innenbild*) of the artist, that psychological construct of sensual/emotional ecstasy that was the origin of the picture.[67] This result, Kirchner argued, could not be achieved by a mimetic reconstruction of the original stimulus, but only by the production of "unfamiliar effects" that were truly "the origin of the artistic impression."[68] "The lines of force," intended to convey "the feeling that pervades a city," would be an example of this. It is clear, then, that for all of their carefully calculated effects of spontaneity, the so-called distortions of Kirchner's pictures should not be naively read as merely reactive—as symptoms of alienation, acts of aggression against a hostile milieu, or nightmarish visions of a collapsing world. Like the distortions of his contemporary, Matisse, these are aspects of a sophisticated aesthetic strategy.

But it is not Kirchner's Berlin style alone that has inspired the negative readings of his urban imagery: his street scenes with prostitutes, widely regarded as icons of urban decadence, have been seen as consummate expressions of the alienation Kirchner experienced in the city. This group of ten

Figure 14. Ernst Ludwig Kirchner. White Dancer in a Little Variété, *1914. Lithograph, 59 x 51 cm. Städelsches Kunstinstitut, Frankfurt am Main.*

paintings, executed in 1913–14, rightly enjoys a privileged place in Kirchner's oeuvre, but it has tended to be the dominant, occasionally even the exclusive focus in discussions of his images of Berlin. Yet these works were created within a period spanning less than a year, while there are other urban subjects that Kirchner drew and painted repeatedly between 1908 and 1915—parks and gardens, rows of houses and railroad bridges, dance halls and cafés, variété dancers (figure 14) and circus performers (figure 15). These motifs tend to get perfunctory notice in the discourse on Kirchner's

Figure 15. Ernst Ludwig Kirchner. Circus Rider, 1914. *Oil on canvas, 202 x 153 cm. The St. Louis Art Museum, bequest of Morton D. May.*

supposed urban anxiety, probably because such subject matter is difficult to reconcile with the currently prevalent "anxious" reading of his art.

Just as these subjects have been neglected, so have the texts that help to illuminate Kirchner's attraction to them. Kirchner was as articulate about his subject matter as he was about his style, and while no text has come to light that supports the moralistic reading of his prostitutes, a number of sources suggest that he saw his mission as an artist, at least during the decade he spent in Dresden and Berlin, as a commitment to an art based on direct experience, and this of necessity involved urban life. In an autobiographical text from the 1930s, Kirchner recalled how as a student in Munich, in 1904, he had found the Secessionists—the progressive German artists of that era—uninspiring because of their neglect "of the colorful, sunny life outside. And that was what I as a young student would so like to have seen in pictures, our life, movement, color. . . . And I attempted it, drew in the streets and squares, in restaurants, in cafés."[69] This same commitment to the vibrancy of contemporary life found expression in two Kirchner texts from the Berlin period. In the "Chronik der Brücke," drafted in early 1913, Kirchner declared that the goal of the Brücke artists was "to draw their stimulus for creation from life, and to subordinate themselves to lived experience" (*Erlebnis*).[70] And the brochure for the MUIM Institut (Institute for Modern Instruction in Painting), which Kirchner operated briefly with Pechstein in Berlin in 1911–12, proclaimed: "The life of our new age (*das neuzeitliche Leben*) is the starting point of artistic creation." The students were to be taught to draw and paint with new means in the new manner, "sketching from life."[71]

If one surveys Kirchner's production, in paintings, drawings, prints, and pastels from 1908 to 1914, the life of the "new age"—a certain segment of it, at any rate—is what one finds. Alongside the numerous motifs of nudes, in the studio or bathing outdoors, which were important to his and the group's ideology of sexual liberation, the dominant subject matter is drawn from the life of the city. Moreover, the majority of Kirchner's urban motifs are the same ones of urban spectacle favored by some of the major French impressionists and postimpressionists.[72] These same subjects were ignored by the German impressionists—Slevogt was drawn to the world of entertainment, but only to the highbrow world of opera through the traditional genre of portraiture.[73] By contrast Kirchner, like his French precursors, chose "vulgar" entertainments that were genuinely popular products and expressions of modern urban culture.

Kirchner's published correspondence from this period documents his enthusiasm for this culture. He frequented such places regularly in Dresden and Berlin and, apparently, whenever he traveled. Many of his postcards to Erich Heckel contain sketches of dancers, evidently made on the spot, which evolved into prints or paintings.[74] And these entertainments were modern not only in origin; as Peter Jelavich demonstrates in his essay in this volume, their content was explicitly affirmative of that modern Berlin that was ignored by artists and lamented by writers with more traditional aesthetic values. Jelavich writes, for example, that in one such revue, *Das muss man seh'n!* (You gotta see it!), presented in the Metropol Theater in 1907:

> The majority of the numbers praised Berlin for its modernity. The *Weltstadt* was welcomed with open arms: its vitality, its hectic tempo, its commercialism and consumerism were hailed. In songs and skits, praise was lavished on new urban phenomena ranging from the elevated rapid-transit municipal train to novel forms of mass-cultural entertainment like the Lunapark, cinema, and sports events. (p. 101, this volume)

It is not merely coincidental that Karl Scheffler, seeking an analogy for those rare and accidental aesthetic pleasures to be found in the dismal urban landscape of Berlin, looked to such forms of popular culture.

> One acts in the city like the aesthetically sensitive person does in the variété or the circus, where he loathes the intended effects of the harshly colorful, coarse entertainments and where he knows how, with the aid of a certain refinement, to discover and to enjoy aesthetic values that are unintended and in which precisely for that reason the enchantment of the natural is inherent.[75]

Scheffler here equates these "coarse entertainments" with the "capital city of all modern ugliness" that spawned and nurtured them. Both assault the refined sensibility; it is only by chance that such things can be the source of aesthetic pleasure, never by design.

In contrast to the cultivated visual arts, in which, as Hermann lamented, the Berlin artist seemed ashamed of his city, these popular entertainments were at once a manifestation of the new urban culture and an explicit celebration of it. This vividly marks a dividing line between Kirchner and the German impressionist sensibility. The topics of the songs and skits described by Jelavich strikingly coincide with many of Kirchner's motifs, and it is arguable that he conceived of his art in the same spirit. It is precisely the "harshly colorful" aspects of the city in which Kirchner discovered a new beauty. He did not seek aesthetically to "redeem" such phenomena from their innate "ugliness" by transfiguring them according to impressionist criteria of beauty; his abstraction of the object aimed rather at capturing its raw vitalism. As Dube writes, Kirchner was drawn to "the music hall and circus . . . as expressions of intensified life."[76]

Viewed purely in terms of motifs, putting aside for the moment questions concerning the artist's moral attitudes or emotional state, Kirchner achieved within German painting between 1908 and 1914 what the French avant-garde—above all Manet and Degas, Seurat and Toulouse-Lautrec—accomplished for French painting from the 1860s to the 1890s: he became the first major German painter of modern life. Curt Glaser noted this achievement in 1923, when he wrote of Kirchner, "He loved the public places where people gathered, the street itself as well as places of nocturnal amusement, the café or the *Tingeltangel*. . . . Kirchner gave artistic form to this world."[77]

But what of the prostitutes? How do they relate to Kirchner's program of giving artistic form to modern city life? Can one reconcile a positive reading of Kirchner's Berlin pictures with the subject matter of his most ambitious series of paintings from these years? Clearly they must be central to any reading of Kirchner's Berlin imagery and of what it reflected about his attitude toward the city. As I have already stated, these are the images that have been the focus of the discourse on urban alienation. For Dube these scenes are expressions of the "lovelessness of all toward all."[78] For Gordon, Kirchner's prostitutes are "the unconscious agents of urban anxiety"; the street scenes reveal "an active distaste for the image of urban sin. . . . The Dresden champion of instinct in nature has become the Berlin critic of sex in the streets."[79]

Rosalyn Deutsche, linking the street scenes with the spirit of Simmel's essay on prostitution (1907),[80] attributes a more specific moral critique to Kirchner. In these works, she wrote, the artist "went beyond a mere depiction of alienation to observe its actual cause—the dominance of a money economy." "Contemplating the city crowd," Deutsche continues, "Kirchner depicted its members as commodities. . . . By choosing as his subjects prostitutes and their clients, Kirchner focused on the objectification of human relations inherent in economic exchange."[81] In developing this interpretation, she emphasizes an iconographic element that occurs in two of the street scenes: the presence of shop windows. This motif appears in the earliest work in the series, *Five Women on the Street* (figure 16), and again in the slightly later composition, *The Street* of 1913 (figure 17). The linkage of this sign of merchandising with prostitutes "effectively situates them as objects for consumption." For Deutsche, this meaning is also implicit in other works. In *Berlin Street Scene* (figure 18), for example, the rhomboid geometric design "circumscribes an interaction between buyer and seller"; the work "presents an implied, condensed narrative of perusal and selection of goods (and perhaps rejection, depending on the man's averted face)."[82] She sees the prostitutes as emblems for a specific social order.

> Whereas 19th-century artists portrayed prostitution as the antithesis of respectable sexuality—marriage—Kirchner depicted it as the fundamental transaction in a society ruled by exchange. Kirchner's metamorphosis of his prostitutes into commodity-like things effectively locates the origins of human alienation in the commodification of human functions—in this case of sexuality.[83]

Yet, for Deutsche, these same Kirchner paintings strove to counter, through their pictorial means, the alienating motifs that they depicted. The intense feelings they conveyed, their "spiritual and emotional presence," were an at-

Figure 16. Ernst Ludwig Kirchner. Five Women on the Street, *1913. Oil on canvas, 120 x 90 cm. Rheinische Bildarchiv, Cologne.*

tempt to "reinfuse some measure of humanity into a world from which it had been alienated."[84]

But can we be sure that Kirchner regarded these as scenes of alienation? There are at least two problems with Deutsche's interpretation. The first is her reading of Kirchner's style: that style, in her view, is directly conditioned by the moral critique she attributes to these pictures: "the angular hardening of organic form in all the paintings," she writes, "is a perfect

Figure 17. Ernst Ludwig Kirchner. The Street (Berlin), *1913. Oil on canvas, 120.6 x 91.1 cm. Collection, The Museum of Modern Art, New York. Purchase.*

visual analogue for the process of thingification."[85] Yet, this is the same Berlin style Kirchner used for all of his paintings, including those of popular culture (see figures 14 and 15), his beloved Erna Schilling, and his erotic idylls, such as *Striding into the Sea* (see figure 20), which he painted during

Figure 18. Ernst Ludwig Kirchner. Berlin Street Scene, *1913. Oil on canvas, 121 x 195. Brücke-Museum, Berlin. Copyright by Dr. W. and I. Henze, Campione d'Italia, Switzerland.*

the summers on the Baltic island of Fehmarn. Are we then to assume that these scenes, too, are expressions of alienation, yet other examples of the reduction of human beings to objects under a money economy? The second problem is that, if we do accept this reading, we are faced with a contradiction between Kirchner's art during the Berlin period and what he and those closest to him wrote about it, then and later. Kirchner himself described his Berlin style not as an expression of his emotional estrangement from his motifs but as an attempt to capture, in a carefully worked out composition, "the ecstasy of the initial perception."[86] The artist's closest friend, the art historian Botho Graef, described Kirchner's art of this period as inspired by a spirit of friendship toward the world.[87] One cannot, to be sure, accept such sources uncritically, but where they appear to contradict one's own analysis neither should they be ignored.

There is also the problem of documentation concerning Kirchner's attitudes toward prostitutes. Other than references to picture subjects, Kirchner's known writings and correspondence contain few remarks on them. In none of them, however, is there any trace of moral condemnation or of other attitudes attributed to him by the writers I have quoted. Two of these sources date from the winter of 1915–16. Kirchner, ill, tormented by a pathological fear of being recalled to the military, and consequently unable to work, compared the precariousness of his own existence to that of the streetwalkers he painted. In December 1915, he wrote to Carl Hagemann: "New draft calls of the reserves stay close at my heels and who knows when they will stick me in again and then one can't work anymore; one is more frightful of that than any prostitute." The following March he wrote to Gustav Schiefler, describing the same situation: "I am now myself like the prostitutes I painted. Whisked away, gone the next time."[88] These references suggest not a revulsion toward the prostitute but a sympathy and perhaps even an identification with her.

Kirchner's identification with the vulnerability of the whore to civil authority could have been nurtured by a traumatic incident of August 1914. En route back to Berlin from Fehmarn after war had broken out, Kirchner and his companion, Erna Schilling, were twice briefly detained by police under suspicion of being Russian spies. After this incident, Erna reported, Kirchner suffered from deep anxieties of being arrested again: he developed a phobia toward uniforms, and was afraid to go out of his studio, except at night. This signaled the beginning of the psychological deterioration that marked his last years in Germany.[89] In any case, however one may interpret these documents, neither they nor any other known statement by Kirchner attest to a clear antipathy toward prostitutes.

If there is scant textual documentation of Kirchner's feelings toward prostitutes, he did write often in later life about the street scenes in which they appear, yet he never did so in the moralistic terms that have become the norm in the recent literature. On the contrary, he wrote about the sensory excitement of the street, about the problems of rendering such dynamism of movement in a static medium, about his geometrical compositional schemas. This discrepancy between Kirchner's words and the ostensible content of these images was noted by Gordon, who seemed mildly puzzled that Kirchner wrote about these Berlin street scenes "more in esthetic than in ethical terms," while remaining silent about "the ambivalent feelings for prostitutes that these pictures revealed."[90] But again, can we be sure that those feelings were Kirchner's own?

One element that has been ignored in the discussion of these images is the practice of prostitution itself in Berlin at the time Kirchner painted these works. Prostitution was rampant in the city during this period of rapid growth, as it was in other industrial centers of Europe. Most of the prostitutes appear to have come from immigrant working families, and were usually forced onto the streets by low pay or unemployment to help meet their families' needs. Berlin differed from Hamburg, Paris, and Vienna, however, in that it was not a brothel city—brothels had been outlawed in the mid-nineteenth century. And since this law was strictly enforced, prostitutes were forced to solicit in the streets, cafés, taverns, and dance halls.[91]

In Kirchner's time prostitution was officially illegal in Berlin, but it was openly tolerated, and the police sought to regulate it by inscription. Only a fraction of prostitutes actually followed this procedure, however; as one streetwalker retorted to the inquiry of Abraham Flexner, the author of a book on the subject: "Nur die Dummen werden inscribiert!" (Only the dumb ones register).[92] An inscribed prostitute was permitted to function under certain conditions set by the police. She had to practice her trade discreetly so as not to give scandal; accordingly, she was forbidden to solicit on major thoroughfares, or in the immediate vicinity of cultural institutions, public parks, railroad stations, or army barracks. A registered prostitute who violated these laws, or an unregistered woman who practiced prostitution under any circumstances—and these were many times more numerous—was liable to arrest and imprisonment. And arrest was a real risk, since the Morals Police (*Sittenpolizei*)—200 strong—patrolled the Berlin streets undercover, in pairs.

Consequently, the typical prostitute had to be extremely circumspect in seeking clients. According to Flexner, the streetwalker was "noticeable by reason of slow gait, furtive expression, and more or less striking garb. Her demeanor is usually restrained. If no response is made to the invitation conveyed in a glance, she passes on; doubtful or encouraged, she stops at a show-window or turns off into a café or street."[93] The undercover agents of the Morals Police had to be almost equally cautious: since solicitation took discreet and often ambiguous forms, they were, Flexner reports, "bound to proceed with great circumspection. They are indeed instructed that a hundred omissions are preferable to a single error, or apparent error." They dared not touch "the most sophisticated forms of prostitution," because proof was so difficult; consequently, they arrested only "the most obvious and flagrant offenders."[94] As a result, the laws were ineffectual, not only with regard to inscription, but also in interdicting prostitution on the proscribed public thoroughfares. Flexner explained:

> The inscribed woman who conducts herself without scandal on streets in
> which she is tolerated, soon begins unobtrusively to invade those which are
> forbidden: and so long as her demeanor is circumspect, no notice is taken.
> . . . But other consequences follow. What is allowed to the inscribed
> woman cannot be forbidden to the uninscribed; it is not in human nature
> to forbid to the one what is so freely allowed to the other.[95]

Indeed, some of those places that were interdicted became the most notorious for prostitution. As Flexner reported, the streetwalker sought "by preference the main channels of retail trade."[96]

The restraint necessitated on both sides obviously produced a considerable ambiguity. One could not always be sure: was a glance perhaps innocent? Was a woman perhaps *really* only window-shopping or en route from work or to meet a friend? Dress and demeanor were not always conclusive: some dressed flamboyantly, others simply; many looked the part, but some looked like respectable girls from bourgeois families.[97] The ambiguities were even more pronounced, Hans Ostwald reported, in the fashionable western part of the city.

> In the streets between the Zoo Railway Station and Wittenbergplatz and
> along the Kurfürstendamm there is, at every time of day, a crowd of
> strollers in which women predominate. Young women, schoolgirls,
> youthful-looking mothers with their grown daughters. Sometimes in a
> smart dress, sometimes in furs, . . . sometimes in a fluttering shawl or a
> modest raincoat. Sometimes with the serious face of a school teacher or a
> student, sometimes with longing lips and eyes, mouth blood red with
> lipstick or blackened eyelashes and eyebrows and a pallid powder-coated
> face. Or motherly, with defensive glances. And yet, an infinite number of
> sideward glances: "Make me yours!"—Intermingling with them are old and
> young men, mostly tradespeople, lawyers, engineers, a few with an artistic
> look. . . . And the glances of the women divided between the men and the
> gleaming display windows of the milliners, . . . of the jewelers and the art
> galleries, of the delicatessens and the bookshops with the handsomely
> bound volumes, the furriers and the cinema posters. . . . The woman over
> there—she could perhaps be a famous film actress,—that one—a cabaret
> dancer. But here one often doesn't know: perhaps she is the daughter or the
> wife of the man who walks beside her—for here the glittering color of the
> demimonde is also the style of dress. And that plain woman over there is
> perhaps soliciting. . . .[98]

The scene Ostwald describes certainly echoes that association of sex with merchandise that Deutsche and Hanne Bergius have expounded. But what is more significant here for Kirchner's street scenes, I believe, is the element of pervasive erotic ambiguity.

This same ambiguity is a feature of most of Kirchner's street scenes. With one exception, their titles seem innocent enough — *Berlin Street Scene; Two Women on the Street; The Street*.[99] This has led some commentators to misinterpret the actual subject of these pictures or to pass over it in discreet silence.[100] However, the showy plumed hats worn by the women — a feature of each of the ten Berlin street scenes — were associated with prostitutes.[101] And interestingly, the only paintings in the series that bear specific topographical titles, *Friedrichstraße* (figure 19), *Potsdamer Platz*, and *Leipziger Straße with Electric Tram*, refer to places notorious for prostitution. The Friedrichstraße had the reputation of being a "public love market," yet, since both it and Potsdamer Platz were officially off limits for prostitution, circumspection was especially in order.[102]

Significantly, none of Kirchner's street scenes show women in the act of overt solicitation,[103] — they exchange glances, walk singly or in groups, look in shop windows, or gaze directly at the viewer. Where men figure in the picture, as they do in all but *Five Women on the Street*, they are usually relegated to the background. In none of them do we see direct eye contact between a man and a woman, but *The Street* and *Berlin Street Scene* seem to show the prelude to such an encounter. In the former, the woman on the left may be attempting to catch the male window-shopper's eye by means of her reflection in the glass. In the latter, the man who looks away may not be rejecting the prostitute who gazes upon him, as Deutsche and Leopold Reidemeister have suggested, but cautiously surveying the scene before making an overture.[104] In several other cases, Kirchner seems to have been specifically interested in the disguises employed by streetwalkers. *Potsdamer Platz* and *Two Women on the Street* (figure 13) show them in widow's veils, which, after the war began, were adopted by some Berlin prostitutes as a means of signification that nevertheless retained a particularly delicate ambiguity.[105] They were surely an excellent deterrent to the already cautious Morals Police, since a false arrest of a genuine war widow would be particularly embarrassing.

The ambiguities in Kirchner's street scenes, then — ambiguities that led some early critics to overlook the actual subject matter of these works — approximate very closely the contemporary descriptions of the modus operandi of prostitution in the capital, and in this sense these pictures seem to be very much a part of Kirchner's program of giving pictorial form to modern urban life. Indeed, for Will Grohmann, who did recognize the subjects of these pictures, such images of Berlin were neither celebratory nor critical in spirit; the artist stood outside of his subject matter, merely registering what he saw and giving it artistic form.[106] But such an interpretation does not explain why precisely this subject should have occupied such a prominent place within Kirchner's art of the Berlin period.

Figure 19. Ernst Ludwig Kirchner. Friedrichstraße, Berlin, *1914. Oil on canvas, 121 x 95 cm. Staatsgalerie, Stuttgart. Copyright by Dr. W. and I. Henze, Campione d'Italia, Switzerland.*

Surprisingly, no one has yet commented on the paradoxical fact that Kirchner, the most erotic of German artists, was never sexually explicit in his treatment of this theme. The classic modern images of prostitutes — Manet's *Olympia* and *Nana*, the coarse brothel scenes of Degas and Toulouse-Lautrec, Picasso's *Demoiselles d'Avignon* — all depict women nude or in provocative states of partial undress. In 1911, the year Kirchner moved to the capital, the Berlin impressionist Lovis Corinth painted an image of Nana as a voluptuous nude writhing in a state of obvious arousal, manifesting a "sexual nature . . . strong enough," in Zola's words, "to destroy the whole crowd of her admirers and yet sustain no injury."[107] In the same year Max Beckmann painted his Rubensesque *Battle of the Amazons*, a bloody scene of combat between males and fleshy females, interpreted as a metaphor for prostitution in Berlin, the deadly "struggle for existence by means of sex."[108] Images like Beckmann's and Corinth's, which treat the prostitute as the incarnation of destructive female sexuality while yet titillating the male viewer, were of course extremely common in the late nineteenth and early twentieth centuries. Other than Kirchner, only moralists like Baluschek produced images of prostitutes that were not flagrantly sexual. But, unlike Kirchner's images, these have no ambiguity: they spotlight the act of solicitation, and have an overtly anecdotal character.[109]

Kirchner's treatment of prostitutes is even more striking when one considers his devotion to the nude. In the "Chronik der Brücke" he called the nude "the foundation of all plastic art,"[110] and it is the most constant motif in his work in all media and periods. Moreover, he never treated the nude in a merely academic way: male and female nudes are shown together in life situations—engaged in sexual play in the studio or bathing nude at a secluded beach; they evoke a world of sexual freedom very much at odds with the bourgeois mores of the time. The work of these years is particularly rich in explicit sexual imagery, and many compositions seem born of an amoral fascination with the polymorphous flowerings of sexual instinct. Kirchner's images of the young Dresden models Fränzi and Marzella explore pubescent sexuality; a series of lithographs of 1914 pictures a couple in various coital positions (Dube L 185–90); another lithographic cycle from 1915 depicts the varieties of sexual perversion (Dube L 267–74); and a Kirchner sketchbook from that year is filled with nude drawings of his homosexual friend Botho Graef and his young lover.[111] Kirchner even decorated his Berlin studio with erotic wall hangings he executed himself. Yet, with the exception of a few minor works, in his depictions of prostitutes Kirchner restricted himself to showing them in full dress within the hectic tempo of the urban landscape.[112]

Some commentators have explained Kirchner's separation of prostitution from his overtly erotic subjects precisely through his ostensibly negative feelings toward it. In this view, a work like *Striding into the Sea* (figure 20), evocative of a primordial state of sexual bliss, constituted a deliberate contrast with the crass commodification of sexuality within the "dehumanized" metropolis.[113] But such a moralizing attitude seems incompatible with the relationship to the erotic that emerges from those other works of Kirchner cited above. In them he approached sexuality as a natural phenomenon be-

Figure 20. Ernst Ludwig Kirchner. Striding into the Sea, *1912. Oil on canvas, 146 x 200 cm. Staatsgalerie, Stuttgart. Copyright by Dr. W. and I. Henze, Campione d'Italia, Switzerland.*

yond moral judgment, as the manifestation of a vital primordial energy. Might he have seen even prostitution in this way? Such a view was not alien to men of his time. After witnessing an encounter of two prostitutes with two potential clients on the Friedrichstraße one evening in 1909, Max Beckmann wrote that this urban manifestation of sexual magnetism, "particularly on the street, always fills me with admiration for the immense splendor of nature."[114] It is precisely in this conception of the erotic that we may perhaps find the key to the centrality of the street scenes in Kirchner's paintings of Berlin.

It should be remembered that Kirchner was of provincial origin: born and raised in a bourgeois family in the Saxon town of Chemnitz, he moved to Berlin from Dresden at the age of thirty-one, and was still a relative newcomer to the city when he painted his street scenes. While decidedly no puritan himself, he does seem to have shared that provincial fixation that identified Berlin with sexual indulgence, giving it the reputation of being the most lascivious city in Germany. Hanne Bergius has written of how precisely Berlin's notorious reputation as the Whore Babylon constituted a major part of the city's appeal to artists and writers of Kirchner's generation.

For many of them this myth, stirred up by the provinces, meant liberation from the narrowness of provincial morality and succumbing to the magic of the urban "femme fatale," instead of dozing eternally at the breast of provincial Mother Nature. Sexual desires and the first experience of the metropolis become interwoven. For at first it was not a moralizing Christian interpretation of the Whore Babylon that characterized the avant-garde artists and literati, but rather a Dionysian avowal of the real, sensual world.[115]

This attitude seems much more consistent with the generally Dionysian tone of Kirchner's descriptions of the city, free of any trace of moralizing, as it does with his fascination with all manifestations of sexuality. The prostitute, simultaneously threatening and fascinating to fin-de-siècle artists who treated her as a subversive force within the bourgeois social order, may have appealed to Kirchner for precisely that reason. Robert Hessen wrote that "nowhere does prostitution have as many traits in common with free love as in Berlin."[116] If this reading is correct, Kirchner would not have seen the prostitutes, as did so many males of that era, as "tempting sirens and vampires of the streets";[117] nor would he have viewed them, as Simmel did, as victims of a degrading, dehumanizing financial transaction that reduced them to sexual commodities. Instead, Kirchner would have seen them as allies in his campaign for the liberation of instinct. What would have attracted him to these subjects, then, was not that sex was being sold like hats and furs and jewels—which, in any case, it was not, for there was no need for circumspection in those trades—but that, through discreet glances and coded words and gestures, the bourgeois city—this world of labor, industry, and commerce, of crowded sidewalks, omnibuses, and automobiles—had been *eroticized*. The prostitutes who promenaded the streets of this clean, orderly, industrious metropolis would thus constitute a kind of erotic epiphany, an irrepressible, triumphant manifestation of the primordial id in an artificial world built by the superego. Kirchner's street scenes would then function not as the negative antithesis of his erotic Baltic idylls, but as a glorification of those same primordial energies within the modern metropolis.

This, too, may well have been a factor in Kirchner's attraction to the dances of the *variétés*. Not only were the dances expressions of libidinal energy; such places were themselves notorious as rendezvous for prostitutes. As Flexner wrote: "the Variety Theater, the café and other establishments largely derive their profit, direct or indirect, through affording an ever increasing supply [of prostitutes] an abundant opportunity to work up a demand. . . . Beyond all doubt . . . a fair, perhaps a very large, share of the immorality connected with these establishments is incited in them."[118]

To be sure, to present Berlin as Kirchner did during this period was to present it selectively. Clearly he was not truly interested in being the chronicler of urban life in all of its variety. One need only look at the posthumously discovered photographs of Berlin life by Heinrich Zille from roughly those same years—a far more diverse visual chronicle of "das neuzeitliche Leben"—to realize how narrow was Kirchner's choice of urban motifs.[119] He avoided the horrible poverty, the dreadful housing conditions, the class tensions; he ignored the city at work. Similarly, Kirchner's idealization of the prostitute as a sign of the eroticized city ignored, whether out of romantic naïveté or callousness, the brutal social realities that forced so many women into this role. At the same time, these street scenes have a social dimension that the images of prostitution in the work of Degas, Rops, Picasso, Beckmann, and others do not. Kirchner's images are unique in linking prostitution explicitly with the emergent metropolis while avoiding the explicity erotic, and as such they document a particular sociohistorical moment: the epidemic spread of prostitution that accompanied the rapid urbanization brought on by industrialization in the nineteenth and early twentieth centuries—a process for which Berlin offered the most extreme example in Europe. In this sense there was an element of truth in the myth of Berlin as the "Whore Babylon." As Richard Evans has written:

> Large-scale conspicuous prostitution was a by-product of the first,
> explosive stage in the growth of the modern industrial city. It was a
> functional consequence of the rise of the urban society created by early
> industrial capitalism. It constituted a social problem that disappeared, or at
> least dwindled to more manageable proportions, as modern industrial
> society became more sophisticated and the pressures that created the
> prostitution problem gradually diminished.[120]

Kirchner's primary intention, however, was to document not a social reality but an aesthetic one. Berlin for him was above all a domain of intense sensuous excitement, a stimulus to aesthetic ecstasy. He represented Berlin as a place of vibrant pleasures, a city that up to then—to quote Scheffler once more—had seemed "a place in which there was much work and little enjoyment, good order and discipline, but not the poetry of exuberance."[121] The "new beauty" that Kirchner found in this "capital of modern ugliness" is to be explained neither by a sudden transformation in the physiognomy of Berlin nor simply by a change of taste. For Kirchner beauty was not an attribute of form—whether human, mechanical, or architectural—but of movement. Out of movement, he declared, "there comes to me the intensified feeling for life that is the origin of the work of art."[122] In the dynamism of the "artificial" city of Berlin, Kirchner sensed a manifestation of vitalist energies. Whether the buildings were ugly or beautiful, whether the Berliners were vulgar or elegant, whether the urban landscape was arbitrarily or harmoniously shaped had become irrelevant to this aesthetic.

NOTES

Parts of this essay first appeared in "Images of Berlin in the Art of the Secession and Expressionism," in an exhibition catalogue for the High Art Museum, Atlanta: *Art in Berlin, 1815–1989* (Atlanta, 1989). In preparing the present text I have been helped by the suggestions and criticisms of several colleagues: Barbara C. Buenger, John Czaplicka, David Frisby, Jane Hancock, Reinhold Heller, Beth Irwin Lewis, Peter Petzling, and Thomas Steinfeld.

1. Georg Hermann, "Um Berlin," *Pan* 2 (22 August 1912): 1101.

2. On the impressionist treatment of Paris, see Theodore Reff, *Manet and Modern Paris* (Chicago, 1982), and T. J. Clark, *The Painting of Modern Life: Paris in the Art of Manet and His Followers* (Princeton, 1984).

3. Liebermann was never interested in modern cityscapes as motifs, although he was drawn to urban recreational scenes of a kind associated with French impressionism. See, e.g., his two Amsterdam scenes, *The Parrot Man* and *Parrot Walk*, both of 1902, and his *Summer Evening on the Alster*, painted in 1911, a motif from Hamburg—illustrated in *Max Liebermann in seiner Zeit*, exhibition catalog, Nationalgalerie Berlin (Munich, 1979), 301, 303, 333.

4. Charles Huard, *Berlin comme je l'ai vu* (Paris, 1907), 11–12.

5. Werner Hegemann, *Das steinerne Berlin: Geschichte der größten Mietkasernenstadt der Welt* (Berlin, 1930), 13.

6. Karl Scheffler, *Berlin: Ein Stadtschicksal*, 2d ed. (Berlin, 1910), 200.

7. Ibid., 50, 55ff.

8. Ibid., 163.

9. Ibid., 190.

10. Karl Baedeker, *Berlin and Its Environs: Handbook for Travellers* (Leipzig, 1903), 51.

11. Georg Hermann (see note 1), 1101.

12. Huard, 33.

13. Scheffler, *Berlin*, 17. On the parallels drawn between Berlin and America, see the essays by Lothar Müller and Heidrun Suhr in this volume.

14. In 1905, for example, over half of Berlin's 2 million inhabitants lived in dwellings averaging between three and thirteen occupants per heated room. (42 percent of the population lived in one-room dwellings, 75 percent in dwellings with two rooms or less). Berlin had the worst housing conditions of any city in Europe except for Budapest, but masked this condition behind ornate eclectic facades of four- and five-story buildings. See the data reproduced in Hegemann (see note 5), plates 4, 5.

15. Jost Hermand, "Das Bild der 'großen Stadt' im Expressionismus," in *Die Unwirklichkeit der Städte: Großstadtdarstellungen zwischen Moderne und Postmoderne*, ed. Klaus Scherpe (Reinbek bei Hamburg, 1988), 65.

16. Emil Waldmann, "Die künstlerische Entdeckung der Großstadt," *Vossische Zeitung*, 2 December 1917, Morgenblatt.

17. I have taken the phrase from Andreas Freisfeld's study of the response to urbanization in German literature, *Das Leiden an der Stadt: Spuren der Verstädterung in deutschen Romanen des 20. Jahrhunderts* (Cologne, 1982).

18. Kirchner moved to Berlin from Dresden in October 1911, and it remained his primary residence until May 1917, when he settled in Davos. Nevertheless, Kirchner spent relatively little productive time in Berlin after 1915, and the city ceased to be a major theme in his art thereafter. From September of that year, when he was granted leave from the military for medical reasons (after only two months of duty in Halle), until he settled in Switzerland in 1917, Kirchner was plagued by a series of health problems, and much of 1916 and 1917 was spent in sanatoriums. See the chronology by Hans Bolliger and Georg Reinhardt, "Ernst Ludwig Kirchner 1880–1938: Eine biografische Text-Bild-Dokumentation," in *Ernst Ludwig Kirchner 1880–1938*, exhibition catalog, Nationalgalerie Berlin (Berlin, 1979), 60, 70ff.—hereafter cited

as Berlin, *Kirchner*. For the most complete narrative account of this period of Kirchner's life, see E. W. Kornfeld, *Ernst Ludwig Kirchner: Nachzeichnung seines Lebens* (Berne, 1979), 54–110.

19. Donald E. Gordon, *Ernst Ludwig Kirchner* (Cambridge, Mass., 1968), 86.

20. Charles Baudelaire, "On the Heroism of Modern Life" (from *The Salon of 1846*), in *The Mirror of Art: Critical Studies by Baudelaire*, trans. and ed. Jonathan Mayne (Garden City, 1956), 130.

21. Curt Glaser, *Die Graphik der Neuzeit: Vom Anfang des XIX. Jahrhunderts bis zur Gegenwart* (Berlin, 1923), 540.

22. Karl Scheffler, "Ernst Ludwig Kirchner," *Kunst und Künstler* 18 (1920): 217ff. One of the first to make the connection was Wilhelm Hausenstein, *Die bildende Kunst der Gegenwart* (Stuttgart, 1914), 304. See also G. F. Hartlaub's remarks on Kirchner, note 72, below.

23. Paul Westheim, *Helden und Abenteurer: Welt und Leben der Künstler* (Berlin, 1931), 212. The characterization is of course inspired by Walter Ruttmann's classic film of 1927, *Berlin, die Symphonie einer Großstadt*.

24. Will Grohmann, *E. L. Kirchner* (Stuttgart, 1958). It is significant in this regard that Grohmann had been a leading proponent of Kirchner's art in the 1920s, publishing the first general monograph on the artist: *Das Werk Ernst Ludwig Kirchners* (Munich, 1926).

25. Annemarie Dube-Heynig, *E. L. Kirchner: Graphik* (Munich, 1961), 49.

26. See Peter Selz, *German Expressionist Painting* (Berkeley, 1957), 139; Bernard S. Myers, *The German Expressionists: A Generation in Revolt* (New York, 1957), 131–32.

27. There have been exceptions to this. Jost Hermand (see note 15) has recently offered a fresh look at this issue. He writes, for example, that although Kirchner's street scenes with prostitutes may have been shocking to bourgeois sensibilities, they are not "ripe for collapse (untergangsreif) or apocalyptic" (64). Indeed, he suggests that, contrary to the conventional view, only Ludwig Meidner's urban scenes truly fit into this category. Reinhold Heller has also taken a more nuanced look at Kirchner's urban imagery. Although he does not focus on Kirchner's Berlin imagery, he does write about Kirchner's first major street scene, *Street* (Museum of Modern Art), executed in Dresden in 1908, and suggests that there are positive as well as negative elements, notably, "a fascination (with) . . . the city's dynamism and intensified life." (" 'The City is Dark': Conceptions of Urban Landscape and Life in Expressionist Painting and Architecture," in: Gertrud Bauer Pickar and Karl Eugen Webb, eds., *Expressionism Reconsidered* [Munich, 1979], 50–51.)

28. The most comprehensive historical treatment of the pictorial representation of Berlin is to be found in *Stadtbilder: Berlin in der Malerei vom 17. Jahrhundert bis zur Gegenwart*, exhibition catalog, Berlin Museum (Berlin, 1987).

29. The *Berlin-Potsdam Railway* (1847), which shows a distant panorama of the city with a steaming locomotive in the foreground, is one example; the best known is Menzel's unfinished painting inspired by the 1848 Revolution, *The Lying-in-State of the Dead of March 1848*. Although it is in its subject a modern "history painting," its manner of composition and treatment of the subject anticipate French impressionism. For illustrations, see the exhibition catalog *Menzel der Beobachter*, ed. Werner Hofmann (Munich, 1982), 38, 83.

30. See *Parisian Workdays* (1869), ibid., 25; and *In the Tuileries* (Dresden, Albertinum).

31. Hans Mackowsky, "Hans Baluschek," *Kunst und Künstler* 1 (1902–03): 338. Compare John Czaplicka's discussion of Baluschek in this volume. See also Margrit Bröhan, *Hans Baluschek (1870–1935): Maler-Zeichner-Illustrator* (Berlin, 1985).

32. John Czaplicka, "Prolegomena to a Typology of Großstadt Imageries: The Pictorial Imagery of Berlin, 1870–1930," unpublished dissertation, Universität Hamburg, 1984. 217ff. On the pictorial treatment of Berlin by Ury, Hübner, Skarbina, and other impressionists, see also Rolf Bothe, "Stadtbilder zwischen Menzel und Liebermann: Von der Reichsgründungsepoche zur wilhelminischen Großstadt," in Berlin Museum, *Stadtbilder* (see note 28), 185–96, and cat. 112–15, 117, 118, 121, 122.

33. August Endell, "Abendfarben," *Die neue Gesellschaft*, 1905: 81. I am grateful to John Czaplicka for bringing this article to my attention and making a photocopy of it available to me. These observations were further developed three years later in Endell's book, *Die Schönheit der großen Stadt* (Stuttgart, 1908). For a detailed examination of Endell's views, see Lothar Müller's essay in this volume.

34. Endell, "Abendfarben," 81–82.

35. Scheffler, *Berlin* (see note 6), 201–2.

36. Ludwig Meidner, "Anleitung zum Malen von Großstadtbildern," originally published in *Kunst und Künstler* 12 (1914): 299ff; here and elsewhere quoted from Thomas Grochowiak, *Ludwig Meidner* (Recklinghausen, FRG, 1966), 78–80.

37. August Endell, *Die Schönheit der großen Stadt* (Berlin, 1984), 18–19.

38. Meidner, in Grochowiak, 80.

39. Ibid., 78.

40. For illustrations, see Gustav Vriesen and Max Imdahl, *Robert Delaunay: Light and Color* (New York, n.d.), 23, 27, 31. On Delaunay's importance for Meidner and the Berlin avant-garde generally see Thomas Gaehtgens, "Delaunay in Berlin," in *Delaunay und Deutschland*, ed. Peter-Klaus Schuster (Cologne, 1985), 264–84.

41. Victor Miesel, "Ludwig Meidner," in *Ludwig Meidner*, exhibition catalog, University of Michigan Museum of Art (Ann Arbor, 1978), 6.

42. Illustrated in Grochowiak, *Meidner*, Plate IX.

43. Heller (see note 27), 46–47. For a less apocalyptic view of Meidner, see Charles W. Haxthausen, "Images of Berlin in the Art of the Secession and Expressionism," in *Art in Berlin, 1815–1989*, exhibition catalog, High Art Museum (Atlanta, 1989), 68–73.

44. Wolf-Dieter Dube, "The Artists Group Die Brücke," in *Expressionism: A German Intuition, 1905–1920*, exhibition catalog, Solomon R. Guggenheim Museum (New York, 1980), 101.

45. Rosalyn Deutsche, "Alienation in Berlin: Kirchner's Street Scenes," *Art in America*, January 1983:69.

46. Donald E. Gordon, *Expressionism: Art and Idea* (New Haven, Conn., 1987), 139. Kirchner commentators such as Ewald Rathke, Karlheinz Gabler, and Lucius Grisebach, who have refrained from this type of reading, have generally confined themselves to stressing the formal issues in Kirchner's street scenes, without directly addressing the issue of his attitude toward the city or placing his images of Berlin in a larger historical context. See Ewald Rathke, *Ernst Ludwig Kirchner: Straßenbilder* (Stuttgart, 1969); Karlheinz Gabler, "Die Gemälde Ernst Ludwig Kirchners," in *Ernst Ludwig Kirchner*, exhibition catalog, Kunstverein für die Rheinlande und Westfalen (Düsseldorf, 1960), and *E. L. Kirchner: Zeichnungen*, exhibition catalog, Museum der Stadt Aschaffenburg (Aschaffenburg, FRG, 1980), 21ff. See Grisebach's catalog commentaries in Berlin, *Kirchner*, catalog 150, 173ff and passim; and in particular his *Ernst Ludwig Kirchner: Großstadtbilder* (Munich, 1979). Anton Henze's brief Kirchner monograph also belongs in this company: *Ernst Ludwig Kirchner: Leben und Werk* (Stuttgart, 1980), 37ff.

47. [ies] "Bilder der Angst und Einsamkeit: Kirchner-Gedenkausstellung im Kunsthaus Zürich," *Neue Zürcher Zeitung*, 23 June 1980.

48. Deutsche, "Alienation in Berlin," 65. For Deutsche, however, Kirchner's painting style was an attempt to overcome the alienation that he painted: "The tense, jagged strokes . . . are direct records of the artist's presence and desperate attempts to touch the alienated world he depicted."

49. Silvio Vietta, "Großstadtwahrnehmung und ihre literarische Darstellung. Expressionistischer Reihungsstil und Collage," *Deutsche Vierteljahrsschrift für Literaturwissenschaft und Geistesgeschichte* 48 (1974):359–73.

50. Georg Simmel, "The Metropolis and Mental Life," in *On Individuality and Social Forms: Selected Writings*, ed. Donald N. Levine (Chicago, 1971), 325—hereafter cited as Simmel, *Selected Writings*.

51. Vietta, "Großstadtwahrnehmung," 361.

52. Kirchner, "Die Arbeit E. L. Kirchners," in Kornfeld, *Kirchner* (see note 18), 332–44. The cited passage can be found on 339. The text dates from the mid-1920s. Hereafter cited as "Arbeit ELK."

53. Ibid., 341.

54. *E. L Kirchners Davoser Tagebuch: Eine Darstellung des Malers und eine Sammlung seiner Schriften*, ed. Lothar Grisebach (Cologne, 1968), 86. Hereafter cited as Kirchner, *Davoser Tagebuch*.

55. "The Exhibitors to the Public," quoted from Herschel B. Chipp, *Theories of Modern Art* (Berkeley, 1968), 294–95.

56. Ibid., 298. The shared concept of "lines of force" ("Kraftlinien" in Kirchner's text and "Linienkräften" in the original German translation of the futurist text) is especially striking. See the exhibition catalog, *Zweite Ausstellung: Die Futuristen*, Galerie "Der Sturm" (Berlin, 1912), 22.

57. Simmel, *Selected Writings*, 326.

58. Ibid., 329.

59. E. L. Kirchner, "Über die Malerei," text of 1913, in Berlin, *Kirchner* (see note 18), 67.

60. E. L. Kirchner to Eberhard Grisebach, 31 January 1918, as quoted by Bolliger and Reinhardt, in Berlin, *Kirchner*, 77. In an undated diary entry from 1927 (*Davoser Tagebuch*, 157), Kirchner writes: "The work originates in impulse, in ecstasy." See also the entry for 18 February 1926 (128).

61. Berlin, *Kirchner*, 98. Unfortunately, the bulk of Kirchner's published statements on the art of his Dresden and Berlin periods dates from his later residence in Switzerland. Yet, with regard to urban experience, Berlin was clearly the reference, and Kirchner sometimes mentioned his Berlin cityscapes and street scenes in this context. While the dates of these statements may place their reliability in question, given Kirchner's notorious mendacity in other areas, it is striking that despite a wealth of letters and diary entries documenting past and present anguish, such as the difficult war years, there is not a single negative statement about Berlin or urban experience, and there are on the other hand a number, spread over many years, that are positive. Donald Gordon acknowledged the gap between Kirchner's statements and the meanings that he, Gordon, read into these images, but this discrepancy apparently did not lead him to question his reading. See Gordon, "Ernst Ludwig Kirchner: By Instinct Possessed," *Art in America*, November 1980: 95.

62. "Arbeit ELK," 341. Simmel (*Selected Writings*, 325). "The essentially intellectualistic character of the mental life of the metropolis becomes intelligible as over against that of the small town which rests more on feelings and emotional relationships."

63. Vietta, "Großstadtwahrnehmung," 359.

64. Kirchner (1930), quoted from Berlin, *Kirchner*, 97. The contrast of Kirchner's Berlin style with that of the early Grosz is interesting in this context. It is in Grosz's aggressive cubo-futurist style of 1914–18, used to create works presenting a nightmarish vision of the city as a cauldron of crime, vice, and violence, that we find a visual parallel to the fragmentation of the *Reihungsstil*. See, for example, figures 22 and 24, illustrating Beth Irwin Lewis's article in this volume, and particularly the paintings *The City* (1916–17), *Explosion* (1917), and *Dedicated to Oskar Panizza* (1917–18). For illustrations see Hans Hess, *George Grosz* (New York, 1974), 71, 74, 82.

65. Kirchner, writing under the pseudonym *L. de Marsalle*, "Zeichnungen von E. L. Kirchner," originally published in *Genius* (1920), quoted in Kirchner, *Davoser Tagebuch*, 185.

66. Umberto Eco, *A Theory of Semiotics* (Bloomington, Ind., 1979), 203–4.

67. "From this actual artistic image, which we take from the scene as an inner image, emerges the actual vision which it is our task to render on canvas, and [it] will arise in . . . [the viewer] anew if we have strongly and properly constructed it on the canvas." "Arbeit ELK" (see note 52), 342.

68. Ibid.

69. This is taken from a "Lebensgeschichte" that Kirchner included in a letter to Carl Hagemann, 30 June 1937, quoted from Berlin, *Kirchner* (see note 18), 48.

70. "Chronik der Brücke," quoted from Berlin, *Kirchner*, 65. An English translation can be found in Chipp, *Theories* (see note 55), 175–78. Kirchner's choice of the word *Erlebnis*, translated here as "lived experience," suggests a unique moment as opposed to experience (*Erfahrung*) as knowledge gradually acquired through repetition and with the aid of tradition. The significance of Kirchner's terminology is illuminated by Hans-Georg Gadamer's discussion of the etymology of *Erlebnis*, which entered the German language only in the 1870s, when Germany was undergoing a period of rapid industrialization and urbanization. Gadamer's characterization of the word aptly suits Kirchner's aesthetic: "In the notion of experience (Erlebnis) there is . . . a contrast of life with mere concept. The experience has a definite immediacy which eludes every opinion about its meaning." (*Truth and Method* [New York, 1985], 55–63, particularly 60.) Walter Benjamin would later build on the distinction between *Erlebnis* and *Erfahrung* in his writings. See for example, "On Some Motifs in Baudelaire," in: *Illuminations*, ed. Hannah Arendt (New York, 1969), 154–200.

71. The text of the brochure is reproduced in Karlheinz Gabler, ed., *E. L. Kirchner—Dokumente: Fotos, Schriften, Briefe*, exhibition catalog, Museum der Stadt Aschaffenburg (Aschaffenburg, FRG, 1980), 90. "Sketching from life" (*Skizzieren nach dem Leben*) should not be confused with what in English is called "life drawing," or drawing from the nude, since there can be no semantic confusion in German, where the latter is *Aktzeichnen*.

72. This iconographic parallel was noted by G. F. Hartlaub in 1920: "In their subject matter Kirchner, Heckel, Schmidt-Rottluff and Pechstein have long remained *impressionists*. They have captured impressions of the circus, variété and ballet, nudity in the bath and boudoir or out of doors, harbor and beach. . . . " Specifically referring to Kirchner, Hartlaub wrote, "Like his companion Pechstein, the autodidact (Kirchner) also comes out of an admiration for impressionism, above all in that movement's boldest and most daring expressions, in the drawings and prints of a Degas, Lautrec, . . . among others. He in particular has shown a fondness for impressionist subjects . . . ." (G. F. Hartlaub, *Die neue deutsche Graphik*, Tribüne der Kunst und Zeit: Eine Schriftensammlung, 14 [Berlin, 1920], 49–50, 52–53.) This relationship was reaffirmed by other writers of the time, and was reaffirmed in the Kirchner literature of our own era by Dube-Heynig, *Kirchner Graphik* (see note 25), 54. Since the appearance of Dube-Heynig's book, however, this insight seems to have been ignored, with few exceptions. One of them is Hans Wentzel. Reviewing Donald Gordon's 1968 monograph in *Kunstchronik* 24 (February 1971): 48, he observed, "Kirchner's iconography corresponds roughly to the French impressionists from Degas to Manet," but he did not develop this idea. Although Wentzel gained this insight from Gordon's monograph, Gordon himself did not make the connection.

73. In the early 1900s, Slevogt initiated a series of portraits of the Portuguese singer Francisco d'Andrade in the role of Don Giovanni, which he performed at the Theater des Westens in the Kantstraße. Later, in 1920, Slevogt did forty-seven etchings based on Mozart's *Die Zauberflöte*.

74. See Annemarie Dube-Heynig, *Ernst Ludwig Kirchner: Postkarten und Briefe an Erich Heckel im Altonaer Museum in Hamburg* (Cologne, 1984).

75. Scheffler, *Berlin* (see note 6), 202.

76. Dube, "The Artists Group Die Brücke" (see note 44), 98.

77. Glaser (see note 21), 540.

78. Wolf-Dieter Dube, "Kirchners Bildmotive in Beziehung zur Umwelt," in Berlin, *Kirchner* (see note 18), 13. Dube takes the phrase, "Lieblosigkeit aller gegen alle," from a novel by Otto Flake, *Die Welt des Hirns*.

79. Gordon, *Kirchner* (see note 19), 92; Gordon, "By Instinct Possessed" (see note 61), 89.

80. See Simmel's essay, "Prostitution," in *Selected Writings* (see note 50), 121–26. Deutsche ("Alienation in Berlin" [see note 45], 71) writing from a Marxist perspective, criticizes both Simmel and Kirchner for failing to see, following Marx, that "prostitution was 'only a specific expression of the *general* prostitution of the laborer' in a capitalist economy."

81. Deutsche, "Alienation in Berlin," 69, 71.

82. Ibid.

83. Ibid., 72.

84. Ibid. Since Deutsche, Hanne Bergius has pursued this theme of commodification. She writes that Kirchner's manner of presenting his prostitutes in major arteries like Friedrichstraße, displaying themselves like merchandise, was intended to show that they belonged to the readily available enjoyments of the city, "like the snack at Aschinger, the leisurely cigarette in a café, the pleasure ride in an automobile—amusements that at just this time were achieving a certain popularity within the city." See Hanne Bergius, "Berlin als Hure Babylon," in *Die Metropole: Industriekultur in Berlin im 20. Jahrhundert*, ed. Jochen Boberg, Tilman Fichter, and Eckhart Gillen (Munich, 1986), 108.

85. Deutsche, "Alienation in Berlin," 69.

86. Kirchner, *Davoser Tagebuch* (see note 54), 18 February 1926, 128.

87. Graef, "Über die Arbeit von E. L. Kirchner," originally published in 1919 as the foreword to the catalog of a Kirchner exhibition at the Galerie Ludwig Schames in Frankfurt, reprinted in Berlin, *Kirchner*, 78. Since Graef died in 1917, the reference is clearly to the works of the artist's Berlin period.

88. Both letters, unpublished, are quoted from Gordon, *Kirchner*, 27.

89. See Kornfeld, *Kirchner* (see note 18), 54–55, and Kirchner's own mention of the incident in "Arbeit ELK" (see note 52), 337.

90. Gordon, "By Instinct Possessed," 95.

91. For an account of the development of prostitution in Berlin see Hans Ostwald, *Kultur- und Sittengeschichte* Berlins (Berlin-Grunewald, n.d. [1924?]), 613–52. An informative contemporary source, with a chapter devoted to Berlin, is Robert Hessen, *Die Prostitution in Deutschland* (Munich, 1910). For a general discussion on the social background of German prostitution during this era, and state and local attempts to regulate it, see Richard J. Evans, "Prostitution, State and Society in Imperial Germany," *Past and Present*, no. 70 (February 1976): 106–29. For a literary portrayal of the life of a Berlin prostitute during this period, see *Tagebuch einer Verlorenen*, "edited" by Margarete Böhme (Berlin, 1903). Published as an "authentic" diary recording the life of a provincial girl, Thymian Gotteball, from confirmation to seduction, pregnancy, and ultimately the Berlin demimonde and an early death, it had gone into its 100th printing within two years. It is now generally held to be the work of its "editor," and has recently been reprinted as such (Frankfurt/Main, 1989). Even if fictional, the pattern of Thymian's life was a common one, and the novel's treatment of Berlin prostitution seems founded on an intimate knowledge of this subculture.

92. Abraham Flexner, *Prostitution in Europe*, Publications of the Bureau of Social Hygiene (New York, 1914), 157. Flexner's book was published in January 1914 and his account is based on the practice of prostitution in Berlin during the years in which Kirchner painted his street scenes. Flexner also published the Berlin regulations governing prostitution at that time, which went into effect in February 1912 (415–19).

93. Ibid., 157.

94. Ibid., 146–47.

95. Ibid., 160–61.

96. Ibid., 157.

97. Contributing to this ambiguity was certainly the phenomenon of "casual prostitution," i.e., women who practiced prostitution only sporadically, to augment their inadequate income from respectable employment or to help their families through difficult financial periods. See Evans, "Prostitution, State and Society," 112, also 107.

98. Ostwald, *Kultur- und Sittengeschichte*, 640–41. Huard was momentarily fooled by such a case of ambivalent identity while watching the street traffic from the Café Kranzler, on Unter den Linden and Friedrichstraße. See Huard (note 4), 13.

99. According to Gordon's catalog of the paintings (Gordon, *Kirchner* [see note 19]), it seems that Kirchner gave only one of these works a title with an explicit reference to prostitution (*Street with Red Cocotte*, 1914–25, Gordon, 366). However, there are a number of prints with such titles.

100. For example, in the 1920s, Scheffler, Gustav Schiefler, and Curt Glaser discussed Kirchner's street scenes without any reference to prostitutes. In a long commentary on *The Street*, just acquired by the Berlin Nationalgalerie in 1920, Ludwig Justi (the institution's director), characterized it as a "poem in planes and colors"; there was not a word about "cocottes." (L. Justi, *Neue Kunst: Ein Führer zu den Gemälden der sogenannten Expressionisten in der Nationalgalerie* [Berlin, 1921], 31). Discussing the same work in 1957 Peter Selz, *German Expressionist Painting* (139–40) also omitted any mention of prostitutes, describing the motif as a "perfectly ordinary scene" of a Berlin street.

101. See George Grosz, *Ein kleines Ja und ein großes Nein* (Reinbek bei Hamburg, 1974), 98; Ostwald, *Kultur- und Sittengeschichte*, 644; also Bergius, "Berlin als Hure Babylon" (see note 84), 125.

102. The quote on Friedrichstraße is by Edmund Edel, as cited by Dieter und Ruth Glatzer, *Berliner Leben, 1900–1914: Eine historische Reportage aus Erinnerungen und Berichten* (Berlin, 1986), 2: 359. Compare also George Grosz, *Ein kleines Ja*, 98; and Ostwald, *Kultur- und Sittengeschichte*, 638, 644. See the police regulations in Flexner, *Prostitution in Europe*, 416, wherein Potsdamerplatz and Friedrichstraße are listed among the streets and places forbidden to prostitutes.

103. In his prints, Kirchner does show such episodes. For example, among a series of twelve etchings of the street scene motif from 1914, several show eye contact and verbal exchanges. See Dube R 177 (*Ansprachen auf der Straße*), R 179 (*Ansprachen II*), and R 182 (*Sich anbietende Kokotte*). Compare also the woodcut of the same year, Dube H 238 (*Am Schaufenster*). The titles, first published by Gustav Schiefler, may be Kirchner's own. In any case the images present open exchanges not found in the paintings.

104. Deutsche, "Alienation in Berlin," 71. Leopold Reidemeister interpreted this figure as a self-portrait of the artist, who, by his bearing, reveals himself "at once attracted and repelled by the seductions of the metropolis. . . . Kirchner is one of these endangered urbanites, to whom he erects an ingenious monument in his Berlin street scenes." Leopold Reidemeister, "Ernst Ludwig Kirchners Berliner Straßenszene von 1913: Eine Neuerwerbung des Brücke-Museums," *Brücke-Archiv* 11 (1979–80): 13.

105. Gordon, *Kirchner* (see note 61), 98.

106. Grohmann, *E. L. Kirchner* (see note 24), 54.

107. For an illustration and commentary on the painting, see Charles W. Haxthausen, "Modern German Masterpieces," *The Saint Louis Art Museum: Bulletin*, Winter 1985: 37–38.

108. Hans Kaiser, *Max Beckmann* (Berlin, 1913), 41–42. Beckmann dealt directly with subjects of prostitution in his graphic work of these years. Compare, for example, the lithograph *Ulrikusstraße in Hamburg* (1912, Gallwitz 27), which differs from Kirchner's street scenes in its flagrantly sexual imagery; and the drypoint, *The Night* (1914, Gallwitz 54), a sordid image of a murder in a brothel, in which the victim is male.

109. See the illustrations from the graphic cycle, *Opfer* (Victims), in Ostwald, *Kultur- und Sittengeschichte*, 642–43.

110. "Chronik der Brücke," in Berlin, *Kirchner* (see note 18), 65.

111. I was shown this sketchbook on a visit to the late Leopold Reidemeister, director of the Brücke Museum. It had been sent to him by a private collector for purchase consideration, an option he did not take. I do not know its current provenance.

112. The only exceptions, within Kirchner's cataloged paintings and prints, are: the painting *Two Whores* (1908, Gordon 52), and the lithograph *Cocotte* (1910, Dube L 147).

113. See, for example, Dube, in Berlin, *Kirchner*, 12.

114. Max Beckmann, *Leben in Berlin: Tagebuch 1908–1909*, ed. Hans Kinkel (Munich, 1983), entry of 10 January 1909. Compare Sarah O'Brien-Twohig, "Beckmann and the City," in *Max Beckmann Retrospective*, ed. Carla Schulz-Hoffmann and Judith C. Weiss, exhibition catalog, St. Louis Art Museum (St. Louis, 1984), 96–97. The picture in question, Göpel 124, is lost.

115. Bergius, "Berlin als Hure Babylon" (see note 84), 102.

116. Hessen, *Die Prostitution in Deutschland* (see note 91), 111.

117. I borrow the phrase from Bram Dijkstra, *Idols of Perversity: Fantasies of Feminine Evil in Fin-de-Siècle Culture* (New York, 1986), 357.

118. Flexner, *Prostitution in Europe*, 97–98. See also Ostwald, *Kultur- und Sittengeschichte*, 634ff.

119. See Winfried Ranke, *Heinrich Zille: Photographien, Berlin 1890–1910* (Munich, 1975). Zille's photographs were, however, not published or even known at the time that he made them; they are a posthumous discovery.

120. Evans, "Prostitution, State and Society (see note 91)," 106–7.

121. Scheffler, *Berlin* (see note 6), 100.

122. "Über Leben und Arbeit" (1930), in Berlin, *Kirchner*, 97.

CHAPTER 4

Modernity, Civic Identity, and Metropolitan Entertainment: Vaudeville, Cabaret, and Revue in Berlin, 1900–1933

Peter Jelavich

In his essay on "The Invention of Tradition," Eric Hobsbawm asserts that "traditions which appear or claim to be old are often quite recent in origin and sometimes invented." He notes that we should expect them "to occur more frequently when a rapid transformation of society weakens or destroys the social patterns for which old traditions had been designed, producing new ones to which they were not applicable, or when such old traditions and their institutional carriers and promulgators no longer prove sufficiently adaptable and flexible, or are otherwise eliminated." Hobsbawm notes that in Europe, such "invention of tradition" was particularly intense during the decades preceding the outbreak of World War I: the rapid economic and social changes of those years gave a sense of urgency to the project of "establishing or symbolizing social cohesion or the membership of groups, real or artificial communities." He contends, however, that the "new" traditions filled only "a small part of the space left by the secular decline of both old traditions and custom." Whereas customs regulated much of preindustrial life, modern society is held together by "the external compulsions of the economy, technology, bureaucratic state organization, political decision and other forces which neither rely on nor develop 'tradition' in our sense." Without using such words, Hobsbawm implies that the "invented traditions" form part of a superstructure that masks the "real" forces that are simultaneously holding society together and impelling it in new directions; they are attempts to act out persistence in eras of unstoppable change.[1]

Hobsbawm focuses on the modern nation-state and the creation of national traditions to underscore his thesis. Many of his arguments can be applied, with qualifications, to urban communities as well. The modern city at the turn of the century was the locus of change in its most concentrated form: the rapid and continuous influx of immigrants and the transformations occasioned by industrialization made civic identity increasingly problematic. As individuals came to see themselves more as citizens of a nation than as burghers of a local community, the invented national traditions that Hobsbawn describes might often conflict with civic ones. The maintenance of a sense of urban identity in the face of immigration, industrialization, and national homogenization required the invention of new forms of civic self-definition. By focusing on Berlin, this essay will attempt to show how novel types of popular and mass entertainment — vaudeville, cabaret, revues — responded to the need for a new urban identity. Not only the content, but also the form of these shows corresponded to perceptions of the "Berlin experience" in 1900, perceptions that had to be reformulated after the disaster of 1918.

Civic identity was particularly problematic in Berlin, which underwent rapid growth throughout the later nineteenth and early twentieth centuries. Every year tens of thousands of immigrants were attracted to a city that was the capital of Prussia and the Reich, as well as the major center of German commerce, finance, and industry. For much of the modern era, this city turned metropolis (*Weltstadt*) had a primarily nonnative population, hence the majority of its residents were faced with the question: What does it mean to be a Berliner? An answer to that query had never been easy, inasmuch as Berlin, like the United States, traditionally had been a melting pot of various ethnic and professional groups. By the end of the eighteenth century, the city had already experienced an influx of French Huguenots, Jews, craftsmen from Holland, Bohemia, and the Pfalz, and laborers from Silesia, Pomerania, and Poland. The melting down of these groups was never complete, and a fully homogeneous citizenry was never achieved. Nevertheless, there arose (supposedly) a certain Berlin "character type." Even Goethe noted "that one doesn't get very far with politeness in Berlin, because such an audacious race of men lives there that one has to have a sharp tongue in order to keep oneself afloat." To this image of pushiness and audacity was added a sense that Berliners had a corresponding style of humor (*Witz*), one marked by disrespect of authority and cynical scepticism toward received values.

Whether the average Berliner in reality betrayed these characteristics in the early nineteenth century is hard to determine. What is more certain is the fact that this stereotype of the Berliner became accepted by many people as early as 1822, with the performance of Julius von Voss's play, *Der Stralauer Fischzug*. This was the first popular farce (Possenspiel) to present local characters speaking Berlin dialect in a typically *berlinerisch*, i.e., aggressive fashion. It had numerous imitators during the *Vormärz*, both on stage (e.g., the skits of Adolf Glassbrenner) and in illustrated comic journals. A roster of characters was developed in these media that depicted the average lower-class Berliner as half-educated yet cunning, self-assured, and slyly subversive of authority. Major representatives of this attitude were cabdrivers, hawkers, shoemakers' apprentices, and the *Eckensteher* figure (a man-for-hire who stood at streetcorners). It would be difficult to come down on a single side of a chicken-or-egg argument — did the reality shape these images, or did the images shape actual behavior? At least one can say that over time, the continued presentation of such characters in the popular media led to a perception of Berliners (by people within and outside the city) in a manner summarized thus by *Meyers Konversations-Lexikon* in 1874: "The Berliner is always quick at repartee, always able to find a sharp, suggestive, witty formulation for every event and occurrence. . . . But the Berliner also has the tendency to find fault with anything greater or more profound that he encounters."[2]

The original image of the Berliner thus had been fashioned before 1848. However, the characters that populated the popular farces and comic journals of that time had little relevance to the Berlin of 1900, when the *Reichshauptstadt* was undergoing precisely those types of rapid social change that Hobsbawn considers so crucial to the invention of traditions. As hawkers, apprentices, and *Eckensteher* gave way to employees of department stores and heavy industry, new images of Berlin had to be fashioned for public consumption. Those images were created and propagated primarily in revues and cabarets.

A "Modern" Form: The Variety Show

The appearance of cabarets and revues after 1901 was itself an expression of the change that had taken place in the nature of Berlin and its inhabitants. Cabarets and revues were attempts to come to terms with the growing popularity of vaudeville or variety shows in the years following the unification of the Reich. As their name suggests, such *variétés* provided a "variety" of unconnected entertainments, primarily songs, acrobatic stunts, and animal acts. At the upper end of the vaudeville spectrum were large commercial establishments that seated well over a thousand spectators, such as the famous Wintergarten. When the Central-Hotel opened in Berlin in 1880, it boasted an enormous (2300-square-meter), glass-decked winter garden. Its owners soon put it to more profitable use, first as a ballroom, and eventually (by 1887) as a vaudeville hall. They proceeded to book the most famous stars of the vaudeville circuit, and the Wintergarten eventually became Europe's most prestigious variety theater. Among its featured attractions were Yvette Guilbert, Loie Fuller, La belle Otéro, Cleo de Mérode, Saharet, the Five Sisters Barrison, and Lillian Russell. Indeed, the world's first film projection took place at the Wintergarten on November 1, 1895, when the Skladanowsky brothers presented their *Bioskop* as part of the evening's entertainment.[3]

By the turn of the century, variety shows were becoming so popular that they were driving conventional theater out of business. This trend was especially pronounced in Berlin at an early date. The Tonhallen-Theater (founded 1870), the Bellevue-Theater (1872), the Neues American Reichs-Theater (1877), and the Reichshallen-Theater (1881) were among those that switched, within a few months after their opening, from concerts or spoken comedy and drama to variety shows. By the 1880s it had become apparent that broad segments of the middle class, which had initially looked down upon vaudeville, were being won over to its popular theatricality. The Wintergarten played a key role in this transition, inasmuch as attendance there became fashionable for Berliners as well as tourists. A cabaret journal of 1902 noted in retrospect that "Julius Baron, the former director of the Wintergarten, was probably the first person to build a large and wide bridge between vaudeville artistry and bourgeois society [zwischen Artistentum und bürgerlicher Gesellschaft]." The success of the Wintergarten and other prestigious variety theaters (e.g., Apollotheater, Passagetheater) was so great that Conrad Alberti, a noted naturalist writer and critic, could write in 1901: "The fact that vaudeville halls have increasingly supplanted and diminished interest in theater has caused a stir for quite some time in all circles which still take an interest in the fate and the future of art in Germany. Perhaps this has never been so apparent as this winter in Berlin, where attendance at the performances of theaters dwindles day by day and has become limited almost exclusively to inferior farces, while the vaudeville halls can boast of sold-out houses nearly every evening."[4]

Various attempts were made to explain the abandonment of theater in favor of variety shows. Among the most common, as well as intriguing, was the assertion that vaudeville was a quintessentially modern art form, a logical and inevitable outcome of urban life. The hustle and bustle of the modern city, with its crowds and traffic, its constant variation of sights and sounds, fragmented consciousness and shattered all sense of stability and continuity. Ernst von Wolzogen, the founder of Berlin's (and Germany's) first cabaret, noted that vaudeville's popularity was "a sign of our nervous, precipitate age, which finds no repose for long and prolix entertainments. We are all, each and every one of us, attuned to aphoristic, terse and catchy tunes." In the introduction to *Deutsche Chansons* (1900), an influential collection of lyrics that helped usher in the cabaret movement, Otto Julius Bierbaum wrote, "The contemporary city dweller has vaudeville nerves; he seldom has the capacity of following great dramatic continuities, of tuning his senses to the same sound for three hours. He desires diversity — Variété." The fragmentation and intensification of sense experience in everyday metropolitan life transformed the perceptual apparatus of modern urbanites to such an extent that they were no longer capable of the type of continuous reflection demanded by conventional drama. Stage presentations thus had to become as multiform and disjunct as the presentation of everyday life in the streets, the shops, and the offices of the modern metropolis.[5]

Such observations paralleled those of contemporary sociologists such as Georg Simmel, whose analyses of social interaction, commerce, and culture in the modern world were determined by lifelong observations in his native Berlin. He noted repeatedly that "the development of Berlin from a large city to a metropolis (von der Großstadt zur Weltstadt) in the years around and after the turn of the century coincides with the period of my own strongest and broadest development; . . . perhaps in another city I would have achieved something that also would have been valuable, but the special achievements that I made during these decades are undoubtedly tied to the Berlin milieu." Simmel was an extremely popular lecturer among both students and a broader educated public, and his published essays were (and are) considered some of the most trenchant analyses of the society and culture of modernity. Unlike many of the later social thinkers that he influenced— Siegfried Kracauer, Ernst Bloch, Walter Benjamin—Simmel never directly discussed vaudeville, cabaret, or revues, but many of his observations paralleled and complemented other ongoing debates about the nature of modern life and popular culture.[6]

Simmel contended that "the psychological foundation" of individuals in the metropolis was "the intensification of nervous life, which proceeds from the rapid and uninterrupted fluctuation of external and internal impressions." In contrast to "the slower, more customary, more uniformly flowing rhythm" of small-town life, the modern metropolis confronted its inhabitants with a dizzying variety of sensations. "With every walk across the street, with the tempo and multiplicity of economic, professional and social life," human consciousness came to be shaped in a uniquely modern and metropolitan manner: urbanites became accustomed to a multiplicity of sensations, but needed to be given direction and stimulation amid the bewildering confusion of impressions. Novel commercial and cultural forms sought to take advantage of this situation. While the display of innumerable commodities in shop windows, department stores, and exhibitions replicated the wealth of impressions experienced in everyday life, modern advertising and entertainment sought to attract the attention of the distracted urbanite. Observing the plethora of commodities presented at the Berlin Trade Exhibition of 1896, Simmel noted that "precisely this wealth and variety of fleeting impressions is appropriate to the desire for stimulation of irritated and exhausted nerves."[7]

To direct attention amid these variegated impressions, modern advertising became necessary. In situations where the supply of commodities exceeded the demand, goods needed to have not only use-value, but also an "enticing exterior": they needed to be fashioned, packaged, and displayed in an aesthetic manner to increase their "external appeal," since "internally" there often was little differentiation among competing products. The "shop-window quality" (Schaufenster-Qualität) of commodities thus came to supersede their practical utility for the consumer. At the same time, "ordinary advertisement has advanced to the art of the poster," since ever more extreme means were required to catch the attention of the shopper. As commodities and their advertisements acquired aesthetic traits, shopping and "window-shopping" became forms of entertainment. Conversely, the forms of art favored by the modern urbanite came to reflect the diversity and fragmentation of the world of commodities: he or she responded to the "charm of the fragment, the mere allusion, the aphorism, the symbol, the undeveloped artistic style." The metropolitan consumer ultimately felt at home amid a fragmented multiplicity of objects and styles in both the aesthetic and the commercial spheres, which increasingly overlapped.[8]

It should be obvious that Simmel's analysis of the metropolitan psyche and its effects on the marketing of commodities paralleled in many respects the arguments advanced by the proponents of cabaret and revues. Both contended that modern life fashioned citizens who felt increasingly "at home" in surroundings that changed constantly. Indeed, too much apparent stability would create excessive demands on the concentration of the modern observer. Moreover, ever more extreme means were needed to attract the attention of modern urbanites, bewildered and exhausted by the plethora of external stimuli. As Wolzogen said, everyone was "attuned to aphoristic, terse and catchy tunes." The melodies of modern life needed to be not only succinct, but also "catchy"; they had to reach out and ensnare the consumer. This became a vicious circle: as the number and intensity of stimulations increased, the observer became more confused and exhausted, which necessitated ever greater exertions to attract his or her attention. Shop-window displays became more extravagant, advertisements became more colorful and catching, and entertainments became more lavish and "sexy" in order to feed the hunger for overt stimulation. Just as window displays and trade exhibitions presented an increasing diversity of goods attractively packaged and presented, vaudeville provided a variety of different entertainments that increasingly claimed to be "the world's best," "the most beautiful," "the most daring," "the sensation of Europe."

A "Modern" Character Type: The "Berliner" according to the Metropol Revues and Claire Waldoff

The cabaret movement launched in Berlin in January 1901 adopted the variegated format of variety shows, which was now deemed most appropriate to the metropolitan psyche. Cabarets attempted to ennoble this form with higher artistic quality (e.g., lyric poetry) and a modicum of political criticism. Although the forty-odd cabarets that sprang up by the summer of 1901 tried various recipes to attract their audiences, no formula was completely satisfactory, and the first wave of the German cabaret movement ended in numerous closings and bankruptcies by 1903. That same year, however, many of the formal and thematic characteristics of cabaret were successfully appropriated by the revues that began to be staged by the Metropol-Theater. Like the cabaret, the revue was topical in content, and included a juxtaposition of songs, dances, and skits. It differed from cabaret insofar as it was performed on a larger stage before a larger audience, offered "production numbers" with lavish sets and costumes, and had a meager plot line that pretended to hold the various numbers together. These revues, which were staged annually from 1903 to 1913, were immensely successful with both native Berliners and tourists to the capital. Each different revue could count on approximately 300 performances—an immensely successful run for a Berlin theater of that age—and opening night became de rigueur for Berlin's high society. As the title of the 1907 revue smugly proclaimed: *Das muss man seh'n!* (You gotta see it!).

The popularity of such shows was due in part to the lavish productions, the witty texts by Julius Freund, and the peppy music by Viktor Hollaender and, less frequently, by Paul Lincke and Rudolph Nelson. But much of the attraction of the revues was also attributable to their thematic content, which, unlike that of the cabarets, centered on Berlin. To be sure, there were rare—very rare—songs or dances portraying Biedermeier idylls, suggesting that life was much more *gemütlich* before the *Gründerzeit*. However, the majority of the numbers praised Berlin for its modernity. The *Weltstadt* was welcomed with open arms: its vitality, its hectic tempo, its commercialism and consumerism were hailed. In songs and skits, praise was lavished on new urban phenomena ranging from the elevated rapid-transit municipal train to novel forms of mass-cultural entertainment like the Lunapark, cinema, and sports events. The consumerism of Berlin department stores like Wertheim was applauded as well. One show even contended that Berlin was one big Warenhaus, not only for material goods, but also for culture and politics; indeed, the revue presented itself as a department store that collected and displayed the year's events.[9] By explicitly equating modern Berlin with the form of both the department store and the revue, these scenes corroborated Simmel's assertion that variegated objects, attractively packaged and put on display, constituted the entertainment most appropriate to the modern urbanite.

The image of the Berliner projected in the revues was a combination of traditional and novel characteristics. What was new was the image of the thoroughly modern metropolitan person. Whereas the older Berlin character types were somewhat slow and phlegmatic, despite their wit and sarcasm (e.g., the *Eckensteher* figure), the revues projected a novel personality, one that could keep up with the increasingly hectic tempo of the *Weltstadt* and follow the changing fashions of the times. Simultaneously, certain traits of the older *Vormärz* (i.e., pre-1848) tradition were retained. Indeed, the crassness and critical spirit of the "typical Berliner" of yesteryear were brought up-to-date. Many numbers were indirectly critical of the Kaiser and directly critical of members of his cabinet and of the Reichstag: a distinction was made between Berlin, the fulcrum of commercial and cultural modernity, and the not-quite-so-progressive imperial offices that just happened to be located in the same city. Specifically Wilhelmine additions to Berlin, such as the Siegesallee with its lineup of Hohenzollern statues, were often ridiculed; and all of the Reichstag parties, from the Social Democrats to the Junkerite "agrarians," were chastised for being narrow class-interest groups that failed to take the national good to heart.

The Metropol revues thus treated Berliners as well as the city's thousands of tourists to an image of the metropolis that was lively, lavish, liberally open-minded, self-assured, *mondän*. If certain aspects seemed crass or excessive, it was because Berlin was still a very youthful metropolis. "Metropolinchen," a female personification of the capital in *Das muss man seh'n!*, sings:

> I have the foibles of my youth,
> I'm still a young metropolis!
>
> (Ich hab' die Fehler meiner Jugend,
> Ich bin als Weltstadt noch so jung!)[10]

Moreover, the revues repeatedly contended, it was better to live in Berlin than in Vienna or, heaven forbid, London, where "the fun's over at twelve-thirty" (der Spass aus [ist] um halb eins).

> Soon after day has turned to night,
> All of London's shut up tight!
>
> (Doch in London bei der Nacht
> Wird die Großstadt zugemacht!)[11]

Only Paris could compete with Berlin as a true metropolis, according to the Metropol revues. In the face of a large body of literature (and not merely "provincial" literature) condemning the "German Chicago," Berliners were exhorted to be proud of their modernity and tourists were told that they should marvel at and enjoy the novelties of their capital.

This was bait that many visitors were happy to swallow, and it was a picture that imperial officials were also pleased to have projected, despite the revues' attenuated barbs at official culture and the kaiser's cabinets. In July

1905, Theobald von Bethmann Hollweg, then with the Ministry of the Interior, wrote to Berlin's chief of police that although some restrictions on cabarets and revues might be necessary, he opposed any excessive curtailment of forms of entertainment appropriate to a *Weltstadt*. Even the chief of police summoned Julius Freund, the author of the revues, into his office to tell him: "I have asked you to see me so that you can hear from my own mouth: With me you can do whatever you like." This exchange suggests not only that the police were willing to give the Metropol-Theater freer rein than other theaters and cabarets, but also that social prestige was attached to being portrayed, even if satirically, in the immensely popular revues.[12]

Themes similar to those of the Metropol revues were taken up by some performers in those few cabarets that survived the bankruptcies of 1903. That was certainly true of Claire Waldoff, one of the most popular cabaret performers of the Wilhelmine and Weimar eras. In her songs she portrayed various lower-class Berlin characters, both male and female, speaking Berlin dialect. As in the Metropol revues, her tone was upbeat and up-to-date; little mention was made of the harsh working and grim housing conditions of Berlin's proletariat. Instead, she portrayed what purported to be the leisure-time activities of Berlin's lower-middle and working classes, and she touted the sexual freedom and mass-cultural entertainments (cinemas, the Lunapark) that the city offered even its poorer inhabitants. The metropolis in all its modernity was there to be enjoyed by one and all. To be sure, Waldoff sentimentalized and even "kitschified" the life of the lower classes in her presentations, but she cannot be accused of nostalgia for a vanished past. The opening lines of her "Kremserlied" proclaimed:

> Anyone who has reflected
> On these times will surely see:
> Everything our dads respected
> Seems to us stupidity.

> (Wenn man die Zeit von heut' betrachtet,
> Dann merkt man leicht als Philosoph,
> Was uns're Eltern einst geachtet,
> Das scheint uns Kindern 'n'bisken doof.)

After describing the nostalgic reminiscences of the older generation, she sings the refrain:

> Now that's all gone, it's a dead letter,
> Don't waste your tears on that old score.
> You might have liked those days much better,
> But what is gone is here no more.

(Das ist vorbei, das ist vorüber,

Wein' keine Träne hinterher.

War Dir die Zeit auch damals lieber,

Ja das was war, das jibt's nicht mehr.)

Indeed, extant recordings of Waldoff's performances indicate that she sang the last line in a decidedly forceful and positive manner.[13]

Although Waldoff portrayed lower-class characters, she appealed to all social strata, and she performed in mass-cultural vaudevilles and revues as well as the most expensive cabarets. She probably can be accused of trivializing social issues before middle-class audiences; like Heinrich Zille in his later graphic works, she gave the impression that after hours, life was a ball for the lower classes as well. Her major function, though, was to establish a sense of community among Berliners of all social strata, to foster pride in their city and its modernity, and to make them activate their assertive, self-assured character.

It is important to note that this "character" was something that one acquired, developed, and cultivated. Although Waldoff and Zille were regarded as the two prime embodiments of "the Berliner," neither of them was native to that city: she grew up in Gelsenkirchen, he in Saxony. Waldoff noted in her autobiography, "Everyone says that the true Berliner comes from Breslau." The Berlin character type was a product of "becoming" rather than "being." Describing her adoption of the Berlin dialect and *berlinerisch* qualities in her cabaret acts after 1908, she noted, "I began to become *the* Berliner, a prototype of the Berliner, a representative of modern Berlin." By the 1920s, Kurt Tucholsky was equating her with the statue of Berolina on the Alexanderplatz. The fact that an "outsider" could become the ultimate "insider" gives some indication of the degree to which "being a Berliner" was a social role that one could appropriate with sufficient practice. It was, moreover, a role that was modeled, recreated, and refurbished on the stages of revues and cabarets.[14]

Form as Content:
Cabaret and Revues in Weimar Berlin

In imperial Berlin after 1900, new types of commercial popular entertainment were created whose form and content addressed the style of life arising in the modern metropolis. A fractured "variety" format was paired with a novel image of the Berliner as a person who was able to cope with the increased tempo of the big city. After World War I, however, this mixture fell apart. Germany's defeat in the war meant that "modernity" came to be defined in international and increasingly abstract terms. Thus while the shows' "content"—the definition of a Berliner—fell into the background, the revue "form" came even more to the fore, so that the formal aspects of revue became the new content of entertainment.

The prewar Metropol revues had been an expression of the self-confidence of the imperial capital, the hub of the greatest power on the European continent as well as the world's second greatest industrial nation (after the United States). Though critical of some aspects of the Wilhelmine regime, the writers of antebellum cabaret and revue texts could rightly proclaim that their city was one of the very few centers of modernity (along with New York, London, and Paris). That assertion was shattered by the defeat of 1918, as well as the civil strife and the devastating inflation that ensued. After the war only a few avant-garde cabarets, whose writers often belonged to the Berlin dada movement, celebrated the hectic nature of the metropolis. This was especially true of Walter Mehring, whose song of 1921, "Heimat Berlin," proclaimed:

> Giddy-up! Down the Linden! Don't act dead!
> On foot, on horse, in twos!
> Got a watch in my hand and a hat on my head
> No time! No time to lose!
>
> (Die Linden lang! Galopp! Galopp!
> Zu Fuss, zu Pferd, zu zweit!
> Mit der Uhr in der Hand, mit'n Hut auf'm Kopp
> Keine Zeit! Keine Zeit! Keine Zeit!)[15]

These lines obviously tried to reformulate radically the cozy, homey, and communal qualities evoked by the word *Heimat*. This was, however, something that only a few members of the literary elite and their hangers-on wanted to hear. Having suffered military humiliation and economic catastrophe, most members of the Berlin audience craved a type of nostalgic looking-back that had been spurned by prewar revues. In 1919 Rudolph Nelson, who had been the manager and in-house composer of the most upscale cabaret in antebellum Berlin (the "Chat noir"), set a song by Willi Prager that began: "How days gone by were full of bliss . . . " (Wie war die alte Zeit so voll Glückseligkeit . . .). The refrain contained the lament:

> Berlin, Berlin, you just aren't what you were—
> Where is your humor, levity and wit?
> Where are the good old songs we used to hear?
> The Friedrichstadt now looks like Myslowitz!

(Berlin, Berlin, ich kenne dich nicht wieder
Wo ist dein Leichtsinn, dein Humor, dein Witz?
Wo sind die lieben guten alten Lieder?
Die Friedrichstadt sieht aus wie Myslowitz!)

Now that the capital (represented by the Friedrichstadt entertainment district) came to look like the provinces (Myslowitz), Berlin could hardly be considered a fulcrum of modernity, and had even lost its characteristic wit.[16]

The revues of the early and mid-1920s had relatively few numbers dealing with Berlin, and they were usually of a highly sentimental and nostalgic nature. When the Metropol revived its revues in 1926 after a hiatus of over a decade, it included a song entitled "The Fairy Tale of Long-Lost Berlin" ("Das Märchen vom verklungenen Berlin," in *Wieder Metropol!*). Walter Kollo, the composer of the music of the "Haller revues" of the mid-1920s, was perhaps the major cultivator of that genre, with songs such as "Then Everything Will Be Alright Again" (Dann ist es wieder richtig, in *Achtung! Welle 505!* [Attention! Radio station 505!], 1925) and especially the famous "Linden March" (in *Drunter und Drüber* [Over and under], 1923). The latter's refrain has become the epitome of Berlin nostalgia.

As long as lindens greet us
There where they've always been,
Then nothing can defeat us.
Berlin, you're still Berlin.

(So lang noch Untern Linden
Die alten Bäume blüh'n,
Kann nichts uns überwinden,
Berlin, du bleibst Berlin.)

Indeed, Marlene Dietrich was to revive that song after 1945. By then, it was the 1920s that seemed like the Golden Years.[17]

The revues of the Weimar era continued to provide images of modernity, but if they were localized, then they were attributed to the United States. The 1920s witnessed a seeming Americanization of popular entertainment. The music of the prewar revues derived from waltzes, polkas, mazurkas, folk songs, and marches; only occasionally would the tango, the Boston, the two-step, and the cakewalk be added as exotic interludes. After the war, however, the specifically Central European musical element was lost, and the music of the revues came to be dominated increasingly by foxtrot, tango, and jazz rhythms (even when composed by Germans). This music was used to back up images of modernity that included another import from America, namely the kick-line of "girls" (also called thus in German) in various states of undress. With the abolition of censorship after the war, the path lay open for the public display of women in near-total nudity. The worst offender among revue producers was James Klein, whose shows at the Komische Oper had titles like *Berlin ohne Hemd* (Berlin without a blouse), *Die Sünden der Welt* (The sins of the world), *Streng verboten* (Strictly prohibited), *Zieh dich aus* (Take it off), and *Donnerwetter—1000 Frauen!* (Goddam—1000 women!). Not all producers and directors were as crass as Klein, but nearly all revues had to include large doses of the "girl" element, which was considered indispensable for attracting an audience in a highly competitive market.

These shows attracted the attention not only of the average theatergoer, but also of some of the most significant social theorists of the day. Siegfried Kracauer was interested not so much in the obvious sexuality of the "girls" as in the fact that they appeared in great numbers in identical, interchangeable form. His essay on "The Mass Ornament" (1927) was a reflection upon the American Tiller Girls and similar troupes that appeared on revue stages in Berlin. In such shows, according to Kracauer, the individual woman was lost in a constantly changing pattern of abstract, geometric forms. Indeed, the unit of composition was no longer the whole person, but the body part: "The Tiller Girls cannot be reassembled retrospectively into human beings; the mass gymnastics are never undertaken by total and complete bodies, whose contortions defy rational understanding. Arms, thighs and other parts are the smallest components of the composition." These shows were devoid not only of personal characteristics, but also any sense of national identity: they symbolized the masses as a mass, a truly impersonal, supranational and modern phenomenon. After all, such revues could be seen not just in Berlin, but throughout the world, from America to India and Australia, and even in "the smallest village" owing to the medium of film.[18]

Kracauer suggested that the meaning of these numbers resided in their form: "The ornament is an *end in itself*" (*Selbstzweck*), and "the constellations have no meaning beyond themselves." They were not even primarily sexual, but rather "a system of lines that no longer has an erotic meaning, but at best signifies the place where the erotic may be found." Their fascination was a product of the fact that they reflected the actual condition of the mass audiences. On the one hand, autonomous individuals were reduced to economically useful attributes: "the legs of the Tiller Girls correspond to the hands in the factories." On the other hand, peculiarities of civic, regional, and national identity became eradicated by an international economy and mass culture.

Regardless of the validity of Kracauer's Marxist analysis in particular, it is hard to deny that increasingly supranational forms of mass culture combined with the trauma of Germany's defeat to attenuate the specifically *berlinerisch* elements of the postwar revues. Berlin could not, in the immediate postwar years, claim to be a capital of modernity, at least not in a positive sense. Only for a brief period—1926 to 1929—did the revues regain some of the previous self-confidence in the city. Beginning with Rudolph Nelson's revue of 1926, significantly entitled *Es geht schon besser* (It's getting better), Berlin again began to be portrayed as a locus of hectic consumerism. The high point of this renaissance of prewar themes was the 1928 revue *Es liegt in der Luft* (It's in the air), with music by Mischa Spoliansky and lyrics by Marcellus Schiffer. Once again, the whole plot took place in a department store, which came to represent various aspects of Berlin's political, social, and cultural life. The crash of 1929 and the de facto cessation of parliamentary democracy the following year buried this short interlude of optimism.

Even though Berlin did not play the same thematic role that it had in the antebellum Metropol revues, social theorists tended to agree that the revue form itself was most appropriate to the nature of that city. Whereas Simmel had not reflected explicitly upon the significance of revues, they became an important concern of not only Kracauer, but also Ernst Bloch. Both noted the congruence between Berlin's mutability and the formal aspects of the revue. For Bloch, that metropolis appeared to be "a city that is perenially new, a city built around a hollow space, in which not even the mortar becomes or remains hard." The revue seemed to Bloch to be congruent with such a "hollow" and perpetually transmutable Berlin, since revues were "one of the most open and unintentionally honest forms of the present, a cast of that hollow space. . . . The appeal of the revues comes precisely from the sensual power and turbulence of loosely-strung scenes, from their ability to change and to transform themselves into one another. . . . " Likewise, Siegfried Kracauer noted, "The Berlin public behaves in a profoundly truthful manner when it increasingly shuns [conventional forms of high art] . . . and shows its preference for the superficial luster of stars, films, revues, and production numbers. Here, in pure externality, it finds itself; the dismembered succession of splendid sensory perceptions brings to light its own reality." For Bloch and Kracauer, a hollow, commercialized city constantly seeking to give itself form sought a cultural expression that could keep abreast of consumerist and mass-cultural trends. That form was the revue.[19]

Conclusion

After 1900, Berlin's revues and cabarets had responded to the transformation of their city into a metropolis by touting attitudes and character types that made the most of the city's hectic consumerist and mass-cultural life. An older image of the Berliner was refurbished to appear as up-to-date as possible. Indeed, there was a happy paradox in the solution proffered by the prewar revues and cabarets: they posited the traditional Berliner as someone who was as untraditional as possible. Unlike Hobsbawm's national invented traditions, which sought to establish a sense of permanence in an era of actual change, the image of the Berliner projected by revues and cabarets was that of a person whose character traits—crass, critical, self-assured—allowed him or her to live with and relish a permanent sense of impermanence, to change with the changing times.

This fact forces one to reformulate Hobsbawm's thesis in certain instances. Whereas his "invented traditions" were attempts to act out persistence in eras of instability, it seems that other forms of tradition could foster change by applauding and sustaining modern character types. Nevertheless, to Hobsbawm's credit, it should be admitted that Berlin was an exceptional case, and its message could not have worked in Germany at large. Moreover, it is obvious that not all Berliners evidenced those traits imputed to them by the prewar revues and cabarets, which also neglected or prettified many serious social issues. Needless to say, for radical cultural conservatives, Berlin remained the Whore Babylon. Still, at least in the imperial era, the revues and cabarets did provide positive values and role models to those Berliners and visitors to Berlin who wanted to accept and enjoy the city's new metropolitan character. Both in their themes and their variety-show format, they sought to make modernity—or at least certain aspects thereof—palatable and comestible to urbanites. However, this felicitous fusion of form and content dissolved after the war. Excepting a few revues in the years of "relative stabilization," most Weimar shows depicted Berlin through the veils of a nostalgic past, and represented modernity through the abstract formal means of human ornament and the revue pattern. This perpetual reordering of human fragments into evanescent visual structures not only entertained, but also mirrored the Weimar polity.

NOTES

This essay was originally presented at the conference "In Search of 'Central Europe': 20th Century Culture and Society in the Capital Cities," at the Wilson Center of the Smithsonian Institution, 5–6 May 1988, and is published here with the permission of the Woodrow Wilson International Center for Scholars. Copyright 1988, Woodrow Wilson International Center for Scholars, Washington, D. C.

1. Eric Hobsbawm, "Inventing Traditions," in *The Invention of Tradition*, ed. Hobsbawm and Terence Ranger (Cambridge, 1983), 1, 4–5, 9, 11.

2. "Berlin," in *Meyers Konversations-Lexikon*, 3d ed. (Leipzig, 1874), vol. 3, 13–14.

3. A thoughtful contemporary survey of vaudeville halls is Eberhard Buchner, *Varieté und Tingeltangel in Berlin* (Berlin, 1905). See also Ernst Günther, *Geschichte des Varietés* (Berlin, 1978); and Ingrid Heinrich-Jost, *Auf ins Metropol: Specialitäten- und Unterhaltungstheater im ausgehenden 19. Jahrhundert* (Berlin, n.d.). For more information on the Wintergarten, see the commemorative booklet, *Festschrift 50 Jahre Wintergarten, 1888–1938* (Berlin, 1938).

4. Günther, *Varieté*, 125–26, 138; anon., "Ueberbrettl und Varieté" *Modernes Brettl* 1 (15 January 1902): 49; and Conrad Alberti, "Die Chansonnière," *Münchener Salonblatt* 3 (2 June

1901): 363. For a detailed account of how one Munich theater that opened as a home for modern drama was rapidly converted into a vaudeville hall, see Peter Jelavich, *Munich and Theatrical Modernism* (Cambridge, Mass., 1985), 115–25.

5. Wolzogen in the *Vossische Zeitung*, 31 October 1900; and Otto Julius Bierbaum, ed., *Deutsche Chansons* (*Brettl-Lieder*), 3d ed. (Berlin, 1901), xi–xii.

6. Hans Simmel, "Auszüge aus den Lebenserinnerungen," in *Ästhetik und Soziologie um die Jahrhundertwende: Georg Simmel*, ed. Hannes Böhringer and Karlfried Gründer (Frankfurt/ Main, 1976), 265.

7. Georg Simmel, "Die Großstädte und das Geistesleben," *Jahrbuch der Gehe-Stiftung zu Dresden* 9 (1903): 188, 193, 195; "Berliner Gewerbe-Ausstellung," *Die Zeit* (Vienna) 8 (25 July 1896): 59.

8. Simmel, "Berliner Gewerbe-Ausstellung," 60; and *The Philosophy of Money*, trans. Tom Bottomore and David Frisby (Boston, 1978), 474.

9. Rudolph Nelson and Julius Freund, *Chauffeur—in's Metropol!!* (Berlin, 1912), act 2.

10. Viktor Hollaender and Julius Freund, *Das muss man seh'n!* (Berlin, 1907) act 1.

11. Viktor Hollaender and Julius Freund, *Hurra! Wir leben noch!* (Berlin, 1910), act 1, part 3.

12. Letter by Bethmann Hollweg of 5 July 1905 in Staatsarchiv Potsdam, Pr. Br. Rep. 30 Berlin C, Pol. Präs. Tit. 74, Th 1499; and conversation cited in Walter Freund, "Aus der Frühzeit des Berliner Metropoltheaters," in *Kleine Schriften der Gesellschaft für Theatergeschichte*, no. 19 (Berlin, 1962), 63. For more information on revues in general, see Franz-Peter Kothes, *Die theatralische Revue in Berlin und Wien, 1900–1938: Typen, Inhalte, Funktionen* (Wilhelmshaven, FRG, 1977).

13. For information on Waldoff, see her 1953 autobiography, *Weeste noch . . . ? Aus meinen Erinnerungen* (Berlin, 1969); Helga Bemmann, *Wer schmeisst denn da mit Lehm? Eine Claire-Waldoff-Biographie* (Berlin, 1982); and Bemmann, ed., *Die Lieder der Claire Waldoff* (Berlin, 1983). There are also several reissues of her recordings. The "Kremserlied" may be heard on Claire Waldoff, "Es gibt nur ein Berlin," EMI/Electrola (No. F 667 949/50).

14. Waldoff, *Weeste noch . . . ?*, 31, 55; and Kurt Tucholsky, "Berolina . . . Claire Waldoff," *Die Weltbühne*, 27 August 1929.

15. Walter Mehring, "Heimat Berlin," in *Das Ketzerbrevier: Ein Kabarettprogramm* (Munich, 1921).

16. Rudolph Nelson and Willi Prager, *Berlin, ich kenne dich nicht wieder!* (Berlin, 1919).

17. "Linden-Marsch," in Walter Kollo and Herman Haller, Rideamus and Willi Wolff, *Drunter und Drüber* (Berlin, 1923).

18. Siegfried Kracauer, "Das Ornament der Masse" (1927), in *Das Ornament der Masse: Essays* (Frankfurt, 1977). Citations in this and the following paragraph from 50–54.

19. Ernst Bloch, "Berlin, Funktionen im Hohlraum," and "Revueform in der Philosophie" (1928), both reprinted in Bloch, *Erbschaft dieser Zeit* (Frankfurt, 1962), 212, 368–69; and Kracauer, "Kult der Zerstreuung" (1926), in *Das Ornament der Masse*, 314–15.

CHAPTER 5

Lustmord: **Inside the Windows of the Metropolis**

Beth Irwin Lewis

At the end of June 1917, two months after being discharged from a military mental asylum, George Grosz, writing to his close friend Otto Schmalhausen, discussed his new large paintings of city scenes. His description of the chaotic street scene intermingled violence and sex with the technology of the modern city. Screams of women giving birth, jangling telephones, knuckle-dusters and Solingen knives resting in the trouser pocket of the pimp, Circe turning men into swine, gramophone music, and murder by strangling in a dusty cellar—all these Grosz called the "emotions of the metropolis," which he executed with a remarkable palette of reds.[1] In this letter, Grosz was probably referring to two of his major paintings of 1917–18, *Metropolis* and *Dedicated to Oskar Panizza*; however, the theme of the suspicious and bestial world of the streets and of the life inside the windows was not a new one for him. It was the dominant subject in his first published works, both drawings and poetry, in journals and portfolios. In the *Erste George Grosz Mappe* (1917), seven of the nine lithographs were street scenes in which windows in multistory buildings revealed scenes of seduction, assault, and suicide. In the twenty prints of the *Kleine Grosz Mappe* of the same year, not only did fourteen show street scenes, but the long, expressionist title-page poem was a verbal counterpart to the drawings, in which the windows of the city displayed drinking, sex, murder, and mayhem.[2] The windows serve as a catalog of the signs of degeneracy—the "sickness of the age" according to Max Nordau—attributed to the modern metropolis.[3] In his poem Grosz expressed this view of the degeneration within the city characterizing those who inhabit the dingy streets and toppling tenements as:

> and always evil people, degenerate,
> meaty-handed, with ball-like feet.

111

(und immer böse Menschen, entartete,
großhändig, mit Ballenfüßen.)

Looking from the outside in, Grosz presented domestic scenes during the
First World War in which people commit suicide, fight and murder, or stare
in bleak desolation out onto streets where funeral hearses mingle with respectable burghers and degenerate figures.

The first critics who wrote about Grosz concentrated upon his brutal vision of the metropolis and his disturbing view inside the windows. Theodor
Däubler, in the earliest review of his work in 1916, described Grosz's penchant for portraying the windows of the city with violent scenes within
and, in the following year in a major art journal, stated that in Grosz's drawings one did not look, as is usual, *out* of a window, but instead looked *into*
windows like stacked boxes containing quarrelsome, sentimental, murder-
ous people. Even the deep cellars, Däubler said, contained raging suicides,
sadists, drunks, gamblers, and whores.[4] By 1918, Däubler developed his
theme further, seeing Grosz as passionately affirming violent modern urban
life, even the bitter life within the tenements of the great city. Grosz's tenements virtually exploded, said Däubler, from the force of the emotions raging within: itching, cringing, rioting, rutting.[5] Each of Däubler's articles
was accompanied with drawings and poems by Grosz that confirmed his
observations (figure 21).

Within this catalog of passion that Grosz portrayed in word and line and
that critics discussed was the *Lustmord* (sex or rape murder). In the second
part of the title-page poem, published in 1932 under the title "Berlin, 1917,"
Grosz intimated a scene of sexual violence.

> Gloomily the overcoat flaps at the pimp's bones,
> Back bent, brass knuckles fixed,
> Descending with a sharp Solingen knife
> Deep into tenements
> Into fur shops and silk houses
> Or coal cellars
> Afterwards one sometimes finds a bloody
> Piece of taffetta or a wool stocking
> Or the bill with a handprint.
>
> (Schwarz schlägt der Paletot ans Zuhältergebein
> Rückenkrumm, schlagringfest
> Mit scharfem Solingmesser gehts bergab
> Mietskasernen tief
> In die Pelzgeschäfte und Seidenhäuser

Figure 21. George Grosz. People in the Street, *1915–16. Transfer lithograph in* Erste George Grosz Mappe, *Malik Verlag, 1917, pl. 5, 27.6 x 21.7 cm. Los Angeles County Museum of Art, The Robert Gore Rifkind Center for German Expressionist Studies.*

Oder Kohlenkeller
Nachher findet einer mal ein blutiges
Stück Taft oder einen Wollstrumpf
Oder die Rechnung mit Handabdruck.)[6]

Figure 22. George Grosz. World of the Bourgeoisie, *1918, Offset lithograph in* Ecce Homo, *Malik Verlag, 1923, pl. 18, 21.0 x 26.3 cm. Los Angeles County Museum of Art, The Robert Gore Rifkind Center for German Expressionist Studies, purchased with funds provided by Anna Bing Arnold, Museum Acquisition Fund, and Deaccession Funds.*

In his drawings and paintings of sexual murders, Grosz was more explicit. Several of the paintings were published in the early reviews of his work and the descriptions by avant-garde critics are surprisingly matter-of-fact, concentrating upon the formal elements of the works. For example, Däubler wrote in 1917, "Grosz also painted many a *Lustmord.* . . . The red of the blood stains and marks intertwined with the arabesques of the imitation Genoese damask carpet."[7]

This acceptance of sexual murder as an expected manifestation of the nasty underworld of the metropolis can be viewed as an extension of the bourgeois preoccupation with the degeneracy and corruption of urban life at the end of the century. Grosz himself clearly viewed the prostitute, both alive and dead, as very much part of bourgeois life. In *World of the Bourgeoisie* (figure 22), drawn in July 1918, Grosz integrated both respectably conventional prostitutes and those engaged in sadistic practices into a crowded urban scene presided over by a top-hatted aristocrat and a straight-laced burgher seated at a table. In this corrupt metropolis, Grosz included a truncated image of the *Lustmord:* a bloody knife and a dismembered female torso with lash marks on her buttocks rest on the burgher's table. Furthermore, the bloody knife connects the torso to the profile of the artist himself.[8]

★ ★ ★

In this essay, I shall address the question of why Grosz and other avant-garde artists of his generation chose to present images of violated and dismembered women in bleak urban settings. I shall argue that these artists portrayed domestic violence in its extreme form—the *Lustmord* or sex murder—because of pervasive social anxieties about the role of women that many of the artists and intellectuals shared with the middle classes in this period. Anxiety about the "woman question" constituted one of the burning social issues of the day, debated by intellectuals, artists, and politicians. An underlying theme of the essay is that these artists, who constituted the second generation of German expressionists, or the generation of 1914,[9] consciously turned to popular urban culture for artistic themes to express their own anxieties.

Reinhold Heller and Bram Dijkstra have both analyzed the misogynistic response of artists at the turn of the century to the increasingly strong women's movement and to social changes within the industrial world. These artists of the 1890s, they argue, objectified their anxiety about women in the images of the seductive femme fatale and the dangerous animalistic woman.[10] The artists who came of age on the eve of the war—the generation of 1914—were affected by a different complex of cultural and and social changes. As adolescents, they consumed the violent and pornographic trash literature and itinerant films that had their heyday in the decade before the First World War. As young men, they became enamored with the misogynistic ideas of the earlier generation of Symbolists, shortly before most of them had to confront service in the war, which was, for many, traumatic. Most of these young men were aware of the turn-of-the-century sexology that sought to define normative sexual activity for both male and female. At the same time, troubling social problems associated with the metropolis—such as the rising visibility of prostitution, contraceptive usage, abortion, venereal diseases, sexual promiscuity, and pornography—combined with Darwinian ideas, produced on the part of many intellectuals a preoccupation with degeneracy that was linked with woman. A critical factor associated with all of these phenomena was anxiety about sexual roles that was accelerated by the social changes brought about by the women's movement and later by the war.

★ ★ ★

Grosz started drawing sex murders in 1912–13, several years before the war. The earliest examples of the *Lustmord* theme in his work were presented in a hazy, stylized fashion, clearly inspired by images from popular culture and from his reading of horror novels. Grosz often recounted in later years that he was fascinated as a child by the horror stories shown in primitive peep shows in country fairs. He liked to read newspaper accounts of sensational murders and he devoured trashy pornographic, adventure, and detective novels. A voracious reader of fantastic and demonic writers, he was particularly fond of Gustav Meyrink, Hanns Heinz Ewers, and E. A. Poe; hence, the title of one of his early depictions of a man murdering a woman: *Double Murder on the Rue Morgue, dedicated to E. A. Poe.* In the decades before the war, pulp novels, sold in installments, and cheap pamphlet stories constituted a lucrative trade throughout Germany, so extensive that one scholar has claimed that "the world picture of millions of late 19th century Germans was formed more by pamphlet stories than anything else."[11] Estimates of annual sales on the eve of the war range from 25 to 300 million. The most popular colporteur novels combined violence and sex; Victor von Falk's *The Executioner of Berlin*, possibly the best-selling novel in nineteenth-century Germany with over a million copies sold, included graphic descriptions of murders, executions, dismemberments, torture, and kidnapping in its 3,000 pages[12] Beginning in the 1880s, the covers of the pamphlet stories displayed multicolored scenes of sensational, violent acts.[13] Itinerant films, introduced in 1895, did not lag far behind in portraying endless cycles of violence and sadism. The cinemas spread so rapidly that by 1914, millions of lower-class Germans were viewing films each day in over 2,500 cinema houses.[14] Together, the trash novels and the cinema constituted a burgeoning urban culture, providing the working urban classes with escape into the windows of distant exotic worlds or nearby urban underworlds.

Grosz attested to the power of the pamphlet novels and primitive films over his imagination in his autobiographical statements, first published in 1929, in which he recounted both titles and plots of the ones he most relished, and reproduced an illustration from *Jack the Mysterious Maiden Killer*, a childhood book he still owned.[15] In 1943 he planned to dedicate his autobiography to several men, including the author of his favorite dime novels.[16] Not surprisingly, given Grosz's penchant for expressing the same ideas in written and visual form, a long series of Grosz drawings from 1912–14 have the gruesome and exotic quality of the pulp novels. Scenes of harems, family tragedies, modern Bluebeards, and sailors of death disposing of female victims mixed with the predominant image — that of the *Lustmord*. These sex murders took place in prostitutes' rooms, disordered, with indications of alcoholism and debauchery, both believed at that time to be characteristics of urban degeneration. The sense of uncanny agitation in most of these images was emphasized by Grosz's use of fine, spidery lines to envelop the figures.

Although Grosz reveled in these tales, many in the educated middle and upper classes did not. Reacting against the widespread popularity of these cheap, colorful, and trashy manifestations of popular culture, middle-class crusaders by the late 1890s mounted campaigns against the pornographic and violent books and films, which they charged had deleterious effects upon young people and the lower classes. Forming a large number of morality associations, the purity crusaders agitated in journals, newspapers, and demonstrations in front of various city councils and state legislatures. By 1912, limited forms of censorship were put into place. These crusades were significant for the public debate and attention that they generated over the linked themes of sexuality and violence in popular culture at the time when Grosz and his peers were adolescents. Scholars who have examined these crusades speak of the "unprecedented obsession with and fear of sexuality" at that time.[17]

This obsession with sexuality also emerged in the high culture of the pre-war period. The fear of women became visible in misogynist writings by intellectuals and in the preoccupation with sexuality in the medical world throughout Europe. The "science" of sexology that emerged in the late nineteenth century was both a response to and a manifestation of anxiety about moral and national degeneracy. Sexology was an attempt to define and then regulate sexual pathologies that were perceived to underlie patterns of national degeneration. A basic axiom among sexologists was that sexuality was biologically determined, not socially constructed. The concern was to define respectable bourgeois roles or, conversely, to liberate people from social constraints and enable them to fulfil "normal" biological needs. Whether reformist or conservative, the sexologists agreed that woman is determined by her biology, that her being is overwhelming sexual, and that her purpose is reproductive.[18] This concentration upon woman's sexual nature and reproductive purpose indicated that underneath the concern for respectable and healthy sexual norms lay considerable anxiety about the threat to the traditional male-dominant role that the "woman question" was posing. That a woman's normal nature was fulfilled by sexual relations and reproduction was a powerful argument for maintaining traditional roles against women's demands for equal rights and independence.[19]

The assumption of the fundamentally sexual nature of woman underlay the misogyny of writers in Germany, Austria, and France who cultivated a reactionary view of women. Drawing on Schopenhauer's pessimistic study *On Women*, which was reissued in 1908 in an edition of 50,000, on Nietzsche's brief aphoristic condemnation in *Beyond Good and Evil* of woman as a mindless and soulless being, and on Strindberg's unbounded hatred of and fascination with strong aggressive women, writers and artists compulsively explored the nature of the battle of the sexes. In *Die Frau und die Kunst* (1908), Karl Scheffler, editor of *Kunst und Künstler*, attacked the women's rights movement because it denied the fundamental, eternal, and natural polarity of the sexes. Arguing that man's true nature is active, creative, and individualized, but that woman's true nature is passive, imitative, undifferentiated, and childlike, Scheffler insisted that man fulfils his nature by creative activity. When woman, however, attempts to become active or creative, she either becomes a poor imitation of man or she destroys herself.[20] The ultimate statement of pseudoscientific sexology and pseudo-philosophical writing came from Otto Weininger in his 1903 book on *Sex and Character*, in which he defined woman totally as a sexual being (*Geschlectswesen*) who has no consciousness, no soul, and no existence beyond her sexuality. As pure sexual being, the female, living only for the phallus, threatens all that is transcendent and godlike in the male. Men, as moral beings, can only be destroyed by the immoral sensual omnipotence of the female.[21] Weininger himself chose suicide after he completed his passionate discourse, but Weininger's woman, possessed by her sexual organs and her omnivorous appetite for the phallus, emerged in startling clarity in the images of the femme fatale in turn-of-the-century German art.[22]

Weininger's woman appeared around 1912 in a series of Grosz's drawings of Circe, whose imperious sexuality reduced men to degraded cringing animals. In other drawings, under her direction an ape with knife and ax slaughtered and beheaded a man, handing her the gory head. The images conflate Salome, Judith, Circe, Poe, and cheap novels. Grosz's drawings, expressing the pessimism of high culture, were indebted to the images of urban mass culture. When he came to Berlin in 1912, Grosz was not only reading horror novels, he was enamored—as were most young artists—by fashionable writers, all of whom were noted for agonizing over woman's sexuality.

> We worshipped Zola, Strindberg, Weininger, Wedekind—naturalistic enlighteners, anarchistic self-tormenters, devotees of death, and erotomaniacs.[23]

Filled with the diatribes of Nietzsche and Schopenhauer, Grosz was particularly drawn to "the truly great Huysmans and Strindberg,"[24] whose works he read, admired, and wrote about throughout his life. He remembers seeing a series of Strindberg plays in Berlin at this time. His letters, poetry, and drawings were awash with his own fascination, influenced by his reading, with sex and death. In a letter to his friend Otto Schmalhausen in 1916, he used language from Weininger to analyze Otto's problems.[25] Däubler, describing the denizens of Grosz's street scenes in 1917, referred to "a criminal, in Weininger's sense." Yet Grosz also shared Weininger's awe before the eternal reproductive power of women. Writing about a childhood experience—whether actual or fantasy—of peering through a window and finding within a woman undressing, Grosz, transfixed by the fleshy vision, concluded:

> It was as if someone I don't know had shown me a symbol, something eternal—for as long as we exist, there will be the symbol of nudity: woman as the everlasting source and continuation of our species.[26]

Enthralled by the power of sex, fearful of women embodying that power, Grosz and his generation of artists, like Bohemians before them, glorified and vilified the prostitute. He read Flaubert and de Maupassant and reveled in the prostitutes of Berlin, for, as he said, "The Friedrichstadt was alive with whores."[27]

Grosz's observation coincided with contemporary controversies over the conspicuous growth and visibility of prostitution in German cities in the decades before the First World War. As a result of social and economic changes produced by rapid industrialization, prostitutes not only increased in numbers but spread out of the old police-regulated bordellos into the streets of the industrial cities in Germany. In 1897, Berlin police regulated 3,000 registered prostitutes, but estimated there were another 40–50,000 unregistered prostitutes in the city. By 1900, estimates for prostitutes in Germany varied between 100 and 200,000. By 1914, 330,000.[28] In addition to prostitutes becoming more visible and, therefore, more threatening to middle-class morals, a whole lower-class entertainment industry grew up around prostitution in the cities: cafés, cabarets, beer-halls, and music halls. With the prostitutes also came venereal diseases that reached epidemic proportions in the early years of the century; according to one source, VD was second only to tuberculosis in the number of cases treated in hospitals.[29] Women as prostitutes were perceived as carriers of sickness and death. The connection between sex and death was concrete and physical. Prostitutes, usually as victims, were also involved in the rising crime statistics. The number of sexual crimes and homicides increased: in Prussia in 1900, 191 women were killed; that number rose to 365 in 1914. While the raw numbers seem low to our violence-saturated minds, they caused alarm in the prewar period, particularly the female homicides, because the newspapers tended to run lurid stories on murdered women, heightening the perception of women as victims of the industrial city. Women who were single, living and working independently in Berlin and other cities, were more likely to be murder victims than women who remained in traditional roles in rural areas.[30] Women, therefore, became visible symbols for fears about the degeneration and corruption produced by industrial city life. Morality associations, as well as crusading against pornographic books and films, were actively trying in the years before the war to cleanse the city streets of the social disorder represented by the prostitutes.[31]

Another form of degeneration—again connected with women—that raised national anxieties at this time was the declining birth rate and rise of abortions in Germany. Both of these phenomena were occurring in other European countries, but the proportions of each in Germany were sufficient to alarm authorities, who began to talk about a "birth strike." The downward trend of the birth rate, begun in the 1870s, became most visible after the turn of the century, and declined precipitously during and after the First World War. In 1914 there were 27 births per 1,000 persons; in 1922, 11.5 per 1,000.[32] Particularly worrisome was the declining birth rate among the lower-middle and lower classes. Motivation for the refusal to bear children appears to have gone, in many cases, beyond fear of pregnancy to a rejection of male sexual demands.[33] Despite increased prosecution of women, abortions increased from an estimated 100,000 in 1912 to 1 million in 1931. In 1914, half of all German women were estimated to have had at least one abortion. By 1930, that estimate became two abortions per woman and abortions exceeded live births.[34] Already by 1914, fears raised by illegal abortions and by the specter of a birth strike brought debates in the Prussian parliament and the Reichstag. Newspaper articles not only blamed socialism and feminism for this decline of births, but charged the birth strike with undermining the health and strength of the nation.[35]

Anxiety over all these forms of degeneration, from venereal disease, pornography, and crime to abortions and the falling birth rate, reached levels of active agitation and publicity in the decade before the war. Observers believed that sexuality and confused sexual roles lay at the basis of the degeneration. As early as 1888, in his exhaustive catalog of contemporary sexual pathologies, Richard Krafft-Ebing had posited that advanced urban cultures generated degenerate sexuality that would undermine the nation unless controlled.[36] The locus of this degenerate sexuality was generally seen to be the modern metropolis that accelerated vice and perversions. For many, a fundamental factor in urban degeneracy was the women's movement, with its heatedly debated effort to overturn traditional sexual roles. It was in the cities—Hamburg, Berlin—that women were organizing and clamoring for rights that had hitherto been the prerogative of men. Both the liberal and the socialist women's movement, begun in midcentury, came actively to the political scene in the 1880s. Their period of most vocal and radical agitation lasted until women were granted the right of assembly in 1908. This coincided, as I have outlined above, with the period of the most intense agitation and discussion on questions of prostitution, pornography, and sexuality. Karl Kraus, an acerbic observer of his time, complained in a lead article in *Die Fackel* in 1912:

My head is whirring from the women's movement, the women's

exhibition, and such things at home and at work. Everywhere people are jewing about problems, sexual problems. . . . [37]

After 1908 women's organizations increased substantially in number and size, although some historians argue that they became less militant. After supporting the war effort, in part, by entering the work force in large numbers, women were granted the vote in the November Revolution of 1918.[38] Among the women's continuing demands were the rights to education, to enter the professions, and to gain civil and marital equality.

Most of the avant-garde artists and writers in Germany were not receptive to these demands that would bring women into equality within bourgeois society. There was sympathy among some—for example, *Brücke* or the circle around Otto Gross—for freeing women from the moral strictures of bourgeois marriage, but this was based on a view of woman as essentially a sexual being who should be free to become totally sexual. Women, in this view, should not aspire to education or careers because that might inhibit their sexuality.[39] Grosz expressed a Nietzschean rejection of intelligent women in a 1918 letter, even as he was later in his autobiography to exalt their reproductive force and sexuality:

> Between us: I shit on profundity in women, generally they combine it with a hateful predominance of masculine characteristics, angularity, and skinny thighs; I agree with Kerr (the critic): "I alone have intelligence—"[40]

All of his drawings, letters, and poems in the years before and during the war indicate that Grosz not only was unsympathetic to the women's movement, but that, even while he was fascinated by woman, he saw her as a creature of the city who demonstrated various degrees of sexually degenerate behavior. This became focused during the war for Grosz, and many other young artists, into the harshly punitive image of the *Lustmord.*

An acquaintance in the circle of friends around Grosz in Berlin suggested an explanation for this violent turn against woman. Magnus Hirschfeld, a radical sexologist who founded the Institute for Sexual Science in Berlin in 1919 and who strongly supported the women's movement, claimed in the twenties that the war constituted a major turning point in moral history, marked by the emergence of women in considerable numbers in the work force and by the dissolution of the old bourgeois moral standards.[41] Women were mobilized during the war to take positions of all kinds left by men called to the front. They entered into the heaviest forms of construction work and outnumbered men by 75 percent in light industry. The proportion of women in industrial jobs rose from 22 percent in 1913 to 35 percent in 1918. Not only did women leave domestic work to invade the industrial sector, they were increasingly employed in visible official positions such as mail deliverer, postal clerks, and railroad guards.[42]

Although women became a decisive economic factor in the war machine, male resistance to women stepping into male jobs began almost immediately. Magda Trott, writing in 1915, described organized action in offices by men against the new "intruders."[43] Meta Kraus-Fessel, a colleague of Hirschfeld's, agreed with him about the great changes wrought by the war in women's economic and social position, but she also pointed out that men were threatened by the possibility of women achieving equality with them and made considerable efforts during and after the war to curtail those gains.[44] Hirschfeld himself cited frequent instances of brutal and violent acts by returning soldiers against wives who were suspected of exhibiting too much freedom. He accused newspapers of deliberately fostering suspicion and violence on the part of the veterans against women. He also, however, charged women—as did other writers, including Freud—with widespread sexual aggressiveness that elicited the violent male response.[45]

Popular medical books about sex-starved women appeared at the time with titles like *The Rape of Men by Women* by Hans Menzel or *The Sexual Infidelity of Woman*.[46] The latter was written by a much-published physician, Dr. E. Heinrich Kisch, in 1917. Within a year, it had gone through three editions and had been enlarged from 208 pages into two volumes, titled *The Adulteress* and *The Mercenary Woman [Weib]*. These titles and the violent acts against women suggest the heightened anxiety about sexuality that the war engendered. As early as September 1914, at a meeting of the medical Society for Sexual Science, a speaker discussed the problem of antisocial perversity being released by the war, especially the danger of sexual inversion or crossing of sexual lines as women wanted to become soldiers and men refused to bear weapons. The implication of the talk was clear: that the war was a proving ground for masculinity and that failure to meet that test could create disturbances in sexuality and sexual roles.[47] The disruption of traditional patterns on the home front, the threat that women posed to male jobs, and the sexual anxiety produced by the war experience appeared early in the war in the work of artists.

During the war years, Kokoschka, Kirchner, Klinger, and Barlach—all artists who had already achieved recognition—created graphic cycles and paintings on the theme of the artist's violent struggle against a woman who would stifle his creativity. Ernst Kirchner painted his *Self-Portrait as a Soldier* in 1915, after a brief period of artillery service. In it he expressed his neurotic anxiety about the destruction of his creative ability—through his fear of war, but also through his fear of woman. The castration imagery of the bloody stump and the female nude behind him connect the fear of loss of artistic potency with contact with woman. This fear seemed to have been precipitated for Kirchner, and for other older artists, by the war. In 1905 and 1918, he executed two graphic cycles in which man and woman encounter each other. In the first woodcut cycle, the meeting is untroubled, though rather odd. The same meeting portrayed after his military service in the 1918 cycle is tense and fraught with hostility. In the whole second cycle, Kirchner made it very clear that the "wide and dreadful" battle could only be resolved through the woman's submission to the artist's need for creative dominance.[48] Shortly before the second cycle, Kirchner created a series of explicit lithographs of perverse forms of sexuality—a visualization of Krafft-Ebing's catalog of sexual perversions.[49] In the middle of the war, an older artist, Max Klinger, shifted from allegorical portrayals of women to an eerie series of images in a graphic cycle depicting the demonic power of woman and the necessity of violently subduing that power.[50] Klinger, whose work was closely based on his reading of Schopenhauer, played with both phallic and castration references.

While the older artists seemed to link their attack on woman to fears of loss of their already established artistic power, the younger generation moved to an artistic assault upon woman that is stylistically much more nasty and vicious. Grosz served for six months in the military before being discharged as unfit for service in May 1916. Until he was recalled to service in January 1917, he experienced a period of intense dread of being called up again that resulted in the poetry and drawings discussed at the beginning of this essay. Three images drawn by Grosz at this time demonstrate the basic iconography of the *Lustmord* that emerged in his work and the work of other artists: the degenerate man wielding fist or knife and the sexually aggressive female. The hostile relationship between them is epitomized in *Married Life*, where the symbolic battle of the sexes of the late nineteenth century has turned into an ugly fistfight in a barren, boxlike tenement room with windows looking out onto the factories of the industrial city. Grosz leaves no doubt in this scene that the man will brutalize the woman.[51] In a 1916 self-portrait, Grosz depicted himself as the artist dandy or voyeur of the violent relationship that takes place in the modern metropolis. Significantly, Grosz here linked himself not only with the bloody body of a woman, but also with the stereotype of the urban criminal degenerate, defined by Cesare Lombroso and recalling his own poetic assertion that cities are inhabited by "böse Menschen, entartete." In a 1915 drawing, Grosz's identification with the degenerate criminal was more explicit (figure 23). The brutal figure, barely recognizable as a human, standing over a bloody distorted woman's body, carries the slender reed cane, Grosz's trademark that he adopted from reading Barbey d'Aurévilly.[52]

Grosz's second brief tour of duty was spent in a hospital and a mental asylum, from which he sent vivid descriptions of his nightmarish experiences, his overwhelming sense of death, his longing to escape to exotic lands, all conveyed with a heavy dose of sex and obscenity. Writing to Schmalhausen from the sanitarium in April 1917, he exclaimed:

Figure 23. George Grosz. [Untitled], 1915. Ink drawing, 19.8 x 16.7 cm. Reproduced with permission of the George Grosz Estate, Princeton, N.J.

Where have the nights gone, Pierrot? . . . Where are the women? The adventurers??—And my friends hacked up, scattered, duped, bewitched into battle-grey comrades of slaughter!! . . . Oh finale of the inferno, of vile murdering here and murdering there—end of the witches' sabbath, of the most gruesome castration, of slaughter, cadaver upon cadaver, already green rotting corpses glow among the rank and file!—If only it would end soon!!—[53]

Figure 24. George Grosz, Sex Murder in the Ackerstraße, *1916–17. Offset lithograph in* Ecce Homo, *Malik Verlag, 1923, pl. 32, 18.6 x 19.0 cm. Los Angeles County Museum of Art, The Robert Gore Rifkind Center for German Expressionist Studies, purchased with funds provided by Anna Bing Arnold, Museum Acquisition Fund, and Deaccession Funds.*

He was released from the asylum when Magnus Hirschfeld testified that he was not fit to serve.[54] Back in Berlin, he produced two of his strongest and best-known drawings: *Sex Murder in the Ackerstraße* and *After It Was Over, They Played Cards* (figures 24, 25). The fanciful quality of Grosz's prewar sex murders gave way here to hard, crisp depictions of matter-of-fact brutality. "Jack, the Killer"—another title for the first drawing that recalls Grosz's favorite book, *Jack the Mysterious Maiden Killer*—is washing his hands after his bloody assault on the woman whose head is nowhere to be seen. This room displays all the symbols of a petty bourgeois existence in the metropolis. Located in a working-class district of Berlin that can be glimpsed through the window, it is identified by the reference in the title to

Figure 25. George Grosz. After It Was Over, They Played Cards, *1917. Offset lithograph in* Ecce Homo, Malik Verlag, pl. 58, *titled* Apaches, *20.2 x 27.1 cm. Los Angeles County Museum of Art, The Robert Gore Rifkind Center for German Expressionist Studies, purchased with funds provided by Anna Bing Arnold, Museum Acquisition Fund, and Deaccession Funds.*

Ackerstraße, a tough street in Wedding.[55] In the second drawing, the criminal degeneracy of the murderers is displayed by their casual card play after dismembering, with ax and razor, the female body in the box. Grosz carefully delineated the basement tenement room in which live these Lomborosian figures or urban apaches, one of whom displays his wealth with his cigar and watch chain. Another *Sex Murderer* from 1916 depicted an aggressive, degenerate man, knife in hand, trousers open, standing in a barren room between a bed with two mutilated women's bodies and a table topped with liquor bottle and glass. All of these works were rooted in the themes of the prewar pulp novels or newspaper accounts of murders, but the stylistic shift to brutal clarity must be related to Grosz's own experience of the insanity of the war and grotesque encounters with men in the hospitals.

By 1918, Grosz moved from drawings and watercolors of *Lustmords* in shabby rooms to oil paintings of assaulted women in the streets of the metropolis. Titled variously *The Little Woman Killer*, or *John the Woman Killer* (figure 26), these paintings present desperate males—"böse Menschen, en-

Figure 26. George Grosz. John the Woman Killer, *1918. Oil on canvas, 86.5 x 81 cm. Kunsthalle, Hamburger. © the George Grosz Estate.*

tartete, großhändig" — who have just slaughtered a woman. The degenerate character of the men is firmly established in all of these drawings and paintings not only by the vicious act, but also by the stigmata of urban degeneration that had been defined by criminologists and anthropologists in the nineteenth century: sloping forehead, large nose, jutting jaw, small eyes, dark visages. In one image, there is the strong suggestion that the murderer is a Jew, a factor that further emphasizes the urban locus of the degenerate act.[56] Wielding knives, teeth clenched, the men grimly pursue their victim or leave the mutilated and bloody body in the street. Fully clothed in all of these murder scenes, they are dwarfed by the sexually powerful woman, whose hacked off head and arms serve to emphasize her potent and threat-

Figure 27. Heinrich Maria Davringhausen. The Sex Murderer, *1917. Oil on canvas, 119.5 x 148.5 cm. Munich, Bayerische Staatsgemäldesammlungen.*

ening sexuality by focusing attention on her breasts and torso.[57] Ravished and decapitated, the corpse remains palpably and bloomingly sexual. In all of these works Grosz used cubistic displacement and windows that are simultaneously mirrors to create an interpenetration of interior and exterior space in the urban world in which these crimes take place.

Images of despoiled women and degraded men were not confined to the works of Grosz at this time. In 1918 Max Reinhardt, for whom Grosz was later to design sets, was able to mount the first public production in Berlin of Frank Wedekind's *Pandora's Box*, in which Lulu, the precocious, flamboyantly sexual femme fatale, became the victim of Jack the Ripper. In the last years of the war, another friend of Grosz's, Heinrich Maria Davringhausen, painted a series of oils in which he picked up the theme of the sex murderer whose actions take place in commonplace rooms within the city. In *The Sex Murderer*, 1917 (figure 27), an Olympia-like woman, modeled on Manet's portrayal of aggressive sexuality, shares the canvas space with a huge window overlooking a cityscape crowded with high apartment buildings. The relaxed domestic scene with a cat on the end of the bed is disturbed by one other figure in the room: a man under the bed, looking at a pistol on the bedside table.[58] This oil was displayed at the Goltz Gallery in Munich in 1919, where two of Grosz's "Woman Killer" paintings were exhibited the following spring.

Another artist infamous for his appalling depictions of ravaged women was Otto Dix. Dix, a friend of Grosz from their Dresden days who was as laconic a writer as Grosz was effusive, spent the whole war at the front, where he had firsthand experience of conditions in the trenches and behind the lines. Examining those conditions throughout the war, Hirschfeld insisted that the war produced five years of "unchained atavistic impulses" and, at the same time, a repression of normal sexuality.[59] Months spent in the trenches, he wrote, produced pathological and perverse forms of sex. Military brothels behind the front lines resulted in the brutalization of sex.[60] In his *War* portfolio (1924), Dix portrayed soldiers raping nuns and depicted whores, obscenely bloated from their lucrative trade, dwarfing soldiers who have returned from the front. Strongly influenced by his reading of Nietzsche, Dix wrote brief aphorisms in his war diaries in which he suggested an integral relationship between war and sexuality: "Money, religion, and women have been the impetus for war, but not the *fundamental cause*—that is an *eternal law*. And again: "Actually, in the final analysis *all* war is waged over and for the vulva."[61]

Upon his return to civilian life, Dix continued to explore the Nietzschean cycle of life and decay, of sexuality and death.[62] From 1920 to 1922, this took the form of a series of grotesque sex murders. In 1920, he produced an *Altar for Gentlemen* (figure 28), an oil on wood painting of a woman and man walking past a city residence with large shuttered windows. This innocuous work, however, masked Dix's vision of the disparity between external appearances in postwar Dresden and the inner reality of the metropolis. The shutters open up to show scenes of a brothel, in which the central window becomes an adoration of two prostitutes by wealthy customers. The right shutter of this altar is dominated by a disproportionately large prostitute, stabbed, with her throat cut, and draped off a bed—in what we could call Dix's favorite *Lustmord* pose. To emphasize the sexuality and death found within the respectable facades of the city, Dix also unveiled the smartly dressed, voluptuous young woman to reveal an ancient hag with enlarged genitals whose clothes contained patented false breasts, buttocks, and thighs. The fraternity student's head opened to a steamy racist brain filled with right-wing anti-Semitic slogans.

Dix's penetration behind surfaces and windows applied to himself and his own world. In two self-portraits, Dix presented himself, standing in his own biedermeier room, dismembering a woman with vicious glee. Dix created the image, which he titled *The Sex Murderer: Self-Portrait*, both as an oil painting and as an etching that was included in a major graphic cycle

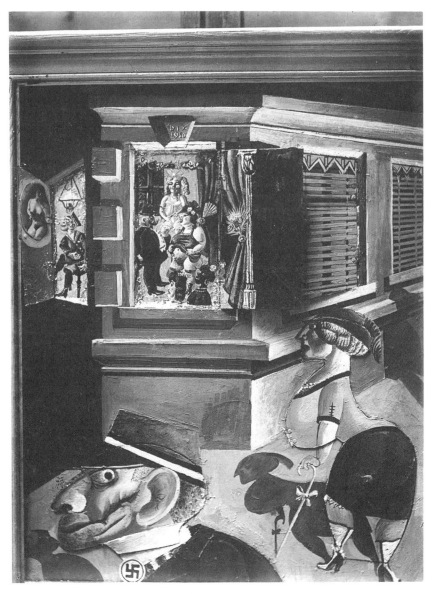

Figure 28. Otto Dix. Altar for Gentlemen, *1920. Oil on wood with montage [measurements unavailable]. Private collection, Berlin. Photograph with windows partially open. Reproduced by permission of Otto Dix Stiftung, Vaduz, Liechtenstein.*

(figure 29). Fully clothed like a cosmopolitan dandy, Dix wildly waves a bloody knife and a detached leg; pieces of a gigantic woman litter the room; her decapitated head is still screaming; blood gushes from the limbs and from his mouth. Dix dissected her with a surgical precision that allowed for

Figure 29. Otto Dix. The Sex Murderer: Self-Portrait, *1920. Oil on canvas [measurements unavailable], destroyed. Reproduced by permission of Otto Dix Stiftung, Vaduz, Liechtenstein.*

a jarring anatomically correct rendition of the genitals and reproductive system, which is particularly clear in the etching. He then placed his own bloody hand prints all over the pieces of the figure in the oil painting, as if to paw brutally over the body. Dix executed both of these works in 1920, when he was back in Dresden as a student at the Art Academy. A fellow student years later recalled going to Dix's room—the scene of these murders—and watching Dix show off this self-portrait by standing behind the oil and moving the arm with the bloody knife.[63] Another friend recalled Dix saying that if he had not been able to create these artistic sex murders, he could well have committed actual murder.[64] Whether either of these reminiscences was accurate, Dix definitely chose to cultivate the myth of being a wild man capable of mayhem and murder. In 1921, he portrayed another fantasy vision of himself surrounded by prostitutes, including one marked by the sores of venereal disease. Directly in front of his face, he placed a female corpse, raped, bleeding, and disemboweled. He balanced this with a castrated penis on the other side of the watercolor.

The following year, Dix created five more versions of raped and violated corpses. He gave a watercolor of a woman with her throat slit, sprawled off a pillow on the floor, titled *Murder*, to his wife on her birthday.[65] Two other watercolors include a man in the scene, one of which presents his attack and rape of a woman and the other his departure from the murdered woman. He included a gruesome disemboweling and slashing of a woman in a cycle of graphic works called *Death and Resurrection*. Copulating dogs in the foreground of this etching underlined the sexual nature of the murder and the bestiality of sexual intercourse (figure 30). Another even more shocking oil painting depicted a meticulously detailed corpse whose throat and torso have been slit (figure 31). She is draped half off a bed, again in Dix's student room in Dresden. In this room, Dix painted with fastidious care his lamp, an overturned cane chair, elaborately embroidered table covers, filmy curtains, a blood-filled wash basin, and a mirror placed strategically to reflect the mutilated body. Outside the large window that dominates the back wall is a view of middle-class apartment buildings.

Dix's fascination with death and dismemberment led him to study corpses in morgues and police photographs of horrendously mutilated corpses. The iconographic source of at least two of Dix's ravaged women was in police photographs published by Erich Wulffen in his 1910 book, *The Sexual Criminal*.[66] Dix was reported to have owned and carefully studied this book shortly before he did the *Lustmord* oil of 1920.[67] Paul Westheim, writing in *Das Kunstblatt*, recognized that Dix's sex murders were virtually illustrations to Wulffen's text.[68] In the late twenties, Wulffen published a study in which he argued that both art and crime were human responses to the explosive drive of sexuality; therefore, he explained, criminal sexual acts were a natural and consistent theme in the history of art. His book was illustrated by visual images of *Lustmord* executed by contemporary German and French artists, including two of these by Dix and others by Willi Geiger, Alfred Kubin, Walter Trier, Frans Masereel, Max Beckmann, Käthe Kollwitz, and Ernst Stern.[69]

Figure 30. Otto Dix. Sex Murder, 1922. *Etching in* Radierwerk V: Tod und Auferstehung, *Dresden, Selbstverlag, 1922, pl. 2, 27.5 x 34.6 cm. Reproduced by permission of Otto Dix Stiftung, Vaduz, Liechtenstein.*

Dix's *Lustmord* images all date from the immediate postwar period, a period perceived at the time, even in government reports, as one marked by a wild disintegration of morals.[70] Commentators blamed this moral chaos on the war and the inflation, but particularly on the New Woman, who was loath to give up her work and return to her family role. Hans Ostwald, who published a *Moral History of the Inflation,* cited the women's rights movement as a significant factor in the "hellish carnival" of those days.[71] The eroticism of women in the inflationary years formed a leitmotif in his book. He devoted a chapter to the social problems resulting from women's leaving the home to seek work, though he ended with the certainty that good German women would return to home and hearth. Ostwald was not alone. A chorus of voices held the New Woman responsible for the break-up of the family, the epidemic of venereal diseases, illegitimate children, abortions, dancing, and cultural decadence.[72] Men blamed women for taking their jobs, even though the demobilization laws required women to give up their

Figure 31. Otto Dix. Sex Murder, 1922. Oil, 165 x 135 cm. Reproduced by permission of Otto Dix Stiftung, Vaduz, Liechtenstein.

jobs to returning veterans. With demobilization, wrote one observer, "a horrible war broke out between male and female over bread and work."[73]

The war may have been over bread and work, but the antagonism had its roots in sexual anxieties. Carried out in visual images, the violent and sa-

Figure 32. Rudolf Schlichter. Sex Murder, *1924. Watercolor, 69 x 53 cm. Private collection, Munich.*

distic attack went beyond Dix and Grosz. In 1920, Georg Scholz, who returned to Karlsruhe from three years at the front, created images of rape and torture, including a sexually perverse crucifixion of a woman that was reminiscent of Felicien Rops.[74] In 1921, Gert Wolheim, who also had three years of front-line duty, created a dreadful collage of a servant girl who was tortured to death with rakes and pitchforks. The collage combined the newspaper report of her death with a drawn image.[75] After two years at the front, Erich Wegner enrolled at the Kunstgewerbeschule in Hannover, where he produced a long series of crude sex murders and dismemberments in attic rooms.[76] Also in Hannover, Kurt Schwitters placed a model of an "abominably mutilated corpse of an unfortunate young girl, painted tomato-red," into the Sex Crime Cavern in his Cathedral of Erotic Misfortune.[77] In his drawings and watercolors, Rudolf Schlichter plunged deep into the world of overt sexual perversity popularly associated with postwar Berlin. One of Grosz's closest friends, Schlichter shared Grosz's love of carnival peep-shows, trivial literature, and adventure stories. Schlichter, whom Grosz satirized sharply as a foot fetishist, portrayed in his work the underground world of the twenties in Berlin. Like Dix, Schlichter was deeply influenced by Nietzsche's dionysian negation of traditional values, but Schlichter combined his study of Nietzsche with his fascination over the exotic crimes and massacres of trash novels and films. Sexual murders, suicides, hanging women, and murders in public and private proliferated in Schlichter's drawings. The images that emerged from his compulsive fantasies in the early 1920s are, however, almost like calm reports of urban atrocities, visions of lonely women murdered in the great empty rooms and back streets of the modern Babylon of the great metropolis (figure 32).[78]

I have tried to suggest the range and intensity of images of violence against woman created by this group of avant-garde artists in the industrialized German metropolis during and after the Great War. I have also argued that these works can only make sense if they are viewed in the context of the pervasive cultural and social struggle over sexual roles that took place in German urban industrial society in the first decades of the century. In each of these images, there is an overpowering fear of sexuality and an obsessive dread of woman. In the midst of the profound unsettling of boundaries between the sexes that the war accelerated, these artists' apprehension and anxiety produced vicious images that grew out of complex emotional and social responses to women's changing role. The sentence of death against woman pronounced in these works was a reactionary response that had its roots deep in contemporary cultural and social misogyny. The presence of these *Lustmord* images in the art of the avant-garde at that time is a sharp reminder that artistic works cannot be understood outside of their social and cultural context. Within that context, these particular images force us to go beyond the celebration of the artist as a perceptive interpreter of the period to recognize the extent to which artists shared contemporary fears and anxiety.

NOTES

An early version of this essay grew out of a graduate seminar that I taught at UCLA, and was first presented for criticism at Stanford University in 1985. I received further constructive criticism from presentations at UCLA, Pomona College, SUNY/Stony Brook, Iowa, Harvard, Wisconsin, and New Hampshire. I thank Peter Paret, Arnold Lewis, Susan Figge, Joan Weinstein, and Sanda Agalidi for their uncomfortable, but sustaining criticism. I also thank the Robert Gore Rifkind Center for German Expressionist Studies, Los Angeles County Museum of Art, in whose extensive library and print collection I was able to complete the research for this essay.

1. George Grosz, *Briefe, 1913-1959*, ed. Herbert Knust (Reinbek, bei Hamburg, 1979), 53–54.

2. *Erste George Grosz Mappe* (Berlin, 1917), published in the spring; and *Kleine Grosz Mappe* (Berlin-Halensee, 1917), published in the fall.

3. Max Nordau, *Degeneration* (New York, 1895). For the development of the concept of degeneration, see J. Edward Chamberlin and Sander Gilman, ed., *Degeneration: The Dark Side of Progress* (New York, 1985), and Robert A. Nye, *Crime, Madness and Politics in Modern France: the Medical Concept of National Decline* (Princeton, 1984).

4. Theodor Däubler, "Georg [sic] Grosz," *Die Weissen Blätter* 3 (October–December 1916): 167–70; and "George Grosz," *Das Kunstblatt* 1 (March 1917): 80–82.

5. Theodor Däubler, "George Grosz," *1918: Neue Blätter für Kunst und Dichtung* 1 (November 1918): 153–54.

6. Grosz, *Gedichte und Gesänge. 1916–1917* (Litomysl/Czech., 1932).

7. Däubler, in *Das Kunstblatt.* See also "George Grosz im Spiegel der Kritik," *Der Ararat* 1 (July 1920): 84–86; "George Grosz," *Der Ararat*, Erstes Sonderheft (Munich, 1920); Alfred Salmony, "George Grosz," *Das Kunstblatt* 4 (April 1920): 97–104.

8. Grosz recorded in his accounting ledger that Goltz had sold thirty-four copies of the lithographic version by the end of February 1922.

9. Robert Wohl, "The Generation of 1914 and Modernism," *Modernism: Challenges & Perspectives*, ed. M. Chefdor et al. (Urbana, Ill., 1986), 66–78.

10. Reinhold Heller, *The Earthly Chimera and the Femme Fatale* (Chicago, 1981); Bram Dijkstra, *Idols of Perversity* (New York, 1986).

11. Ronald A. Fullerton, "Toward a Commercial Popular Culture in Germany: The Development of Pamphlet Fiction, 1871–1914," *Journal of Social History* 12 (Summer 1979): 489–511.

12. Rudolf Schenda, *Volk ohne Buch: Studien zur Sozialgeschichte der populären Lesestoff, 1770–1910* (Munich, 1977), 310–14; Ronald A. Fullerton, "Creating a Mass Book Market in Germany: The Story of the 'Colporteur Novel,' 1870–1890," *Journal of Social History* 10 (March 1977): 271.

13. Fullerton, "Toward a Commercial Popular Culture," 496.

14. Gary D. Stark, "Cinema, Society, and the State: Policing the Film Industry in Imperial Germany," in *Essays on Culture and Society in Modern Germany*, ed. Stark et al. (College Station, Tex., 1982), 122–27.

15. Grosz, "Jugenderinnerungen," *Das Kunstblatt* 13 (June 1929): 172–74; and *Ein kleines Ja und ein großes Nein* (Hamburg, 1955), 21–26. The German title was *Jack der Geheimnisvolle Mädchenmörder* (Berlin, 1899). For an analysis of the Ripper murders in London in 1888 and the construction of the Jack the Ripper myth, see Judith R. Walkowitz, "Jack the Ripper and the Myth of Male Violence," *Feminist Studies* 8 (Fall 1982): 542–74.

16. In his typed notes, he listed several names, including James Fenimore Cooper and Adolph von Menzel in one list and then: "UND Arvid von Falk, Verfasser des Romans: Der Rauberhauptmann Zimmermann, der Schrecken der Tyrannen, der Beschutzer der Armen,

oder Hass und LIEBE oder Zwei Frauen unter einem Dache." Archives of the History of Art, The Getty Center for the History of Art and the Humanities, Los Angeles, Calif., #850703.

17. Gary D. Stark, "Pornography, Society, and the Law in Imperial Germany," *Central European History* 14 (September 1981): 203. See also R. J. V. Lenman, "Art, Society, and the Law in Wilhelmine Germany: The Lex Heinze," *Oxford German Studies* (1973): 86–113; and Fullerton, "Toward a Commercial Popular Culture," 500–503.

18. The literature on this subject is extensive. See Sander Gilman, *Difference and Pathology* (Ithaca, N.Y., 1985); George L. Mosse, *Nationalism and Sexuality* (New York, 1985); Jeffrey Weeks, *Sex, Politics and Society* (London, 1981).

19. For a persuasive statement of this argument about sexology, see Sheila Jeffreys, *The Spinster and Her Enemies* (London, 1985).

20. Karl Scheffler, *Die Frau und die Kunst* (Berlin, 1908). For an analysis of Scheffler's views, see Silvia Bovenschen, *Die imaginierte Weiblichkeit* (Frankfurt, 1979), 24–43.

21. Otto Weininger, *Sex and Character* (London, 1906; originally published in Vienna, 1903), Pt. 2, chap. 12.

22. See Nadine Sine, "Cases of Mistaken Identity: Salome and Judith at the Turn of the Century," *German Studies Review* 10 (February 1988); Patrick Bade, *Femme Fatale* (New York, 1979); Gerd Stein, ed., *Femme Fatale-Vamp-Blaustrumpf* (Frankfurt, 1984); Virginia M. Allen, *The Femme Fatale* (Troy, N.Y., 1983).

23. "Man verehrte Zola, Strindberg, Weininger, Wedekind—naturalistische Aufklärer, anarchistische Selbstquäler, Todesanbeter und Erotomanen." Grosz, *Ein kleines Ja*, 98.

24. Grosz, *Briefe*, 352.

25. Ibid., 37.

26. "Es war, als hätte mir jemand, den ich nicht kenne, ein Sinnbild gezeigt, etwas Ewiges—denn so lange wir existieren, wird es das Sinnbild der Nacktheit geben: das Weib als die unvergängliche Quelle und Fortsetzung unseres Geschlechths." Grosz, *Ein kleines Ja* (see note 15), 35.

27. Ibid., 91.

28. Richard J. Evans, "Prostitution, State and Society in Imperial Germany," *Past and Present* 70 (1976): 106–9; Lenman, "Art, Society, and the Law" (see note 17), 89.

29. Lenman, "Art, Society, and the Law," 89.

30. Randolph E. Bergstrom and Eric A. Johnson, "The Female Victim: Homicide and Women in Imperial Germany," in *German Women in the Nineteenth Century*, ed. John C. Fout (New York, 1984), 346–57.

31. See Evans, "Prostitution, State and Society," 120–29.

32. Hans Ostwald, *Sittengeschichte der Inflation: Ein Kulturdokument aus den Jahren des Marksturzes* (Berlin, 1931), 159.

33. Anneliese Bergmann, "Frauen, Männer, Sexualität und Geburtenkontrolle. Die Gebärstreikdebatte der SPD im Jahre 1913," in *Frauen suchen ihre Geschichte: Historische Studien zum 19. und 20. Jahrhundert*, ed. Karin Hausen (Munich, 1983), 81–92.

34. Ibid., 86; and Atina Grossman, "Abortion and Economic Crisis: The 1931 Campaign against Paragraph 218," in *When Biology Became Destiny: Women in Weimar and Nazi Germany*, ed. Renate Bridenthal et al. (New York, 1984), 80–81. Grossman discusses the unreliability of all of these estimated figures.

35. Bergmann, "Frauen, Männer, Sexualität und Geburtenkontrolle," 92–103.

36. Sander Gilman, "Sexology, Psychoanalysis, and Degeneration: From a Theory of Race to a Race to Theory," in *Degeneration*, ed. Chamberlin and Gilman, 77–79.

37. "Mir schwirrt der Kopf vor Frauenbewegung, Frauenausstellung and so Sachen in Haus und Beruf. Überall jüdelt es von Problemen, Sexual Problem. . . . " Karl Kraus, "Glossen," *Die Fackel* (31 März 1912): 1.

38. See Richard J. Evans, *The Feminist Movement in Germany 1894–1933* (Beverly Hills, Calif., 1976) and Barbara Greven-Aschoff, *Die Bürgerliche Frauenbewegung in Deutschland 1894–1933* (Gottingen, FRG, 1981). For a useful bibliography of the German women's movement, see John C. Fout, *German Women in the Nineteenth Century* (New York, 1984), 385–94.

39. For analyses of expressionist critics and writers, see Marion Adams, "Der Expressionismus und die Krise der deutschen Frauenbewegung," in *Expressionismus und Kulturkrise*, ed. Bernd Hüppauf (Heidelberg, 1983), 105–30; and Barbara D. Wright, " 'New Man,' Eternal Woman: Expressionist Responses to German Feminism," *The German Quarterly* 60 (Fall 1987): 582–99.

40. "Unter uns: ich scheiße auf die Tiefe bei Frauen, meistens verbinden sie damit ein häßliches überwiegen männlicher Eigenarten, Eckigkeit und Schenkellosigkeit; ich denke wie Kerr (der Kritiker) 'Jeist hab ick aleene—' " Grosz, *Briefe* (see note 1), 58. See M. Kay Flavell, "Über alles die Liebe: Food, Sex, and Money in the Work of George Grosz," *Journal of European Studies* 13 (1983): 279.

41. Magnus Hirschfeld, *The Sexual History of the World War* (New York, 1943; German edition, 1930), introduction; and Hirschfeld, *Sittengeschichte der Nachkriegszeit* (Leipzig, 1931), vol. 1, ch. 1.

42. Ursula von Gersdorff, *Frauen im Kriegsdienst* (Stuttgart, 1969), 20–27, 218–19; "Frauendienst," in *Ein Krieg wird ausgstellt* (Frankfurt am Main, 1976), 144–54; Ute Frevert, *Women in German History: From Bourgeois Emancipation to Sexual Liberation* (Oxford, Eng., 1989), 156–59; Renate Bridenthal and Claudia Koonz, "Beyond *Kinder, Küche, Kirche*: Weimar Women in Politics and Work," in Bridenthal et al., *When Biology Became Destiny*, 48–49.

43. Magda Trott, "Frauenarbeit, ein Ersatz für Männerarbeit?," *Die Frau* 3 (1915), reprinted in *Women, the Family, and Freedom: The Debate in Documents*, ed. Susan Groag Bell and Karen M. Offen (Stanford, Calif., 1983), vol. 2, 277–79.

44. Meta Kraus-Fessel, "Frauenarbeit und Frauenemanzipation in der Nachkriegszeit," in Hirschfeld, *Sittengeschichte*, ch. 6.

45. Hirschfeld, *Sexual History*, ch. 2, 11.

46. E. Heinrich Kisch, *Die Sexuelle Untreue der Frau: Eine soziale-medizinische Studie* (Bonn, 1917). His book, *Das Geschlechtsleben des Weibes in physiologischer und hygienischer Beziehung* (Berlin, 1904), was translated into English by M. Eden Paul in 1910 and went through six editions by 1931.

47. E. Burchard, "Sexuelle Fragen zur Kriegszeit," *Zeitschrift für Sexualwissenschaft* 1 (January 1915): 373–80.

48. *Zwei Menschen*, 1905; *Petrarka, Triumpf der Liebe*, 1918. See Guenther Gercken, *Ernst Ludwig Kirchner: Holzschnittzyklen* (Stuttgart, 1980).

49. Annemarie and Wolf-Dieter Dube, *E. L. Kirchner: Das graphische Werk* (Munich, 1980), nos. L 266–74. Titles included, among others, *Der Sadist, Der Masochist, Der Busenfreier, Der Fußfreier*.

50. *Zelt, Opus XIV*, 1915. See Alexander Dückers, *Max Klinger* (Berlin, 1976), ch. 7.

51. For a remarkable playing out of this image of violence against a woman, see the multiple variations on Grosz's drawing created by Concetto Pozzati, *Dal Suicidio di Grosz* (Bologna, 1972).

52. Grosz, *Ein kleines Ja,* 84.

53. "Wo sind die Nächte hin, Pierrot . . . Wo sind die Weiber? Abenteurer??—Und die Freunde zerhackt, zerstoben, genarrt, verhext in feldgraue Schlachtgesellen!! . . . O Finale des Infernos, des wüsten Hin und Hermordens—Ende des Hexensabbat, grausigster Entmannung, Hinabschlachtens, Kadaver über Kadaver, schon glotzt grün verwesende Leiche aus Gemeinen!—Wenn doch bald ein Ende herankäme!!—" Grosz, *Briefe* (see note 1), 49–50.

54. Lothar Fischer, *George Grosz* (Reinbek, bei Hamburg, 1976), 42.

55. According to notes in his accounting ledger, Grosz sent one proof and fifty lithographs of this drawing to Hans Goltz in December 1920. All were sold by the end of February 1922.

56. On attempts to identify Jack the Ripper as a Jew, see Walkowitz, "Jack the Ripper" (note 15), 555–56.

57. For interpretations of dismemberment of female bodies in art, see Renate Berger, "Pars pro toto: Zum Verhältnis von künstlerischer Freiheit und sexueller Integrität," in *Der Garten der Lüste: Zur Deutung des Erotischen und Sexuellen bei Künstler und ihren Interpreten* (Cologne, 1985), 150–99; and Susan Gubar, "Representing Pornography: Feminism, Criticism, and Depictions of Female Violation," *Critical Inquiry* 13 (Summer 1987): 712–41.

58. Wolf-Dieter Dube, " 'Der Lustmörder' von Heinrich Maria Davringhausen," *Pantheon* (April-June 1973): 181–85. See also *Heinrich Maria Davringhausen: 'Der General,' Aspekte eines Bildes* (Bonn, 1975), 22–28.

59. Hirschfeld, *Sexual History* (see note 41), 21; see also chs. 17–18.

60. Ibid., chs. 8–9.

61. "Geld, Religion und Weiber sind der Anstoß zu Kriegen gewesen, nicht aber *die Grundursache*, diese ist eine *ewiges Gesetz*." "Eigentlich wird im letzten Grunde bloß *aller* Krieg um und wegen der Vulva geführt." Dix (in his "Kriegstagebuch") quoted from Otto Conzelmann, *Der andere Dix: Sein Bild vom Menschen und vom Krieg* (Stuttgart, 1983), 133.

62. For thorough analysis of this theme, see Eva Karcher's books: *Eros und Tod im Werk von Otto Dix* (Münster, FRG, 1984) and *Otto Dix* (New York, 1987); and her essays in exhibition catalogs on Dix at the Rupertinium Salzburg (1984) and the Villa Stuck, Munich (1985).

63. Lothar Fischer, *Otto Dix: Ein Malerleben in Deutschland* (Berlin, 1981), 23.

64. Diether Schmidt, *Otto Dix im Selbstbildnis* (Berlin, 1978), 58.

65. Dix inscribed this 1922 watercolor: "Mutzli zum Geburtstag." Mutzli was Martha Koch, the daughter of a well-to-do family and wife of Dr. Hans Koch, a surgeon and a patron of Dix's work. In 1922 when these works were created, Martha had left her husband to live with Dix, whom she married in 1923. Their marriage lasted until their deaths.

66. Erich Wulffen, *Der Sexualverbrecher: Ein Handbuch für Juristen, Verwaltungsbeamte und Ärtze mit zahlreichen kriminalistischen Originalaufnahmen* (Berlin, 1910), 459, 476.

67. Fischer, *Otto Dix*, 81–82. Fischer also states that there was a copy of Hirschfeld's book on sexual criminals (possibly *Geschlecht und Verbrechen*, published in 1932) in Dix's library in Hemmenhof.

68. Paul Westheim, "Dix," *Das Kunstblatt* 10 (1926): 144.

69. Erich Wulffen, *Sexualspiegel von Kunst und Verbrechen* (Dresden, n.d.). The Dix works were the oil painting of 1922 and the self-portrait oil of 1920.

70. Atina Grossman, "The New Woman and the Rationalization of Sexuality in Weimar Germany," in *Power of Desire: The Politics of Sexuality*, ed. Ann Snitow et al. (New York, 1983), 156.

71. Hans Ostwald, *Sittengeschichte der Inflation: Ein Kulturdokument aus den Jahren des Marksturzes* (Berlin, 1931), 7.

72. Grossman, "The New Woman," 156–57; Bridenthal et al., *When Biology Became Destiny,* (see note 34), 1–14. See also Hirschfeld, *Sittengeschichte* (see note 41), chs. 1 and 8.

73. Matilde Wurm, quoted in Claudia Koonz, *Mothers in the Fatherland: Women, the Family, and Nazi Politics* (New York, 1987), 26.

74. *Georg Scholz: Das Druckgrafische Werk* (Karlsruhe, FRG, 1982). I am indebted to Vernon Lidtke for bringing these works to my attention.

75. *Eine Dienstmagd zu Tode gemartert*, 1921; see *Am Anfang: Das Junge Rheinland* exhibition catalog (Düsseldorf, 1985), 210.

76. *Erich Wegner* exhibition catalog (Munich, 1987).

77. John Elderfield, *Kurt Schwitters* (London, 1985), 161.

78. *Rudolf Schlichter, 1890–1955* exhibition catalog (Berlin, 1984).

CHAPTER 6

The City as Megaphone in Alfred Döblin's *Berlin Alexanderplatz*

Harald Jähner

A mountain can be viewed from two perspectives: standing before it, one sees it differently than after descending from its peak. It is similar with the observation of Berlin, perhaps even with cities in general. As social entities, they have long since passed their prime. While today in the so-called Third World the earlier urbanization process of the West is being repeated, in the Western nations themselves the development of cities has abated, and urbanity, undermined by television, electronic communication, and automobile traffic, is threatened with extinction. Today one looks back with longing to the density of the city, a quality that only a few decades ago was still considered depressing, but which has now become almost everywhere the elusive ideal of city planning proposals. In our nostalgia we are inclined to view this earlier process of urban concentration in retrospect as more harmonious, less dramatic than it in fact was. For example, Berlin: in the 1920s, uncertainty about the future profoundly influenced the view Germans had of their turbulent, rapidly developing capital. Everyone was convinced that the metropolis would fundamentally change the human person; whether such change would be a blessing or a curse was the topic of much bitter debate. As a social phenomenon, the modern city awakened passionate hopes and deep anxieties. With our more sober view of today, when the city has lost its portentous mystery, we have difficulty identifying with either position, as we do with the sentiment Alfred Döblin expressed in 1930 about his relationship to the city.

> Whether explicitly or not, all my thinking, all my spiritual labors belong to
> Berlin. This city provided and continues to provide the crucial impulses
> and direction for it. In this great and sober city I have grown up, this is my
> native soil, this sea of stone is the native soil of all my thoughts.[1]

Does this mean simply that the city is a vital place, a continual source of stimulation, such as one would describe life in the cities of today? If so, then the concept "native soil of all my thoughts" would be a badly overdrawn metaphor.

In 1929, responding to a survey of the *Vossische Zeitung* on the question: "Does Berlin inhibit or impair artistic creation?", Döblin wrote:

> The city as a whole has an intensely inspiring, energizing power; this agitation of the streets, shops, and vehicles provides the heat I must have in order to work, at all times. It is the fuel that makes my motor run.[2]

Taken literally, this "fuel" metaphor describes the city's participation in the intellectual process, in that consciousness and city constitute an energetic unity. To be a city dweller is for Döblin a fundamentally new way of being human, which distinguishes him, down to the very depths of his consciousness, from a provincial.

Döblin is a city dweller by conviction. "Fantasy based on facts" (*Tatsachenphantasie*) is what he demands in his "Berlin Program" of 1913.

> I am not myself, but the street, the street lamps, this and that occurrence, otherwise nothing. That's what I call the "stony style" (*steinerner Stil*). . . . Depersonalization! . . . Have the courage for kinetic fantasy![3]

This rigid euphoria makes unmistakably clear how much separates today's sober comprehension of the city from the image of Berlin in the first decades of this century. This metropolis, whose population increased from 2 to 4 million in only two decades, was something outrageously novel for a Germany just awakening from the era of the Kaiser. It was despised by those who held it responsible for the deterioration of all traditional values; others cynically praised it as an exciting intensification of the human tragicomedy; still others—Döblin among them—perceived Berlin as the laboratory of the new democratic republic, which was supposed to make the Germans civil, democratic, and vivacious (or stated simply, was to change them into new persons). As it was for Heinrich Mann, Berlin was for Döblin a *Menschenwerkstatt*, a workshop that was producing a new type of human being, producing them for a Germany that had slept through 200 years of bourgeois democracy and now had a lot of catching up to do—also in the development of its mentality and social psyche. To be sure, for those authors, too, this city that had exploded its traditional identity was a problem, but only Berlin seemed capable of producing human beings who could solve it. This self-portrait of Berlin as a *Menschenwerkstatt* had many facets: now stylized as gigantic machinery, now as an encampment of workaholics, or as a psychedelic vaudeville show.

All of these visions of the city play their respective roles in Döblin's novel, *Berlin Alexanderplatz*, published in 1929. Döblin expected the transformations brought forth by the city to affect not only the contents of consciousness, but also its forms. It is the literary application of this concept that will be the subject of this essay: the literary forms of narration and reportage used to represent the experience of the city dweller. In Döblin's perception the city had so profoundly altered the relationship of individuals to their environment and to the apparatus of their own consciousness that it was no longer possible to write about its inhabitants in classical narrative forms. As a makeshift solution he invented the constructive device of textual montage. In his novel, the author's relationship to the city, "the native soil of [his] thoughts," becomes evident through contrast of narration and montage.

Berlin Alexanderplatz is set in 1927–28, at the time of its writing. In the book, Döblin undertakes a systematic literary examination of the relationship between an individual consciousness and the city. At the beginning of the novel, as if conducting a scientific laboratory experiment, Döblin allows his protagonist, a former transport worker named Franz Biberkopf, to confront the city.

As the novel opens, Biberkopf stands tightly against the red wall of the prison in Tegel, a suburb north of Berlin. Having served a four-year sentence, he has just been released and turned out of the prison gate. As though ejected from his mother's body, from whose exterior he still seeks warmth and protection, Biberkopf literally now takes his first steps. But he still clings anxiously to the prison wall, hesitates, delays the beginning of the tale. Opposite lies the city that will provide the space for his unfolding story. What will happen when the two elements, the individual and the city, collide?

As though pressing a button, Döblin opens the experiment with the imperative "start" (*los*). Biberkopf detaches himself from the red-brick prison wall and "steps into Berlin."

> He shook himself, gulped. He stepped on his own foot. Then he made a run and was sitting in the streetcar. In the midst of people. Start. At first it was as if one was at the dentist, who has grabbed a root with the forceps and pulled, the pain grows, one's head wants to burst. He turned his head back toward the red wall, but the streetcar raced on with him along the tracks, then only his head still faced the prison. The streetcar made a turn, trees, houses intervened. Busy streets sprang up, *Seestraße*, people got on and off. Something inside him screamed with terror: Look out, look out, it's starting now. The tip of his nose turned to ice; something was whirring over his cheek. "Zwölf Uhr Mittagszeitung, B.Z., Die neuste Illustrirte, Die Funkstunde neu." "Any more fares please?" . . . Unnoticed, he got off the streetcar, was among people. What was the matter then? Nothing. Chest out, you starved sucker, pull yourself together or I'll give you a crack on the jaw! A swarm, what a swarm of people! How they hustle and bustle! . . . On the outside everything was moving, but—behind—it—was nothing! It—wasn't—alive! . . . He had been discharged from prison and

had to go into this, deeper and deeper into it. . . . I'll go into it alright but I don't want to, my God, I can't. . . . The cars roared and jangled on, house front after house front raced along without end. And roofs were on the houses, they soared atop the houses, his eyes wandered upward: if only the roofs don't slide off, but the houses stood upright. Where shall I go, poor devil. . . .[4]

Biberkopf flees into a quiet, dark hallway. He feels that the city has "thrown him off" (259). With his first few steps into the universal motion of the scene, his first movement into the space of the narrative, the protagonist has been rebuffed. The city sucks him in, spins him through its traffic tubes, dashes with its hundredfold impressions against his senses, and finally throws him out on his ear at a remote spot, similar to the secluded spot in front of the red wall, opposite the city. "He clung to the banister-post" (Er hielt den Geländerpfosten fest, 16). This sentence corresponds exactly to the inversion of the motion that was supposed to start Biberkopf's story.

Even if things calm down considerably at this point, the trauma induced by the independent motion of objects, concentrated in the vision of the sliding roofs, will stay with Biberkopf until the end of the novel. Each blow of fate he suffers actualizes the independence of the world, a leitmotif that recurs in numerous variations. In every case it is a subjectivity that has been stripped from human beings and invested in inanimate things that makes the city into Biberkopf's antagonist.

Beginning a story with the movement of the hero into the world is a device as old as narration itself. The traversal of space is an archetypal action in the narrated story: a fair share of medieval and classical epic poems begin with the hero's departure. By so expressly subverting the theme of the hero confronting the world in Biberkopf's relationship to the city, Döblin puts the centuries-old tradition of narrative to the test. Just as the hero in the chivalric romances rides out looking for adventure in order to prove himself in battle, so, too, the growing self-awareness of the protagonist in this later genre of the *Bildungsroman* is linked to the traversal of a space that presents obstacles which the hero surmounts, thereby developing toward maturity.

These classical epic structures of the mastery of space, with their relatively clear subject-object distinctions, are no longer adequate to the subject matter of the metropolis. In contrast to the penetration of space in the adventure novel, the theme of the big city presents the independent dynamism of traffic in which the hero must participate. It is no longer the world of objects that stands in opposition before the human subject, but a society that has itself been configured as a subject, that demands that the individual adjust to its dynamic structures. The individual must adapt his movements to the structures of traffic and rely passively on the means of public transportation. From the beginning, it is clear to Franz Biberkopf who is the stronger: the failure of his pathetic gesture of mastering space as he becomes a helpless object within a universal movement is a signal that the power of making stories has shifted from the individual into the social totality.

However, Biberkopf, who "would rather have no truck with others," (lieber nichts mit die andern haben, 67) does not give up yet. He challenges his anonymous enemy to the next round. Stubborn and proud (for which he is later reproached by the personification of death, symbolizing the last stage of pitiless socialization), Biberkopf insists on his right to maintain the sovereignty of his ego, and thus tries to push his way through the confusing city of Berlin. "What's the matter with them?" (Was ist denn mit die?), he exclaims when feeling threatened by a pair of glistening window panes. "Well, you can go ahead and break them" (Kannst sie ja kaputtschlagen, 14), is his hostile response. Clinging to his motto, "Behave yourself and keep to yourself" (Anständig bleiben und für sich bleiben), an assertion of sovereign individuality phrased in the language of the *Lumpenproletariat*, Biberkopf fights to clear a path for his story which, time and again, gets entangled with the tumult of the big city.

There are more than fifty references in *Berlin Alexanderplatz* to forward motion, to the movement of Biberkopf, who can literally still feel "in his bones" the trauma brought on by his eruptive vision of the city. "Trample down, shout down" (Niedertreten, niederbrüllen, 99) becomes Biberkopf's motto. His pace intensifies, ranging from fear-ridden, aimless cruising (Loskarriolen) to marching about. In the end, as he moves through the peaceful Berlin of 1927 he hallucinates that he is marching through an artillery barrage at Arras in World War I. Even during the few more detached moments in which he strolls, seemingly without anxiety, through the city streets, his feet are unconsciously and repeatedly testing whether the ground beneath them is still solid, whether the city is not perhaps trying to shake him off, whether, once more, the roofs are threatening to slide off the houses. And they do it again and again. The city wins each new round. The mirage of sliding roofs mutates and intensifies into ever more terrifying visions of a world with a will of its own, which buries Biberkopf, nails him down, topples him, tears him apart.

The contrast with Leopold Bloom in James Joyce's *Ulysses* (1922)—a novel to which *Berlin Alexanderplatz* is often compared—is striking. Bloom is ruminative, sensual, given to lively association; the city, in its myriad facets, permeates his monologues as a welcome presence. Biberkopf, gripped by a panic fear, is impervious to the dazzling spectacle of the city; his consciousness remains completely mute. As Günther Anders has remarked, Biberkopf remains "a human being only in a barbaric sense."[5] His story consists of nothing but its contested demand that it be allowed to continue. Consequently the novel repeatedly abandons the device of narration, abandons Biberkopf as its focal point, and liberates the text to move away from the protagonist. With the "courage for depersonalization," the text branches out into the city; it is there that it finds its way back to Biberkopf.

In the second chapter, after introducing the oppositional narrative structure that pits Biberkopf against the city, Döblin begins his literary construction of Berlin, outside of the narrated story. He reprints the graphic emblems of the individual municipal agencies — for transportation, commerce, finance, art and education, etc. He then proceeds to construct the intricate web of the city: by listing the stations of a streetcar line; by fleeting observations ranging from the open spaces of large squares to the glandular functions of some random passersby; by describing the unfolding network of streets, the administrative structure of a large electrical concern, and the transport of cattle from pasture to slaughterhouse; by describing the patterns of traffic as an observer looking down from a watchtower. The listing of street names, intersections, and streetcar lines forms a cartographic textual structure, which Döblin develops further by means of literary montage.

While the narrative unfolds as a line, sequentially arranged according to the protagonist's movements, in literary montage the material is arranged on a plane. Line and plane — the red thread of narration and the planar tableau of montage — constitute the opposing constructive principles of the novel. Just as Biberkopf makes his way through Berlin, often resembling "a dog who has lost the scent of his trail," the story takes its course through the impersonal fabric of associations, which irritate, divert, and delay it.

Newspaper clippings, news dispatches, letters, court records, song lyrics, recurrent advertising slogans, parts of dime novels, quotes from scripture, magical and mythological elements from various religions, user manuals, statistics, quotes in various styles and fictional subplots are linked by Döblin into an immeasurable textual fabric that, like a city of words, extends into the vastness of the textual body. Döblin describes the structural devices of the epic novel as "stacking, piling up, rolling, pushing"; the epic poet does not narrate but rather constructs. He assembles, rearranges, combines, and varies. In contrast to the line of narration, in which each episode has a fixed position on the terrain of the action, the single elements of textual montage have a paradigmatic function. Thus they stand for a virtually infinite variety of other elements that could substitute for them. As Döblin commented in his "Bemerkungen zum Roman" (Remarks on the novel), "A novel is worth nothing, unless — analogous to an earth worm — it can be dissected into ten segments, each of which moves on its own."[6] While a narrative can integrate into its chain of events only those elements that are reflected upon by either the author or the protagonist, the material of the montage stands within the space of the text without a sender or addressee. While this textual material is combined without reference to a concrete personal speech act, it can only be quoted from existing texts — from weather forecasts, love letters, court records, and so on. Accordingly, a multitude of social discourses—fragmentary to be sure but unaltered—penetrates the textual space and, as anonymous, objective material, stands opposed to the subject and his story.

Spread out upon a plane and constructed of quotations, the textual space of *Berlin Alexanderplatz* resembles a city. Just as the pedestrian must make his way through the city, the story of Franz Biberkopf must make its way through the montages of texts. Yet, as the novel progresses, it gradually becomes clear that the opposition of story and montage, of line and plane, is only superficially an opposition of the ego and the city, and that the conflicts of the text run straight through the subject himself. Therefore the anonymous textual space permits the fixing of those fugitive, prerational impressions and conditions of speech that are excluded from a plot centered in subjective consciousness. The assembled textual fabric imitates, for example, the crude, undigested, unconscious perceptions of a stranger hastening through the urban space. The disparate impressions are linked to a continuously roaring, anonymous field of language, of urban noise, which, in spite of Biberkopf's monadic armor-plating, unceasingly addresses him as he roams through the city, and entangles him in a volatile and multilayered text.

> Hahn's department store has gone way downhill, otherwise all the
> buildings are crammed with shops. But it only looks like they're shops.
> Actually they're calls, mating calls, chirping, knick, knack, a twittering
> without a forest.[7]

The world of inner voices blends with the sonorities of the urban roar, fusing with the anonymous text into an indissoluble synthesis. Over the naturalistic rendering of the urban babble there flows a fantastic stream of language having little to do with the blatant reality of the city.

> A criminal, an erstwhile God-accursed man (how do you know that, my
> child?); Orestes killed Clytemnestra at the altar; it's hard to say, that name,
> anyhow his mother. (Which altar do you mean then? Here you can look for
> a church that's open at night.) I say, times have changed. . . . Without
> harps, as the song says, the dance of the furies, they embrace the victim, a
> mad frenzy, delusion of the senses, preparation for the booby-hatch.[8]

Over the incomplete topography of the real city, Döblin designs a surrealistic map—a collective memory. It encompasses virtually the entire field of cultural, social, and historical influences, to which—consciously or unconsciously—an individual life is subject. This field of associations lines Biberkopf's path through the city with words and images that he has probably never consciously heard nor seen but that shape, in however mediated a form, his life and his thinking.

At the same time the text proceeds not primarily according to sense or meaning, but according to material aspects: it is guided by associations of sound, by rhythms, by the twisting and mutilating of words, by alliteration and meaningless yet ingenious rhymes. Language flows by in playful self-reference, without suppressing its sensuous materiality — what Döblin called "the alogical in the individual word" (*A-Logische im Einzelwort*)[9] — and lets the signified, the sphere of meaning, be swept along as though accidentally on its current, whose motion generates meaning often only as an incidental effect.

In a remark that is equally apt for *Berlin Alexanderplatz*, Ernst Bloch wrote that in *Ulysses* language hangs into the story as from a gridiron above the stage.[10] The materiality of the stream of language replaces the speaking subject, who differentiates himself from the objects to which he refers and thereby creates a clear dichotomy between the internal and the external, between subject and object, between speech and its referent.

When Death, the great mentor, breaks through Biberkopf's armor at the end of the novel, the protagonist is forced to realize something that has long become a reality in the literary practice of montage: he has to eliminate the boundaries that divide the inner from the outer within a subjectivity bound by the "cogito." With this step, the trauma of the novel's tumultuous beginning is dispelled. There Döblin portrayed the city as a subject that confronts the human subject, threatening and overpowering it. The textual montages trigger the countermovement by constructing the human subject as a city. They add a spatial dimension to language, memory, and the psyche, as a city created out of words. The surrealistic projection of the city is born of the desire to hear oneself speak in what is alien: not merely to talk about something or belligerently to confront objects, but to reach to the boundaries of the self, to see oneself and to hear oneself speak in the variegated configuration of the literary city.

In contrast to the ponderous one-dimensionality of Biberkopf's thinking and his tale of woe, within the apparatus of consciousness created by a language objectified as a textual fabric, the subject experiences itself as an immeasurably extended yet still unfamiliar and anonymous space. It is left to him either to be fascinated by the extensive vastness, or to be frightened by the desolate expanses and anarchy of some quarters.

"Who is speaking?" asks the despairing Job, whose lament is one of the pervasive leitmotifs of Döblin's *Berlin Alexanderplatz*. "My head, my brain. And now I am also being driven mad, now they are taking from me even my thoughts." And an anonymous voice replies: "And if they do, is that such a shame?" (154). The depersonalization of the textual applies to the protagonist, the reader — and the author. "One believes one is speaking, and one is being spoken; one believes one is writing, and one is being written," noted Döblin in *Der Bau des epischen Werkes* (Composition of epics).[11] In a letter to the German literary scholar Petersen, he commented on his work on *Berlin Alexanderplatz*: "It was hopeless. All my intentions went for nought. The book developed contrary to my plan."[12]

Döblin's textual montages resemble the *écriture automatique* of the surrealists. Being themselves in part a result of an autonomous stream of language, these montages contribute to its preservation, regeneration, and renewal. The assembled textual configurations are restless, unstable, incessantly active. Döblin spoke of the "throb of conception" (*Pochen der Konzeption*),[13] of a "dynamic mesh" (*dynamisches Netz*), which, once exposed, independently calls forth associations that generate new material and a surrealistic stream of language, which the author infuses into the text. In this manner, the city Döblin reconstructs as a speaking fabric of texts becomes a source of inspiration even for the author, "the native soil of my thoughts." Döblin speaks the text, as Benjamin suggests, as the breakers of the sea wash flotsam ashore. Döblin, however, releases himself from the compulsions of conscious composition and self-assured authorship. He leans back, "dreams, listens, collects,"[14] receiving the text before he writes it. For him, the textual fabric that he had already partially constructed became the megaphone[15] of the psychic apparatus; it became an apparatus of inspiration.

With his literary construction of Berlin, Döblin designed an eccentric image of humanity, through which he cheerfully affirmed the autonomy of social systems ranging from language to traffic. He did not ignore the violence that is thereby inflicted on human beings who persist in the belief in their self-determination. His openly contradictory novel ends with a scene that functions as an open question: parades of demonstrators—it is not clear whether of the left or right—march through the streets past Biberkopf. The motif of motion, of walking and marching, which throughout the novel was used to express the contradictions between the subject and the autonomous world of objects, is now taken on by the anonymous masses, who carry it into an unresolved conclusion.

Translated by Charles W. Haxthausen
with the assistance of Virginia Steinhagen
and Jerry Gerber

NOTES

1. Alfred Döblin, untitled typescript, in *Alfred Döblin 1878–1957: Katalog zur Ausstellung des Literaturarchiv Marbach* (Munich, 1978), 214. "Mein Denken und Arbeiten geistiger Art gehört, ob ausgesprochen oder nicht ausgesprochen, zu Berlin. Von hier hat es empfangen und empfängt es dauernd seine entscheidenden Einflüsse und seine Richtung, in diesem großen nüchternen Berlin bin ich aufgewachsen, dies ist der Mutterboden, dieses Steinmeer der Mutterboden all meiner Gedanken."

2. Döblin, "Berlin und die Künstler," in *Schriften zu Leben und Werk* (Olten, Switz., 1986), 38. "Das Ganze hat mächtig inspiratorisch belebende Kraft, diese Erregung der Straßen, Läden, Wagen ist die Hitze, in die ich mich schlagen lassen muß, wenn ich arbeite, daß heißt eigentlich immer. Das ist das Benzin, mit dem mein Wagen läuft."

3. Döblin, "An Romanautoren und ihre Kritiker. Berliner Programm," *Der Sturm*, 158–59 (May 1913): 17f. "Ich bin nicht ich, sondern die Straße, die Laternen, dies und das Ereignis, weiter nichts. Das ist es was ich den steinernen Stil nenne. . . . Depersonation! . . . Mut zur kinetischen Phantasie!"

4. Döblin, *Berlin Alexanderplatz* (Olten, Switz., 1961), 13–14. All subsequent references in the text are to this edition. "Er schüttelte sich, schluckte. Er trat sich auf den Fuß. Dann nahm er einen Anlauf und saß in der Elektrischen. Mitten unter den Leuten. Los. Das war zuerst, als wenn man beim Zahnarzt sitzt, der eine Wurzel mit der Zange gepackt hat und zieht, der Schmerz wächst, der Kopf will platzen. Er drehte den Kopf zurück nach der roten Mauer, aber die Elektrische sauste mit ihm auf den Schienen weg, dann stand nur noch sein Kopf in der Richtung des Gefängnisses. Der Wagen machte eine Biegung, Bäume, Häuser traten dazwischen. Lebhafte Staßen tauchten auf, die Seestraße, Leute stiegen ein und aus. In ihm schrie es entsetzt: Achtung, es geht los. Seine Nasenspitze vereiste, über seine Backe schwirrte es. 'Zwölf Uhr Mittagzeitung,' 'B.Z.,' 'Die neueste Illustrirte,' 'Die Funkstunde neu,' 'Noch jemand zugestiegen?' . . . Er stieg unbeachtet wieder aus dem Wagen, war unter Menschen. Was war denn? Haltung, ausgehungertes Schwein, kriegst meine Faust zu reichen. Gewimmel, welch Gewimmel. Wie sich das bewegte. . . . Draußen bewegte sich alles, aber — dahinter — war nichts! Es — lebte — nicht! . . . Er war aus dem Gefängnis entlassen und mußte hier hinein, noch tiefer hinein. . . . Ich geh auch rin, aber ich möchte nicht, mein Gott, ich kann nicht. . . . Die Wagen tobten und klingelten weiter, es rann Häuserfront neben Häuserfront ohne Aufhören hin. Und Dächer waren auf den Häusern, die schwebten auf den Häusern, seine Augen irrten nach oben: wenn die Dächer nur nicht abrutschten, aber die Dächer standen grade. Wo soll ick armer Deibel hin."

5. Günther Anders, "Der verwüstete Mensch," in *Festschrift für Georg Lukacs*, ed. F. Benseler (Neuwied, FRG, 1965), 420.

6. Döblin, "Bemerkungen zum Roman," *Die neue Rundschau* 28 (1917): 410–11. "Wenn ein Roman nicht wie ein Regenwurm in zehn Stücke geschnitten werden kann, und jeder Teil bewegt sich selbst, dann taugt er nichts."

7. Döblin, *Berlin Alexanderplatz*, 399–400: "Das Kaufhaus Hahn ist ganz runter, sonst stecken alle Häuser voll Geschäfte, sieht aber bloß aus, als ob es Geschäfte sind, tatsächlich sind es lauter Rufe, Lockrufe, Gezwitscher, knick, knack. Zwitschern ohne Wald."

8. Ibid., 103: "Ein Verbrecher, seinerzeit gottverfluchter Mann (woher weißt du, mein Kind?) am Altar, Orestes, hat Klytämnestra totgeschlagen, kaum auszusprechen der Name, immerhin seine Mutter, (An welchem Altar meinen Sie denn? Bei uns können Sie ne Kirche suchen, die nachts auf ist.) Ich sage, veränderte Zeiten . . . Harfenlos, wie es im Liede heißt, der Erynnientanz, schlingen sich um das Opfer, Wahnsinnsverstörung, Sinnesbetörung, Vorbereitung für die Klapsmühle."

9. Döblin, *Aufsätze zur Literatur* (Olten, Switz., 1962), 35.

10. Ernst Bloch, *Erbschaft dieser Zeit* (Frankfurt/Main 1962), 243.

11. Döblin, "Der Bau des epischen Werkes," *Aufsätze zur Literatur*, 131. "Man glaubt zu sprechen, und man wird gesprochen, man glaubt zu schreiben, und man wird geschrieben."

12. Döblin, "Letter to Julius Petersen," *Briefe* (Olten, Switz., 1970), 445. "Es war rettungslos. Mir schwammen die Felle davon. Gegen meinen Plan entwickelte sich das Buch fort."

13. Döblin, "Der Bau des epischen Werkes," 122.

14. Walter Benjamin, "Krisis des Romans: Zu Döblins *Berlin Alexanderplatz*," *Die Gesellschaft*, 7 (1930): 522–66. Cited in Matthias Prangel, *Materialien zu Alfred Döblins "Berlin Alexanderplatz"* (Frankfurt/Main, 1975), 108.

15. Benjamin, "Krisis," in Prangel, *Materialien*, 111.

CHAPTER 7

Deciphering the Hieroglyphics
of Weimar Berlin: Siegfried Kracauer

David Frisby

> *This landscape is that of raw Berlin. Unintentionally, there is expressed in it . . . its contradictions, its ruggedness, its openness, its simultaneity, its glamour. Knowledge of cities is bound up with the deciphering of their dreamlike expressive images.*
>
> "Berlin Landscape"

> *Spatial images are the dreams of society. Wherever the hieroglyphics of any spatial image is deciphered, there the basis of reality presents itself.*
>
> "On Employment Exchanges"

> *This crisis, despite the plush upholstery and the glamorous perspectives that so quickly reveal themselves to strangers, is certainly not invisible. On the contrary, its signals loom up like the masts of a sunken ship above the mirror-flat surface.*
>
> "Beneath the Surface"

I

Well before the First World War, Baedeker's staid guide to *Berlin and Its Environs* was proclaiming that although Berlin did "not compete in antiquity or historical interest with other great European capitals," it did possess a special attraction as "the greatest purely modern city in Europe," whose "streets are a model of cleanliness."[1] Such guidebook claims were still being made in the postwar period, especially after the surface of the metropolis had been seemingly cleansed of revolutionary upheaval, putschist rabble, and hyperinflationary chaos. For then the anonymous populace of the guidebooks had come to celebrate, in this period of "relative stabilization," all that was glittering and absolutely new about the vanguard city of

152

Berlin.[2] Siegfried Kracauer (1889–1966), a review editor of the *Frankfurter Zeitung* and its Berlin review editor from 1930 to 1933,[3] was aware of such artificially constructed images of the Berlin *Metropole*. In one of his essays originally entitled "Berlin Landscape" (10 August 1931), he draws the following distinction between such images and those that interest him.

> One can distinguish between two types of images of the city: those that are consciously formed, and others that reveal themselves unintentionally. The former have their origin in the artificial intention that is realized in squares, vistas, groups of buildings and perspectival effects that Baedeker illuminates with a small star. In contrast, the latter emerge without having been previously planned. They are not compositions . . . but rather fortuitous creations [*Geschöpfe des Zufalls*] that do not allow themselves to be called to account. Wherever masses of stones and lines of streets are to be found together, whose elements emerge out of quite diversely oriented interests, there such an image of the city comes into existence that is itself never the object of some interest or other. It is no more constructed than is nature and is similar to a landscape in that it unconsciously asserts itself. Unconcerned with how it looks, it continues to glow through time.[4]

Hence, Kracauer does not take the ready-made totality of "consciously formed" images of the metropolis as anything more than constructs whose facticity must be explored and exploded. Rather, as Inka Mülder has persuasively argued, his starting point is "the experience of the city as a labyrinth of fragmentary signs."[5] It is what lies on the surface, the superficial, the fortuitous constellation that is Kracauer's starting point—not in order to reproduce such phenomena, but to deconstruct them, to reveal a hidden reality submerged beneath them. Indeed, as Mülder suggests, Kracauer's aim is "to release 'mute' and 'unconscious' phenomena from their natural-like reification, 'enlighten' them as historical, to leave them as alive."[6]

How does Kracauer confront the task of "recovering contingency from oblivion?"[7] How does he decipher the complex labyrinth of signs and spatial configurations that constitute the phenomenal reality of the metropolis? Kracauer's "confrontation with a piece of the everyday world, a build-up Here, a live-out Now,"[8] suggests a critical phenomenological intention, a description—often metaphorical—that wrenches the object from its everyday self-evidentness, that explodes our conventional experience of it and that, in the process of unmasking its reified nature, reveals its historical nature. On occasion, Kracauer forces us—in a manner reminiscent of Benjamin—to confront fragments of metropolitan modernity by restoring childhood's gaze and astonishment as we look upon its familiar spatial constellations, such as trains crossing a bridge by Charlottenburg station, "emerging suddenly from behind a larger than life wall of tenements," or "heavy express trains rushing toward famous cities such as Warsaw and Paris that are built up just around the next corner."[9]

But Kracauer's aim is not merely a phenomenological description of fragments of urban experience. It is also a deconstruction of that experience, and especially of the dominant view from above, in order to reveal what lies beneath the surface of the world taken for granted. Sometimes this intention is announced in the titles of Kracauer's vignettes, as in "Beneath the Surface," or, critically, in a section of *Die Angestellten*, "Viewed from Above."[10] And if Kracauer's unmasking intention is vital to his mode of procedure, then it is neither that of the sociology of knowledge, whose diagnoses are "lacking in content," nor that of an orthodox Marxism, which comes fully armed with a ready-made theory of the totality.[11] Kracauer's own "material dialectics" was fashioned in deliberate contrast to the assertion of Lukácsian totalities, as he made clear in his exchanges with Ernst Bloch: "The notion of totality should not blind us to the instances of superficial life. To start from the substantive and the superficial seems to me not to be banished from a genuine revolutionary theory."[12]

Furthermore, his aim of the "destruction of all mythical things around us and within us" was to be demarcated from that of much of the radical Berlin intelligentsia who opposed capitalism's "extreme instances: war, crass miscarriages of justice, the May unrest, etc., without appreciating normal existence in its imperceptible dreadfulness."[13] Kracauer does of course concern himself with "exemplary instances" of metropolitan modernity, with "extreme" instances, but they are located in superficial, profane existence. In contrast, much of the radical intelligentsia "castigates blatant instances of corruption and forgets in so doing the consequences of minor events out of which our normal social life is composed. . . . The radicalism of these radicals would carry more weight if it really penetrated the structure of reality instead of meeting its instructions from the *bel étage* above. How is the everyday world to change when those who were called upon to transform it also fail to give any attention to it?" (ibid.).

Kracauer's approach should not be confused with the thirst for reportage, which was also taken up by sections of the radical intelligentsia, but which he saw as the result of German thought's undernourishment by German idealism. "The abstract nature of idealistic thought . . . is countered by reportage as the self-advertisement of concrete existence." However, as Kracauer points out:

> A hundred reports from a factory do not lend themselves to being added up to the reality of the factory, but rather remain for all eternity a hundred views of the factory. Reality is a construction. Of course life must be observed for it to come into being. But in no way is it embodied in the more or less arbitrary series of observations of reportage. Rather, it is embodied solely in the mosaic that is assembled together from out of the individual observations on the basis of knowledge of its content.
> (ibid., 216)

A similar indictment is provided by Bloch in his review of Kracauer's *Die Angestellten* when he suggests that "mere reportage no longer helps; where everything becomes so construed and artificial as in present day life, naive recording is not appropriate, the overlit foreground merely envelops once more the true background."[14]

Kracauer, then, addresses the "insignificant superficial manifestations" of an epoch, the spatial, temporal, and social constellations that exist in the metropolitan context of Weimar Berlin.[15] He interests himself in its architecture, its streets, its interiors, its social types, its cultural pastimes and ephemera. With some important exceptions, it is above all the culture of the growing white-collar strata—the "new middle class"—that preoccupy Kracauer, rather than its working class. In this respect, like many other social theorists writing on Berlin, Kracauer does not make it apparent that Berlin is also a major industrial city.

II

Trained as an architectural engineer whose practical experience consisted largely in the design of war cemeteries and memorials in the immediate post-First World War period, Kracauer understood only too well what sometimes lay hidden behind the "forest of symbols" (Baudelaire) generated by architectural practice. For him, "the fragments of architecture are ciphered communications that only the initiated can decipher. Just like the lover to whom half a word discloses the secrets of the loved one, so he too draws them out of the avenues, the streets, the squares which do not all immediately reveal themselves."[16] As a critical erstwhile student of Georg Simmel—author of the first essay on "The Sociology of Space" as well as the more widely known "Metropolis and Mental Life"—Kracauer was attuned to the social significance of spatial configurations. Further, as a critical materialist with an interest in the demythologization of reality, and, like Bloch, with a recognition of the complexity of the interaction between mythology and modernity, theology and the profane, Kracauer identified many spatial images with mythical images, with "the dreams of society." Hence, in reply to Adorno's criticism that he seemed to have accepted "the Benjamin hypothesis of buildings as the dreams of the collectivity," Kracauer retorts that "certain spatial images I did speak of as the dreams of society, because they present the existence of this society that is veiled by its consciousness."[17]

In his early city images, Kracauer often deals with Paris (as in "Parisian Observations" and "Street People in Paris" [1927], and "Analysis of a City Plan" and "Memory of a Paris Street" [1930]) as a spatial and temporal labyrinth in which its ordinary population constitutes "an improvised mosaic."

Above all, Paris remains a city permeated by history, however much it might appear to the Berlin traveler as "a huge provincial town."[18] Indeed, by confronting his images of Paris with those of Berlin we become aware of Kracauer's response to the vanguard modernity of Berlin through the juxtaposition of the historical with the absolutely new, the dream with the nightmare, humanity with emptiness. Kracauer's images of Berlin highlight, as it were, the dark side of Baedeker's proud pronouncement of its status as "the greatest purely modern city in Europe." Kracauer is concerned with its "unhistorical nature," with "the formless disquiet with which it is permeated,"[19] with the time of its fashionable and western suburban streets as an empty, unhistorical time. "Street without Memory" (1932) commences, "If some street blocks seem to be created for eternity, then the present-day Kurfürstendamm is the embodiment of empty flowing time in which nothing is allowed to last."[20] Its ever-changing facades, its rapidly disappearing shops and enterprises, are such that many of them "no longer make the effort to create the feeling of a securely grounded concern but rather from the very first awaken the impression of improvisation." Each enterprise that disappears

> is not merely superseded but is so completely displaced as if it never existed at all. From its complete presentness it is plunged into a state of being forgotten from which no force can any longer rescue it, it then becomes *the fortuitous* over which the everyday world quickly closes once more. Elsewhere, what has passed remains fixed to the place that during its lifetime was its home; on the Kurfürstendamm it makes its exit *without leaving behind any traces* . . . the new enterprises are always absolutely new. . . . What once existed is on its way to being never seen again, and what has just been claimed is confiscated one hundred percent by today. *A frenzy predominates* as it did in the colonies and gold rush town even though veins of gold had hardly been detected in these zones. Many buildings have been shorn of the ornaments that formed a kind of bridge to yesterday. *Now the plundered facades stand uninterrupted in time and are the symbol of the unhistorical change that takes place behind them.* Only the marble staircases that glimmer through the doorway preserve memories: those of the prewar first class world.[21]

The spectral objectivity created by the circulation of urban capital is, as Zohlen has suggested, that of "the ever-same prevailing actuality or, more precisely, the frenzy of the fetish 'nouveauté' as an unhistorical presentness."[22] It is present in all showplaces of modernity, as Benjamin sought to demonstrate in his unfinished "Prehistory of Modernity," as Harvey has finely illustrated for Paris of the Second Empire in *Consciousness and the Urban Experience*, as Kracauer himself sought to do in his own *Jacques Offenbach and the Paris of His Times* (1937), and as Berman has argued for New York today (in *All That Is Solid Melts into Air*).[23]

The experience of absolute presentness in the absolutely new, unhistorical actuality of Berlin is again highlighted by Kracauer in "Repetition" (1932).

> It appears as if this city has control of the magical means of eradicating all memories. It is present-day and, moreover, it makes it a point of honor of being absolutely present-day. Whoever stays for any length of time in Berlin hardly knows in the end where he actually came from. His existence is not like a line but a series of points; it is new every day like the newspapers that are thrown away when they have become old. . . . Only in Berlin are the transformations of the past so radically stripped from memory. Many experience precisely this life from headline to headline as exciting; partly because they profit from the fact that their earlier existence vanishes in its moment of disappearing, partly because they believe they are living twice as much when they live purely in the present.[24]

An ever-disappearing present is, of course, a central constituent of the transitory nature of the experience of modernity, whose concomitant is the destruction of historical memory.

The permanent destruction of dimensions of the urban environment, which Kracauer highlights with reference to the Kurfürstendamm or the new Alexanderplatz, combined with the accelerating sociopolitical and economic crisis of the early 1930s, creates an increase in tension, in "the nervousness in the everyday world" that permeates everyday experience. One of its counterparts is distraction from crisis, the creation of an artificial glamour. In *Strassen in Berlin*, Kracauer speaks of the "profane" lighting surrounding the Kaiser-Wilhelm Gedächtniskirche, giving it a "glamour full of secrecy." This illumination is in fact "a reflection of the facades of light" that "make night into day in order to banish the dread of the night from the working day of its visitor."[25] More generally, Kracauer comments on the extensive use of neon lighting and the neon advertisement: the latter "rises up to a heaven in which there is no longer an angel but also not merely business. It shoots beyond the economy, and what is intended as advertisement is transformed into illumination." These facades of discordant light constitute "an attack on tiredness that wishes to take over, on the emptiness that wishes to escape at any price. They roar, they pummel, they hammer with the brutality of the insane upon the crowd" (ibid., 47).

But it is not only artificial glamour that heightens the tension it is supposed to dispel. In suburbia, too, there are "less obvious symptoms of the real state of affairs." The underpass ("The Underpass," 1932) beneath a railway also contains a "sense of dread" in its contrast between "the enclosed, unshakeable construction system and the vanishing human motley that produces the terror."[26] In "Screams on the Street" (1930), Kracauer detects in the "friendly and clean" streets of western Berlin with their "nice green trees before its houses" an inexplicable "angst," a "panic horror."[27] The origin of the angst pervading these suburban streets perhaps lies in the fact that they "lose themselves in infinity; that buses roar through them, whose occupants during the journey to their distant destinations look down so indifferently upon the landscape of pavements, shop windows and balconies as if upon a river valley or a town in which they would never think of getting off; that a countless human crowd moves in them, constantly new people with unknown aims that intersect like the linear maze of a pattern sheet. In any case, it sometimes seems to me as if an explosive lies ready in all possible hidden places that, in the very next moment, can indeed blow up."[28] Kracauer contrasts these middle class suburbs with "whole city areas to which there clings the penetrating odor of political riots: Neukölln or perhaps Wedding. By their very nature, their streets are streets for parades." In contrast:

> There flows in these streets in the west a terror that is without an object. They are neither inhabited by the proletariat, nor are they witnesses to rebellion. Their populace does not belong together and the atmosphere in which communal actions emerge is completely lacking in them. Here, no one expects anything from anyone else. Uncertain, they extend themselves, without content and empty." (ibid., 29)

The questionable outcome of the crisis of the early 1930s is felt not merely in the suburbs but also in the center too: "A cold wind sweeps through the streets that are lacking in gentleness. On the Bülowplatz illuminations with the names of Lenin and Stalin light up. And yesterday, yet again, a German beauty queen was elected."[29]

III

Kracauer concerned himself not merely with the exterior public space of Weimar Berlin but also with some of its equally revealing interiors. Sometimes they appeared as an ambiguous symbol of decline ("Farewell to the Linden Arcade," 1930), sometimes as indicative of the socioeconomic crisis ("On Employment Exchanges," 1930, or "Refuge for the Homeless," 1931), sometimes as an escape ("Luck and Fate," 1931, or "Beneath Palm Trees," 1930).

The Linden Arcade, "like all bourgeois arcades," constituted an *extérieur* within an *intérieur*, a passage into a world of fantasy, a "passageway through bourgeois life. . . . Everything that was cut off from it because unworthy of representation or even ran counter to the official world view nestled itself in the arcade." It was the repository of objects that satisfy those ideas that appear in a waking dream: an anatomical museum displaying "the excrescences and monstrosities" of the body, pornography—always "at home in the twilight," photographs, stamp collectors' shops, and the like. What they all had in common was "withdrawal from the bourgeois front," in order "to organize an effective act of protest in the twilight of the passageway against the facade culture outside. They laid bare idealism and exposed its products as kitsch." However, by the time the arcade was due for demolition, their "critique" of the bourgeois world had become ineffective, they were no longer sensational. Rather, "all the objects are stricken with muteness. Shyly, they crowd together behind the architecture that once upon a time held them completely neutral and later once more will hatch out who knows what—perhaps fascism or even nothing at all. What is the point still of an arcade in a society that is itself only an arcade?"[30]

If Kracauer's "Farewell to the Linden Arcade" is tinged with melancholy—shared by Aragon in *Paris Peasant*, where he regrets the passing of the Passage d'Opéra, though not by Benjamin, at least in the later phase of his *Passagenwerk* (Arcades project)—and if the arcade in this form had long outlived its function (the circulation of commodities was not rapid enough to necessitate its modern successor, the shopping mall), then this is not the case with his treatment of the public *intérieur* of the employment office.

The employment exchange is also an arcade, one "through which the unemployed should once more attain a gainfully employed existence. Today, unfortunately, the arcade is heavily congested."[31] Kracauer's "On Employment Exchanges" (1930) is one of the best instances of his critical deciphering of spatial images. At the outset, he declares that he visited several employment exchanges in Berlin, not "in order to indulge the enjoyment of the reporter" in the exotic but rather

> in order to ascertain what position the unemployed actually occupy in the system of our society. Neither the diverse commentaries on unemployment statistics nor the relevant parliamentary debates give any information on this. They are ideologically permeated and, in one sense or another, iron out reality; whereas the space of the employment exchange is filled by reality itself. (ibid.)

This social space for the unemployed is often one that is buried away from "normal places of work," hidden away behind other buildings. It is a location that reflects its inmates' position "in the present production process. They are secreted from it as waste products, they are the leftovers that remain. Under the prevailing circumstances, the space accorded to them can hardly have any other visage than that of a junk room." Its empty space is filled with bare minimal furniture and grim warnings such as "Unemployed! Protect and Preserve Common Property!" Kracauer takes this grandiose imperative for the preservation of a minimum of common property as indicative of society's rhetoric for the preservation and protection of property: "It fences it in, even there where its defense is not at all necessary, with linguistic trenches and ramparts. It probably does it unintentionally, and perhaps one of those affected hardly notices that it does it. But that is precisely the genius of the language; that it fulfills instructions that it has not been informed of, and erects bastions in the unconscious." The rhetoric of protection and preservation does not extend to the inmates of such institutions; rather, they are shut off from "the serene heaven" of dominant classes and their illusions. In these and similar social spaces, "human entrails are hung out in the back courts of society like pieces of wash" (ibid.).

More fortunate are those existing within a minimum of living space: that expanding lower middle class—once described as "new"—whose culture Kracauer took to be the prevailing mass culture in Berlin. On the one hand, their social living space is extremely confined: "As the characteristic location of the small dependent existences who still very much like to associate themselves with the sunken middle class, more and more suburbs are formed. The few inhabitable cubic meters, which cannot even be enlarged by the radio, correspond precisely to the narrow living space of this strata" (ibid.). On the other hand, this very confinement requires as its counterpart a seemingly expansive "cult of distraction" from such a constricted existence, "oases" from everyday tribulations. In an early piece, "Das Mittelgebirge" (1926), Kracauer detects a search for the pastoral idyll by those so constrained by "the narrowness of the illusory private sphere," which "strengthens the urge to flee from their own four walls." The urge is fulfilled, in part, by those fortunate to possess a small automobile, which itself becomes "the major ornament of the Mittelgebirge."[32] As we shall see, that pastoral idyll or an even more exotic escape from the everyday world was also to be found in Berlin itself.

IV

In his most sustained work on Berlin in the Weimar period, *Die Angestellten* (whose full title, in English translation, is *White-Collar Workers: Out of the Newest Germany*), Kracauer deliberately focuses on Berlin, where "the situation of white collar workers [is] presented at its most extreme. Only from its extremes can reality be opened up." Indeed, "in that it goes in search of white-collar workers it leads at the same time into the inner reaches of the metropolis," and of course that metropolis is Berlin,

> the city of decidely white-collar culture; that is, a culture made by white-collar strata for white-collar strata, and taken by most white-collar workers to be a culture. Only in Berlin, where the bonds of origin and native soil are so repressed that the weekend can be the epitome of fashion, can the reality of white-collar workers be comprehended. It is also a good part of the reality of Berlin itself.[33]

It should not be assumed, of course, that Kracauer was unaware of "the reality of the proletariat" in Berlin. In "Girls at Work" (1932), he indicates the need to examine this reality, pointing out, however, that "the proletariat is even more unknown and even more difficult to get to know than the lower white-collar strata that border them," and is "only insufficiently to be grasped with imported bourgeois concepts."[34]

Kracauer's focus upon white-collar employees in Berlin may be justified, as Schröter suggests, by the fact that "the white-collar workers are the agents or consumers of all the phenomena around whose analysis Kracauer's work in these years gravitated."[35] *They* are the audience for the new culture of the distraction industry in the cinema and elsewhere, the culture of the "mass ornament"; *they* constitute the social specifics of a mass culture theory (which subsequently degenerated into theories of anonymous masses); and, above all, *they* illustrate the significance of the relationship between leisure, work, and ideology in the context of a universal process of rationalization. The face of the city is transformed not merely by new constructions but also by the growing illusion that its center is given over increasingly to leisure, to distraction.

Of particular note in Kracauer's construction of the reality of Berlin white-collar employees' existence out of "the illegal grammar of everyday language," interviews, and observations, is the delineation of the cultural interests and consumption of these disparate strata seeking an "asylum for the homeless" (in the sense of ideological homelessness). Kracauer views these "intellectually homeless" strata—especially their younger members—as being intent upon the distraction of glamour. In a telling interview a stenographer maintains that "the young girls came mostly from a poorer milieu and are attracted by the glamour." In a highly remarkable way she justifies the fact that the young girls in general avoid serious conversations. "Serious conversations," she says, "only distract and divert from the environment that one wishes to enjoy."[36] If a serious conversation is credited with distracting effects, then distraction is an inexorably serious matter.

The "glamour" of the rationalized typing pool must be compensated for, however, by expenditure on distraction in "free time." Similarly, employees' participation in the consumer wonderland of the large Berlin department store, within "the cheerful rooms flooded with light" and "the higher strata" customers, may bewitch them as well as their customers. But perhaps "the light deceives more than it enlightens, and perhaps the wealth of light, which more recently flows over our cities, serves not least to increase the darkness" (ibid., 284).

More commonly, however, compensation for the absence of the glamour of work is sought in the "pleasure barracks," "distraction factories," and "oases" that have their place in filling in leisure time. This is because, Kracauer argues:

The more the monotony of the workday predominates, the more must leisure time be distanced from it as much as possible. . . . The precise counterattack against the office machine . . . is the richly colored world. Not the world as it is, but as it appears in the hit tunes. A world that even in its most obscure niches is cleansed of the dust of the everyday world as if with a vacuum cleaner. The geography of the asylum for the homeless is born of the hit tune. (ibid., 287)

The brief flight into paradise that is embodied in film fantasies and their "daydreams of society" is also incorporated into the exotic interiors of bars ("Beneath Palm Trees," 1930, for instance), such as Haus Vaterland, whose "core forms a kind of enormous hotel lobby," one that:

takes to excess the *Neue Sachlichkeit* style, for only the most modern is good enough for our masses. The secret of *Neue Sachlichkeit* cannot be anywhere more decisively unmasked than here. In fact, behind the pseudostrictness of the lobby architecture Grinzing's grin exudes itself ("grinst Grinzing hervor"). Just another step into the depths and one lingers in the midst of the most sumptuous sentimentality. This, however, is the most characteristic feature of *Neue Sachlichkeit*, namely, that it is a facade that hides nothing behind itself, that it does not release any depth but rather it merely feigns to do so.[37]

The exotically decorated bars of Haus Vaterland recall the world of "the panorama of the nineteenth century," a paradise lost and not one to be aimed for. Those not enamored of the "magic of images" could, in turn, be distracted from within, as it were, in "the whole body culture," in sport. Unlike those who argued that sport destroyed individual complexes, Kracauer maintained that "the expansion of sport does not destroy complexes but is, amongst other things, a phenomenon of repression on a large scale; it does not support the transformation of social relations but is as a whole a major means of depoliticization"—a means used to its full mobilizing and politicizing effect a few years later.

V

It is clearly difficult in the scope of a few pages to indicate the richness of Kracauer's presentation of Berlin in the years before 1933—increasingly precarious years for Kracauer on the *Frankfurter Zeitung* since its takeover in 1929–30 by I. G. Farben, culminating in his dismissal in 1933.[38] His important contribution to film criticism has recently been treated in an issue of *New German Critique* (No. 40), part of which concerns explicitly the Ufa productions in Berlin. And anyone who now peruses the pages of the *Frankfurter Zeitung* from the late 1920s until 1933 will be rewarded with a wealth of essays by Kracauer on Berlin, including a regular column on "Berliners among Themselves" (Berliner Nebeneinander) and "Berlin Figures" (Berliner Figuren). In the literary sphere, there are his critical reviews of the Threepenny Opera trial, of Döblin's *Berlin Alexanderplatz*, of Benjamin's *Einbahnstrasse*, and his early reception of Tretjakov's work in Berlin, among others.[39]

But what is the significance of Kracauer's illuminations of the social space of Weimar Berlin? For Kracauer the metropolis is the site of both ordered and fragmented constellations of buildings, structures, artifacts, and people. Those who move about in the metropolis do so either without being *aware* of what these constellations are signifying or without being able to *read* these fragmentary signs. This is a feature of the everyday world's unawareness, of its forgetfulness. Kracauer does not present us with a single fixed focus of the metropolis, but deciphers its spatial images in a variety of media, in a variety of ways. What he reveals is at times the daydreams of society embodied in its artifacts; at others, the seemingly impenetrable meaninglessness of spatial configurations (the empty, unhistorical time that pervades the west end); at still others, the complex manner in which ideology is embedded in spatial forms themselves. His starting point for such attempts at demythologizing the present is always the fragmentary, fractured experience of the surface phenomena of the urban landscape and its inhabitants: its spatial "fortuitous creations," its inhabitants' "illegal grammar," their unreflected daydreams. This fractured experience is also manifested in the world "viewed from above," its ideology, its facticity, beneath whose surface lies a constructed normalcy.

Above all, we should be struck by Kracauer's sensitivity to the nuances of everyday metropolitan life as experiencing both illusions and utopian dreams, the depiction of the fortuitous social and spatial configurations in the urban context, however seemingly insignificant they may appear. His illumination of the "exemplary instances of reality" by deliberately shunning the view from above and "the euphemistic whispering of sociology" (Benjamin) enabled Kracauer to realize a materialist dialectics that had abandoned the fixed categories of base and superstructure. His critical materialism enabled him to reveal "socially necessary illusion," not in order to be denounced as the product of "ideological state apparatuses," but rather, as Benjamin suggested in one of his reviews of *Die Angestellten*, to recognize that "the products of false consciousness are like picture puzzles in which what is essential merely peeps through from out of the clouds, the foliage and the shadows."[40] (The ragpicker, as Benjamin termed Kracauer, moving through the modernity of late Weimar Berlin, redeemed its fragments and rendered them intelligible in a precarious mosaic. As Benjamin said of the author of *Die Angestellten*, "At the moment in which the first traces of an active love of the metropolis show themselves, one goes in search for the first time for its defects.")

164   David Frisby

NOTES

1. Karl Baedeker, *Berlin and Its Environs*, 5th ed. (Leipzig, 1912), v. and 54. See also 6th ed., 1923.

2. On the pecularities of the construction of reality for the tourist, see Dean MacCannell, *The Tourist* (New York, 1976).

3. On Kracauer's life and work to 1933, see the excellent study by Inka Mülder, *Siegfried Kracauer: Grenzgänger zwischen Theorie und Literatur* (Stuttgart, 1985), which also contains the most comprehensive bibliography of Kracauer's work. In English, see Martin Jay, "The Extraterritorial Life of Siegfried Kracauer," *Salmagundi* 31–32 (1975–76): 49–106; Martin Jay, "Adorno and Kracauer: Notes on a Troubled Friendship," *Salmagundi* 40 (1978): 42–66; as well as David Frisby, *Fragments of Modernity* (Cambridge, Mass., 1986).

4. Siegfried Kracauer, *Strassen in Berlin und Anderswo* (Frankfurt, 1964), 51.

5. Inka Mülder, *Erfahrendes Denken. Zu den Schriften von Siegfried Kracauer*, dissertation, Tübingen University (1984), 155–56. See also Inka Mülder-Bach, "Der Umschlag der Negativität," *Deutsche Vierteljahrschrift für Literaturwissenschaft und Geistesgeschichte* 61 (1987): 359–73.

6. Ibid.

7. Jay, "The Extraterritorial Life," 50.

8. Walter Benjamin, *Gesammelte Schriften* 3 (Frankfurt/Main, 1980), 221.

9. Kracauer, *Strassen in Berlin*, 52.

10. See Kracauer, "Unter der Oberfläche," *Frankfurter Zeitung*, 11 July 1931; Kracauer, *Die Angestellten* in *Schriften* I (Frankfurt, 1971).

11. See Kracauer's critique of Karl Mannheim's Ideology and Utopia: "Ideologie und Utopie," *Frankfurter Zeitung*, 23 April 1929.

12. Letter from Kracauer to Ernst Bloch, 27 May 1926.

13. Kracauer, *Die Angestellten*, 298.

14. Ernst Bloch, "Künstliche Mitte. Zu Kracauers *Die Angestellten*," *Die Neue Rundschau* 41 (1930): 861.

15. Some of these are collected in Kracauer, *Strassen in Berlin*. Otherwise, the bibliography to Mülder, *Siegfried Kracauer*, should be consulted.

16. Kracauer, "Die Berührung," *Frankfurter Zeitung*, 18 November 1928. It would be fruitful to compare Kracauer's procedure with that of two of his contemporaries who also provided topographies of Berlin in this period: Bernard von Brentano (whom Kracauer succeeded as review editor in Berlin in 1930) also published Berlin vignettes in the *Frankfurter Zeitung*—now assembled in B. von Brentano, *Wo in Europa ist Berlin?* (Frankfurt, 1987). Of greater interest is Franz Hessel's *Spazieren in Berlin* (Berlin, 1929), now reprinted as *Ein Flaneur in Berlin* (Berlin, 1984), which was reviewed by Benjamin. Hessel and Aragon are the immediate sources of inspiration for Benjamin's Arcades Project.

17. Cited in Mülder, *Erfahrendes Denken*, 259, n. 17.

18. Kracauer, "Pariser Beobachtungen," *Frankfurter Zeitung*, 13 February 1927.

19. Kracauer, "Berlin in Deutschland," *Frankfurter Zeitung*, 14 August 1932.

20. Kracauer, "Strasse ohne Erinnerung," *Frankfurter Zeitung*, 16 December 1932. Reprinted in Kracauer, *Strassen in Berlin*, 19–23.

21. See *Strassen in Berlin*, 19–23.

22. Gerwin Zohlen, "Text-Strassen," *Text + Kritik* 68: 64.

23. On Benjamin see my *Fragments of Modernity*; David Harvey, *Consciousness and the Urban Experience* (Oxford, 1985); Kracauer, *Jacques Offenbach and the Paris of His Times* (London, 1937); Marshall Berman, *All That Is Solid Melts into Air* (New York, 1982).

24. Kracauer, "Wiederholung," *Frankfurter Zeitung*, 29 May 1932.

25. Kracauer, *Strassen in Berlin*, 47.

26. Kracauer, "Die Unterführung," *Frankfurter Zeitung*, 11 March 1932. Reprinted in *Strassen in Berlin*, 48–50.

27. Kracauer, "Schrei auf der Strasse," *Frankfurter Zeitung*, 19 July 1930. Reprinted in *Strassen in Berlin*, 27–29.

28. Kracauer, *Strassen in Berlin*, 28.

29. Kracauer, "Wärmehalle," in *Strassen in Berlin*, 84.

30. Kracauer, "Abschied von der Lindenpassage," *Frankfurter Zeitung*, 21 December 1930. Reprinted in *Das Ornament der Masse* (Frankfurt/Main, 1977), 326–32.

31. Kracauer, "Über Arbeitsnachweise. Konstruktion eines Raumes," *Frankfurter Zeitung*, 17 June 1930. Reprinted in *Strassen in Berlin*, 69–78.

32. Kracauer, "Das Mittelgebirge," in *Strassen in Berlin*, 122–24.

33. Kracauer, *Die Angestellten*, 215–16.

34. Kracauer, "Mädchen im Beruf," *Der Querschnitt* 12 (1932): 242.

35. M. Schröter, "Weltzerfall und Konstruktion" in *Text + Kritik*, 68.

36. Kraucauer, *Die Angestellten*, 282f.

37. Kracauer, *Die Angestellten*, 286–87. See also "Unter Palmen," *Frankfurter Zeitung*, 19 October 1930.

38. For details of this see Mülder, *Siegfried Kracauer*, 147, n. 8. For a recent brief discussion of Kracauer as a reporter see Karl Prümm, "Die Stadt der Reporter und Kinogänger bei Roth, Brentano und Kracauer," in Die *Unwirklichkeit der Städte*, ed. Klaus R. Scherpe (Reinbeck bei Hamburg, 1988), 80–105.

39. See Kracauer, "Ein soziologisches Experiment? Zu Bert Brechts Versuch 'Der Dreigroschenprozess,' " *Frankfurter Zeitung*, 28 February 1932; Kracauer, "Was soll Herr Hocke tun?", *Frankfurter Zeitung*, 17 April 1931; Kracauer, "Der operierende Schriftsteller," *Frankfurter Zeitung*, 17 February 1932; and Kracauer, "Zu den Schriften Walter Benjamins," *Frankfurter Zeitung*, 15 July 1928; reprinted in *Das Ornament der Masse*, 249–55.

40. Benjamin, *Gesammelte Schriften* 3: 225.

CHAPTER 8

Retrieving the City as *Heimat:*
Berlin in Nazi Cinema

Linda Schulte-Sasse

Not surprisingly, Berlin as a focal point of the modern or, to quote Luzie in Edgar Reitz's *Heimat*, of "*Welt*," ceased to play the central role in Nazi cinema that it had in the Weimar period. On the contrary, precisely the cosmopolitan side of Berlin life, when represented in Nazi films, served to demonstrate a state of disintegration and debasement that needed to be overcome by National Socialism. Nazism's critique of modernity as embodied in ideologemes like blood and soil, the nation, *Heimat* (homeland), or *Volk* is amply manifested in the "mountain" film genre produced before and during the Third Reich (associated with Arnold Fanck and Leni Riefenstahl), and in films such as *Das verlorene Tal* (The lost valley, 1934), *Ewiger Wald* (Eternal forest, 1936), or *Die goldene Stadt* (The golden city, 1943). These "blood and soil" narratives privilege agrarian life, while the city becomes a paradigm for dissolution, eroticism, and degeneracy that must be contained.

Yet it would be reductive to claim that the city per se embodies evil in Nazi cinema or to expect every Nazi film to feature a pastoral utopia, since the spatial terms of the oppositions structuring Nazi film narratives vary considerably. The city-country opposition is indeed merely a narrative manifestation of the more fundamental opposition between alienation and community, between the fragmented and the whole, the rootless and a sense of place—an opposition that can be defined by a variety of terms and that determines narratives juxtaposing the urban with the agrarian, the German with the foreign, as well as those located exclusively within one city or one rural setting. The city, when thematized at all, can represent dissolution *or* a locale of collectivity, a *Heimat* that needs to be secured, protected, and constantly reaffirmed. I intend here to demonstrate the invocation of Berlin as a collective space (or at least a potential collective space) in both early and later Nazi cinema, but will first briefly demonstrate how the predominant binary opposition "community versus alienation" adapts itself to a variety of spatial configurations.

National Socialism targets the dispersing, alienating, and fragmenting effect of modern life but does *not* necessarily identify industrialized society as evil in itself. Veit Harlan's *Der Herrscher* (The ruler, 1937), for example, "freely" based on Hauptmann's *Vor Sonnenuntergang* (Before sundown), valorizes industry as a guarantor of progress. The film depicts the conflict between industrial magnate Matthias Clausen, whose empire embodies the values of community, and his egotistical family. Both the film's narrative and its imagery champion industry, as when Clausen is presented with a model of the factory he has founded, or when he passes in front of giant ovens symbolizing the crucible to which he is subjected when his own children attempt to declare him mentally incompetent. Similarly, Jürgen von Allen's *Togger* (1940), one of relatively few flattering portrayals of journalists in the Nazi era,[1] copies and affirms the aestheticized big-city iconography of films such as Ruttman's *Berlin, Symphonie einer Großstadt* (Symphony of a great city, 1927) by featuring montage sequences of thundering printing presses churning out antimonopolistic headlines. What counts in these films is not the fact that industry and machines are portrayed, but the spirit that inhabits them; they can be employed in the service of the *Volksgemeinschaft* (community of the people) or in the service of egotism. At the same time, remnants of the antimodernist urban-rural dichotomy often color even the most positive portrayals of urban environments, when the city betrays a dependency on provincial Germany. In *Togger*, the last newspaper in Berlin to take a stand against the conspiracy of international capital, *Der neue Weg* (The new way), is saved from financial ruin by a journalist from the provincial *Siebenbürger Bote*.[2] In *Der Herrscher*, Clausen finds salvation in his provincial secretary Inken Peters, who is semiotically linked with "nature," as her mother owns a nursery, referred to pejoratively as a *Grünkramladen* (literally "green stuff store") by an urbane daughter-in-law.

Another characteristic form that the fundamental opposition in Nazi cinema between community and alienation assumes is of course the juxtaposition of a German with a foreign context. Harlan's *Die goldene Stadt*, which epitomizes the classic blood-and-soil narrative of romantic anticapitalism, is set in a German village in Bohemia, but significantly locates the narrative source of dissolution in Prague, lending foreign accents to the figures who cause the heroine's downfall. These figures are accompanied by a predictable series of negative semantic markers: plus materialism, egotism, eroticism, excessive drinking; minus honesty, a work ethic, "heart," or "moral fiber." The film portrays the penetration of the German organism or "body" at the fringes, and the consequent necessity of spatial armament or containment. The threat to these spatial peripheries is analogous to the threat to the German city as portrayed in Nazi cinema: both are besieged by foreign penetration, both subject to the psychological threat of dissolute otherness. The necessity for geographical containment also takes on a biological dimension in *Die goldene Stadt*, since the heroine Maria is the product of a German father and a (deceased) Czech mother, whose basic character flaw — fascination with city life — Maria inherits. Figures too susceptible to the lure of the foreign are killed off by the Nazi narrative, as is Maria or the musician Klaus, in *Kolberg*, whose years in Strasbourg (again, at the spatial fringes of the "German" empire) have turned him into a "World Citizen," always a pejorative epithet in Nazi discourse. Characters with a stronger ego often barely escape the dissolution linked with the foreign, but the popular topos of returning "home" (compare the title of *Heimkehr*, 1941) reinforces the territorial superiority of "the German" with its opposition to the material egotism of modernity — as when Hans Albers returns home in the films *Flüchtlinge* (Refugees) and *Gold*, Zarah Leander returns to her village in *Heimat*, or Luis Trencker and Willi Birgel return from America in *Der verlorene Sohn* (The prodigal son) and *Amerika — Ein Mann will nach Deutschland* (America — A man wants to go to Germany), respectively. The recurrence of this motif illustrates the parallel between the need for spatial, geographical containment and personal containment: A spatially contained, homogeneous "German" environment provides a context in which the individual can avoid contamination and in which community can come to fruition.

In the following I will explore the special connection between Berlin and the notion of *Heimat* in a number of films that specifically thematize this relationship. I will focus mainly on the three programmatic Nazi films produced in 1933, the best known of which is Hans Steinhoff's *Hitlerjunge Quex* (Hitler youth quex), and on a number of films from the early 1940s based on the experience of war, in particular Eduard von Borsody's *Wunschkonzert* (Request concert). I will argue that early Nazi films concentrate on reinvesting Berlin with the wholeness and patriarchal authority perceived as lost in the process of modernization epitomized by the Weimar Republic. Later films shift their focus to outside forces of disunion, particularly war, against which the community must fortify itself. Films like *Wunschkonzert* communicate an increasingly abstract and imaginary experience of Berlin as a collective space invoked on the level of memory and mobilized through the technologically produced spectacle. Yet all the films discussed allow Berlin to transcend mere physical space in favor of an emotional space that is or needs to be spiritually permeated by the "community of the people."

1. Early Cinema

Berlin plays a significant role in shaping the popular memory of the Weimar Republic as encouraged by the NSDAP. A series of early films that are essentially filmic articulations of the "stab in the back legend" trace the ori-

gins of the National Socialist movement in the twenties as an effort to restore community, homogeneity, and a hypostatized "Germany" in face of
the strife or *Zerrissenheit* Weimar came to signify. The films focus first on
communism as the adversary of community, as a movement whose very
precondition and aim is the continuance of strife, and second, on capitalism,
whose profit orientation likewise precludes the reinstatement of "old" German values—although, to be sure, the critique of capitalism is restricted to
a transparent semantic system centering on the notion of greed.

Many of these films are set in anonymous locations, but in a few Berlin is
highlighted, and is likewise hypostatized as a space plagued by disunion,
but longing to be returned to community. Of the three programmatic films
made immediately after Hitler's ascension to power in 1933, two, *Hitlerjunge Quex* and *Hans Westmar*, are set specifically in Berlin, and the third,
S.A. Mann Brand, in an unnamed city. The three films are similar in structure and style mainly because they participate in a kind of Nazi "master narrative" based on the Horst Wessel myth, on whose name Hans Westmar is a
fictional variation. In all three films a paradigmatic hero dies for "the
cause"; in all three, communists are the enemy, and all three feature young
communist women who to varying degrees develop sympathy for the Nazi
hero. All three denigrate "internationalism," signified in part by the constant presence of "Die Internationale," which is always juxtaposed with a
song invested with nationalistic connotations, such as "Die Wacht am
Rhein" (The guard at the Rhine) or the Hitler Youth Song.

A sequence from *Hans Westmar* epitomizes the *Überfremdung*, the stifling
of German culture by foreign elements in Weimar Berlin. Westmar gives a
tour of the city to a German emigré to the United States and his American
daughter. Both Westmar and the father express outrage at the foreign influence that has taken over Berlin: The father remarks, "You find everything
here—only nothing German. This is Berlin? This is Germany's capital? I
don't recognize it." As they drive through the dark, neon signs cut diagonally across the screen from all directions: "On parle français," "English
spoken," names of international restaurants intersect with each other.

The group makes a vigil to the older man's *Stammkneipe*, his favorite pub
from his youth, which now bears the name *Chez Ninette*. In the bar they are
greeted by a doorman and a black coat boy, both of whom speak only
French, provoking the father to ask sarcastically: "Can one speak German
here, too?" The uncomprehending coat boy answers: "*Naturellement!*" and
gestures toward the men's toilet, next to which theater posters advertise
plays with titles like: *A Jew Goes through the World* and *Berlin without a Blouse*.
The scene thus links visually the usage of a foreign language in a "German"
environment with human waste, Jewry (another signifier for capitalism),
and indecent exposure. When the group attempts to order beer, they are told
the bar carries only English beer. A French singer provides—again multi-

lingual—entertainment, and the clientele consists of men bearing signifiers of the capitalist that abound in Nazi film: obesity, baldness, cigar smoking, boisterousness, lechery. One of the drunken men tells the orchestra to play "Die Wacht am Rhein," and the drunkards begin dancing. Seeing German tradition defiled in this way overwhelms Westmar, who protests loudly and, near tears, stalks out of the bar, remarking to the American girl, "Germany—is somewhere completely different" (ganz wo anders).

The scene illustrates how the corrupt domination of international money violates Germany's sovereignty—even its essence—as gravely as a military invasion by France or Austria in Frederick's era of the Seven Years War could have. Moreover, the penetration of "German" space by capitalism, by exchange value, effects a homogenizing of the culture; the specific of Germany gives way to the abstractness of international capitalism. Yet National Socialism counters this general not with a specific, but with another general: that of emotional collectivism. Just as in Klaus Theweleit's definition of the *nation* as existing in the individual or in the male group,[3] Westmar's remark that "Germany" is somewhere else suggests that it exists at this point only within him, the Volkish, soldierly man. Berlin is important not as a specific location, but as a representative element of the greater whole, Germany. Berlin in its present state provides a spatial metaphor for the threat of capitalism.

Yet Berlin and even "Germany" cease to be spatial categories, but rather emotional ones: Germany is "inside"—at this point only inside an individual, but it must begin penetrating all people. Once "Germany" as an abstract emotional force has been internalized by the masses, its spatial boundaries can likewise be secured. The very notion of a "German" identity is dependent upon such bodily and psychological containment, since identity always already means containment and the demarcation of boundaries.

Variations on the nightclub scene recur periodically in Nazi films set in Weimar, like *Pour le Mérite* (1938), *Um das Menschenrecht*, (For human rights, 1934), and *Togger*. Although the details may change, invariable elements include the pejorative depiction of the nightclub or *Bumslokal* atmosphere, the linkage of scantily clothed women and the capitalist "type," the predominance of foreign languages,[4] foods, and drink, and of course the protagonist's revulsion. Moreover, this scenario is one of the few in Nazi cinema to specifically thematize blacks as a race imported by imperialist forces antagonistic to Germany, and as a sexual threat or what one might call in Theweleitian terms a black—as opposed to red—"flood." Invariably blacks appear in the nightclub context, represented naked on wall murals or as strip-tease dancers, threatening the containment of sexuality essential for the armored man's self-preservation. *Togger* even features a black man dancing with a white woman, an "obscenity" (*Schweinerei*) that provokes near-nausea in the protagonist. Typically, such representations of debauchery function on two levels, permitting the spectator a voyeuristic pleasure in the forbidden and a simultaneous feeling of indignation. They allow, in other words, an imaginary decentering experience, while never threatening the spectator's real containment within a morally superior identity.

The *Bumslokal* paradigm is only one example for the demoralizing and disharmonious effect of Weimar capitalism on Berlin as portrayed in Nazi cinema. The discursive and visual signifiers in the initial sequence of *Hans Westmar* already reveal the sense of despair and *Zerrissenheit* (disunion) pervading Berlin. The film opens as Westmar reminisces about Berlin from the point of view of a "gay, troublefree" Vienna where he is vacationing. A pan across the romanticized outdoor Viennese restaurant is followed by a cut to a workers' meeting in Berlin, where a man's offscreen voice screams: "Crush the whole shebang!" (Schlag doch die ganze Bude in Klumpen!) The camera travels past haggard, disheveled men to a sign saying "Welfare Office" and another saying "Homeless Shelter, Room VII," while the men discuss rumors of a better life in Russia.

S.A. Mann Brand, Um das Menschenrecht, and *Pour le Mérite* likewise depict urban areas as centers of corruption as well as despondency. Hanno Möbius has pointed out the indebtedness of such urban depictions to the "Zille" film genre of the twenties.[5] The protagonists of these three films — all former soldiers — face alienation and displacement in a society that does not share their code of "honor." They either are unable to obtain jobs or they lose them because of their political affiliation or their unwillingness to compromise themselves. In *Pour le Mérite*, Captain Prank fails repeatedly in his business ventures, ironically because of his honesty. He first opens an auto repair shop, but refuses to play the game and invent problems with customers' cars, even though "everybody in this business does it." Consequently the business fails. The captain then tries unsuccessfully to become a liquor dealer, an even more unsavory occupation since it forces him to deal with "capitalist" types and visit sleazy bars. Again, the disorder of Weimar culture is signaled by the repeated humiliation of the "born" leader Prank, who becomes increasingly depressed to see "strong men" robbed of their social function: "Men are needed everywhere; only not here!"

All of these films exploit the memory of soldiers fallen in the war, whose sacrifices make the obscenity of Weimar all the more blatant. Hans Westmar's remark that Germany is "elsewhere" in reference to the Berlin nightclub is followed by a montage sequence of dancing couples seen through distorted lenses and in blurred focus, which dissolves into a sequence of battle scenes from World War I, and finally to a shot of military graves. Westmar exclaims: "Three million had to die. And they (*gesturing toward the club*) — they are dancing . . . boozing . . . howling!" Similarly, in *Um das Menschenrecht* the close-up face of a dead comrade reappears periodically as a kind of conscience or warning to the protagonist and to the spectator.

In the context of Nazi cinema, the Weimar democracy is of course regarded as a betrayal of the soldiers who fought for the fatherland, as a loss of pride and "manhood" in the name of an illusory peace. Hans Westmar's liberal university professor invokes the notion of the "world citizen" — which is tantamount to one who has "sold out" to the international conspiracy of world capitalism — to legitimate Germany's humiliation: "The treaty of Versailles, which brought us the peace we yearned for, drew the political borders of Germany even tighter. But . . . with narrower borders we became border*less*. We have become Europeans, world citizens. We have been taken up as equals into the great cultural nations. . . . Down with weapons!" A cut to two raised fencing swords follows the professor's final words — a typically phallic image in response to the professor's pacifism.

Steinhoff's *Hitlerjunge Quex* differs from the other early Nazi Berlin films in its focus on a specific district, the Berlin working-class neighborhood Beuselkiez. Yet while *Berlin Alexanderplatz*, like other Weimar works, celebrates the uniqueness and local color of a certain part of the city, the specific in *Hitlerjunge Quex* again exists only to be surrendered to the general. Beuselkiez, Berlin, the river Spree all gain significance in the film as entities that need to be reincorporated into the large community, the transcendental anchor Deutschland, which is less a place than an "armored" mentality. This hypostatized "Germany" can function as a transcendental anchor because it reconciles the containment in an "armored" identity and the pleasurable release in merging the lonely self with a whole; it combines *Begrenzung* (containment of boundaries) and *Entgrenzung* (loss of boundaries).

This valorization of the general over the specific, the community over the individual self, is best illustrated by a discussion in the film between a communist (whose family name is, significantly, Völker) and a Hitler Youth leader. The protagonist, Heini Völker, the communist's son, has joined the Hitler Youth but is nearly asphyxiated when his destitute mother commits suicide. Father Völker predictably disapproves of his son's newfound allegiance, but is given a lesson on community during a hospital visit with the Hitler Youth leader.

YOUTH LEADER: Hello, Heini! The doctor says you can leave the hospital now.

HEINI: But where am I to go?

FATHER: What sort of question is that? With your father, of course, where you belong.

YOUTH LEADER: But that's precisely the question. Where does the boy belong today? My parents were well-meaning, but when I was fifteen, I ran away . . . many boys did the same. . . .

FATHER: Rascals, that's what they were, all of them.

YOUTH LEADER: Ah, but that is their nature, and it always has been. Once they reach a certain age they all want to roam. Where then does a boy belong? Why don't you ask your son?

FATHER: Well then, what have you to say for yourself?
[*Heini starts to answer*]

YOUTH LEADER: Tell me, were you in the war?

FATHER: Why, of course I was . . .

YOUTH LEADER: Well then, over two million boys volunteered for action. All of them had families, fathers, and mothers. Tell me, where did they belong?

FATHER: I am a simple man of the people, a proletarian (*ein Prolet*).

YOUTH LEADER: You've heard of the Movement, haven't you?

FATHER: [*gesticulating*] Movement! Up one, two, — Up one, two — that's the movement I understood. Until I was hit by a bullet and then the movement stopped. From then on I had to limp to the labour exchange. Week in, week out, year after year. It drove me crazy. Do you think that I got fat through eating too much? Of course not, it was because I was out of a job. Sitting around made me fat. So where do I belong? I belong with my friends, from my own class. And where I belong, my son belongs too.

YOUTH LEADER: With your own class? By that, I take you to mean the Internationale?

FATHER: Yes, of course, the Internationale.

YOUTH LEADER: [*pauses*] Where were you born?

FATHER: Why, in Berlin.

YOUTH LEADER: Yes, but where is Berlin?

FATHER: [*impatient*] In Germany, of course.

YOUTH LEADER: Yes, of course, in Germany—in *our* Germany. Now I want you to think about that.[6]

Father Völker is a drunkard who squanders the little money his family has and beats his son into singing "Die Internationale" instead of the Hitler Youth Song. But in the course of the film, foremost in the preceding scene, we come to understand the conditions that made the father the way he is. *Hitlerjunge Quex* courts the working-class viewer by showing Father Völker to be not fundamentally bad, but misguided.[7] The persona of Heinrich George, who carries on here the tradition of proletarian roles he has skillfully portrayed since Jutzi's *Berlin Alexanderplatz* (1931), further assures a sympathetic audience response. Moreover, within the context of Nazi film and the tradition of what Karl Prümm calls "soldierly nationalism,"[8] the fact that Völker served in World War I and sacrificed his health to the defense of his country is an important signifier, however incidental to the plot, of Völker—read: the worker—as a salvageable figure.

In fact, Völker soon repeats the exact same phrases about "our" Germany to a comrade—thus, the foundation for a conversion of the worker to Nazism, to community, appears to be laid. (At the same time, Völker's corpulent body, which contrasts markedly with the slender erectness of the Youth leader, suggests that at best he is fit to be a follower, not a leader in the movement.) More important for my purposes is the manner in which the specific gives way to the general, in which the scene uses community as a response to communist ideology. As a proletarian, Völker's allegiance is class specific; he is well aware of class differences separating him from privilege. The Youth leader uses the idea of a German Volk united by blood, by common origin, as an antidote to Völker's Marxist concept of society as a struggle between different classes for hegemony. The idea of "one" (that is, "our") Germany that Völker begins to accept serves merely to cloud his earlier perception of his class as victimized by an economic system and an imperialist war. "Community," or the Volkish concept of socialism, had the emotional appeal of allegedly effacing social differences, yet it was accompanied by few changes in the real social structure, especially after the left wing of the party was eliminated in 1934. Unlike Berlin and the Spree, for which Völker feels no ideological fervor, "our" Germany again begins to transcend the geographical as a purely emotional locale. It thus gains a compensatory appeal to the underprivileged Völker, while acting as a palliative to stabilize the economic system.

The film's central opposition of the chaos, unleashed sexuality, and violence linked with communism versus the order, containment, and inner peace linked with National Socialism underscores this compensation. Moreover, *Hitlerjunge Quex* semiotically interweaves an antimodernist city/nature opposition with the above opposition. The film associates communism with a local carnival, where Heini tries to win a knife with which he is later murdered, and particularly with the dizzying spinning movement of a carousel; hence communism appears as a decidedly urban phenomenon. Heini's first encounter with National Socialism, by contrast, occurs in a forest outside Berlin, where he witnesses a Hitler Youth outing with singing, ritual fire, and a display of community spirit. Moreover, it is significant that the scene crucial to Father Völker's conversion is located in a natural enclave within the city; a parklike area surrounding Heini's hospital. Thoughout the film National Socialism thus represents a return of the city to the principles of nature, to what Hanno Möbius refers to as an intended "renaturalization" of the urban environment.[9] Heini's turn toward Nazism is never explained in terms of social programs or ideology, nor need it be. The film's persistent use of such oppositions as his family's cramped apartment versus his Nazi friends' warm, bourgeois comfort; the sexually aggressive communist girl Gerda (linked with the carousel) versus the deeroticized Ulla of the League of German Girls (BDM), the neat columns of Hitler Youth versus the boisterous disorder of communist youth on the train platform; the buoyant enthusiasm of Heini's Hitler Youth Song versus the drunken slurring with which his father belts out the "Internationale" all serve as legitimation of Heini's intuitive preference for the mystified "others" over the communists. Eventually the nurturing, maternal qualities of Nazism supplant those of the family. In a plot line borrowed from Piel Jutzi's leftist film *Mutter Krausens Fahrt ins Glück* (Mother Krause's journey to happiness, 1929), Heini's mother commits suicide in despair and attempts to take her son with her. She dies, but Heini lives and is subsequently cared for by his (apparently parentless) Hitler Youth friends. As alluded to in the earlier quote, when the Hitler Youth leader expounds on the need for young boys to leave home, Nazism increasingly takes over the family's function; its compensatory appeal pervades all aspects of the private and public spheres and becomes a substitute for structural social change.

Hans Westmar's romantic, i.e., "true," socialism has the same compensatory function as Nazism in the preceding film. Westmar, a university student, gives up his studies to become a worker and begins successfully converting other workers to National Socialism. To a friend's remark that workers are the "real enemy," he responds: "We [the intellectuals] must fight side by side with the workers. . . . There must not be classes any more! We, too, are workers! We work with our heads—and our place is next to our brother who works with his hands." Westmar's comment of course recalls the much maligned solution to social conflict in Fritz Lang's *Metropolis*, its call for mediation of the "heart" between the "head" (management) and the "hand" (labor). Both films avoid any real confrontation of social problems by proposing a harmony guaranteed by good intentions, or what Axel Eggebrecht called an "unscientific sympathy-socialism."[10]

The importance of Berlin in early Nazi films lies in its function as *Heimat* of the past that needs to be retrieved, restored to its inherent function as the heart of "Germany"—which can only be achieved by a protagonist who has never lost *Heimat*, i.e., mental erectness and fortitude on the inside. The films thus have an anticipatory function, often pointing to a future when Germany will be "ours," when the forces of community will constitute a majority and not a threatened minority. Many early films thus end with the triumph of the Nazis in 1933 or at least on a hopeful note—as when one figure in *Um das Menschenrecht* remarks just before 1923, "The party I am thinking of doesn't exist yet." The films imply that only a movement like National Socialism can transform Berlin into a metaphor of community rather than one of dissolute modernity, can recuperate a Berlin that is pervaded by otherness. This quality of otherness stems, in the films examined thus far, from the masses that grew with the urbanization accompanying Germany's swift, late industrialization. The mass of Weimar Berlin takes essentially two forms: first the sexualized, degenerate, parasitic middle class of the *Bumslokal* paradigm, and second, the destructive, aggressive, likewise sexualized proletarian masses. Both of these urban phemonena are viewed in fascist discourse as feminized; especially the latter, which, as Klaus Theweleit has analyzed, is associated with a flood of uncontained sexuality. Gustave Le Bon's *The Crowd* (1895), which was an important source for Hitler's analysis of mass behavior, also links the masses to woman, since he sees both as unpredictable and capable of going to extremes. Given the increasing power of *both* the industrialized classes and the proletariat in modernity, subjugation of mass behavior became synonymous with self-preservation for the fascist male: "The haunting specter of a loss of power combines with fear of losing one's fortified and stable ego boundaries, which represent the sine qua non of a male psychology in that bourgeois order."[11] Since, as Patrice Petro has demonstrated,[12] twentieth-century writers have repeatedly envisioned Berlin as a woman, it is no surprise that the city should play a special role as an object waiting to be reconquered by the soldierly male.

   S.A. Mann Brand literally gives credit to the Nazi takeover for the reinstatement of "correct" gender roles in an amusing mininarrative involving Brand's middle-aged Nazi landlord Anton and his wife, Genoveva. Genoveva repeatedly forces the henpecked Anton into a "feminine" position by forcing him to don an apron and wash dishes while she attends meetings. Anton generously lends back to a destitute war-widow the money she pays him in rent, but Genoveva greedily insists on trying to squeeze money out of renters whether they can pay or not. Anton is thus forced to hide money in a box disguised to resemble a copy of *Mein Kampf*, which presumably Genoveva, as a member of the anti-Nazi Catholic Women's League, will never touch. The news that Hitler has been appointed chancellor provokes a transformation in Anton.

ANTON: Germany Awake!

GENOVEVA: [shrill] Anton! That gets on my nerves!

ANTON: Genoveva, in the Third Reich we can't be concerned with your nerves!

GENOVEVA: Anton!

ANTON: [interrupting]—Quiet! Anton has awakened!

In one of Nazi cinema's most blatant politicizations of gender, Anton's potency and, in psychoanalytic terms, Ideal-I is suddenly restored by secondary identification with Hitler, which enables him to cast off all traces of femininity and "handle" his astonished wife. This transformation, although couched in a humorous vignette, is another paradigm for the containment of otherness, the restoration of male cultural authority necessary for returning *Heimat* to Germany.

2. Films from the Early 1940s

What role then is left for Berlin or other cities to play once the Third Reich has been consolidated? Although the community of the people is represented as a fait accompli in films set *in* the Third Reich, various forces of *Zerrissenheit* or disunion are potentially ever-present. From about 1940 on, the narrative disruption by the enemy from within increasingly shifts to that of an external enemy. The borders of the homogeneous whole have been secured and the (juxtaposed) otherness so essential to the self-identity of the fascist character is displaced to the outside. Specifically, war becomes the force testing the endurance of the community, as illustrated by the topos of separation in many films from the period, such as Rolf Hansen's *Die große Liebe* (The great love, 1942), or Helmut Käntner's *Auf Wiedersehen, Franziska!* (Good bye, Franziska, 1943). In this context the city again finds filmic expression as a locale of collective experience, only increasingly this experience is limited by historical circumstances to the level of memory and/or media representation. In other words, the invocation of Berlin as community depends even less on spatial constraints and shifts, already on the level of diegesis, more into the imaginary.

This is clearly Berlin's role in Borsody's *Wunschkonzert* (1940), which directly exploits the city's emotional appeal. The second most popular film in the years 1940–42 (following only *Die große Liebe*), *Wunschkonzert* begins at the 1936 Berlin Olympics, where the two protagonists, Lieutenant Koch and Inge Wagner, meet and fall in love. Again a specific Berlin location becomes the film's spatial focal point, but again the specific location of the Olympic stadium acquires a far greater significance as a collective symbol of German unity. The opening shots of the film recall Riefenstahl's work and even use some documentary footage that also appears in her *Olympia* (1938): a montage sequence begins with a close-up of large bells, superimposed with the Olympic insignia, followed by close-ups of flags set against a sky with the cumulus clouds that earmark the Riefenstahl style. As in Riefenstahl's films, the beginning of *Wunschkonzert* conveys to the spectator a sense of participation in an awesome and monumental historical moment, particularly when the camera sweeps dramatically from the elevated flags down the poles to the city below, or suggests the enveloping nature of the event by traveling in a panoramic, circular motion around the decorated poles. An aerial shot travels into the stadium, capturing its concave shape as container of the popular euphoria, and then on outside, to the crowd flocking toward it. The images are underscored by music, beginning with the dramatic "Olympia Fanfare," which will play an important diegetic role by reuniting the protagonists later in the film.

The grandiose monumentality of the film's beginning quickly gives way to the comedy-of-errors style of its diegesis, as Inge's aunt frets over the tickets she inadvertently put in the wrong purse, which forces her to leave and clear the way for the chance meeting of the two protagonists. Koch has an extra ticket and offers it to Inge, who balks at the invitation until— significantly—Hitler arrives at the games, causing a great excitement in the crowd, which is magnetically drawn to the stadium. Inge abandons her hesitation and enters the stadium with Koch. The magnetic effect of Hitler and the Olympics is a catalyst for the magnetic attraction of the couple; Inge's decision to plunge into a *Gemeinschaft* (community) with Koch coincides with the community experience of the crowd. This correlation between public and private events is characteristic of *Wunschkonzert*, which follows multiple plot lines but always interweaves the fate of the individual protagonists with that of the nation. Correspondingly, the film's style oscillates between the monumental overt narration of the beginning and the more covert narration of the personalized story lines.

The Olympic spectacle in *Wunschkonzert* recalls Walter Benjamin's description of fascist art as executed *for* the masses but also *by* them. According to Benjamin, fascist politics placed "the participants as well as the audience under a spell, in which they appear to themselves as monumental, which means incapable of . . . independent action. Thus art strengthens the suggestive energies of its effect at the expense of the intellectual and enlightening energies."[13] Siegfried Kracauer's description of the techniques with which the Nazis hypostatized the masses applies equally to the film: "a) The masses are forced to see themselves everywhere (mass gatherings, mass pageants, etc.); they are always aware of themselves, often in the aesthetically seductive form of an ornament or an effective image. b) With the aid of the radio, the living room is transformed into a public place. c) All the mythical powers which the masses are capable of developing are exploited for the purpose of underscoring the significance of the masses as a mass. To many it then appears as though they were elevated in the masses above themselves."[14]

In *Wunschkonzert*, as in *Olympia*, the icon of the Olympic stadium functions as a transcendental anchorage of unity and collectivity in which the masses can indeed watch themselves and each individual can identify with the group, feel stabilized, and overcome the perceived ill effects of modern society. The stadium is a symbol both of containment—enhanced by its solidity and shape—and of ecstatic dissolution (*Entgrenzung*) within the contained boundaries, which allows the individual to merge safely with the whole. Indeed, Germany can presumably afford the presence of the "international" at the Olympics because it has become too strong to be threatened, and the presence of the other serves only to underscore Germany's physical and spiritual strength. During the opening Olympic march a variety of national teams are welcomed, but the film again breaks its diegetic flow and returns to the epic style of the beginning as Inge notices the arrival of the German athletes. Her euphoric exclamation—"There are the Germans!"—is followed by a shot of a perfect column of white undulating figures crosscut with shots of the frenetic crowd saluting and cheering. The aesthetic fusion of the athletes into a "mass ornament" (Kracauer) becomes another visual metaphor for public harmony. The scene plays with popular memory, invoking the "glory" of 1936 in a public now (in 1940) experiencing the effects of war. Throughout the entire film, the Olympics continue on the level of memory to stand for the unity of the nation *and* of the individual lovers, despite the dispersing effect of war. The games provide a vehicle through which the personal and the collective harmonize, are *gleichgeschaltet*.

Although *Wunschkonzert* presents the most tangible functionalization of Berlin as a locale of collectivity, one can draw analogies with other films. Karl Ritter's *Urlaub auf Ehrenwort* (Holiday on word of honor, 1937) tells the story of a World War I regiment that stops briefly in Berlin on its way to the front. Since most of the soldiers are from Berlin, the regiment's young captain allows them all a few hours' vacation before their departure—thus risking a court-martial, since he bears full responsibility if a single man fails to return on time. The men stem from a broad variety of social backgrounds, and are thus able to serve as a cross-section of German society. Here a platform at the Potsdam train station provides the specific location in which the captain tensely awaits the return of the men. The narrative suspense revolves around the question: will they return, or, in broader terms, will disunion or community prevail? The enigma is underscored by conventional crosscutting and by recurring icons of the clock and the sign "Potsdam Train Station." While the train platform appears to be a location marked by dispersal or absence throughout the film, the conclusion predictably reverses it into a locale of unity, when in the nick of time three missing men return, including a man who was supposed to be promoted to the leadership of the Communist Party. The dispersal of and in space proves not to be threatening in itself as long as it is contained, or balanced, by each individual's inner strength and secure identity—again the specificity of location is transcended by the general concepts of "Germany," fidelity, and the "cause."

Die große Liebe, which was seen by more Germans during and after the war than any other German film, likewise locates collective experience in an unlikely place: the Berlin revue hall dominated by Zarah Leander. The *Revue*, derived from "review" or military inspection, already embodies in its spectacle the notion of geometric, hierarchal containment or order. In what he calls a "reciprocal transference from the military to the theatrical sphere," Karsten Witte points out how the revue anticipates in the realm of entertainment a form that finds its expression in war: "The fact that 'girls' are on parade in these uniforms may heighten the erotic appeal, but actually degrades it through the very massive deindividualization of those girls. The director . . . inspects the revue girls as representatives of the female reserve army, who hold up the home front even as the war front of male armies is collapsing."[15] Of the three musical numbers Leander performs in the film, especially the last two, "That Won't Be the End of the World" and the climactic "I Know Someday a Miracle Will Happen," are musical invocations of community—which may be applied to the personal love story between Leander and her air force officer as well as to Germany's plight in the war. The sense of community is enhanced by the fact that constant shots and countershots allow the *Revue* film audience to watch its surrogate, the fictional audience, watching the unifying spectacle. Yet *Die große Liebe* does not make such a state of unity seem automatic, but rather thematizes it as an end result of human sacrifice. The film contrasts the electrifying and instantaneous community Leander achieves in her music with the slow and painful *process* by which her character learns to subordinate personal needs to those of the community. Until the end, she remains guilty of an unwillingness to sacrifice her public role to her man and hence to Germany's needs in the war. The film's narrative strategy is to rectify her indulgence in the needs of the "I" and reincorporate her into the dominant "we," a strategy presumably directed toward the female spectator at whom the film was aimed.

All three of these films are characterized by the dynamics of togetherness and separation. Yet all three stress the maintenance of spiritual togetherness by transcending the physical separation imposed by war. Nazi cinema of course mystifies war as a trial or natural catastrophe that, once withstood, culminates in a deeper fulfillment of personal and collective needs: "War is destiny. No legitimation for it is offered. Each and every one must bear this destiny and stand the test. But if he does, if he makes the required efforts and sacrifices, if he relinquishes his private wishes and interests, then everyone may believe that his efforts to ensure victory will bring him a bit closer to fulfilling his idea of happiness."[16]

According to this formula, all three films displace the real fulfillment of needs (i.e., an end to separation and war) into imaginary fulfillment. The second half of *Wunschkonzert*, set in 1939, is unique in its mobilization of

Berlin as an emotional value that transcends its spatial coordinates, and in its mystification of technology as the means by which this unification is achieved. The bulk of the narrative entails the separation of the central lovers as well as peripheral lovers and family members by the war. Yet the unity of the central and peripheral figures is restored by the popular Sunday afternoon radio program "Request Concert" broadcast from Berlin: first, Koch's request for the music of the '36 Olympics signals to Inge via the radio after three years of silence that he has indeed never forgotten her. (The personal history of the couple is significant, as they are first separated not by World War II, but by Koch's top-secret participation in the Legion Condor during the Spanish Civil War already in 1936. Their emotional trials thus anticipate those of the nation as a whole.) Second, the radio concert vicariously reunites all the film's characters in a grand spectacle at the film's conclusion. As in *Die große Liebe*, music serves to buoy the spirit of the dispersed individuals, only in *Wunschkonzert* the musical experience permeates Germany by means of the radio and is augmented by images. The images allow the aestheticization of politics to extend into an aestheticization of everyday life, which is designed to conceal or reconcile contradictions and tensions in everyday existence under Nazi rule. A militaristic march, for example, accompanies images of industriously working civilians linked by the conspicuous absence of young men, as when the camera dwells on a young woman sewing with her children, or when it tracks out from a radio speaker to reveal a young woman writing a letter next to a soldier's photograph. These images are constantly juxtaposed with those of the front, where the soldiers display equal good cheer. Each of these vignettes is informed by an aestheticized feeling of unity, even though its contents depict an act of sacrifice. Moreover, the concert's technologically dispersed music stands in for "real" community spirit, thus providing an excellent example for the fusion of four aspects of fascism: the aestheticization of politics, the importance of art and of technology, and the emphasis on community (including the "biologizing" of Weltanschauung).

The request concert thus provides a culmination of the harmony that surmounts all negative effects of the war, which appears amazingly free of violence. It articulates the people's experience *for* them—even tracing the cycles of life from birth, as the names of new babies born to soldiers at the front are announced (followed by a predictable montage of children and a lullaby sung by a children's chorus), to death, as the musician-soldier Schwarzkopf is remembered.

The subplot involving Schwarzkopf is thematically crucial to the film in its recurrent exploitation of the harmonizing function of music and "culture." Schwarzkopf's ideological significance is suggested by the fact that he is totally dispensable to the film's main story. Yet structurally he is one of the film's most important images, surfacing three times toward the beginning, middle, and end; thus spanning the entire narrative. He first appears at home playing a Beethoven sonata on the piano. Various characters who live in the same apartment building burst into the room talking and are admonished to reverent silence for the music. Although the figures' reactions differ in accordance with their social class (the comical baker is much more ill-at-ease in the presence of "culture" than the educated teacher), the mere utterance of the word *Beethoven* transports them all into a state of sentimental ecstasy—in a manner analagous to Werther's reaction to Lotte's exclamation "Klopstock!" 150 years earlier. In the midst of war, diverse individuals are made one by the experience of their common German cultural heritage, as they are elsewhere in the film by the Olympics and the radio.[17] Moreover, the scene invokes the cult of genius exploited in so many Nazi films from the same period—mention of the genius's name suffices to communicate a transcendent quality—any further discursive reference would be superfluous.

The second major scene involving Schwarzkopf is an emotional high point of the film—although again peripheral to the film's story. On the Polish front, Schwarzkopf has orders to await in a church the return of his comrades from battle. When the men are unable to find the meeting place due to intense fog, Schwarzkopf begins playing Max Reger's "Ein feste Burg" (A mighty fortress) on the organ to guide them, simultaneously exposing himself as an easy target for the enemy. Predictably, the men are saved and Schwarzkopf is killed by a grenade. Martin Luther's text to "A Mighty Fortress" invokes salvation through "Jesus Christ," just as the scene links Schwarzkopf with the statue of the crucified Christ visible in the church.[18] Again German culture serves as a magnet drawing individuals from all walks of life to one (literally) harmonious point—this time as a matter of survival. The appearance of Luther's "A Mighty Fortress" in a scene aestheticizing and sentimentalizing death is significant for a number of reasons. First, the metaphor of the mighty fortress is suggestive of the ideal and fortified ego-substitute Theweleit describes in his notion of the "armored" individual who is impervious to weakness. Second, "A Mighty Fortress," labeled by Heine a "battle song," had been recited during military actions since the seventeenth century, with its reference to God as "a good defense and weapon," or the final line "the empire (*Reich*) must remain ours," finding a new, more literal meaning. During World War I nationalistic leaders suggested that soldiers recite it as a form of "spiritual rearmament."[19] *Wunschkonzert* capitalizes on the Christian tradition in the scene, while again associating salvation through Christ with salvation through (and sacrifice for) the community of "Germany."

The final encounter with Schwarzkopf occurs during the sentimental conclusion of the radio concert, when he is spiritually reunited with his mother as the orchestra fulfills her request to play his favorite song. Again, the film interweaves the levels of the general and the specific: Schwarzkopf

functions paradigmatically for all fallen soldiers, and his mother for all be-
reft mothers. The displacement from the particular to the general simultaneously tends to be a displacement from the real to the imaginary. Again the
camera makes the most out of the maudlin scene as it tracks (to the sounds
of a male voice singing "Good Night, Mother") from the ubiquitous radio
speaker past Schwarzkopf's empty piano to a photograph of him, and finally to the mother sitting at the same table and with the same stance as in
the Beethoven scene. The Schwarzkopf scenes contribute to the significance
of music and technology by blending art, death or sacrifice, and memory
nostalgically into a vague notion of unity.

It is significant that *Wunschkonzert*, which begins by recycling footage of
the Olympics to revive the spirit of prewar Nazi Germany — and thus locates the collective experience of Germany in a single physical location,
however symbolic this may be — concludes by allowing the location of Berlin to transcend its physical boundaries, as had the newsreel footage of the
Olympics or Riefenstahl's 1938 film. The film does not take technology for
granted, but thematizes it and turns it into a conscious and ideologically important means of transcending space, as in the recurrent close-up shots of
radios in the film.[20] The collective, the imaginary *Gemeinschaft*, or community of listeners, created by the spectacle located in a specific place in Berlin
need no longer be physically limited to the city; technological progress allows the emotional value of Berlin, the center, to penetrate the living room
of the dead musician's mother, the hospital, the air force headquarters, all of
Germany. The displacement of space/geography into an imaginary realm
reconciles the opposition of city and country, center and periphery. Hence
the levels of the particular place and the general space, of the personal and
the public interwoven by the narrative are characterized by an increasingly
abstract experience of togetherness, of wholeness created by the media.
Technology helps synchronize emotions, reflecting the modern antimodernism peculiar to National Socialism.

Technology therefore remains a *means* toward a greater end: the transformation of an actual experience into an imaginary one, which is in turn a
prerequisite for the aestheticization of experience. Aestheticized experience
displaces need fulfillment into the imaginary, provides compensatory satis-
faction, or as Benjamin put it, "helps the masses find their expression, but
by no means their rights."[21] The experience of the Olympics or even that of
Schwarzkopf playing Beethoven are "real" occurrences, but their importance lies in their value as imaginary experiences — both for the characters in
the film and for its viewers. As imaginary experience, the Olympics or a
radio concert can be participated in both by the people actually there and by
those for whom participation is limited to technological reproduction,
which again includes the film audience. The sense of community evoked is
as "real" for one group as for the other, is as successful in displacing the

fulfillment of needs into the imaginary. The narrative trajectory of *Wunsch-konzert* allows the Olympic experience with its relative confinement to a specific locale to represent an earlier stage of aestheticization, while the radio concert with its increased dispersal and abstractness represents a more advanced stage.

Wunschkonzert is symptomatic of National Socialism's promise that private and public happiness are one and the same. It illustrates Benjamin's analysis of how National Socialism mobilizes technology to penetrate all spheres of the personal with the collective, and to reinforce this penetration with the aestheticization of the political and everyday life as well as the politicization of the aesthetic sphere. But the aestheticization of politics, i.e., the replacing of real experiences by imaginary ones, is not the only strategy of fascist narrative discourse. From the eighteenth century on, modern thinking has been a historical or historicophilosophical one, projecting improvements into an idealized future. As Jean François Lyotard has argued, the idea of a better future can never be a representation of something real. Projections of a better state of affairs into the future are therefore always imaginary or aesthetic in nature. The Nazis exploit this elective affinity between the aesthetic and the historicophilosophical: first, by projecting the reconciliation of the imaginary and the real into the future (this they have in common with other popular philosophies of history), and, second, by fusing the abstract level of history with everyday experiences.

I by no means intend to imply an equation between Nazism, which relies on the concept of "eternal" entities transcending history (or "calculates according to millennia"),[22] and, for example, Marxism, which is of course based on a philosophy of history. National Socialism merely *invokes* history and indeed restricts such invocations to either the prehistory of the Nazi State, which is a history of struggle, as in the early films I discussed, or to an anticipation of a conclusion to the war, as in the later films. In the latter sense, the happy conclusion of *Wunschkonzert* (and of other films portraying the trials of wartime separation) has an anticipatory function. Like the famous concluding shot of *Die große Liebe*, in which the reunited lovers look up toward distant planes in anticipation of the "miracle" Leander sings of, *Wunschkonzert*'s end promises the reunification of real individuals separated by a real war.

Wunschkonzert differs from *Die große Liebe*, however, in its fixation of a specific point in time, the *beginning* of the war in 1939, as the narrative point of reunification and resolution. In compensating for current suffering, the film links an earlier and fictitious reconciliation (1936–1940) with a projected real one (1940 to the end of the war), thus envisioning a happy end clearly premature for the population as a whole, yet just as clearly linked to the spirit of *Gemeinschaft* allegedly shared by that population. Hence the displacement from real experience to imaginary community from which these films gain their ideological substance is supplemented with a second, related one: a temporal displacement into a future in which the imaginary experience will become actual.

With their anticipatory promise, all the films discussed have in common the social function Benjamin ascribes to fascist theatrics: "the eternal preservation of the status quo . . . is accomplished in fascist art by paralyzing the participants or spectators, who could change this status quo."[23]

NOTES

1. Journalists in Nazi films, especially when set in the Weimar Republic, often appear as cold-blooded sensationalists who disseminate prejudice and distortion. They are usually coded as physical weaklings, as "little runts" wearing glasses. This no doubt relates to the fact that many large publishing houses previous to the Nazi era were owned by Jews, but relates more fundamentally to the anticapitalism and antiliberalism that in turn underlay anti-Semitism. Compare, for example, *Ohm Krüger, Gold, Urlaub auf Ehrenwort* (Holiday on word of honor), or *Die Rothschild*.

2. Hanno Möbius demonstrates a similar dependence of a Berlin newspaper on a small-town protagonist in *Grosstadtmelodie* (Big city melody, 1943): "Clearly the provincial is valorized: . . . the city is dependent on the provincial woman." Möbius, "Heimat im nationalsozialistischen Film," *Augen-Blick: Marburger Hefte zur Medienwissenschaft* 5 (1988): 39.

3. Klaus Theweleit, *Male Fantasies*, vol. 2, trans. Erica Carter and Chris Turner (Minneapolis: University of Minnesota Press, 1989), 77–94.

4. Compare the portrayal in *Togger* of a conference at the ruthless, monopolistic Reuter corporation, which tries to secure domination of the international market. The scene consists of a long series of corporation board members giving speeches, each in a different language.

5. Möbius, "Heimat im nationalsozialistischen Film," 34.

6. English translation with some modifications from David Welch, *Propaganda and German Cinema. 1933–45* (Oxford, 1983), 69.

7. Compare the portrayal of a communist worker as a Christlike martyr in the second Nazi Bismarck biography, *Die Entlassung* (The dismissal, 1942). A crucial distinction must be made here between the often sympathetic portrayal in Nazi film of the misguided leftist worker (S.A. Man Brand's father is similarly characterized) and communist leadership. The latter, often depicted as Russian, Jewish, or both, appear invariably as inhumane despots treating their constituents "like children" and with no time for "silly sentimentalities" (*Gefühlsduseleien*). When a German communist objects in *S.A. Mann Brand* to cold-blooded murder, his Soviet colleague responds sarcastically: "Still so German?", equating "Germanness" with compassion.

8. Karl Prümm, *Die Literatur des soldatischen Nationalismus der zwanziger Jahre (1918–1933). Grundideologie und Epochenproblmatik*, 2 vols. (Kronberg/Taunus, FRG, 1974).

9. Ibid., 35.

10. Axel Eggebrecht, "Metropolis," *Die rote Fahne*, 1.12.1927. Despite rhetoric to the contrary, Nazi film continues to portray class differences, only it ceases to refer to them as such. Everyone is united by the community of the Volk and differences in education, cultivation, or wealth appear as natural as they do in eighteenth-century drama. As in the latter genre, the lower classes display unwavering solidarity with their superiors, as well as providing comic relief. In *Pour le Mérite*, two proletarian soldiers beg to stay with their Captain Prank during peacetime, and the three perpetuate the male bonding of wartime as well as the same hierarchical order of military bureaucracy, with the educated bourgeois Prank clearly functioning as

leader. Similar constellations exist in *Urlaub auf Ehrenwurt* and *Wunschkonzert* where the working-class men are subservient to their respective superiors.

11. Andreas Huyssen, "Mass Culture as Woman: Modernism's Other," *After the Great Divide* (Bloomington, Ind., 1986), 53.

12. Patrice Petro, "Modernity and Mass Culture in Weimar: Contours of a Discourse on Sexuality in Early Theories of Perception and Representation," *New German Critique* 40 (Winter 1987): 115–18.

13. Walter Benjamin, "Pariser Brief I" (1936), *Gesammelte Schriften* 3 (Frankfurt/Main, 1980): 489.

14. Siegfried Kracauer, "Masse und Propaganda. Eine Untersuchung über die faschistische Propaganda" (Paris, 1939), trans. from Karsten Witte, "Introduction to Kracauer's 'The Mass Ornament,' " *New German Critique* 5 (Spring 1975): 64.

15. Karsten Witte, "Visual Pleasure Inhibited: Aspects of the German Revue Film," *New German Critique* 24–25 (fall/winter 1981–82): 238.

16. Klaus Schönekäs and Martin Loiperdinge, "Die Produktion filmischer Zeichen im Dienste der nationalsozialistischen Propaganda—Dargestellt am Film 'Die große Liebe,' " unpublished paper for the Münchner Semiotik-Kongress (Feb. 1, 1984), n.p.

17. Another example for the exploitation of the German/Austrian cultural canon is the overture to Mozart's *Marriage of Figaro*, played in the request concert with Eugen Jochum as guest conductor. It serves via the radio as diegetic and nondiegetic accompaniment to the resolution of a misunderstanding that clouds the reconciliation of Inge and Koch—thus picking up on the *Lustspiel* tone of Mozart's opera while exploiting the German-Austrian cultural heritage.

18. The status of musicians is ambivalent, as pointed out by Schönekäs and Loiperdinger: "Musicians, especially of keyboard instruments, are a peculiarily ambivalent sign, on the one hand for softness, weakness, and unfitness for life (*Lebensuntüchtigkeit*); on the other hand, for genius and as bearers of 'German culture.' " Compare also the chapter on *Friedemann Bach* (1941) in my dissertation, "The Never-Was as History: Portrayals of the Eighteenth Century in the National Socialist Film" (Minneapolis: University of Minnesota, 1985).

19. Lothar Schmidt, " 'Und wenn die Welt voll Teufel wär'. Zu Martin Luthers 'Ein feste burg ist unser Gott,' " in *Gedichte und Interpretationen. Renaissance und Barock*, ed. Volker Meid (Stuttgart, 1982), 66.

20. Compare also the scene in *Die große Liebe* (The great love) in which Hanna (Leander) sits in a movie theater and, viewing battle scenes, is moved to think about the reality of her Lieutenant Wendlandt.

21. Walter Benjamin, "The Work of Art in the Age of Mechanical Reproduction" (1936), in *Illuminations*, trans. Harry Zohn (New York, 1969), 241. I have modified the translation.

22. Benjamin, "Pariser Brief I" (see note 13), 489.

23. Ibid.

CHAPTER 9

Lyric Poetry in Berlin since 1961

Harald Hartung

In the 1950s, a young German poetry lover was interested in two poets, whose names begin with *B*: Benn and Brecht. He might have preferred one poet over the other; but because he was open and flexible, he was at least irritated by the other, whom he liked less or consequently even rejected. One's love for poetry could create a problem, perhaps even an unsolvable one, an aporia. Aesthetically, one could enjoy both Brecht and Benn, but their philosophies of life—or, one might say later, their ideologies—were incompatible. Yet, one would have liked to believe in both and to accept both: artistic purity as well as political engagement—Gottfried Benn's dictum about the modern poem as the absolute poem, the poem without faith, without hope, addressed to no one; but also Bertolt Brecht's verse "Auf einen chinesischen Theewurzellöwen" (To a Chinese tea root lion).

> Die Schlechten fürchten deine Klaue
>
> Die Guten freuen sich deiner Grazie
>
> Derlei
>
> Hörte ich gern
>
> Von meinem Vers.[1]

Aporia means impassability, the absence of a path. But perhaps there was a path, a path out. It led to a city, whose name also begins with a *B* and in which, coincidentally or not, both writers happened to live. When the young man of whom I am speaking came to Berlin for the first time, both writers were already dead; and as he prepared to live and work there, the one state closed the previously open borders and erected a wall between the west and east sections of the city; and the young man who wrote poems and thought about poems now had to see how he would get along in Berlin— even without the writers B. and B.

To be sure, the construction of the wall in 1961 had nothing to do with lyric poetry, yet in a special way it brought to a head the problem of writing poems, writing poems in this city. The erection of the wall was not the first political event to do this, and certainly not the last. The year 1961 in the title of this essay means more than a specific time in history—and this leads me to my thesis: Lyric poetry in Berlin is different from lyric poetry in Munich, Cologne, Heidelberg, or in the Bavarian Forest—perhaps not categorically different, but different in important nuances. It is different because in Berlin the German reality presents itself differently than in the Federal Republic of Germany—differently, but not necessarily more clearly, more precisely. As a microcosm of the division of Germany, Berlin can blind one; distance can be useful, politically as well as aesthetically.

Lyric poetry in Berlin might be different because there are not only two political, but also two literary systems in the city, a West Berlin and an East Berlin system. But if the poems written on both sides of the wall differ from one another, what they have in common is that they are written in the presence of the wall. This or that half of the city views itself as a metropolis in its own right, either by itself or in a tacit connection with its separated part, and views the rest of the country as provincial. Or is that, too, just a self-deception, an especially insidious one, that the Berlin writer clings to? For one loves nothing more than one's deceptions, one's errors.

I formulate theses, only to relativize them immediately; here my intention is to allow texts to speak. But because I would also like to preserve some distinctiveness for Berlin, and to attach something like hope to the Berlin situation, I shall return to Benn once again. At the end of his famous "Berlin Letter" of July 1948, he speaks of how much he has loved and borne the splendor and misery of the city, and continues, "Yes, one could even predict a future for it: tensions penetrate its sobriety, interferences and phase differences mar its clarity, some ambiguity sets in, an ambiguity from which centaurs or amphibians are born."[2] Forty years have passed since Benn wrote this sentence. The future he speaks of has become the past. Have there been tensions within the sobriety, interferences in the clarity of poetry? Is there an ambiguity within the lyric poetry of Berlin? And where are its centaurs and amphibians?

Questions of a writer, questions cast in poetic language: I will not translate them into the language of the Germanist, into concepts of literary theory. I am not writing as a scholar of literature, but as a critic and author of poems. I have divided my exposition into three sections, three periods. In them the social and the literary come together and act upon one other. I shall refer to discussions and stylistic trends of lyric poetry, but also to individual authors and poems.

1. Between the Wall and the Great Coalition or:
From the Experiential Poem to the Political Poem

On November 17, 1960, not quite a year before the building of the wall, at the International Congress of Writers of the German Language, a conference on "Lyric Poetry Today" took place in the West Berlin Congress Hall. Walter Höllerer, the conference director, moderated the readings and discussions. Participants were Helmut Heißenbüttel from Stuttgart, Franz Mon from Frankfurt, Peter Rühmkorf from Hamburg; and from Berlin Günter Grass, Günter Bruno Fuchs, and Rudolf Hartung. The positions expressed at the conference were contradictory and incompatible. Heißenbüttel and Mon pleaded for work on linguistic material, for the positions of experimental and concrete poetry. Franz Mon formulated a theory based on the concept of the secondary system developed by the sociologist Hans Freyer: "Real is only that which is expressed in a systematic way."[3] He also could have quoted Benn's lines.

> Eine Wirklichkeit ist nicht vonnöten,
>
> ja, es gibt sie gar nicht, wenn ein Mann
>
> aus dem Urmotiv der Flairs und Flöten
>
> seine Existenz beweisen kann.[4]

But too much emotion was attached to Benn; indeed he had coined the concept of the lyrical laboratory, but he was not an experimental poet. Helmut Heißenbüttel spoke of his texts as "demonstrations"—demonstrations of linguistic possibilities; the thought of what students would do a few years later most likely did not occur to him at that time. Other participants opposed these positions, especially those who lived and worked in Berlin.

Günter Grass mocked the "experimental writers" as a "chorus of small letter writers" and as "continual tenants" who "reside near silence." He pleaded, ironically of course, for the "occasional poem" and recommended abstaining from all legumes, as soon as a poem lies "in the air," or as an alternative the purchase of green herring. He also told of an occasion or experience, fictive or real: "So I went to the tailor to be measured for my suit. The tailor took my measurements and asked me, 'Do you dress left or right?' I lied and said, 'Left.' " According to Grass the following four-liner, "Die Lüge" (The lie), arose from this occasion.

> Ihre rechte Schulter hängt,
>
> sagte mein Schneider.
>
> Weil ich rechts die Schultasche trug,
>
> sagte ich und errötete.[5]

Here, no doubt, Brecht's laconic style was a model, as was Keuner's comic naïveté. The poem was concerned with reality, not with word games, even though Grass worked with the ambiguity of "right" and "left." The lyrical anecdote showed a reality with hidden political double-talk: The right shoulder does not hang because of carrying the satchel, but rather because the German has a tendency to submit him- or herself, to being knuckled under — and that of course by the *right*. But Grass, who had just become famous through his novel *Tin Drum* began to dress *left* — not to speak of the slightly obscene double-meaning of the tailor's question — a moderate Social Democratic *Left*, for which he also appeared in political rallies in favor of Willy Brandt after 1965.

Günter Bruno Fuchs was even more connected to Berlin than Günter Grass — for Fuchs it meant more precisely ties with the Kreuzberg district, with its large blocks of tenements and their courtyards, and its *Kneipen*, or bars. A "drinker, poet, wood-carver," his friend Robert Wolfgang Schnell once called him. Fuchs was more than a Kreuzberg eccentric; from the commonplace and the fairy tale, from the courtyard and the circus, tavern pieties and a love of reality, he created a poetic cosmos, inhabited by children, drinkers, and dreamers and their adversaries — also of a fairy-tale wickedness — policemen and generals. The cellar child with whom Fuchs identified was on the "run from cops and robbers" all his life, and in vain. His initiatives toward political engagement and social criticism remained closely bound to this fairy-tale and children's world. During that Congress Hall discussion in 1960, Günter Bruno Fuchs addressed with remarkable clarity the social responsibility of poetry. "I try to ferret out a text that is rugged, that can stand up on a pamphlet," he said, and he wished for a text that "renounces making the best of a bad job, and above all is intact enough to be able to assert its own existence between the predominant ideologies."[6] The poem he read at the end of the discussion, "Tageslauf eines dicken Mannes" (A day in the life of a fat man), is one of his most beautiful and characteristic poems, and at the same time something like a portrait of the author, who died in 1977.

> Morgens
> verdingt er sich bei den Kindern am Buddelplatz.
> Er beginnt seine Arbeit und sagt: Liebe Kinder,
> dieser Bauch ist kein Bauch, sondern der große Bimbula.
> Dann lachen die Kinder, schlagen Purzelbäume und sagen:
> Bitte, großer Berg, morgen mußt du wiederkommen.
>
> Mittags
> macht er seine Urwaldfreunde nach.

Er trommelt dann auf seinen Bauch
und manchmal springt er schweren Herzens
auf den Rücken eines Generals und sagt:
Wenn du meinen Bauch mit einer Trommel verwechselst,
so ist das deine eigne klägliche Sache! Dieser Bauch
ist nämlich der große Berg Bimbula
dessen Schönheit du nie erkennen wirst.

Abends
wird er immer sehr traurig.
Er setzt sich unter die Sterne
und trinkt zehn Liter Himmelsbier.
Manche Leute haben ihn singen gehört—
er singt dann ganz einfältig, so einfältig
wie es ihm niemand zugetraut hätte:
Mutter, ach Mutter, mich hungert![7]

"To assert its own existence between the ruling ideologies"—this definition by Günter Bruno Fuchs characterizes very precisely the position of the Berlin poem in the following years—particularly after the erection of the wall. Lyric poetry kept its distance from the official politics that had led to the wall—distance from those of the West as well as of the East. But this also meant that the wall itself was seldom the subject of a poem, it was not *named*—but its consequences often were: the situation of the insulated, western part of the city, whose existence was now threatened. The poetic view was aimed at everyday life, at social detail. Something like a Berlin regionalism developed, for which the Kreuzberg authors, Günter Bruno Fuchs and Robert Wolfgang Schnell, had already done groundwork.

This regionalism is expressed even in the titles of Rolf Haufs's poetry collections, published in the 1960s. *Straße nach Kohlhasenbrück* (Street to Kohlhasenbrück) appeared in 1961. Its title refers to a street on the southwest border of West Berlin leading to Steinstücken, an exclave in the territory of the GDR until 1972; Haufs lived there at that time. In 1964, the volume *Sonntage in Moabit* (Sundays in Moabit) followed. Moabit is not only a district of Berlin, but the site of a prison, where the author had spent fifty-three days in detention, pending investigation after a denunciation. A later poem, "At the Consulate," treats Haufs's interrogation there.

Sie waren nicht fragt die Miss
Mitglied der Kommunistischen Partei
Nein sag ich da hab abgeschworn

> Dem Zeugs von Marx und Compagnie
> In dreiundfünfzig Nächten Moabit[8]

These ironic-sarcastic lines are found in the volume *Vorstadtbeichte* (Suburban Confessions) of 1967. This, too, is a regionalist title. In several poems of these years Haufs portrays the delusions in knowledge that stem from what is called the front-city mentality. That Haufs did not forget the broader perspective of the Berlin problem is shown in an early poem, "Letter to G. S.," which has as its theme his 1960 emigration from Düsseldorf to Berlin and portrays the effects of the wall. Haufs ironically contrasts himself with Joseph Goebbels.

> . . . der fortging ohne den Segen seiner armen Mutter
> Fortging wie Haufs ein Menschenalter später fortging
> Immer fortging nach Steinstücken wo auch wieder
>   Kiefernbüsche
> An denen die Volkspolizei das Wasser abschlägt
> Und in Schach hält marschierende Renter und wissende
>   Embryos
> Aber ich weiß daß du mich hörst immer mich hörst
> Wie ich die Stimme der Interzonenzüge dreimal täglich
> Und wieder dreimal täglich höre und den wütenden
>   Zisch der Dampfkessel
> Und das süße ach süße Gewisper: Haltet bereit seid
>   bereit
> Haltet bereit euren Personalausweis und daß niemand
>   niemand mir
> Daß mir niemand niemand den Zug verläßt
> Denn es warten auf euch Maschinengewehre und finstere
>   Blicke
> Aber ich fürchte du tauchst dein Haupt in Tränen
> In einer Waschschüssel gekauft bei Woolworth
>   Schadowstraße
> Billig gekauft weil für Gedichte nichts gezahlt wird
>   für Gedichte
> Um die wir ganze Nächte trauern während andere unsern
>   Frauen nachsehn . . . [9]

That is an excerpt from a longer poem—unusually long for Haufs, also unusually long for the lyric poetry of the early 1960s, which favored short, laconic verse. The sociopolitical development mentioned here evidently was no longer to be captured only in short snapshots, but tended toward a broader treatment of perspective and subject matter.

The one who recognized this trend very early was Walter Höllerer, organizer of the most important literary events of the 1960s, literary theorist, lyric poet, and theorist of lyric poetry. He acquainted the German audience with impulses from the United States, published in his anthology *Young American Poetry* (1961) — especially with Olsen's theories of "projective verse," the poem as "field-composition," and his interpretation of "form as expansion of content." That did not remain without influence on Höllerer's "Thesis on the Long Poem," which appeared in *Akzente* in 1965 and led to intense and weighty discussions. Two of these theories, which emphasized the sociopolitical moment of the "long" poem deserve special attention.

> The long poem is, at the present moment, already political in its form; it demonstrates a move against the limitation into compartments. It runs counter to petty boundaries of country and spirit. Dead ends here as well as there: in the GDR — idealists entangled by materialism; in the FRG — materialists bent by idealism. The long poem has enough breath to accomplish negations, to clear away infusions of Marx and Hegel, to break down entrenched thought, and obstinately to find new expression to new situations.

And elsewhere in the essay he writes:

> Anyone who writes a long poem establishes a perspective for himself so that he can view the world with greater freedom, he opposes the status quo and lack of breath. The republic that sets itself free is discernible.[10]

That was a plea for a lyrical realism that was aimed not simply at mirroring, but rather at *changing*. *Long* with reference to a poem also meant a new quality: Through its expansion the poem should make a new view of reality possible, include the observed, the elements of a moment in a process. The politically vague statement, "The republic that sets itself free becomes discernible," was meant in a utopian way, far from current politics.

The real "republic" did not free itself. Rather — in the Erhard era — it was faced with an economic and political crisis. To be sure, the parliamentary elections (Bundestagswahl) of September 1965 endorsed Ludwig Erhard as federal chancellor, but in the following year the "Great Coalition" of the SPD (Social Democratic Party) and CDU (Christian Democratic Union) was established: Kurt Georg Kiesinger (CDU) became federal chancellor, Willy Brandt (SPD) foreign minister. In terms of realist politics, this meant stabilization; for the SPD it meant a share in the power for the first time and therefore a chance for the future. For the intellectuals, the writers, the students — or at least for many of them — this was a weak compromise, even a betrayal. Under the initiative of Günter Grass, an "election office of German writers" had been formed in West Berlin in August 1965. Lyric poets such as Nicolas Born, F. C. Delius, Peter Härtling, and Rolf Haufs also assisted with it. It did not achieve any noticeable increase in votes, however, and it protested in vain that the chancellor of the new coalition government was not from the SPD.

Anyone who followed events at that time remembers how great was the disappointment of the intellectual left over the SPD coup. But of course it led to the party's leadership of the government in 1969. With the "Great Coalition," the debate over the Emergency Powers Act (*Notstandsgesetz*), the atomic armament of the military, and the protests against the war in Vietnam, radicalization set in, leading to the student protests of 1967–68. Political lyric poetry, agitprop, pop literature are the corresponding literary catch-words.

2. The Years of Political Protest: From Political Lyric Poetry to the New Subjectivity

At the end of May 1967, Erich Fried called me from London and asked if I would write a reply to an article by Peter Härtling. In the journal *Monat*, Härtling had posed the question: "Can poems be written about Vietnam?" and had answered no. I thought differently at that time and wrote a reply, "Poetry and Vietnam." While I was writing, the Shah of Iran visited Berlin, and I was among the demonstrators in front of the German Opera, where he saw a performance of *The Magic Flute*. I went home to work on my article before the police intervened against the demonstrators. That evening, student Benno Ohnesorg was shot by a police officer. After Ohnesorg's death, the formation of the so-called extraparliamentary opposition (APO) began. It experienced its peak in the demonstrations after the assassination attempt on Rudi Dutschke and in the protests against the Springer newspapers, which had slandered the protesters. "Was a revolution imminent?" the *Spiegel* asked the authors. Opinions were divided.

The Parisian uprising of May 1968 wanted to bring fantasy into power, and Herbert Marcuse believed that the aesthetic potential of the revolts would become lasting political practice. A "New Sensitivity" had become a political power, he believed. We will again encounter the expression, "New Sensitivity," not in politics, but in poetry. How did lyric poetry react to all of these events? At first with a surge of political lyric poetry, but then — or so it appeared — with silence. At the beginning, there was a hailstorm of political poems: against the Vietnam war, the police, the Springer newspapers, against capitalism, the system in general. From the protest poem it went to agitprop texts in lyrical form, finally to the so-called combat texts: someone seriously suggested using texts printed on sharp-edged sheet metal as "weapons." Disappointment was inevitable: Poems are not weapons, they do not change the world—at least not as one had hoped. That realization was the basis of a counterattack on the poems: because they could not change the world, there should be no more poems. Whoever still wrote poems was considered suspicious, at best harmless. Whoever read poems aloud publicly in Berlin and elsewhere had to justify oneself: Who are you writing for? Who is your target group? "I'm not aiming at persons," I used to say, but the people were not satisfied. Why did they even come to readings? Probably because they were still interested in poetry—as in something forbidden, a vice!

Enzensberger's journal, the *Kursbuch*, proclaimed the "death of literature" in 1968. Two years later this proclamation was no longer taken so seriously. Enzensberger by then had returned to the writing of lyric poetry himself. He admitted that at that time he had "shot at sparrows with canons" and wrote, "Sleeping, taking a deep breath, writing: /that is almost not a crime."[11] How accurately this "almost" was set—addressed to disappointed comrades. And how profoundly and beautifully literary writing was again raised to the level of human necessity: "Sleeping, taking a deep breath, writing." All that sounds strange today perhaps, *tempi passati*. It has all become history.

The rehabilitation of poetry occurred on the political left. There some authors had continued writing all along, we can safely say, had continued to write poetry. Another representative example in Berlin is Nicolas Born. He was not dogmatic, for he lived from writing—not only financially, but also as a human being. He was not an opportunist, but he could not divorce himself from the movement of the *Zeitgeist*. So the development between politicizing and "New Sensitivity" can very precisely be demonstrated in his poetry. Born was from the Ruhr area and had been living in Berlin since the mid-1960s. During the last years of his life he worked in the country, in Lüchow-Dannenberg, without ever losing contact with Berlin. He died of lung cancer in 1979. His development falls into three stages: politicization; utopia and "New Sensitivity"; landscape and ecology.

Born prefaced his first volume of poetry, *Marktlage* (State of the market, 1967) with a programmatic declaration: "Get rid of the old poetics, which is only instruction for poeticizing; get rid of symbol, metaphor, of all vessels of meaning. . . . The poems should be raw, at least not polished; and the raw, nonartificial formulation, I believe, will become poetry again, which . . . follows as a direct consequence of the writer dealing directly with things, relationships, environment, that means he doesn't create poetry with words."[12] Born did not deny the influence of William Carlos Williams, the influence of Charles Olson: the notion that form is no more than an extension of content—a conception that was apparently conveyed by Walter Höllerer. In his second volume, *Wo mir der Kopf steht* (Where my inclinations are, 1970), Born showed interest in the concept of openness and quotes Frank O'Hara as a poetic authority, whose *Lunch Poems*—which appeared in 1979 in a translation by Rolf Dieter Brinkmann—had an enormous influence on young German lyric poets at that time.

The example I cite of Born's politicizing appears to have little to do with all that. It has become so dated that the contemporary appeal it found at that time requires an explanation. In 1968, the Springer newspapers had called the protesting students a "small radical minority." Born's text, "Berlin Paraphrases," turns the formulations around dialectically. It begins:

> Unsere Geduld ist am Ende.
> Wir haben es satt uns von einer Mehrheit
> auf der Nase herumtanzen zu lassen.
> Wir haben es satt die Stadt vom Radau-
> verleger beleidigen zu lassen
> (wenn er Berlin unappetitlich findet
> soll er doch in den Osten gehen).
> Wir haben es satt uns das Demonstrationsrecht
> rationieren zu lassen. . . .[13]

This simple reversal must have appeared too simplistic, too shrill, to Born. It was no longer in accord with his more complex concept of truth. It was only for this reason, and not because he wanted to practice self-censorship, that he chose not to include it in his later collection, *Gedichte 1967–1978*.

Born distanced himself more and more from the political poem. He wrote: "The socially critical author holds a subscription to misery. He reacts vicariously for his public. He cannot help becoming a habitual critic and a critical partner of power." In contrast to this, there is Born's utopian concept of poetry: "Our better possibilities must be better displayed and represented. . . . The mad system that is reality must be wrested of its monopolistic claim on representation. . . . Everybody is a dangerous utopia when he rediscovers his wishes, longings, and imaginations under the crammed catalog of reality."[14]

The program is one thing, the poems are another. Reality is not given up in them—reality as everyday Berlin reality, with family, movie theater, eroticism, news, etc. But this reality is superelevated by the introduction of the "discoverer" and the "pilot"—an idea Born obtained from American pop lyrics and from Brinkmann's 1968 book of poetry, *Die Piloten* (The pilots). "Das Auge des Piloten ist voll Zärtlichkeit/ Wir überfliegen den Wendekreis der Realität" (The eye of the pilot is full of tenderness / we are flying over the turning point of reality), we read in one of the poems. One of the shorter poems, "Drei Wünsche" (Three wishes), may serve as example.

> Sind Tatsachen nicht quälend und langweilig?
> Ist es nicht besser drei Wünsche zu haben
> unter der Bedingung daß sie allen erfüllt werden?
> Ich wünsche ein Leben ohne große Pausen
> in denen die Wände nach Projektilen abgesucht werden
>   ein Leben das nicht heruntergeblättert wird von
>   Kassierern.
> Ich wünsche Briefe zu schreiben in denen ich ganz
>   enthalten bin—
> wie weit würde ich herumkommen ohne Gewichtsverlust.
> Ich wünsche ein Buch in das ihr alle vorn hineingehen
>   und hinten herauskommen könnt.
> Und ich möchte nicht vergessen daß es schöner ist
> dich zu lieben als dich nicht zu lieben.[15]

It is a communicative poem. The author is seeking nearness, the sympathetic agreement of the reader. He begins with rhetorical questions: "Facts, are they not painful and boring?" The famous three wishes allowed us by the fairy are put under *one* condition: that they be fulfilled for all. A life without war and exploitation; a full, fulfilled subjectivity; and the book, that is a literature that does not differentiate between life and art: those are the three wishes this poem articulates. It thematizes a demand for happiness, which is always contained in poetry. Yet while poetic work understands itself for the most part aesthetically and is occasionally a *promesse du bonheur*, Born insists on material fulfillment in life. In this regard this poem is still a political poem—as are most of the poems from *Das Auge des Entdeckers* (The eye of the discoverer). "It is important to stand up," one reads in the remarks at the end of this collection, "even if falling always looks better than getting up."[16]

In his last years, ecological themes became important for Nicolas Born. This was influenced by his move to the country, but also by his participation in the discussions over the atomic waste depot and treatment plant in Gorleben. He envisioned with horror a benumbed world, plundered by technology. Some of his poems of the seventies warned of a bunkered-in, drained existence, others searched for the remnants of nature—like the long poem "Notizen aus dem Elbholz" (Notes from the Elbe Woods), or "Entsorgt" (Drained). The latter was marked by a concentrated negativism, a sorrow without comfort.

> Die Trauer ist jetzt trostlos
> die Wut ohne Silbe, all die maskierte Lebendigkeit
> all die würgende Zuversicht
> Gras stürzt, die Gärten stürzen, niemand
> unterm Geldharnisch fühlt die Wunde
> entsorgt zu sein von sich selbst.
> Kein Gedicht, höchstens das Ende davon.
> Menschenvorkommen
> gefangen in verruchter Vernunft, die sich
> nicht einmal weiß vor wissenschaft. . . .

And in opposition to that, the view of a remnant of nature, changing into a vision, into stammering:

> Gekippte Wiesenböschung, Engel, ungewisse,
> warme Menschenkörper und Verstehn
> Gärten hingebreitet, unter Zweigen Bänke . . .
> . . . Schatten . . . Laub . . . im Wind gesprochen
> . . . Samen.[17]

I have written about Nicolas Born and the development of his lyric poetry in such detail because Born is in fact representative of the most important stages of lyric poetry between 1967 and 1977. Other important Berlin lyric poets in these years were F. C. Delius, Yaak Karsunke, Johannes Schenk, and Jürgen Theobaldy. They were connected with the development I sketched, and yet each poet is an individual who cannot be described in terms of period and style categories. If anything unites them to this day, it is the experience of politicization in the 1960s, the view that lyric poetry had something to do with society. Theobaldy once put it this way: "But this represents one of the accomplishments of the newer lyric poetry, not to separate the subject and its life from political history, and precisely this also differentiates it from every other kind of subjectivity."[18]

Is this statement still valid today? As we come closer to the present, the difficulties increase as the distance decreases. I could refer to those trendy terms "Neue Unübersichtlichkeit" (New Obscurity), Postmodernism, posthistoire. But Arnold Gehlen had announced posthistoire already at the beginning of the 1960s, and believed that from then on there would be no more artistically immanent development, but only a "syncretism of the confusion of all styles and possibilities"—exactly posthistoire.

But in view of the divided Berlin, it is quite another thing to speak of posthistoire. The wall is not a phenomenon of "posthistory"—history goes on, and at the moment it appears thoroughly open and flexible. I return to the wall, because my explanation is still missing something: the poetry on the other side.

3. Lyric Poetry in Berlin, East and West: The Balance and the Present Situation

As I wrote at the beginning, the wall was not a theme that West Berlin lyric poets handled directly; they were interested in its effects on the inhabitants of the city. It was different in East Berlin. There opinion was sought after, and this opinion had to be justification, according to the political circumstances at that time—affirmative or modified justification, but always justification—also on the part of the younger authors. And at that time a complete generation of young authors evolved, the generation of those born in the 1930s and 1940s. I call them the generation of Volker Braun. Several of them lived and worked in East Berlin, which is more a metropolis of writers than West Berlin. This generation produced the so-called *Lyrikwelle* (Lyric Poetry Wave), which began in 1962 with lyric poetry evenings in Halle, Jena, Leipzig, and East Berlin. The most important and momentous of the evenings, organized by Stephan Hermlin, took place on December 11, 1962, in the East Berlin Akademie der Künste (Academy of the Arts), and led to Hermlin's punishment, termination as secretary of the Poetry and Language Department of the academy. But that was long ago; Hermlin today enjoys a position of political and literary influence that has gone unchallenged for years.

Wolf Biermann made his debut on that evening—it was not only his first, but also one of his last public appearances in the GDR. Rainer Kirsch also gave offense with his sonnet "Meinen Freunden, den alten Genossen" (To my friends, the old comrades), which ends: "Und die Träume ganz beim Namen nennen,/ Und die ganze Wahrheit kennen" (And call the dreams by name,/ And know the whole truth).[19]

In his lyrical work Volker Braun himself tried again and again to unite the individual and the collective, to reconcile them. "We're working our way into the free society" described his program for a socialist democracy. The political measures of the GDR leadership have not, to this day—so it appears—shaken his utopian faith. One senses some of that in his justification of the building of the wall.

> Schrecklich
> Hält sie, steinerne Grenze
> Auf was keine Grenze
> Kennt: den Krieg. Und die hält
> Im friedlichen Land, denn es muß stark sein

Nicht arm, die abhaun zu den Wölfen
Die Lämmer. Vor den Kopf
Stößt sie, das gehn soll wohin es will, nicht
In die Massengräber, das
Volk der Denker.

Aber das mich so hält, das halbe
Land; das sich geändert hat mit mir, jetzt
Ist es sichrer, aber
Ändre ichs noch?[20]

Those lines are from 1965. The wall is justified—somewhat as a lesser evil, because it prevents war. The crucial question lies at the end of the quote: "now/ it is more secure [the GDR], but/ do I change it still?" To this day, Volker Braun holds fast to the belief that the GDR can be changed from within, also by poets. The number holding this belief has continually dwindled over the last two decades, especially since the expulsion of Wolf Biermann from the GDR in 1976. Biermann had been allowed to travel to West Germany to present a concert in Cologne in November 1976, at the invitation of the Metal Workers Association (IG Metall). After his concert was recorded by West German television and broadcast to the GDR, he was stripped of his citizenship and prevented from returning. Twelve authors from the GDR, among them Sarah Kirsch, Christa Wolf, Volker Braun, Franz Fühmann, Stephan Hermlin, Günter Kunert, and Heiner Müller, protested with an open letter against the action of the GDR government; over seventy artists joined the protest (in vain, as we know). At the end of 1976, an exodus of writers began, which has not yet ended. One would have to list at least two dozen authors' names. I shall only name those lyric poets who lived in West Berlin or have stayed here since their departure: Sarah Kirsch, Kurt Bartsch, Thomas Brasch, Jürgen Fuchs, Frank-Wolf Matthies, and Sascha Anderson.

For a while it appeared as though the GDR would bleed to death artistically—and East Berlin with it. But in the meantime something like a regeneration appears to be taking place. Marxism is no longer the dominant theme of most young authors—that reduces the possible points of conflict, but it does not exclude political repression. Quite a few young lyric poets forgo the recognition that accompanies official literary activity, thereby forgoing possibilities for publication. There is a kind of underground public for their efforts: in small circles, including church circles, poems are read and texts circulate. These activities are at risk of coming into conflict with the officials. Many young authors have experienced police interrogations and searches.

But there are also counterexamples: the young author who, encouraged

by older colleagues, may publish his poems, is printed by the leading pub-
lisher, the Aufbau-Verlag, and may even have editions in the West by Suhr-
kamp in Frankfurt. This exception—under the given circumstances in the
GDR there can only be exceptions—is Uwe Kolbe, born in 1957, one of the
most talented lyric poets in the GDR, living in East Berlin, and author of
three volumes of poetry. The title of the first volume, *Hineingeboren* (Born
into, 1980), means more than that a person was born in 1957 into the GDR
state. The short poem consists of two pictures from nature, placed side by
side without a synthesis.

> Hohes weites grünes Land,
> zaundurchsetzte Ebene.
> Roter
> Sonnenbaum am Horizont.
> Der Wind ist mein
> und mein die Vögel.
>
> Kleines grünes Land enges,
> Stacheldrahtlandschaft.
> Schwarzer
> Baum neben mir.
> Harter Wind.
> Fremde Vögel.[21]

But how can one report about contemporary Berlin? What trends are
there? Which authors are important? A book of Berlin's local authors, *Berliner Autoren Stadtbuch*, published by the Akademie der Künste in 1985 lists
111 authors, of whom 60 are identified with lyric poetry. Among the writers nearly all kinds of style are found: from political poem to experimental
text, from surrealism to pop art. That does not help us. Again, one must call
attention to a few examples.

My more-or-less clear thesis was that lyric poetry in Berlin has a distinct
relationship to reality, to the reality of a threatened, bipartite city. Three authors, three examples shall once again illustrate or question it: Hans Magnus
Enzensberger, Botho Strauß, and Thomas Brasch.

In 1965 Walter Höllerer had demanded the "long poem" in which "the
republic frees itself." In 1977 Enzensberger's *Untergang der Titanic* (Sinking
of the Titanic) appeared, a long poem in the comedy genre. In the image of
the sinking luxury steamer, the failure of social and political utopias is described. The poem deals with the shipwreck of the philosophical dialectic,
with the end of our knowing our way and of our optimistic arrogance. That
is also expressed in the date at the end: La Habana 1969—Berlin 1977. These

dates mark, respectively, the end of his faith in the Cuban revolution and in the revolt of the German intellectuals. The *I* of the poem is writing in a room where soot flakes are falling.

> Dies schreibe ich in Berlin. Wie Berlin
> rieche ich nach alten Patronenhülsen,
> nach Osten, nach Schwefel, nach Desinfektion.
> Langsam wird es jetzt wieder kälter.
> Langsam lese ich die Vorschriften durch.
> Weit entfernt hinter zahlreichen Kinos
> steht unbemerkt die Mauer, hinter der,
> weit entfernt voneinander, vereinzelte Kinos stehn. . . .[22]

Berlin in the winter, the penetrating image of a frozen city, the image of historical stagnation. Enzensberger, who lived there for over twenty years, interrupted only by travels, moved to Munich in 1979. The Berlin theme appeared closed for him. Some critics had accused his *Untergang der Titanic* of being too smooth, too carefully calculated, to be taken seriously as a long poem and as a diagnosis of the time. Enzensberger proved himself once again as unpredictable, unreliable. In another poem, "The Frogs of Bikini," he had demanded: "Let's leave Dr. Benn alone."[23] Benn instead of Brecht—one would expect something else from one on the Left. A return to aesthetics was announced.

Botho Strauß, the dramatist and novelist, surprisingly challenged the critics with a long poem in 1985. The peculiar title, *Diese Erinnerung an einen, der hier nur einen Tag zu Gast war* (This remembrance of one, who was a guest only for a day), finds its explanation in the Song of Solomon, where the "hope of the godless" is compared to dust, snow, and smoke, and "how one forgets one, who has been a guest for only a day." In this poem Botho Strauß tried to fulfill the demands he had formulated in his prose book, *Paare, Passanten* (Couples, passersby): the "hymnic beauty" and "the difficult big yes: . . . The singing, Pound and Rilke again, may never become silenced!"[24] Critics argued that Strauß had not yet reached the aesthetic quality of Pound or Rilke. Other critics turned against some ideological or political statements of the poem. I tend to agree that Strauß's lyrical attempt was unsuccessful. Nonetheless, the following passage shows that he touched on a theme that has hardly ever been handled with so much pathos in postwar poetry.

> Kein Deutschland gekannt zeit meines Lebens.
> Zwei fremde Staaten nur, die mir verboten,
> je im Namen eines Volkes der Deutsche zu sein.
> Soviel Geschichte, um so zu enden?

Man spüre einmal: das Herz eines Kleist und
die Teilung des Lands. Man denke doch: welch ein
    Reunieren,
wenn einer, in uns, die Bühne der Geschichte
    aufschlug!

Vielleicht, wer deutsch ist, lernt sich ergänzen.
Und jedes Bruchstück Verständigung
gleicht einer Zelle im nationellen Geweb,
die immer den Bauplan des Ganzen enthält.[25]

Is this seen and spoken with grandeur? Is it pathos or merely embarrassing? Political utopia or reactionary resentment? Gottfried Benn, my key witness from the beginning, said art is the opposite of the well-intended. But doesn't the attempt, the failure, also count in literature? Botho Strauß tried to think of Germany as a whole once again in his poem. He attempted it in West Berlin, as someone who conspicuously keeps a distance from cultural and literary activity. That is all to be respected, only it does not put an end to my skepticism. "In this cruel Berlin," to quote Benn once again, "some sentimentality is done away with, it makes one fit and *sec*."

My last example—is it fit and *sec*? Thomas Brasch, son of a high GDR official, but because of his political insubordination repeatedly tormented and arrested, immigrated to West Berlin in 1976 with the permission of the GDR authorities. What I quote is perhaps not great lyric poetry, but in Benn's understanding, perhaps "fit and *sec*." A political fairy tale, unsentimentally worded, it closes with the theme of writing, which was our topic all along: "Sleeping Beauty and Pork."

Wer geht wohin weg
Wer bleibt warum wo
Unter der festen Wolke ein Leck
Alexanderplatz und Bahnhof Zoo

Abschied von morgen Ankunft gestern
Das ist der deutsche Traum
Endlich verbrüdern sich die Schwestern
Zwei Hexen unterm Apfelbaum

Wer schreibt der bleibt
Hier oder weg oder wo
Wer schreibt der treibt
So oder so.[26]

Translated by Lorna Sopeak with
the assistance of Gerhard Weiss.

NOTES

1. Bertolt Brecht, *Die Gedichte von Bertolt Brecht in einem Band* (Frankfurt/Main, 1981), 997. "The bad fear your claws/ The good enjoy your charm/ This/ I would like to hear/ About my verse."

2. Gottfried Benn, "Ein Berliner Brief," in *Prosa und Autobiographie in der Fassung der Erstdrucke* (Frankfurt/Main, 1984), 353.

3. Franz Mon, "An einer Stelle die Gleichgültigkeit durchbrechen," *Akzente*, 1961: 28.

4. Gottfried Benn, "Wirklichkeit," in *Gedichte in der Fassung der Erstdrucke* (Frankfurt/Main, 1982), 426. "It isn't necessary to have a reality/ more than that, there isn't one, if a man/ can prove his existence/ from archetypal flair and flutes."

5. Günter Grass, "Das Gelegenheitsgedicht," *Akzente*, 1961: 10. "Your right shoulder hangs,/ said my tailor./ Because I carried my school satchel on the right,/ said I and blushed."

6. Günter Bruno Fuchs, "Zwischen den Ideologien sein Dasein behaupten," *Akzente* 1961: 6f.

7. Günter Bruno Fuchs, *Akzente*, 1961: 54f. "In the morning/ he works with the children in the playground./ He starts his work and says: Dear children,/ this tummy is no tummy, but the big mountain Bimbula./ Then the children laugh, turn somersaults and say:/ Please, big mountain, you must come back tomorrow.// At mid-day/ he apes his friends in the jungle./ He drums on his tummy/ and sometimes he jumps with a heavy heart/ on the back of a General and says:/ If you swap my tummy for a drum,/ that's your look-out! This tummy/ is really the big mountain Bimbula/ and you'll never see its beauty.// In the evening/ he is always very sad./ He sits down under the stars/ and drinks fifteen pints of heaven's beer./ Some people have heard him singing—/ he sings quite simply, so simply/ no one could have thought it of him:/ *Mother, O Mother, I'm starving!*"

8. Rolf Haufs, *Vorstadtbeichte. Gedichte* (Neuwied, Switz., 1967), 48. "You were not asks the miss/ A member of the Communist Party/ No say I for I have sworn off/ The stuff of Marx and company/ In fifty-three nights at Moabit."

9. Rolf Haufs, *Größer werdende Entfernung. Gedichte 1962–1979* (Reinbek bei Hamburg, 1979), 22. ". . . who went forth without the blessing of his poor mother/ Went forth as Haufs a generation later went forth/ Went forever forth to Steinstücken where again there were fir trees/ At which the Volkspolizei make water/ And controls marching pensioners and knowing embryos/ But I know you hear me forever hear me/ As I hear the voice of the interzone trains three times daily/ And three times daily again and the angry whistle of steam/ And the sweet oh sweet whisper: Make ready be ready/ Make ready your identity papers and nobody nobody should/ Nobody nobody should leave the train/ Machine-guns are waiting for your and dark looks/ But I fear your dip your head in tears/ In a wash basin bought at Woolworth's Schadowstraße/ Bought cheap because for poems nothing's paid for poems/ For which we sorrow whole nights while others look at our women."

10. Walter Höllerer, "Thesen zum langen Gedicht," *Akzente* 1965: 128.

11. Hans Magnus Enzensberger, "Zwei Fehler," in *Gedichte 1955–1970* (Frankfurt/Main, 1971), 162. "Schlafen, Luftholen, Dichten:/ das ist fast kein Verbrechen."

12. Nicolas Born, *Marktlage. Gedichte* (Cologne, 1967), 1.

13. Nicolas Born, *Wo mir der Kopf steht. Gedichte* (Cologne, 1970), 10. "Our patience is at an end./ We're fed up, with letting the majority/ dance round our noses./ We're fed up, with letting the city/ be insulted by this gutter-press publisher/ (if he finds Berlin unappetizing/ he should go to the East)./ We're fed up with letting our right to demonstrate/ be rationed. . . . "

14. Nicolas Born, *Das Auge des Entdeckers. Gedichte* (Reinbek bei Hamburg, 1972), 113.

15. Ibid., 18. "Facts, are they not painful and boring?/ Isn't it better to have three wishes/ with the provision that they will be fulfilled for all?/ I wish a life without long intervals/ in which the walls are searched for bullets/ a life that is not torn off sheet after sheet by cashiers./

I wish to write letters that contain the whole of me—/ How far I would get around without losing weight./ I wish a book that all of you can enter at the front and leave at the back./ And I would not like to forget that it's more pleasant/ to love you than not to love you."

16. Ibid., 115.

17. Nicolas Born, *Gedichte 1967–1978* (Reinbek bei Hamburg, 1978), 222. "Sorrow is now without solace/ the fury without sound, all the masquerading liveliness/ all the choking confidence/ grass collapses, gardens collapse, no one/ beneath the armor of money feels/ the wound to be drained of itself./ No poem, at most the end of it./ Riches in men/ caught in infamous reasoning that cannot see itself/ for the science. . . . tilted meadow slope, angel, uncertain/ warm human bodies and understanding/ gardens spread out, under branches banks . . . / . . . shadow . . . foliage . . . spoken in the wind/ . . . seeds."

18. Jürgen Theobaldy, "Literaturkritik, astrologisch," *Akzente* (1977): 189.

19. Rainer Kirsch, *Auszog das Fürchten zu lernen* (Reinbek bei Hamburg, 1978), 204.

20. Ingrid Krüger and Eike Schmitz, eds., *Berlin, du deutsche deutsche Frau* (Darmstadt, FRG, 1985), 51. "Terribly/ this stone frontier holds off,/ what no frontier/ knows: war. And it holds back/ in a peaceful country, for it must be strong/ not poor, those who buzz off to the wolves/ the lambs./ It offends/ those who want to go where they please, not/ into the mass grave, the/ people of thinkers.// But that which holds me so, the half/ country; that has changed with me, now/ it is more secure, but do I change it still?"

21. Uwe Kolbe, *Hineingeboren. Gedichte 1975–1979* (Frankfurt/Main, 1982), 46. "High broad green land,/ Fence-dotted plain./ Red/ Sun-tree on the horizon./ The wind is mine/ and mine the birds.// Small green narrow land,/ Barbed wire landscape./ Black/ Tree beside me./ Hard wind./ Strange birds."

22. Hans Magnus Enzensberger, *Der Untergang der Titanic. Eine Komödie* (Frankfurt/Main, 1978), 14. "I am writing this in Berlin. Like Berlin,/ I smell like old cartridge-cases,/ like the East, like sulphur, like disinfectant./ Slowly it gets colder./ Slowly I read through the regulations./ Far removed, behind numerous cinemas/ Stands the wall, unnoticed, behind which,/ far removed from one another, stand isolated cinemas. . . ."

23. Hans Magnus Enzensberger, *Die Furie des Verschwindens. Gedichte* (Frankfurt/Main, 1980), 46.

24. Botho Strauß, *Paare, Passanten* (Munich, 1981), 15.

25. Botho Strauß, *Die Erinnerung an einen, der nur einen Tag zu Gast war. Gedicht* (Munich, 1985), 48. "I have known no Germany in my lifetime./ Only two strange states, that forbid me/ ever to be a German of the German nation./ So much history, to end this way?// Try to feel this once: the heart of a Kleist and/ the division of the country. One might still think: what a unification,/ if someone were to put up the stage of history in us!// Perhaps he who is German learns to make himself whole./ And each fragment of agreement/ is like a cell in the national tissue,/ which always retains the plan of the whole."

26. Thomas Brasch, *Der schöne 27. September. Gedichte* (Frankfurt/Main, 1980), 42. "Whoever goes away to where/ Whoever stays why where/ Beneath the fixed cloud a leak/ Alexanderplatz and Bahnhof Zoo// Goodbye from tomorrow arrival yesterday/ That is the German dream/ Finally the sisters will be brothers/ Two witches beneath the apple tree// Whoever writes he stays/ Here or away or where/ Whoever writes he drives forward/ This way or that."

CHAPTER 10

Berlin: Backdrop, Stage, or Actor?
Images of the City in Recent GDR Fiction

Dorothy Rosenberg

Since the division of the city, Berlin has existed simultaneously as at least three ideological entities: East Berlin, West Berlin, and the Divided City. As a rule, the last two have received the bulk of attention in the West and have come to dominate our thinking about the city in the postwar period.

Viewed from the West, the cultural history of the city tends to follow a relatively straight line of development and then suddenly shifts to a cultural history of its western half. We may call it West Berlin (or Rest Berlin), but references to the city reflect a generally unexamined assumption that there is no postwar cultural history in its eastern half. Many West German maps of Berlin show the streets of the East in gray. This attitude is reinforced by infrequent one-day forays to the "other side" to view an itinerary of cultural monuments to Berlin's past: the Bode and Pergamon Museums, Brecht's house, the imperial architecture along Unter den Linden, or a pilgrimage to Wolf Biermann's apartment, more recently a visit to a Prenzlauer Berg poet.

From the East (which bears the official title Berlin, Capital of the GDR) looking West — East German maps of Berlin show the West in white without the streets — the view is even more exotic. To the middle aged, it was movies and jazz before the construction of the wall, to the young it is everything television promises, to the elderly it is a trip to see relatives (or their funerals). To some it is a tour or trip that is a privilege or a reward, to all it represents a complex mixture of threats and temptations.

The East looking at itself, however, finds a coherent whole with an unbroken history (now being reclaimed step by ideological step), along with its traditional central city core and the old neighborhoods radiating out from it. From this point of view, what has been lost are a number of large department stores and the western suburbs. Given the combination of arrogance, habit, and propaganda, it is difficult, looking from the West, to see life in East Berlin as just possibly being as self-absorbed and calmly self-evident as life in the western part of the city.

In the following, I shall explore both the range of attitudes toward and meanings of Berlin as seen from the perspective of its historic center, and the sometimes critical, but nonetheless general, acceptance of not merely the legitimacy, but the perfect ordinariness of saying Berlin and meaning East Berlin. I will discuss, with somewhat diverse purposes, which of the roles listed in the title the city plays in a selection of recent works of fiction. The problem is not one of finding works of fiction set in East Berlin, but of choosing among them.

1. The City as Backdrop

The central districts of Mitte, Prenzlauer Berg, and Friedrichshain carry with them the aura of working–class history, poverty, and overcrowding. By locating a story within one of these neighborhoods, an author can automatically set the parameters of her characters and their conditions, playing on the milieu from the bottom: tenements, back courtyards, corner taverns, the romance of the slums. The crowd scenes: third-generation working class with authentic Berlin accents. The immediately identifiable living conditions in these districts offer authors like Ulrich Plenzdorf, Klaus Schlesinger, and Günter de Bruyn a simple device for establishing a ready-made foundation of nostalgic realism for their various adventures of "the common man."

Klaus Schlesinger begins *Alte Filme* (Old movies) by describing his main character's daily commute on the S-Bahn.

> Kotte's days are filled. Every morning at 6:00 a.m., five days a week, he takes the train from Alexanderplatz to Schöneweide to the transformer works and disappears behind a door marked Technical Design, sits down at his drawing board which, except for breaks, he doesn't leave again until 3:45, boards the 4:16 train at the Schöneweide station and is at the kindergarten on Schönhauser Allee forty-three minutes later, ten minutes after that at the grocery store on the corner and at his own front door at about 5:30, a full shopping bag in his right hand and his daughter in his left.[1]

The framework thus established contains Alexanderplatz and the working class districts and slums behind it and carries the rest of the story, which can be quickly summed up as Kotte getting off the track and then getting back onto it, a procedure that involves a large amount of alcohol, a small amount of sex, a few artistic hippies, a patient wife, and an understanding boss.

The plot of Schlesinger's novella is nearly irrelevant. Very little actually happens, and Kotte is left not much wiser after his binge than before it. The real center of the story is the Prenzlauer Berg "scene." In *Alte Filme*, young "drop-outs"—artists, musicians, and assorted hippies who hold temporary or part-time jobs, listen to Crosby, Stills & Nash, and drink like fish — talk about life, self-expression, and freedom to poor Kotte, who, having lived his whole life in the slums as a fully employed native tenement dweller, has failed to recognize that his surroundings are romantic.

The old working-class districts with their high-ceilinged apartments and established neighborhood infrastructures are enjoying something of the same vogue in East Berlin as in the West. The drop-outs of the 1970s, rebelling against middle-class, success-oriented values and pressures, have been followed in the 1980s by young professionals, who have moved into and renovated the rundown cold-water flats as their working-class inhabitants have moved out into the new, centrally heated apartment blocks being built in "satellite" districts around the city proper. Today, Prenzlauer Berg is a mixture of newcomers and locals who have not yet made it to the top of the Housing Authority waiting list, as well as those too old, or too settled, or too well integrated to want to make the move to the suburbs. Change, renovation, and resettlement have enhanced rather than diminished the popularity of the old neighborhood, with its traditions, characters, and gossip, as a narrative backdrop.

Ulrich Plenzdorf begins *Legende vom Glück ohne Ende* (The legend of happiness without end) with an even more detailed geographical detour, using the concrete physical setting of the action to establish the reliability of his eyewitness testimony. The fact that the buildings have been torn down and the streets renamed underscores the nostalgic flavor of the storyteller's narrative.

> This is where they lived. Here on Singerstraße. And not on Krautstraße or Blumenstraße the way some people say. Or in Prenzlauer Berg or Weißensee. Or finally in Lichtenberg. They lived here on Singerstraße in Friedrichshain. Their building stood right here, right there . . . and right next door were others just like it. And over there, where the telephone booth is now, there was an old green cast-iron pump, where they all played as children and where the whole street fetched its water in 'forty-five.
>
> In those days, Singerstraße went through to Fruchtstraße, now the Street of the Paris Commune. Right at Küstrinerplatz, now Mehringplatz, was where it ran into Fruchtstraße. . . . There was Schubert's big lamp store right across from Neumann's tavern, then Hellwig's bakery, Lehmann, the shoemaker, and the glass store. . . . We had everything on Singerstraße.[2]

Having established both the context of lost community and a sense of oral history, the narrator goes on to tell the story of Paul and Paula as a modern legend and community event. By embedding the love affair in the neighborhood gossip surrounding it and presenting the lovers exclusively from the perspective of a curious neighbor, Plenzdorf elaborates a mythological

dimension for the story, simultaneously emphasizing its physical uniqueness and its universal folk-tale character.

In "Freiheitsberaubung" (Deprivation of liberty), Günter de Bruyn takes
this factual approach to its logical extreme by prefacing his story with the
cast of characters, street, house number, floor, and apartment before beginning his narrative in the dry tones of an official report.

> It begins with the minor character Ströhler. Coming from work at the Bear
> tavern shortly after midnight, tired naturally and slightly inebriated, he
> enters the building, Linienstraße 263, in which he lives, middle apartment
> fourth floor in the rear and leaves it again five minutes later to go to the
> telephone booth at the Oranienburg Gate, which, however, is broken,
> whereupon he quickly . . . returns to the Bear tavern, calls the police
> station and asks the officer on duty to immediately send a radio patrol to
> Linienstraße where in the left apartment, fourth floor, rear, a person, more
> exactly: a man, is pounding on the door with his fists and screaming that
> he has been deprived of his freedom and is urgently demanding the state
> authorities.[3]

De Bruyn uses exactly the same kind of tenement setting and slum gossip
that Plenzdorf sentimentalizes to illustrate why *his* characters' only wish is
to move out. Plenzdorf's nostalgia focuses on an intact community, while
filtering out the rats, falling plaster, and faulty plumbing that are also integral parts of slum life. In contrast, de Bruyn's pay phones are realistically
out-of-order, his description of the redevelopment policy in practice is a
model of clarity, and his love story is modern. His rat stories are classics of
their kind, and the authenticity of his description of a visit to the KWV
(Municipal Housing Administration) is borne out in both truth and fiction.

> Ströhler drinks another schnapps without delaying himself and makes his
> way back to Linienstraße 263, which he does not know was built exactly
> 100 years ago with the money of a man whose great-grandchildren now
> live in Hamburg and allow their property to be municipally administered.
> Ströhler knows only that the building was last renovated in 1930 and the
> Housing Administration does not intend to repeat the process because it
> has been slated for demolition since 1950; the date has always been firmly
> set: 1960, 1963, 1968, 1972. This time, the year after next has been named
> the year of hope, upon which only new tenants with little experience based
> any illusions. (11)

As the story develops, the main character, Anita Paschke, explains to a
police lieutenant why she has locked her lover into her apartment. It seems
that he, Siegfried Böttger, Director of a VEB (State-Owned Corporation),
after first going into nostalgic raptures over her apartment being just like his
grandmother's, had promised her a newly constructed apartment (which

would mean an inside toilet and central heating, among other amenities).
He was motivated not by love, but fear.

> What had transformed him was not she, but the rat sitting in the toilet
> bowl that spoiled his appetite for Sunday morning breakfast. Anita tells
> this in far more graphic detail than the reader can be expected to tolerate.
> A brief sketch will suffice: Still in his pajamas, he lifts the lid to sit down,
> the wet, sewage-smeared beast stares at him, jumps back into the bowl and
> paddles with its snout above water; he flushes, it disappears, pops up again
> and climbs back onto the platform, the next flush won't be possible for
> three or four minutes because the tank has to refill. Who can hit the beast
> with a poker? Besides, the toilet bowl is made of porcelain. (15)

As it turns out, the lieutenant is more than sympathetic. He surprises Anita
by offering practical advice based on his own long experience as a tenement
dweller. He suggests using coal tongs to grab and then drown the rat. Earlier in the evening, Böttger, her lover, had told her that he was leaving her
to move into his now-completed apartment with his family. He had just
stopped by to explain to her that she didn't love him in the proper way, before going to collect his wife and furniture in Leipzig the next morning.
Outraged at having been cheated of the use of her lover's connections (her
best chance to move out of the slums), Anita had locked him into the apartment and gone off to her graveyard shift job. Satisfied that he has missed the
last train to Leipzig, she gives the lieutenant the key.

Having gotten started on the subject of her apartment, however, Anita
pours out the details of her intolerable living situation: the rats in the gar-
bage cans, the frozen pipes in the winter, and the stench in the summer.
Much of the dialogue consists of Anita's narrative of her life in the slums
and the long story of her attempts to get out of them, her campaigns on the
municipal housing office, and her opinions of the entire municipal housing
distribution system.

> Although the sublieutenant really cannot in good conscience listen to such
> comments, especially on duty, he grunts in agreement, after all, he too
> belongs to the hereditary slum dwellers who, compared to the newcomers
> who populate the suburbs, feel like the natives of a conquered nation
> banned to their reservations. (16)

The problems of intolerable living conditions are not a new theme for de
Bruyn. One of the main reasons for the failure of the love affair central to
his novel, *Buridans Esel* (Buridan's ass),[4] was the inability of an older man,
after life in a suburban neighborhood, to readjust to his young lover's standard working-class cold-water flat with its coal stove and hall toilet. In
"Freiheitsberaubung," de Bruyn's story elevates the Berlin slums from
charming local color to pointed social criticism without sacrificing his sense
of humor. His satirical focus on the real problem of living conditions in the

old districts is a welcome antidote to the relentless sentimentalization found in other authors.

2. The City as Stage

A very different part of the city plays quite a different role in Christa Wolf's "Unter den Linden." Wolf neither romanticizes nor satirizes the city, but uses it as a three-dimensional stage set, complete with extras and bit players, for her drama of dream and memory. All of the action of the story takes place along the formal processional main thoroughfare of Berlin, Unter den Linden, which runs from Marx-Engels-Platz to the Brandenburg Gate. Rather than using this historically charged setting to provide a general background mood, Wolf invests these public places with her own private and distinctly personal associations and memories.

> I've always enjoyed walking down Unter den Linden. As you know, I
> prefer to go alone. Recently, after I had avoided the street for a long time,
> it appeared to me in a dream. Now I can finally tell about it.[5]

Wolf begins with the statement, "I am no longer bound to the facts. I am free to tell the truth," and repeatedly states that she is retelling a dream (65). But the author does not introduce the reader to an unreal atmosphere. Instead, the narrator places her dream firmly within the concrete physical context of Unter den Linden from the Neue Wache, past the University, the State Library, and down the street to the Brandenburg Gate and back to Marx-Engels-Platz, telling us both the dream–events connected to each location and the real-life memories called up by each place and commenting on both. The result is an odd mixture of places and settings that are clearly recognizable and so absolutely public that they exist independently for the reader. These public places are invested with a private and specific meaning through the running monologue of multilevel personal associations that the narrator attaches to each physical location that triggers her thoughts, actions, or memories.

The story moves between three levels of reality: the physically real setting; an intermediate level of memories of past events and conversations, as well as thoughts about friends and the quality of their actions and motivations, which could be called speculative reality; and a third level of clearly imaginary dream narrative, which contains within it a cumulative philosophical discourse on the nature of truth.

> Oh dearest, you always want to know the truth. But the truth isn't a story
> and is incredible anyway. . . . For you, so that you can believe me, I now
> set about blurring the transitions between the believable and the
> unbelievable. (74–75)

> Otherwise you're just feeling your way in the dark, he said, and I was
> shocked by how blind he already was. On the day that I'm hoping for,
> because then no one will stand between me and those who want to believe
> me, not even myself—on that distant day they will tear the craziest
> fabrications from my hands as the pure truth and force me to always tell
> the truth, nothing but the pure, crazy truth. Today, however, I am still
> groping for the rough stone pillar that I leaned against, as if it were
> evidence. . . . (90–91)

The narrator inhabits the street, using the physical features of its spaces,
buildings, window displays, and cafes as a solid foundation on which to
build the structure of questions, associations, and memories of her overlapping lives and stories.

Irmtraud Morgner takes similar advantage of a number of major Berlin
architectural landmarks in *Amanda*,[6] using Leipziger Straße, Unter den Linden, and the Tierpark in Friedrichsfelde as scenes of action. Morgner's description of physical geography frequently becomes increasingly detailed as
she inhabits it with ever more flamboyant fantasy, as in her use of the French
Cathedral as the meeting place for her witches' colloquium or a bird cage in
the Tierpark to imprison a winged female Siren.

In another Christa Wolf story "Juninachmittag" (June afternoon), the author injects a note of fragility into her description of an otherwise idyllic
summer day, reminding the reader of wars both hot and cold with a brief
reference to Berlin's curious political geography.

> But this time it was only one of those good, old airliners. . . . I mean: it
> flew, as anyone could see, from east to west, if just this once these terms
> mean nothing more than the directions of the compass; for most of the
> passengers, the airplane flew from West to West.[7]

Public transportation seems almost automatically to bring up the question of Berlin's unusual status and multilayered existence. The fact that there
are other subway lines to forbidden destinations within steps of the daily
commute seems to make the possibility of trains to other times, as in Heinz
Knobloch's "Stadtmitte Umsteigen" (Midtown transfer), or other dimensions, as in Günter Kunert's "Fahrt mit der S-Bahn" (Trip with the
S-Bahn), no more unlikely.

> But one evening between two stations it happens: I look directly into a
> lighted window. . . . The moment of sight is very brief. But I run through
> the half-empty train car to see at least for a fraction of a second longer
> what I have just seen. The speed is too great.
>
> In the room that shot past me so quickly . . . sat none other than myself;
> . . . half turned to someone next to me, a friend who was in fact dead and
> forgotten by me. Several figures were in the room. . . . Among those
> present were only well-known faces, no stranger was among them. Only

many of them had been missing for years, or burned, or killed or
emigrated, or become ancient; but they were all gathered there.[8]

Kunert's narrator describes spending weeks searching for the building he
saw from the train, but fails to locate it. Finally, he gives up and contents
himself with riding the S-Bahn as often as possible, traveling back and forth
and back and forth along the line at least once a week, observing the un-
spoiled, idealized past in the unreachable room.

> Again and again I know as the train carries me away from the window: if I
> could only once walk into that room and reunite myself with me . . . then
> everything would be undone. . . . Enter once at the right moment and I
> would be saved. And the city as well. (228)

Kunert's allegory juxtaposes the gritty and depressing reality of tired
commuters, grimy stations, and blackened fire walls with his tantalizing
glimpses of an age of lost innocence: a fleeting vision of himself as a child
eating a ripe apple in a room full of family and friends before the war that
divided his life as well as the city that he loves and hates.

In an almost mirror-opposite use of the same image, Helga Schubert's
"Das verbotene Zimmer" (The forbidden room) describes a real trip to the
other side, which is colored by an insistent feeling of fantasy.

> You went to West Berlin with a round-trip ticket for 40 pfennigs East.
> The exchange rate was announced every day on the Western news
> broadcasts. . . .
>
> Today you can also go to West Berlin with a round-trip ticket, but it costs
> 2.40. You can buy it at any subway ticket counter without a passport. For
> example, at Alexanderplatz. . . .
>
> I said, "One ticket to West Berlin, please." The ticket clerk answered
> matter-of-factly: "You have to buy a round-trip ticket to West Berlin." . . .
>
> I didn't dream it. Since then I haven't dreamt of West Berlin at all—for I
> was there.

Schubert uses a striking number of fairy-tale references to describe both the
anticipation and the experience of West Berlin. She describes the double
sense of unreality of being in the forbidden West while normal life goes on
at home, shadowed by disbelief that she is really there, and the letdown of
finding the forbidden "other" much too familiar.

> Stairs up to the S-Bahn. Stairs down to the S-Bahn. Transfer to the
> subway. As if it's completely ordinary, I thought. . . .
>
> I get out at the Zoo station. . . . From television, I know that prostitution
> and the drug trade flourish here, that there are teen-age male prostitutes

here. Actually, I already know everything. I know the advertisements, the brands of chocolate, the detergents. . . . (88)

Although the surface of the West is entirely as she anticipated, the narrator has unexpected difficulty in communicating with the people she meets. She finds them friendly and generous, but their assumptions about the East are totally at odds with her own experience. Their complete lack of reciprocal curiosity or interest in listening to her attempts to correct their misconceptions leaves her feeling both frustrated and helpless. She feels uncomfortable with the privilege of being allowed to travel and worries that she isn't using her precious, limited time properly. She, too, fails to relocate her childhood home, not metaphorically but concretely (she ends up at the wrong address). Kreuzberg, where she was born, looks a lot like Prenzlauer Berg, but the racism and poverty that she sees are, although expected, still unnerving.

The story ends with a sense of relief, the narrator safely established back within normality again, happy to be home, but wanting to hold on to the unfulfilled magic of possibility.

> Sometimes, I stand on the lowest level of the subway station at Alex and listen to the sound of the trains. The one above me must be the train to Pankow, and the opposite direction to Thälmannplatz. But where is the through train from Kreuzberg to Gesundbrunnen? I can see it on the schedule. It must be down below. And I remember the man who said he had heard the sound of a train behind a green-tiled wall where it didn't belong. . . .
>
> I was there a long time ago, in the forbidden room. (97)

3. The City as Actor

In a number of works, the city not only frames and colors the narrative, but dominates the action. While many GDR writers avail themselves of the gritty ambience of Berlin's dialect, temperament, atmosphere, and cultural mythology, as well as its physical geography, Heinz Knobloch, a journalist and local historian, has taken Berlin itself as his object. In Knobloch's work, Berlin is more than the setting of action; it has become the main character around which a structure of narrative and anecdote revolve. His biographies of Moses Mendelssohn, *Herr Moses in Berlin* (Mr. Moses in Berlin), and Mathilde Jakobs, Rosa Luxemburg's personal secretary, *Meine Liebste Mathilde* (My dearest Mathilde),[9] several collections of stories and essays, and a weekly newspaper column explore the city through the stories of its visitors and residents. In his latest collection of essays, *Im Lustgarten*,[10] Knobloch uses bits of geography, history, architecture, notable characters and

landmarks, reminiscences, and fantasies, freely mixed with irony and anecdote, to reflect on Berlin as a sum of its past and its parts. While his biographies and volumes of essays and short stories stand as independent works,
taken together they provide an ever-expanding composite portrait of the
city.

Knobloch emphasizes the vital importance of openness and diversity in
Berlin's development into Germany's only truly urban metropolis. The role
played by the Jewish community and the history of journalism are two of
his recurring themes. In "Herbert-Baum-Straße 45," he writes:

> Among the little known sights of Berlin is a cemetery in the Weißensee
> district. It is thought to be the largest in Europe—in all, about 115,000
> Jewish fellow citizens are buried here—and it is recognized as a monument
> of cultural history.[11]

> There are philosophers buried in Weißensee, linguists, famous jurists and
> architects, historians and religious scholars, the Asian specialist Huth, the
> publisher S. Fischer, the philosopher Herrmann Cohen. . . . No one in the
> ranks of honor was born in Berlin. They came from Poland, Hungary,
> Silesia, Moravia, Galicia and the Ukraine, but also from Baden and
> Bavaria, Riga and Magdeburg. (55)

In other essays, Knobloch's gently ironic tone moves easily from self-
deprecating culinary anecdotes[12] to the history of the German Empire and
its consequences. Describing his childhood, Knobloch writes:

> In the district of Berlin to which my parents had moved, the natives in the
> vicinity of the Anhalt station lived in streets whose names sounded like
> harmless places but concealed a lot of bloodshed. Großbeerenstraße, . . .
> Möckernstraße, . . . Königsgrätzstraße, which was then renamed
> Stresemannstraße and in my early days, Saarlandstraße, a street like that has
> to put up with a lot. When the Anhalt station, past which it runs, lay in
> ruins, it was again called Stresemannstraße. (15–16)

In this brief passage, Knobloch juxtaposes the major battles of Prussian imperial consolidation and the failure and collapse of its fascist successor, the
Third Reich, without ever directly mentioning either. The political meanings of the changing street names are clear to anyone familiar with German
history and are not belabored. History becomes a visible framework for the
matter-of-fact observations of a child, ironically recalled with an adult resonance. Knobloch enlists his readers to participate in a joint process of re-
membering and discovering. He expects his audience to know that the ruins
of the Anhalt station are located in Kreuzberg and that the district where he
grew up is now in West Berlin. This fact does not require explicit comment,
nor does the reader need to be told when and why the Anhalt station was

bombed to rubble. Neither does the author emphasize that Pankow, where he now lives, is in the East.

> In our district, Pankow, everything is just the way it is where you live and some things are different. One only needs to be told about Pankow, what all is or was there and each reader will see what he gets out of it. Or wants to get. Or not. . . .

> In our district, Pankow, I say, and I'm not from here at all, although, if I add it up, I've lived in this part of the city for twenty years. . . .(105)

The suggestion that some may expect Pankow to be different from Kreuzberg is touched on obliquely and just as obliquely denied and turned back onto the expectations and motivations of the reader. Knobloch draws his audience into an unspoken dialogue.

> For my son, born in Pankow's Buch clinic, this neighborhood is childhood, home, first playground, path to school. When he says: "In our district, Pankow," it is without irony. (130)

A single literary gesture can touch either on the division of the city or its tradition of residential district stability. Knobloch's style allows him to juggle a number of political and ideological balls at once while pretending to look in the other direction. Simultaneously giving his reader a silent nod, he shifts his ground: only some of us suffer from double vision; for the next generation, experience determines what is normal.

4. Conclusion

There is a distinctly Protestant flavor to the East German attitude toward the West. Deeper than any political analysis is a moralistic vision of a state riddled with sin—decadence, drugs, and prostitution, poverty and unemployment, racism and violence, cheek-by-jowl with conspicuous consumption, wealth, sophistication, fast cars, and aristocrats still using the titles of a defunct nobility—all observed with a mixture of fear and envy by the poor-but-honest, hard-working GDR, pulling itself up by its own bootstraps. The consumer goods, yes—the rest, no. And of course, all of the Nazis fled west. Two societies on rather thin ice over a sea of undigested history.

West Berlin's image as an island cut off from the West rests on geographical reality, and although its propaganda role as "the outpost of freedom" in the 1950s has mellowed considerably in the 1980s, the "West" carries with it the inescapable subtext of a temporary political solution. West Berlin is no longer a capital city. East Berlin is. The eastern half of the city is not cut off from its hinterland, but integrated into it, and it functions as both the political and cultural capital of the GDR. For an East German, a trip to Berlin means shopping and restaurants, theater and museums. It can mean official business, but it is not a political statement.

There is an odd echo in the East of the West German slogan, "Berlin, display window of the West," in the complaints heard in Leipzig and Dresden that Berlin shops are better supplied in order to show off to the West. The mixture of envy and resentment of Berlin's special financial privileges and preferential treatment, stirred up again by the 750-year anniversary, is eerily similar in the two Germanies. The image of the two halves of the city posturing at each other and their respective provinces in a politicized version of sibling rivalry is hard to suppress.

Perhaps Helga Schubert's "Das verbotene Zimmer" catches the mood of the present situation: the tremendous buildup of something kept forbidden for twenty-five years can't fail to be a bit of a disappointment, especially in an age when all secrets are televised. As the level of sophistication and the number of GDR citizens traveling to the West has increased rapidly in the past several years, so has their lack of surprise at what they find there; the complex of responses Schubert describes have become a common phenomenon. As the crowds that followed the opening of the border on November 9, 1989, confirmed, the Kurfürstendamm looks exactly the way everyone expected it to and no one could mistake it for Unter den Linden. But Tiergarten and Mitte or Kreuzberg and Friedrichshain? And where would the uninitiated outsider place Weißensee?

Schubert's story can be used to illustrate another point: the question of the divided status of the city has been neither a taboo topic in the East nor so compelling that it dominated the literature. It is just interesting enough to produce a story about an adventure or an anticlimax before returning to the more pressing concerns of daily life, in the East.

NOTES

1. Klaus Schlesinger, *Alte Filme* (Rostock, GDR, 1975), 7. Translations of this and all passages cited below are my own.

2. Ulrich Plenzdorf, *Legende vom Glück ohne Ende* (Rostock, GDR, 1979), quoted from *Berliner Geschichten* (Munich, 1986), 331.

3. Günter de Bruyn, "Freiheitsberaubung," in *Auskunft 2. Neue Prosa aus der DDR*, ed. Stefan Heym (Reinbek bei Hamburg, 1981), 10.

4. Günter de Bruyn, *Buridans Esel* (Halle, GDR, 1969).

5. Christa Wolf, "Unter den Linden," in *Gesammelte Erzählungen* (Darmstadt, FRG, 1980), 65.

6. Irmtraud Morgner, *Amanda. Ein Hexenroman* (Berlin, 1983).

7. Christa Wolf, "Juninachmittag," in *Gesammelte Erzählungen* (Darmstadt, FRG, 1980), 44.

8. Günter Kunert, "Fahrt mit der S-Bahn," in *Fahrt mit der S-Bahn. Erzähler der DDR*, ed. Lutz Wolff (Munich, 1971), 224, 226–27.

9. Heinz Knobloch, *Herr Moses in Berlin. Auf den Spuren eines Menschenfreundes* (Berlin, 1979); *Meine Liebste Mathilde. Geschichte — um Berühren* (Berlin, 1985).

10. Heinz Knobloch, *Im Lustgarten* (Halle, GDR, 1989).

11. Heinz Knobloch, *Berliner Feuilleton* (Berlin, 1987), 53.

12. "Berlin cuisine naturally comes up short when compared with capital cities of more culinary sophistication. . . . Berlin cuisine is a bit of a problem. How does one make it appetizing to friends from out of town? A friend from Riga sat in front of her boiled pork knuckle, maintaining her composure, but visibly appalled. Until she notices that she doesn't have to eat all of it. Then she likes it.

"Things were different with a young man from the Near East. We went to Nante's Corner for a beer and I asked if he had to observe any dietary laws. No, not at all, he ate everything. No religious restrictions. So I ordered pork knuckle, but he understood enough that he wanted to have the word explained. I tried. He said, 'Actually, I'm a vegetarian.' " (*Berliner Feuilleton*, 101)

CHAPTER 11

Fremde in Berlin:
The Outsiders' View from the Inside

Heidrun Suhr

> *It is not at all easy, the viewing as well as the living in a city that is constantly moving, always in the process of changing, never resting in its past.*
>
> Franz Hessel

"There are a lot of newcomers here, far too many."[1] This sentiment, published in a West Berlin periodical evocatively titled *Niemandsland* (No-man's-land), is frequently heard in West Berlin—often from those who have been there only a short time themselves. Sometimes meant as a complaint, it is more often an affirmation. Recent masses of "Übersiedler," GDR citizens who want to settle there, and the throngs of visitors after the opening of the wall November 9, 1989, populate the streets now. Yet this phenomenon of large numbers of newcomers is hardly historically unique to that postwar urban configuration known as West Berlin; it has been characteristic of this city for most of the past three centuries. Indeed, throughout much of its history Berlin's development has been profoundly affected by the influx of *Fremde*—immigrants either from the provinces or from foreign countries. The reasons for the move to Berlin have varied: many have come in quest of work, others have fled political or religious persecution, still others were drawn to the city by the promise of a life richer in experience. This constantly changing population, bringing with it a multiplicity of influences from the outside, has made Berlin different from any other European city.

The ever-shifting composition of the city's population has contributed to the sense that Berlin has no continuous history, no traditions—an effect that has been aggravated by Germany's difficult history. Its lack of an "organic," gradually developing culture, has been frequently criticized. Walter Rathenau dubbed Berlin the "parvenu of cities,"[2] and Karl Scheffler declared that it was the city's fate "always to be in the process of becoming and never to be."[3]

Others, however, have praised this "city of most heterogeneous elements," as Adolf Glaßbrenner characterized it, regarding it as a basis for a positive sociopolitical development. For the *Vormärz* authors Beta, Ernst Dronke, and Friedrich Saß, Berlin's very fluidity, both socially and culturally, seemed to make it a promising site for a future society shaped by romantic utopian ideas. Beta thought the city's lack of history a virtue, since "for every atmosphere and sentiment of the time, for every task in the future, material and people (are) available."[4] As social rank and tradition diminished in importance, social reformers hoped that the "free and equal" human beings required for the capitalist mode of production could achieve radical change. Later, in the early 1920s, Heinrich Mann was among those who saw Berlin as a model for an egalitarian industrialized society. He believed that this *Menschenwerkstatt*, a workshop for producing a new type of human being, could accelerate the process of democratization and modernization.[5]

A short anonymous guide of 1912, *Berlin für Kenner* (Berlin for experts), gives an insight into the significance of *Fremde* at the peak of Berlin's population surge. It reported that of the city's 2 million inhabitants, 1.3 million were registered *Fremde*, of which one-fifth were from foreign countries. The text included a meticulously drawn up statistical overview of these foreigners, of their numbers and countries of origin, suggesting that the diversity of Berlin's population was a source of pride, a proof of its status as a metropolis. The need to offer such proof, however, is a sign of the city's lingering provincialism.

The social and ethnic diversity of the city was one of the features that made it so different from village and small-town life, and which demanded a new social psyche. For the social psychologist Willy Hellpach, a pupil of Georg Simmel, this diversity was one of the reasons why inhabitants of big cities needed to develop both "intellectual vigilance" and "emotional indifference"[6] in order to cope with this hectic and heterogeneous environment, an environment that made Berliners the embodiment of *homines novi*.[7] However one may assess the validity of Hellpach's theses, the heterogeneity of Berlin's population has undoubtedly had an impact on the city's character. The "Berliner" can hardly be defined—a popular saying is that a typical Berliner was not born in Berlin. This lack of a homogeneous civic identity is usually considered by outside observers and those in positions of power to be an impediment to effective governance.

Today's multifaceted West Berlin prides itself on its openness and multicultural atmosphere. Many current publications on Berlin stress that the city has always welcomed foreigners, political emigrés, workers seeking employment, religious refugees, students, business people, and others. While this has often been the case, today's multicultural city is not as harmonious as those who sing the praises of "oriental market places" like to pretend, nor has its multiculturality ever been free of conflict.

In this article I shall—after a brief historical overview of past immigrations to Berlin—address the contemporary West Berlin literature dealing with the experience of *Fremde* in the city. First I shall discuss Berlin literature *written* by foreigners, who address the "guest worker" situation; then I shall explore the image of *Fremde*—foreigners from other countries and those who come from West Germany to live in West Berlin—in contemporary literature about Berlin written by Germans, specifically, in the so-called *Szeneliteratur* (literature of the Berlin scene). Both categories of literature focus on Kreuzberg, the part of the city sometimes called "Berlin's Berlin."[8]

1. *Fremde* and the Making of Modern Berlin

> *Berlin is newer to the eye than any other city.*
>
> Mark Twain

Berlin has always been a place where outside and non-German influences have mingled and blended. While other German cities, for example Lübeck or Nuremberg with their preindustrial history, or Leverkusen and Ludwigshafen with their more uniform industrial growth, developed with a far more homogeneous population structure and may evoke associations with "German" traditions, already early on in Berlin efforts were made to encourage people to immigrate there. Jewish families were invited to come to Berlin, and toward the end of the seventeenth century 6,000 French Huguenots found a home in this city.[9] Berlin needed skilled workers, and it was expected that the French would improve the level of education. At the beginning of the eighteenth century, Walloons, French-Swiss, people from the Palatinate, and other groups who had been driven out of their respective countries moved to the Prussian city. In 1732, over 2,000 Bohemian Protestants arrived. Frederick the Great expressly proclaimed religious freedom and, as a result, Berlin became an important destination for religious refugees. As part of his political strategy, he also established and renewed political contacts with foreign countries, receiving a Turkish delegation in 1763, for example.[10] Berlin was characterized by a climate of openness and religious tolerance, and it became the center of the German Enlightenment. Yet as always such a development did not exclude restrictions on the "outsiders," on *Fremde*, including Jews.[11] Moses Mendelssohn, who had served the city well and was given the status of "ausserordentlicher Schutzjude" (exceptional, protected Jew), was denied admission to the Akademie der Wissenschaften (Academy of Science). His application for naturalization was granted, but did not extend to his descendants.[12]

Berlin's otherness has been a recurring theme in the literary discourse on the city for centuries. Heinrich Heine's remark that Berlin was not even a city, but only provided a gathering space for a number of people, among them many intellectuals completely indifferent to their surroundings, is often cited. He affirmed Madame de Staël's assessment of Berlin as a "quite modern city" in which, as she said, one does not get "a sense of the history of the land or the character of its people."[13] She drew a comparison to American cities that would become popular in the early twentieth century. Berlin's modernity was often seen in a negative light, and Berlin was generally criticized as a provincial town, although it had already established its reputation as the cultural center of Germany. Even before the university was founded in 1810, many scientists, scholars, and artists were drawn to this city by its stimulating environment. The literary salons, first set up by Henriette Herz and Rahel Levin, also provided an engaging forum for the intellectual community.

By the end of the nineteenth century, Berlin was expanding at an unprecedented pace. It was during this period that the city gained its reputation as the epitome of a modern industrial metropolis. An indispensable component of this growth was the influx of *Fremde*. A rapidly expanding industry needed workers, and they came by the thousands, not for the most part from the regions surrounding Berlin, but from the eastern provinces of the Reich, escaping poverty and unemployment in the countryside. Many who came had expectations similar to those immigrating to the United States. But while conditions in the American frontier sometimes allowed for the realization of the American Dream, this was hardly the case within the rigid social milieu of Berlin.

In this city, the newcomers found appalling living conditions. It was the age of the *Mietskasernen*, literally the rental barracks, set up in a chain of working-class neighborhoods and housing about 90 percent of the city's population. These aptly named tenements were hardly designed for humane living. Writing on Berlin's housing conditions, the architectural critic Werner Hegemann described the city as a "stone-coffin": on the average seventy-eight persons shared the space that in the "island and skyscraper city New York" — a city with its own share of tenements — was occupied by only twenty persons.[14]

The rapid increase of the population — in 1877 Berlin had 1 million inhabitants, in 1905 already 2 million, and in 1920, after Greater Berlin was formed, nearly 4 million — accomplished a sudden change from a provincial capital to a true metropolis. The heterogeneity of the population and all the newly erected modern buildings made Mark Twain describe Berlin as "a European Chicago." Walter Rathenau repeated the analogy in his ironically titled essay, "The Most Beautiful City in the World," calling Berlin "Chicago on the Spree."[15] The comparison with Chicago rather than with New

York implied that Berlin had modernity without urbanity; because of its industry it had economic clout, but no style. Its population he found lacking in ingenuity. In Rathenau's view, the heterogeneous character of Berlin's population and the city's deficiencies were interrelated. "Concerning the Berliners," he wrote, he was not exactly sure "whether there are none left or they just haven't appeared yet. It was not the fertility of the soil alone that increased the population tenfold in three generations. I believe most Berliners are from Posen and the rest are from Breslau," he remarked with obvious distaste (141).

Karl Scheffler, who shared Rathenau's negative opinion of what he called "the capital of all modern ugliness,"[16] also blamed Berlin's failings to a large extent on the influx of immigrants, the workers who were needed in the factories. "All the capitals of Europe grew differently than Berlin" (16), he lamented. Berlin's *Fremde* did not constitute a sound basis for a populace: "Immigrants usually do not represent the highest flowering of a people. The able person who is successful has always remained at home" (18). In his view, it had been precisely the shortcomings of these individuals that had led them to immigrate; economic and social forces, political or religious repression were at best marginal causes. They came from nowhere, these "rejects, refugees, and people without possessions" (24); they were "young, ruthless and enterprising" longing for a modern "Americanism" (144). This mix of immigrants Scheffler called "barbarian colonialists," a population incapable of developing a culture (18, 143).[17] Berlin was "literally a colonial city," with no traditions strong enough to stem the relentless tide of "Americanization" (17, 141, 145).

These analogies with America were misguided, however. For mandarin intellectuals like Rathenau and Scheffler, "American" was a term of aesthetic reprobation. Industrialized Berlin was no unspoilt place that could be exploited for a mother country as the term colonial implies; nor was it truly a pioneer city like the newly established cities in Australia and America he refers to. When the workers thronged into the city from the provinces, harsh conditions of an industrial economy that relied on their labor awaited them. In the industrialized city everybody had the right to pursue individual goals, but there was no frontier, only facts, only factories. "Americanism" was a metaphor for modernity, for Berlin's rapid development at the expense of tradition for the relocation of large segments of the population in search of a decent livelihood. True, it shared similarities with American cities in this respect, but beyond this the experience was very different. The idea of a pioneer city was a romanticization of the free competition in an industrialized society.

World War I and the November Revolution brought great upheavals in their wake, and between 1920 and 1928 an additional 450,000 people arrived in Berlin. It was in the "golden twenties," as they were retrospectively called, that the city acquired a truly metropolitan character. Culturally and economically, Berlin became the center of Europe, and in both respects it also became the European center of American influence. "American" was no longer merely a metaphor of modernity; there were also direct influences during this era—most important, American private capital revitalized the economy. While some companies had previously established businesses, now Berlin became further Americanized.[18] Also American music, and most of all film, attracted wide audiences. The developing mass culture was mostly American and was eagerly absorbed by the public.[19] The new influences were welcomed by the city's bohemians, who regarded the adoption of certain fashionable aspects of the American way of life as, above all, an antibourgeois provocation.

The art dealer, writer, and editor of *Der Sturm*, Herwarth Walden, wrote: "Berlin is America as microcosm. Berlin is timeless movement and timeless life."[20] And there were not only American influences. For a short period during the twenties there were impulses from the Soviet Union as well; it became an "American-Bolshevik metropolis."[21] These foreign influences that fostered Berlin's image as a real metropolis were enthusiastically received. Where before only individual voices had expressed an appreciation of the city, now a fascination took over; a process of general affirmation of urban life had begun.

During the Third Reich, Berlin's role as the capital of Germany dramatically changed. The foreign influences became one of the major targets of propaganda campaigns by the National-Socialists, and with the Third Reich came a vehement critique of Weimar Berlin as a center of internationalism and decadence.[22] Berlin's intellectual and cultural elite was arrested, suppressed, or forced into exile along with over half of its Jewish residents. Much of its foreign population was deported or conscripted as forced labor, and the remnants of its Jewish population murdered along with their coreligionists from the occupied countries.

Postwar Berlin had a slow recovery. By the end of the war it had lost over a third of its residents; in the following years many refugees and others expelled from the eastern territories moved there. West Berlin became the focal point for those who regarded it as an "island of freedom and democracy." And as such it was certainly set up during the era of the cold war; it became a *Frontstadt*, a touchstone of East-West relations. Although the political climate has changed, Berlin has maintained this function.

During the postwar era, a system of financial incentives was developed to support West Berlin's economy, and to encourage West Germans to move there. Colorful buses advertising Berlin were sent through West Germany to attract those who were needed, mainly young qualified blue- and white-collar workers and families. In the early 1960s, when a program to recruit foreign nationals as "guest workers" in the Federal Republic was started, a large number were brought to West Berlin. As mainly unskilled workers, they work in the factories of Germany's largest industrial city, and with the current high unemployment rates they constitute a large contingent of the industrial reserve army. Today there are over 250,000 non-Germans living in the city, about 12 percent of its population. By far the largest group of foreign workers came from Turkey, followed by other minority groups from Greece, Yugoslavia, Italy, and other Southern European and Northern African countries. Originally they were called "guest workers"—now officially "foreign employees"—because their stay was considered to be only temporary. Although many of them have now lived in West Germany or West Berlin for some time, they are still considered temporary residents. As long as the policy of "demand-oriented integration" is maintained, their status will be a transient one. More recently a rather large number of *Auslandsdeutsche* (ethnic Germans), mainly from Poland and the Soviet Union, as well as many seeking asylum from all over the world, have passed through the city. The latter used the German–German situation to their advantage, flying into East Berlin, then crossing over into West Berlin. This permeability of the wall was then heavily criticized by those who generally called for its removal. When too many asylum seekers arrived in 1987, West German politicians actually requested that the GDR keep the wall closed.

Contemporary West Berlin does not have the political power of a capital, but its existence as an outpost of the "free" Western world, the *Frontstadt*, gives it special importance for West Germany and world politics. With the occupying (now called protecting) powers still present and all its special regulations concerning its peculiar status, Jane Kramer correctly observes: "The city as such is a legal fiction."[23] One could ironically characterize it as follows: "a mixture of museum, theater, film studio, convention center, megasized health club, nursing home, and dormitory for students, research lab and administrative maze."[24] This curious mixture of phenomena succinctly conveys the now-prevalent image of Berlin, but what is overlooked is that there always has been a political purpose in making Berlin like this.

2. Literature by *Fremde* in Berlin

> *A guided tour of Berlin: Ahead of us is Oranienplatz. . . . / This neighborhood is also referred to as Little Istanbul/ . . . . You're looking at working-class tenements from the turn of the century,/ when Silesians and East Prussians/ left their native soil in large numbers/ to settle in the industrial metropolis./ At that time, they say, the smell of cabbage/ filled the streets, now it is the smell of mutton, thyme, and garlic.*
>
> Aras Ören

Given Berlin's particular characteristics, the distinction between "outside" and "local" writers of Berlin literature becomes elusive. One anthology, which appeared in 1929, bore the title: *Hier schreibt Berlin* (This is Berlin writing).[25] Berlin speaks for itself, and the problem of determining who belongs to the circle of Berlin authors is thus circumvented. The editor found it necessary, however, to explain that his main criterion was contemporaneity, ignoring whether the selected authors had only recently come to the city or had already moved away.[26] In a recent article Dietger Pforte describes as contemporary "Berlin authors" all those who live in the city at this time, regardless of where they came from and when they arrived in Berlin. He explicitly includes authors from other countries.[27]

There have always been foreign authors who lived in Berlin for a time and documented their stay or referred to the Berlin environment in their fictions. Vladimir Nabokov, the Russian exile who used Berlin as a setting for no fewer than seven of his novels, and Christopher Isherwood are among the most famous. Today's most well-known foreign Berlin author is Aras Ören. He has lived in Berlin since 1969, still writes in Turkish and has his texts translated into German. His main focus is on "guest workers," and he explicitly refers to their situation as essential for his literary work.[28]

A major part of Ören's work is a tribute to the Berlin district of Kreuzberg, part of which is sometimes called "Little Istanbul" because of its heavily Turkish population. It was the first of the old working-class neighborhoods built during the turn-of-the-century population explosion. The *Mietskasernen*, which once housed the first great wave of peasants recruited to work in the factories, were also thought appropriate for the new foreigners, the Turkish peasant population, who could not afford decent housing. The construction of these working-class tenements in the metereologically undesirable eastern parts of the city had led to an almost complete segregation of the social classes.[29] The nonworking-class population never went there; for the bourgeoisie these parts of the city were terra incognita, its inhabitants an unknown species.[30] This division was reinforced when the Turks moved in during the 1960s. The segregation, however, has allowed the foreign population to preserve its way of life to a large extent, to try to re-create village life in a social system that arose within the confines of a limited space, in this distant urban setting.[31] As the Turkish author Güney Dal writes of his compatriots, "For 'them' Berlin was Anatolia, except that the stage-set was in the wrong place; and here they continued their Anatolian lifestyle, practiced for a thousand years."[32] Faced with a multifaceted alterity, differences in social customs, cultural values, and language, this living situation accommodates a need for a sense of community and belonging.

This development is typical of immigrant experience, and the insecurity about the length of their stay seems to make communities of common language and culture even more important for these "temporary immigrants." The transplanting of previous customs has always resulted in a curious mixture of tradition and change. Parts of Kreuzberg may now seem very Turkish to Germans; to Turks, however, they remain very German. Even the Turkish language spoken there has changed. And although many women can be seen wearing the typical Turkish dress—headscarf and wide pants under the dress—this does not necessarily indicate adherence to traditional Turkish norms and values. Studies have shown that women who dress this way here often do it to document a sense of belonging and would reject this clothing in Turkey as too conservative.[33] Those who do adhere more to traditions are nevertheless confronted with a different life-style. It is often said that the Kreuzberg situation made it possible to keep wives and daughters in what is called "Kreuzberg purdah." However, contact with the outside world cannot be completely prevented:[34] all of the areas with large concentrations of foreigners—Wedding, Neukölln, and Kreuzberg, even in the area called "Little Istanbul"—still have some German, mainly working-class, longtime residents and others who have recently chosen to live there. Kreuzberg is today known for "an entirely exotic mix of sixties leftists, seventies squatters, Turkish workers, art people, craft people and various other apostles of what Berliners call 'alternative culture,' punks, pimps, skinheads, addicts, architects, intellectuals."[35] Former citizens of the GDR should be added to this list: they are "the cream in the cocktail of exoticism in Kreuzberg," as Michael Sallmann, a transplant from the GDR himself, puts it.[36]

Berlin is the only German city that officially supports the existence of an "alternative culture." In other cities with a completely competitive free-market structure, small businesses like repair shops or vegetarian food stalls do not survive; in Berlin, however, competition is restricted, and whoever can come up with a project or small enterprise may receive a small share of the subsidies that are distributed. For political purposes Berlin's economy is based on a system of subsidies from West Germany, and one side-effect is a Berlin specialty, an extensive "alternative scene." Since support is limited, movement onto the welfare and unemployment rolls is fluid; but for those willing to live in voluntary poverty, the basic level of subsistence is met. In this environment then, there is space for a variety of communities, which is also why Berlin is the only German city with an urban formation that approximates the status of a ghetto, even though there are other German cities with a higher percentage of foreign residents, such as Frankfurt and Stuttgart.

Most of the Berlin literature by foreign writers on the "guest worker" experience deals with life in Kreuzberg. In the following, I shall relate how this life has been depicted and compare this literary treatment with examples of early twentieth-century Berlin literature on the immigrant experience.

Kreuzberg figures especially prominently in Ören's Berlin poems, the trilogy *Was will Niyazi in der Naunynstraße* (What's Niyazi doing in Naunynstraße, 1973), *Der kurze Traum aus Kagithane* (The fleeting dream of Kagithane, 1974) and *Die Fremde ist auch ein Haus* (A foreign place is a home too, 1980).[37] These texts are not poetry in the strict sense, but a synthesis of epic, dramatic, and lyrical elements. They reflect in content what Ören tries to accomplish with his synthesis in form — an aesthetic anticipation of a harmoniously functioning multicultural society. Since Ören views this as a group endeavor, these books do not have one main protagonist. There are multiple plot lines and the emphasis is continually changing; it is the interaction of a variety of characters that structures the plot. Ören deals with the German as well as Turkish residents, and his ideal of a unified multicultural community develops out of the coexistence of discrete cultural groups.

These works cover the period from 1971 to 1979, during which individuals living in Kreuzberg's Naunynstraße are portrayed in depth, partly by the use of flashbacks that explain the background of their present circumstances. Old Frau Kutzer's family history, for example, relates how workers in the late nineteenth century came from East Prussia, how class-consciousness grew in the Weimar Republic, and how it was crushed in 1933. Different narrative elements are interwoven, and two perspectives clearly emerge: that of the German working-class inhabitants who have lived there for many years, and that of the recent arrivals, the Turks.

The buildings in Kreuzberg, "the kind of houses from whose walls new walls are always emerging,"[38] have remained the same, but the arrival of the "guest workers" has produced clearly noticeable changes: "And Naunynstraße was/ filled with the fresh smell of thyme,/ filled with fresh hatred,/ filled with longing,/ filled with hope/ covered with the fragrance of the steppes" (21). Hatred and longing are found side by side — passages containing such descriptions point to differences and frictions, and show a far more accurate and complex grasp of the situation than Ören is able to convey in his attempts to force understanding. Again and again he articulates hopes for a dynamic pluralistic society with naive expectations of the possibilities of a democratic state. He repeatedly mentions the rights of the workers, and the first volume of the trilogy ends with a German helping Greek and Turkish workers to write letters to colleagues, bosses, and politicians. The assumption is that society can be changed if only the individuals show solidarity and fight for their legitimate rights — i.e., literature is meant to have an impact on the readership, to agitate for political involvement aimed at social transformation. With this approach Ören shows an affinity to the radical Berlin writers of the 1920s, particularly those who in 1928 founded the "Bund proletarisch-revolutionärer Schriftsteller" (Organization of Proletarian-Revolutionary Writers). These writers, too, regarded literature as a political instrument, as a means of changing reality, not merely of representing it.

"And Naunynstraße/ is again a street, where something is happening./ Different than 70 and 50 years ago/ and even more clumsily,/ but sometimes you can see/ what you don't expect: workers, residents of Naunynstraße/ drinking beer together/ discussing politics . . . " (67). Ören refers to political action in the past, often addressed by radical writers of the time. Klaus Neukrantz, for example, in *Barrikaden am Wedding* (1929) also focused on one street, the Kössliner Straße in the working-class district of Wedding. But where Neukrantz described violent street fights then, now the great goal is multiculturality on a very basic level. Ören reveres the solidarity of the victims and reduces the class conflict to a problem of communication.

When, around the turn of the century, hundreds of thousands came from the country to Berlin, the literary treatment of this experience similarly stressed improvement of the deplorable situation of the new urban poor by mutual understanding of people of all classes. Although the immigrants then did not come from a foreign country, they were very much perceived as foreigners in the city, and in some ways there are parallels between their situation and the current one. Those who came were rural people, driven to the city by poverty. Usually they were poorly educated and completely ignorant of life in a metropolis. Individual family members who came were expected to send money home to support the rest of the family. There was fear of the unknown and of city life in general, and a mourning for what had to be left behind. Berlin could just as well have been in the New World, it seemed so far away and alien. In Ingeborg Drewitz's novel, *Gestern war Heute* (Yesterday was tomorrow, 1978), the father of the protagonist, still poor, thinks back to their time of arrival from Silesia: "He had not forgotten the fear of standing somewhere, between the parents and the siblings, the trunks and cardboard boxes, wet snow. America or Berlin, no meadows, where you sink into flowers up to your hips, no creeks. . . ."[39] The newly arrived were apprehensive, but also full of hope that they would be able to make a living.

Most of the literature at the time, classified as social realism and naturalism in its concern for the underprivileged, was antiurban. This is particularly true of Clara Viebig's successful novel *Das tägliche Brot* (Daily bread, 1900). Viebig pointedly focused on the fate of women and gave a voice to the poor and the silent, and to those exploited as servants.[40] Mine and Bertha, two girls from Posen, in the eastern provinces, come to Berlin to seek employment, expecting that "happiness was to be found in the street; easy work, high wages."[41] Yet, from the very beginning, they experience city life at its worst. Their city of hope turns out to be a destructive force. They live in extreme poverty, the work is hard, and nobody can be trusted in this new environment. Only Mine, as the pure country girl still rooted in nature, is able to withstand the destructive forces of the city. There is, however, no simplistic opposition of the idyllic country to the evil city; the country itself does not provide much hope—after all, Mine cannot stay there and is rejected when she tries to return as a single mother. The basic struggle is between nature and the unnaturalness the city embodies. Nature is considered as harmonious, and the nature-city opposition produces mystifications in attributing qualities emerging from the respective source. Those who acquire the traits that seem to be necessary for survival in the city ultimately fail. Only strong, good-hearted "natural" individuals will not be crushed. Or as Fries writes: "Her novel portrays a struggle which originates in and is caused by the existing social situation; but the resolution of this struggle lies within the individual."[42] This view of the destructiveness of the city is typical of the antiurban tendencies of the time. In the savagely competitive urban environment no solidarity could be found; the reliance on individuals to change conditions could be based only on innate goodness. Thus the focus was on one central figure, the course of whose life was followed.

Although most texts in current *Ausländerliteratur* also show antiurban tendencies, in others a different view emerges: the city is seen not as a destructive threat, but as a locus of opportunities, opportunities based in real circumstances, not merely in expectations. Often—especially in Ören's works—there is no central protagonist, but various figures who shift in importance throughout the narrative. The stress on individuals as a decisive force for improving conditions, however, has remained. Workers are to gain insight into the situation and to become politically active.

When *Ausländerliteratur* or *Gastarbeiterarbeiterliteratur* (literature by foreigners or "guest workers") first emerged, it generally depicted the hardships of life in a foreign country, and the resulting loneliness and despair. Since then it has become more diverse, defying easy categorization. Now literary quality tends to be valued more than social documentation. Although some authors find the confines of *Ausländerliteratur* too restrictive, most foreign authors regard this minority literature as a means of raising awareness of discrimination and xenophobia, if not necessarily of effecting fundamental social change.[43] The repressed and silent minority is to be given a voice. In some cases, however, these attempts to politicize through literature suffer from a simplistic social romanticism.

One example is Jusuf Naoum's positive delineation of multiculturality in Kreuzberg. The Lebanese author takes up the story "Sindbad's Last Voyage" (Sindbads letzte Reise)[44] and has the famous seafarer Sindbad travel to Berlin on his magic carpet, which he loses when he lands in the Grunewald during a thunderstorm. He knocks on the door of many big houses, but is always turned away. With great relief he finally sees a dark-skinned man with black eyes—a Turk—who takes him home to Kreuzberg, to his one-room apartment in the rear inside courtyard of a block of tenements. After having seen the better parts of the city first, Sindbad is surprised when he gets to Kreuzberg, assuming it to be in a completely different city. But Mustafa explains: "We are in the same city. This is where we and German workers live" (153). The Turkish friend helps Sinbad to find work and explains the usefulness of trade unions. The solidarity of workers is stressed, the class interests seem to neutralize xenophobia. The fairy tale with well-known figures and forms from the Arabic narrative tradition is a device for calling attention to the life of foreigners in Berlin, to deplorable housing conditions in Kreuzberg, and facts like the residence quotas in certain areas.

Fürüzan, a Turkish woman writer who lived for a year as a guest author in Berlin, also provides an example of the solidarity of the underprivileged, which is, however, better developed. In her story "Frau Elfriede Lemmer," a poor lonely widow lives in a *Mietskaserne* in Kreuzberg that now houses "guest worker" families from Turkey, Greece, Italy, and Yugoslavia. Her own children neglect her, yet in the hospitable family of her Turkish neighbors she finds the warmth she so desperately needs: "She could feel it almost physically, the directness with which they offered their affection."[45] Stereotyped judgments about the impulsive warm-hearted Turks versus the reserved and cold Germans collide glaringly here, and the harmonious picture of the Turkish family is not quite convincing. Again solidarity is stylized as self-praise of the powerless.

Recently Aras Ören has become much less vocal about multicultural solidarity. He seems increasingly disillusioned with Berlin, since his dreams of the harmonious multicultural society have remained unfulfilled. His focus has shifted from the lives of residents in Kreuzberg more to the city itself. Now he looks at Berlin as "a person you love who is being kept alive by intravenous feeding,"[46] and who he occasionally would like to abandon. He describes Berlin as a "provincial metropolis": "Horizon narrow, air polluted, clouds down to the ground,/ ugly buildings, grey and monstrous,/ no coziness,/ no home and the streets/ broad and orderly, but without life."[47]

The idea of the melting pot of emancipation has not been sustained. *Mitten in der Odyssee* (In the middle of the odyssey, 1980) already contains a section on "Laments, Complaints, Songs, and Presentations of Our People in Berlin,"[48] in which Ören speaks for the "guest workers'" plight, stressing the negative aspects. In the volume *Gefühllosigkeiten: Reisen von Berlin nach Berlin* (Without feeling: Journeys from Berlin to Berlin, 1986) his tone is even more resigned: the city has become a ruin of history, "a wreck/ the nightingale is silent/ the rose wilts."[49] He complains: "But Berlin comes no closer, it is still so far away./ Railroad bridges from the old days,/ their sad present terminates on dead-end tracks," and asks: "With what poetic hope have we lived,/ gathering tears that have dried?" (16). The houses are like oriental bazaars, yet what they contain is a strange mixture: "a soap opera on video" and "reduced sale products, leftovers of the affluent society" (13). Turks can only participate at the fringes, leftovers are their appropriate share, "disappointment and sacrifice and patience" are part of their daily life" (12). The belief in the possibility of changing the system and in people's willingness to change their attitudes has been deeply shaken.

Ören's prose texts transmit the same sentiment. *Bitte nix Polizei* (Please no police), a crime story that takes place in Kreuzberg's Pücklerstraße, ends at an impasse, with the suicide of the illegal Turkish alien Ali. Jobless, he feels lost, like a "nonperson, a nobody,"[50] only disdainfully tolerated by the distant relatives he stays with. He is a victim of the conditions. He is homeless, isolated, and lost; and with his death he ultimately becomes a victim of the city. The foreigner can hardly communicate with Germans, but they too have serious communication problems among themselves. After all, the first death occurs because nobody wants to help an old man who has fallen in the snow. All of the street's residents struggle to maintain their lives as they are; they all seem to be helpless and trapped; even in their dreams they cannot project a different world. Reflections of the past, of the immediate postwar years, are used to help explain current attitudes. With multiple plot lines and continual shifts of the narrative *I* to different figures, the feelings and the history of various individuals are illuminated.

Ören's narrative *Manege* (Arena) follows one day in the dreary existence of Bekir Uçal, director of a counseling agency for foreigners. On his walks through Kreuzberg, he becomes lost in thought. Stories from Turkey, memories of his village, dreams and fantasies of the future, and plans for alternative life-styles are interspersed with detailed descriptions of his present environment. The boundaries between reality and dream are fluid. A phenomenon typical of uprooted people in a foreign country is described: the habit of daydreaming, the attempt to reconcile the dissonant fragments of different cultural spheres. Uçal—his name means "the flying"—has lived in Kreuzberg for many years; people know him, and yet he suffers from loneliness and misses the feeling of belonging: "But where is my home? The room in Leibnizstraße is just a place to stay."[51] He longs for a true home, a place within a safe, familiar frame, but he does not idealize what he left behind in Turkey. There is an awareness of home as an illusion of security and coherence; thus he then comments: "My home has always been inside of me, never outside. I carry it around with me. Even though we are fairly distant from one another, we go everywhere together."[52] The displaced person finds means to draw disparate parts of himself together by acknowledging the fragmentary character of the self.[53]

Ören avoids any idealization of the home country. Fontane's dictum: "Only when we are far away do we realize what our home means to us,"[54] seems not necessarily applicable when living conditions in the home country are such that people are forced to leave. In many examples of early "guest worker" literature, as well as in traditional literature by immigrants to the United States, however, the country that was left is seen as an idyllic place that could have fulfilled all needs, if only conditions had been better. In the literature by and about those who came to the Federal Republic for a limited time, the return home is a recurring theme, but none of these texts portrays it as a positive experience. The younger generation often address the problem of *Zerrissenheit*, of being torn between two countries yet belonging to neither, reflecting their own experience. They are foreigners, even when born and raised in the Federal Republic of Germany.

In its traditional sense, *Heimat* connotes nature and the comforting stability of an existing order ostensibly founded on natural law. As a concept this is conservative and antiurban. A loss of this sense of *Heimat* may thus be taken as a positive sign of innovation and progress.

In the Berlin trilogy and other works by Ören are passages describing the beauty of the Turkish countryside and of Istanbul, but the poverty of the people and political repression are also addressed. The foreign workers' motivation for coming to Northern Europe has always been a struggle for economic survival. The specific place of work is not of primary importance to them, nor are they always given a choice of location. Accordingly, they have no great expectations of Berlin; it provides the possibility of making a living and can therefore become a home, as the title of the last part of the trilogy declares: *A Foreign Place Is a Home Too*. The certainty of a *Heimat*, the birthplace as home, no longer exists in this age of mass migration; if at all, the home has to be reestablished in a new environment. The new home then can provide security and a sense of belonging: "Look, this has become our house,/ this means: we are at home here as well."[55] This home then ought to become permanent after such a lengthy stay in a foreign land. In his afterword to *Deutschland, ein türkisches Märchen* (Germany, a Turkish fairy tale, 1978), Ören states, "Having founded little Istanbuls here, we do not want to go back to Turkey and found little Germanies there, all in one lifetime."[56]

Those foreigners who have lived in Berlin so long that they are by now almost natives while technically and legally remaining outsiders have the advantage of bifocality.[57] As has been shown, this is reflected in their literature, in the interweaving of German and Turkish history, of past and new impressions, and of various formal structures, including elements of foreign narrative traditions. Their "otherness" opens new ways of perceiving, of interreference and possibilities of incorporating new concepts into their work. They represent essentially the type of "wanderer," as Georg Simmel characterized it: "He is settled in a particular geographical area . . . but his position there is largely determined by the fact that he has not been part of it right from the beginning, that he brings qualities to this place that did not, and could not, originate there."[58]

Walter Benjamin refers to the perception of place that is peculiar to foreigners. In his review of Franz Hessel's *Spazieren in Berlin* (Walking in Berlin, 1929), for instance, he draws a distinction among descriptions of cities based on where the authors were born. Benjamin states that the exotic, the picturesque, affect only foreigners, while descriptions by native-born authors will always be more like memoirs, since their movement is more into the past than to a distant place.[59] This is certainly true with regard to his own description of Berlin, which he was to write a few years later, *Berliner Kindheit um Neunzehnhundert* (A Berlin childhood around 1900, 1932–1938). This is less so for Hessel, a long-time resident of Berlin, who pays little attention to personal reminiscences, rather deliberately choosing to mingle with strangers and to describe his city from their point of view. In so doing, however, Hessel supports the idea that one's own city does not attract one's attention as something special. This conscious change of perspective facilitates varied perceptions.

This phenomenon, however, is different from the point of view found in the recent literature by foreigners discussed thus far. Clearly they do not present the curious visitor's point of view, and their aim is not to explore the city for pleasure. Most often West Berlin as a whole is not depicted, but only Kreuzberg. There are few references to the attractions of the city, but many to Kreuzberg's miserable housing conditions. In this respect, parallels with the earlier literature of urban immigration are obvious. In Viebig's *Das tägliche Brot*, the setting is largely restricted to Schöneberg as a representative working-class district in this Berlin of the urban poor; the more prosperous or culturally interesting sections are neglected.[60] Viebig obviously concentrates on poverty and the lives of those who hardly ever left their area. The same is true today: Kreuzberg is geographically close, but nevertheless far away from the city of glamour and glitter. As in the earlier literature, the major themes addressed are close to reality: the problems of adjustment, the search for ways to cope, in short, the struggle to adjust in an alien environment. That the struggles and disappointment are so prominently featured shows how central these issues are to the lives of these foreigners and attests to the persistent difficulties of life in an alien environment.[61] The initial hostility—especially toward Turks as originally the least welcomed of all "guest workers"—has subsided. However, xenophobia has certainly not been eliminated, and it is now being fueled again by right-wing political groups. But these foreigners, the "guest worker" population, have by now become accepted as residents. The Turks in particular are occasionally praised for being model citizens and, in reference to some recent radical activities, it has been said that "the feeling among ordinary Kreuzbergers these days is that the only good foreigners here are the Turkish workers."[62]

3. *Fremde* in Berlin Literature

> Hope of the sub-cultures of the provinces
> Artificial soil for the uprooted.
>
> Monica Streit

Most contemporary West Berlin authors now incorporate *Fremde* into their narratives as part of the Berlin setting. As an integral part of the city's local color, they are present, as backdrop, in all forms of fiction. *Szeneliteratur* in particular always includes some reference to foreigners as proof of its authenticity, its direct link to Berlin reality.[63] The Turks have become such a characteristic feature in this city's literature that they are frequently mentioned to signal that the setting is West Berlin. Thus, for instance, in Helga Schubert's short story *Das verbotene Zimmer* (The forbidden room), the first impression of the person coming through the Friedrichstraße checkpoint from East Berlin is of the old-age pensioners and the Turks.[64] Others emphasize the foreign residents as an attractive characteristic of the metropolis and stress the much–desired similarity with New York. Bodo Morshäuser writes, "A Berlin for Berliners only? It's inconceivable!/ Bring in the foreigners! Bring in the foreigners!/ New York with nothing but New Yorkers just wouldn't be New York."[65]

Sympathy for foreigners may improve one's self-image: "What Kreuzberg needs is a minaret," Günter Grass states in his generous philanthropic reflections after a Sunday afternoon walk through this part of the city. He contemplates Kreuzberg as the center for a utopian experiment in international living. In his view, this is a strategy for Berlin's survival, because the city's future cannot be ensured through West German subsidies alone. The internationalization of Berlin's population is needed to prevent "West Berlin from becoming nothing but an old age home."[66] Such utilitarian proposals remain highly questionable; besides, there *are* twenty-five mosques in Berlin—although they lack minarets, since most of them had to be established in existing structures, in most cases deserted factories.

Linie 1,[67] the immensely popular play by the Grips theater group named after the subway line that runs through the very heart of Kreuzberg, presents a complete cross section of Berlin's population, and accordingly foreigners play a major role. Their presence not only adds to the colorful picture, but also serves to provoke xenophobic comments by passengers on the train. This play obviously aims to increase social awareness in its audience, therefore common prejudices appear frequently in this often banal plot that comes dangerously close to social criticism as kitsch. The protagonist, a girl recently arrived in the city from the West German provinces, views Berlin through the lens of its clichés: She is thrilled by the famous "Berliner Luft," this air "that smells of soot and adventure" (3); by its geopolitical uniqueness, "where in all directions it is East/ The sun therefore never goes down/ but always only rises" (40).

A move to Berlin in the quest for personal liberation is nothing new and this theme has always had its place in literature: "Berlin! Berlin! . . . Let yourself be swept away into its wild life" exclaimed Julius Hart nearly a century ago.[68] Hugo Ball's reaction upon his arrival at the end of World War I conveys similar excitement: "This city has initiative, energy, intellect. . . .

Here a new life begins: anarcho-revolutionary . . . contradictory . . . active."[69] This emergent cultural capital of Europe and center of the avant-garde, this "electrified focal point of Germany,"[70] drew artists and writers from all over the world.[71] The myth of the "whore Babylon" was at once alluring and intimidating. In heady anticipation of the city's excitement, animated by a lust tinged with fear, they came from the provinces.[72]

Anything seemed possible, and not only artists and those in quest of work came, but also adventurers and nonconformists of various backgrounds. Doris, the young and naive girl in Irmgard Keun's *Das kunstseidene Mädchen* (The girl in artificial silk, 1932) was drawn to Berlin as an escape from the confines of her provincial existence in pursuit of her dreams of glamour. Fame and fortune, not a regular job, were her goals.[73]

The myth of the wild and flamboyant life in Berlin still attracts new residents every year, but now they are a different sort. They are not the avant-garde, but mainly young West Germans and some foreigners, expecting to find adventure, an "alternative life-style," possibly only for a period of time, passing through en route to a settled professional life. "Although the city has been decreasing in population, there are more and more of us every day," the narrator in *Berliner Simulation* remarks.[74]

After only a few months in the city, a young author recently won the first prize in a literature contest with a badly written text praising Berlin's uniqueness: "baerlin (sic) is not a city—it is a world. . . . berlin is functional, improvised and *directly* alive, unmediated—not as a museum like Vienna; and everybody must take care of his own life in berlin, more so than in other places: otherwise he will perish in the mechanism of the unrestrained will to live in this strange city."[75] The author obviously reiterates old images that have been used to characterize and—according to the position of the commentator—to criticize or praise Berlin for centuries. The challenge for the individual, the adventure, appears most important to him. The sense of mortal danger is reminiscent of the adventure spirit that was prevalent some time ago in Berlin's history. What was once a real struggle, however, has now become a favorite theme for those bored with the banality and monotony of everyday life. As Thomas Steinfeld has argued, the struggle for survival is attractive in that all other questions seem insignificant compared to this ultimate quest for meaning.[76] In a world where real adventure has become rare, the myth of Berlin provides a frame for testing one's mettle. Since New York remains the ultimate challenge, a city whose high crime rate and aggressiveness pose real danger, the description of Berlin as "New York's younger sister"[77] is a tribute to its metropolitan image.

Johann Ritter, in Michael Kleeberg's *Der saubere Tod*, is a typical protagonist of this sort. He comes to Berlin from the provinces, and his initial impressions meet his expectations: "People formed strange patterns, were drawn together around the traffic lights, then were spat out again in all directions. . . . He heard music: New York, New York. He removed his glasses and saw three Turkish kids breakdancing in front of the shop windows."[78] Johann is drawn there to the anticipated excitement in Berlin, and "to acquire, within a year, money, a large old apartment, a sportscar. He believed that there were two ways to accomplish this: One could either sell drugs or oneself. He was prepared for both" (7). He has come to work toward a comfortable lifestyle, but also to prove himself in competitive environment, different from his well-organized background in the province he comes from. He heads directly to Kreuzberg.

The novel captures a current trend: a lot of young "Wessies" (i.e., West Germans) from all walks of life come not just to Berlin, but to Kreuzberg, "trading in the dreary certainties of an apprenticed life in the Federal Republic of Germany for the spacey possibilities of a 'scene' in the shadow of the Berlin Wall."[79] It is a challenge to move there, and this challenge appears as very attractive to many. The struggle for survival may sometimes end tragically: the recent story of a girl from the provinces, whose skeleton was found years after her death in a Kreuzberg attic, is such a case; yet all the press coverage only served to reinforce the Kreuzberg mystique.[80]

"Kreuzberg, brother, is West Berlin's Harlem/ or the Bronx, here/ we call the niggers/ Turks, pensioners, workers," writes Peter Paul Zahl.[81] "This heart and stomach of the city" exudes poverty and despair, just as it did a hundred years ago with its different, but equally poor residents. In this context the analogy to Harlem and the Bronx actually enhances Kreuzberg. It implies its affinity to even more challenging places.

Some of those who move to Kreuzberg are politically active, others see it as temporary diversion on their way up, still others are dropouts and drifters. Other than the workers, those who have chosen to come to Kreuzberg have always been different, have made a point of being "*Verweigerer*, of rejecting the conventions of bourgeois German life."[82] The squatters of the seventies gave Kreuzberg its reputation as a place for radicalism. Street gangs have formed, and violent riots have taken place, especially on May Day. The "Autonomen" thrive on confrontation with the police, representatives of the "system" they abhor, and as Michael Rutschky points out, they show in their constant struggle, in their search for encounters, an almost religious belief in the state.[83] The contrast with those other residents of Kreuzberg is striking: the foreign immigrant population comes to Kreuzberg out of material necessity, and in comparison with some of the district's more extreme "alternative" residents, the Turks have come to be looked upon as normal citizens.

A variety of groups have established a space in Kreuzberg then, but there is hardly any direct contact between them. Michael Sallmann states that not only do Turks remain among Turks, Poles with fellow Poles, but former GDR citizens keep to themselves too. He concludes, "The cultures in

Kreuzberg do not live with each other, but next to each other."[84] Openness
and tolerance, multiculturality as characteristic of the metropolis—this is an
image that does not hold true; Ören's expectations have not been fulfilled.
Kreuzberg has today become a titillating sightseeing spot, a popular destination of tourist buses. The play *Linie 1* includes the following tour guide's
description in English.

> And now ladies and gentlemen, the exiting high point of every Berlin visit;
> the journey to Kreuzberg! SO 36! Their [sic] burns the air, there you are
> from the socks, a mixture out of rive gauche and the Bronx and then still
> singular on the world! There leads only one way: a trip with the undertrain
> line one! Take the A train, as they say in Paris to it. From the zoo till into
> the darkest place of the town are there just ten stations, whose names let
> each Berlin knower showers of luck over body and soul run.[85]

This satire on Kreuzberg as tourist attraction has the ring of truth. On a
daily basis busloads of tourists are driven through this area, and the mayor
has written an introduction to a tourist guide, pointing out Oranienstraße as
a cultural happening.

"Authentic" experiences add excitement and, occasionally, "meaning" to
life; they also provide material for a literature that strives for verisimilitude.
Authentic personal experience is of primary importance in the *Szeneliteratur*,
and, according to Klaus Scherpe, it is this literature that still evokes direct
emotional responses and "real" feelings. It is dominated by "a skewed
yearning for immediacy in the self-contained city district [Großstadt-
kiez]."[86] And Kreuzberg, affectionately called a "scrapheap of a whore"
(*abgewrackte Hure*),[87] provides the setting.

In minority literature depicting the lives of workers in an alien country,
struggle is not sought out but is the inevitable consequence of the friction
that occurs when dreams collide with reality. In the *Szeneliteratur*, on the
other hand, West Germans deliberately seek out struggle, either as adventure or often as a form of survival training in the metropolis. The myth of
the metropolis never had any meaning for the minority workers; for the second group mentioned, it is nourishment for their subjectivity, even if they
become its victims. Despite its sobering reality, Berlin continues to have the
image of a special place where everything is possible. As the West Berlin
periodical *Niemandsland* recently proclaimed, in a gush of urban euphoria:

> Berlin is perhaps the most important refuge in Europe. Berlin is the
> liveliest, most sensual symbol of the remnants of utopia in our civilization,
> for the impossible. Berlin is a hysterical beacon against all social entropies
> because the city incorporates even them, it absorbs, digests, and
> transforms.[88]

The myth of Berlin lives on and continues to be marketed.

NOTES

1. Manfred Mixner, "Heimkehr nach Berlin," *Niemandsland. Zeitschrift zwischen den Kulturen*, 6 (1988): 29. [Translations of this and all other German quotations are my own.]

2. Walter Rathenau, "Die schönste Stadt der Welt," in *Impressionen*, 2d ed. (Leipzig, 1902), 140.

3. Karl Scheffler, *Berlin: Ein Stadtschicksal*, 2d ed. (Berlin, 1910), 267.

4. Beta [Johann Heinrich Bettziech], *Berlin und Potsdam* (Berlin, 1846), 83.

5. Heinrich Mann, *BZ am Mittag*, 23 November 1921. On the *Menschenwerkstatt* see also Harald Jähner, Chapter 6 in this volume.

6. See Willy Hellpach, *Mensch und Volk in der Großstadt*, 2d revised ed. (Stuttgart, 1952), 74.

7. See Gottfried Korff, "Berlin-Berlin. Menschenstadt und Stadtmenschen," in *750 Jahre Berlin. Stadt der Gegenwart*, ed. Ulrich Eckhardt (Frankfurt/Main, 1986), 148.

8. See Jane Kramer, "Letter from Europe," *The New Yorker*, 28 November 1988, 67–100.

9. See Herrmann Schreiber, *Auf den Spuren der Hugenotten* (Munich, 1983); and Rudolph von Thadden, Michelle Magdelaine, eds., *Die Hugenotten* (Munich, 1985).

10. See Gültekin Emre, *300 Jahre Türken an der Spree* (Berlin, 1983), 12. Emre writes that at this point public opinion and the press claimed the end of hatred and wars against the Turks. He explains that this, of course, was a political move to find allies against the Habsburg monarchy.

11. Only certain professions were available to Jews; and although they were granted political equality in 1812, severe restrictions remained until the end of Imperial Germany. See Monika Richarz, "Jüdisches Berlin und seine Vernichtung," in *Die Metropole. Industriekultur in Berlin im 20. Jahrhundert*, ed. Jochen Boberg, Tilman Fichter, and Eckhart Gillen (Munich, 1986), 216–25. See also Manfred Hammer and Julius H. Schoeps, eds., *Juden in Berlin* (Berlin, 1986).

12. See Heinz Knobloch, *Herr Moses in Berlin* (Berlin, 1986). On the significance of foreign scholars for science and the arts, see the three volumes of the exhibition catalog *Wissenschaften in Berlin*, ed. Tilmann Buddensieg, Kurt Düwell, Klaus-Jürgen Sembach (Munich, 1987); also see Stefan Germer " 'Ein dürrer Boden, bis man Fremde hinberuft . . . ,' " in Eckhardt, *750 Jahre Berlin*, 206–17.

13. "Briefe aus Berlin," in *Und grüß mich nicht Unter den Linden: Heine in Berlin. Gedichte und Prosa*, ed. Gerhard Wolf (Frankfurt, 1981),136. (Original quote in French.)

14. See Werner Hegemann, *Das steinerne Berlin: Geschichte der größten Mietkasernenstadt der Welt* (Berlin, 1930).

15. Rathenau, "Die schönste Stadt der Welt" (see note 2), 144. The following quotations in the text are from this essay.

16. Scheffler, *Berlin: Ein Stadtschicksal* (see note 3), 200; the following quotations in the text are from this edition.

17. He mentions the literary salons, but sees them only as coming out of the Jewish family tradition without any impact on the city's culture. See 125.

18. See Hans Dieter Schäfer, "Metropole verinselt," in Boberg, Fichter, Gillen, *Die Metropole*, 282–89. See also the section "Norddeutsches Amerika" in *Im Exerzierfeld der Moderne: Industriekultur im Jahrhundert in Berlin*, ed. Boberg, Fichter, and Gillen (Munich, 1984).

19. See Anton Kaes, "Einleitung," in *Weimarer Republik. Manifest und Dokumente zur deutschen Literatur* (Stuttgart, 1983), 28. See also ch. 5, "Die Auseinandersetzung mit dem kulturellen Amerikanismus."

20. Quoted from Boberg, Fichter, Gillen, *Die Metropole*, 7.

21. See Helmut Lethen, "Chicago und Moskau," in Boberg, Fichter, Gillen, *Die Metropole* (see note 11), 190–213. Concerning the Russian emigrants see Gabriele Gericke, "Russische Emigranten im Berlin der zwanziger Jahre," in *Mythos Berlin* (Berlin, 1987), 181–86.

5240   Heidrun Suhr

22. See Linda Schulte-Sasse's article in this volume.

23. Kramer, "Letter from Europe" (see note 8), 69.

24. *Niemandsland* (see note 1), 29.

25. Herbert Günther, ed., *Hier schreibt Berlin. Eine Anthologie von heute* (Berlin, 1929).

26. Ibid., 16.

27. Dietger Pforte, "Berlin—ein Zentrum der deutschsprachigen Literatur," *Börsenblatt* 21 (13 March 1987): 815. See also the short biographies in the *Berliner Autoren-Stadtbuch* (Berlin, 1985). Only 28 of the 111 writers presented were born in Berlin, and a lot of the others decided to stay after first having been guests of the city.

28. See for example his acceptance speech for the 'Adelbert-von-Chamisso-Prize in *Chamissos Enkel*, ed. Heinz Friedrich (Munich, 1986), 25–29.

29. Hegemann, *Das steinerne Berlin* (see note 14), 240.

30. See Rolf Lindner, "Das andere Ufer. Zwei-Kulturen-Metapher und Großstadtforschung," in *Großstadt. Aspekte empirischer Kulturforschung*, ed. Theodor Kohlmann and Herman Bausinger (Berlin, 1985), 298. Lindner refers here to Gareth Stedman Jones's study on outcast London: *A Study in the Relationship between Classes in Victorian Society* (Harmondsworth, UK, 1976).

31. Recently scholars in urban studies have begun to ask whether the traditional characteristics of the country versus the city are still valid or not, if rather the city, and particularly a metropolis, can provide the setting for new social formations, new group networks, and new neighborhood relationships. See for example Karl Schwarz, "Die Metropolen wollen, Berlin als Metropole wollen," in *Die Zukunft der Metropolen: Paris, London, New York, Berlin*, ed. Karl Schwarz (Berlin, 1984), 15–30.

32. Güney Dal, "Merhabe Berlin! [Guten Tag, Berlin!]," in *Die Vögel des falschen Paradieses* (Frankfurt/Main, 1985), 81.

33. See Nermun Abadan-Unat, "Identity Crisis of Turkish Migrants," in *Turkish Workers in Europe*, ed. Norman Furniss and Ilhan Basgöz (Bloomington, Ind., 1985), 3–22.

34. See Gündüz Vassaf, *Wir haben unsere Stimme noch nicht laut gemacht. Türkische Arbeiterkinder in Europa* (Felsberg, FRG, 1985). Vassaf's study on the effects of migration, particularly in women and children, claims that the traditional unity of Turkish families is threatened by the liberal life-style in Northern Europe.

35. Kramer, "Letter from Europe" (see note 8), 67.

36. Michael Sallmann, "Im Mief von Ost nach West," *Frankfurter Rundschau*, 11 (June 1988).

37. All three volumes were published in Berlin by the Rotbuchverlag.

38. Aras Ören, *Was will Niyazi in der Naunynstraße* (Berlin, 1973), 63. The following citations in the text are taken from this edition.

39. Ingeborg Drewitz, *Gestern war Heute* (Düsseldorf, 1978), 10.

40. For the situation of the servants, the *Dienstmädchen*, see Karin Walser, "Der Zug in die Stadt. Berliner Dienstmädchen um 1900," in *Triumph und Scheitern in der Metropole*, ed. Sigrun Anselm and Barbara Beck (Berlin, 1987), 75–90. For the situation of the working woman in Berlin, see Christiane Seifert and Susanne Rouette, eds., *Unter allen Umständen. Frauengeschichte(n) in Berlin* (Berlin, 1986).

41. Clara Viebig, *Das tägliche Brot*, 10th ed. (Berlin, 1905), 5. For an extensive discussion of this work see Marilyn S. Fries, "The Plight of the Proletariat," in *The Changing Consciousness of Reality* (Bonn, 1980), 74–100.

42. Fries, "The Plight of the Proletariat," 77.

43. For a survey of the development of this literature see Heidrun Suhr, "Ausländerliteratur: Minority Literature in the Federal Republic of Germany," *New German Critique*, 46 (Winter 1989): 71–103.

44. Jusuf Naoum, "Sindbads letzte Reise," in *Als Fremder in Deutschland*, ed. Irmgard Ackermann (Munich, 1982),147–64.

45. Fürüzan, "Frau Elfriede Lemmer," in *Eine Fremde wie ich*, ed. Hülya Özkan and Andrea Wörle (Munich, 1985), 129.

46. Aras Ören, "Meine Bindung an Berlin," *Zeitschrift für Kulturaustausch* 1 (1985): 81.

47. Aras Ören, "Einer provinziellen Metropole grimmige Miene," *Dazwischen* (Frankfurt/Main, 1987), 44.

48. Aras Ören, "Klagen, Beschwerden, Lieder, Darstellungen der Unsrigen in Berlin," in *Mitten in der Odyssee* (Düsseldorf, 1980), 99–106.

49. Aras Ören, *Gefühllosigkeiten: Reisen von Berlin nach Berlin* (Frankfurt/Main, 1986), 16. The following citations in the text are taken from this edition.

50. Aras Ören, *Bitte nix Polizei* (Frankfurt/Main, 1983), 20.

51. Aras Ören, *Manege* (Frankfurt/Main, 1984).

52. Ibid., 120.

53. This concept also occurs in Ören's most recent publication, a semiautobiographical novel that depicts a Turkish intellectual's search for identity in Berlin. See *Eine verspätete Abrechnung oder Der Aufstieg der Gündogdus* (Frankfurt/Main, 1988).

54. Theodor Fontane, "Vorwort," *Wanderungen durch die Mark Brandenburg*, in *Sämtliche Werke*, vol. 1 (Munich, 1966), 9.

55. Aras Öran, in *Odyssee* (see note 48), 55.

56. Aras Ören, *Deutschland, ein türkisches Märchen* (Düsseldorf, 1978), 117.

57. Bifocality has only recently become an important issue in literature, whereas it has always been part of the anthropological rationale. See Michael M. J. Fischer, "Ethnicity and the Post-Modern Arts of Memory," in *Writing Culture. The Poetics of Ethnography*, ed. James Clifford and George E. Marcus (Berkeley, 1986), 194–233.

58. Georg Simmel, "Exkurs über den Fremden," in *Soziologie. Untersuchungen über die Formen der Vergesellschaftung* (Leipzig, 1908), 685.

59. See Walter Benjamin, "Die Wiederkehr des Flaneurs" (review of Franz Hessel's *Spazieren in Berlin*), in *Gesammelte Schriften*, vol. 3, ed. Hella Tiedemann-Bartels (Frankfurt/Main, 1972), 194.

60. See Fries, "The Plight of the Proletariat" (see note 41), 99.

61. See for example the documentary films by Mehrangis Montazami-Dabui, *Männerrecht-Frauenleid. Türkinnen in Deutschland* (1981); *Kindertränen* (1986).

62. Jane Kramer, "Letter from Europe" (see note 8), 67.

63. See for example Ulf Miehe, *Lilli Berlin* (Frankfurt, 1983); Ulrich Peltzer, *Die Sünden der Faulheit* (Zürich, 1987).

64. Helga Schubert, *Das verbotene Zimmer. Geschichten* (Darmstadt, FRG, 1982), 86.

65. Bodo Morshäuser, *Berliner Simulation* (Frankfurt/Main, 1983), 91.

66. Günter Grass, "In Kreuzberg fehlt ein Minarett," in *Berlin, ach Berlin*, ed. Hans Werner Richter (Munich, 1984), 116–18.

67. Volker Ludwig, *Linie 1*, Textbuch, Grips Theater Berlin (Berlin, 1986). Volker Hauff directed the filming of this play. The film was released under the same title in 1988.

68. Julius Hart, "Berlin 1," in *Berlin! Berlin! Eine Großstadt im Gedicht*, ed. Hans-Michael Speier (Stuttgart, 1987), 14–16.

69. Hugo Ball, *Briefe 1911–1927*, ed. Annemarie Schütt-Hennings (Zürich, 1957), 33 and 36, quoted from David Bathrick,"Die Berliner Avantgarde der 20er Jahre. Das Beispiel Franz Jung," in *Literarisches Leben in Berlin 1871–1933*, ed. Peter Wruck (Berlin, 1987), 45–79.

70. Leonhard Frank, *Links wo das Herz ist* (Munich, 1982), 128.

71. See David Bathrick, "Die Berliner Avantgarde der 20er Jahre, 45–76 (see note 69). See also Hermann Kähler, *Berlin—Asphalt und Licht. Die große Stadt in der Literatur der Weimarer Republik* (Berlin, 1986).

72. See Hanne Bergius, "Berlin als Hure Babylon," in Boberg, Fichter, and Gillen, *Die Metropole* (see note 11), 102–19.

73. In Berlin, employment for women was increasingly available during the 1920s. Changes in technology and the expansion of bureaucracy led to overall changes in the structure of society. The group of *Angestellten* (white-collar workers) grew considerably, among them many women who now had the opportunity for an independent income in a white-collar field. For the opportunities for women in Berlin in the 1920s see Sigrun Anselm, "Emanzipation und Tradition in den 20er Jahren," in Anselm and Beck, *Triumph und Scheitern in der Metropole* (see note 40), 253–74. See also Elke Kupschinsky, "Die vernünftige Nephertete. Die 'Neue Frau' der 20er Jahre in Berlin," in Boberg, Fichter, and Gillen, *Die Metropole* (see note 11), 164–72.

74. Morshäuser, *Berliner Simulation*, 65.

75. W. Mondrian Graf v. Lüttichau, ". . . wie eine große schwester," *Tagesspiegel*, 5 April 1987.

76. Thomas Steinfeld, "Metropole, Provinz. Literatur und großstädtisches Selbstbewußsein," *Merkur* 471 (May 1988): 395.

77. Claudio Lange, "Besuch," in Richter, *Berlin, ach Berlin* (see note 66), 128.

78. Michael Kleeberg, *Der saubere Tod* (Munich, 1987) 11ff.

79. Jane Kramer, "Letter from Europe" (see note 8), 67.

80. Marie-Luise Scherer, "Der unheimliche Ort Berlin," *Spiegel* 21 (18 May 1987): 98–125.

81. Peter Paul Zahl, "Kreuzberg, Bruder, ist Westberlins Harlem," in *Berlin, du deutsche Frau*, ed. Ingrid Krüger and Eike Schmitz (Darmstadt, FRG, 1985), 170.

82. Kramer, "Letter from Europe," 71.

83. Michael Rutschky has called them *Staatsfromme*, or pious toward the state, in "Das Reden von Berlin," *Merkur* 476 (October 1988): 888.

84. Michael Sallmann, "Im Mief von Ost nach West" (see note 36).

85. *Linie 1* (see note 67), 47.

86. See Klaus R. Scherpe, "Nonstop nach Nowhere City?" in *Die Unwirklichkeit der Städte*, ed. Klaus Scherpe (Reinbek bei Hamburg, 1988), 9, 148.

87. See Annette Berr, *Nachts sind alle Katzen breit* (Hamburg, 1986), 38.

88. Manfred Mixner, "Heimkehr nach Berlin" (see note 1), 29.

CHAPTER 12

Panem et Circenses:
Berlin's Anniversaries as Political Happenings

Gerhard Weiss

We live in the age of anniversaries. While we are troubled by the present and insecure about the future, we seek refuge and comfort in contemplating the past. We relish the milestones of history — not so much for what they really are, but for what we make of them today. *Habent sua fata anniversarii*, anniversaries, too, have their own fates, and it is usually more interesting to examine the mode of celebration than the event that is being celebrated. Anniversary celebrations tend to have their own agendas, for which history simply offers a convenient forum. They become happenings that reflect, amplify, and popularize the ideologies dominant in a society at a given time.

This is certainly true of any anniversary that commemorates the founding of Berlin. In this case, any reference to history is totally arbitrary. The often-cited date of October 28, 1237, offers documentary evidence of the existence not of Berlin, but of its sister city Cölln. Berlin proper is mentioned only seven years later, in another document dated January 26, 1244. Actually, the settlement history of the Spree River area is shrouded in speculation. Historians are still debating whether it was Germanic or Slavic inhabitants of the river valley who first proclaimed: "Ich bin ein Berliner." During the slow and tedious development from trading post and modest princely residence to the administrative center of Prussia and eventually to the capital of the German Empire, during its growth from a population of a few hundred tough frontierspeople to a sophisticated metropolitan citizenry of over 4 million, it never occurred to the Berliners to commemorate the founding of their city. There was no half-millennium celebration in 1737. In any case, those were the declining years of the Soldier King, whose Spartan rule would not have tolerated public frolicking. Even in 1887, when Berlin had just become the capital of a unified Germany, there were no voices suggesting the celebration of the city's 650th birthday. Berliners had never thought of their city as a museum. They never had developed a sense of

243

their own tradition. Berliners looked to the future, not to the past. They were always ready to tear down the old to make room for the new.

It has been left to our nostalgia-ridden twentieth century to discover the Berlin anniversaries. Initial discussions concerning the possible celebration of a septcentennial began shortly after the end of the First World War, when the country was in a state of hopelessness and despair and the people seemed to have lost faith in their own tradition. Ernst Kaeber, an excellent historian and then director of the city archives, suggested that the year 1237 should be declared the official date of the city's beginnings, so that one could plan a 700th Anniversary Celebration for 1937. The purpose of the jubilee was pragmatic and geared to the needs of post-World War I Berlin: it was to create a sense of history and identity among its citizens, many of whom had only recently moved there or were at best second-generation Berliners. Kaeber hoped to create a sense of roots among Berliners and a pride in and identification with their city's varied past.[1]

When in 1933 the National Socialists seized control of the city government, Ernst Kaeber's festival concepts were quickly pushed aside, and he himself was given early retirement. The new regime had a very different agenda. Now Berlin was to be presented as the capital of a newly awakened Germany. One no longer worried much about commemorating the past or preserving historical accuracy. How little the Third Reich cared about Berlin's historical image can be seen by the fact that on January 30, 1937, at the beginning of the anniversary year, Hitler proclaimed his plan for a new Berlin, the notorious Speer Plan, which envisaged a total rebuilding of the center city and its conversion into a gigantic "Germania," the capital of the Thousand Year Reich. All through 1937, venerable buildings in the heart of Berlin were torn down (such as the Schlüterhaus, the Palais Schwerin, the Ephraim Palais, the Krögel), destroying Berlin's historical substance at the very moment when one pretended to celebrate it.[2]

Kaeber's modest plan for the Septcentennial Celebration was transformed into a typical National Socialist extravaganza. The very founding of Berlin was declared a conscious act of German expansion to the East. Indeed, just before the festival opened in August 1937, the governing mayor and city president, Lippert, publicly announced new archaeological discoveries in the Berlin area that, he promised, would once and for all lay to rest "the old fairy tale of the Sorbic 'fishing village' as the nucleus of Berlin."[3]

The 700-Year Celebration was actually limited to one week, August 14 through 22, exactly one year after the successful Olympic Games in Berlin.[4] It was structured in such a way that the euphoria of 1936 could be revived. Many of the festival events took place in the Olympic Stadium, which had stood empty for almost a year. Berliners were particularly moved when, at least for one week, the suburban railway station "Reichssportfeld" was taken out of mothballs. The spirit of 1936 had obviously returned.[5]

What developed was a typical Third Reich spectacle, with mass events, parades, and omnipresent flags. During the jubilee week, Berlin's central avenue, Unter den Linden, sported special festival columns (which could conveniently be kept up for Mussolini's state visit in September). There was band music everywhere, reminding Berliners that they lived in the capital of a country whose military spirit had been reawakened. The historic residences of those the Nazis considered important Berliners were specially marked. The *Berliner Lokal-Anzeiger* of July 9 lists them in order of significance: Horst Wessel (the notorious pimp who as an early member of the Nazi party had been killed by the Communists) was ranked above classic Berlin literary figures such as E. T. A. Hoffmann and Wilhelm Raabe. All homeowners and apartment dwellers were admonished to fly the swastika flag. At the same time, special warnings were issued reminding Berliners that it was against the law to show the national colors if there were non-Aryans in the house.

Even though the celebration was full of pomp and circumstance, it actually was more a local than a national affair. It was constantly in danger of being overshadowed in the media by the Song Festival in Breslau, the Storm Trooper Sports Festival, and Mussolini's approaching state visit. In contrast to the Olympic Games of 1936, and to the 750th Anniversary Celebration in 1987, there was hardly any international resonance. The *New York Times*, for example, devoted only a brief paragraph to the events. William Shirer never mentioned it in his *Berlin Diary*, even though he was in the city at that time.

Even Hitler and Göring were out of town during the festivities. Hitler was in Nuremberg, making arrangements for the party rally, then in Bayreuth to attend the Wagner Festival; Göring was on vacation. They sent brief congratulatory telegrams that were effusively answered with proclamations of Berlin's loyalty to the Nazi state. Hitler's greetings were particularly telling: "The City of Berlin can look back with pride on its ascent. I hope with confidence that through the truly monumental building projects that will commence next year [Berlin] will acquire more and more the character of a truly worthy capital of the Third, that is to say: the German Reich."[6] Goebbels, the only top-ranking government official in town, opened the festival with a special birthday wish for the *Reichshauptstadt* (Capital of the Reich), a word that was repeated ad nauseam in those days: "I wish for the Reich's capital Berlin that the city may remain for all the future the way it is: industrious, fanatical, generous and full of the joy of life, in a word, National Socialistic."[7]

The dominant themes of the festival were Berlin's military history, the eminence of the princes and rulers as organizers and guarantors of law and order, the Jewish threat and, above all, the worship of authority. That was reflected not only in the various festival publications, such as the special edition of the *Berliner Illustrirte* and the official program booklet, but also in the two major events of the week, the festival parade and the mass spectacle in the Olympic arena. The parade consisted of 1,500 participants. There were fifty floats and fifteen hand-carried displays. It proceeded from the northwestern section of the city through the center and ended at the eastern edge of town. It was a massive march that took more than five hours and was cheered by 2 million spectators. The parade offered segments of Berlin's history, showing knights in armor, princes in battle dress, generals, and soldiers. Civilian life was portrayed in idyllic images taken from the Biedermeier period. The final segment of the pageant presented the accomplishments of National Socialist Berlin, the New Berlin in the New Reich.[8] The *Berliner Tageblatt*, in its report of August 17, 1937, raved:

> But those images of the pageant that really shook one up were the images
> of the third section. Our time! Our accomplishments. And our creative
> forces. The flags of the Third Reich led the way. The tremendous
> achievements of our technology, our transportation industry, the postal
> service, the National Railways, industry, air transport, radio, and then: the
> sound of marching steps. And, rejoicing without end. The Führer's
> personal guards, and behind them, in splendid marching column, the men
> [of the Labor Service] with their spades. The veterans, the SA, the SS,
> Hitler Youth, the National Socialist Transportation Corps, the Civil
> Defense Organization. The Reich Nutrition Service carries its symbols
> past. . . . Wonderful the floats of the organization "Strength through Joy":
> characters from plays currently shown in Strength through Joy theaters,
> high on his horse Götz von Berlichingen, riding with Frau Luna. . . .[9]

Marchers carried banners with quotations from speeches by Goebbels, and the parade closed with a team of Hitler Youth boys, "sun-tanned from their vacations and summer camp," as symbol of the future in the National Socialist state. The message of the festival parade was abundantly clear: it was pure Nazi propaganda.

The event at the Olympic Stadium followed a very similar thrust. It was a carefully orchestrated performance, reminiscent of Leni Riefenstahl's *Triumph of the Will*. The extravaganza showed "Berlin in Seven Centuries of German History." The audience was ecstatic. Searchlights illuminated the flags in the night sky and added to the grandiose spectacle in which masses of people (many drawn from the armed forces) re-created a Nazi version of the history of Berlin. To cite one example, one scene described the arrival of the army of Frederick the Great: "A unique and glorious picture of soldierly discipline and military splendor was the entrance of the 'Langen Kerle' into the stadium. A symphony of the colors blue, red, and white. A thousand men — one step, a thousand men — one line. The joyous shouts of a hundred thousand [spectators] roared until the last man had again marched out."[10]

The 700-Year Celebration closed with massive fireworks, the likes of which, it was said, Berlin had never seen before. The newspapers reported that for thirty minutes the most glorious bombs rained over the Königsplatz in the center of town, and over the Kreuzberg area. Three years later, the first real bombs fell on precisely the same areas of the city—an irony of history.

To be sure, there were also harmless activities during this festival, such as historical marketplaces, vintage buses, shooting contests, and the usual fun and games in period costumes. Yet, the basic ideological message could never be ignored: Berlin is the capital of the Third Reich, the center of an authoritarian state, aware of its German-Aryan heritage and of its Prussian military tradition. Its history had been reinterpreted to fit the National Socialist mold. Berlin, as Goebbels proclaimed, in the past had been the reddest city this side of Moscow. Now it had become a truly German city. That was the lesson to be learned from the 700-Year Celebration.

The week-long festival was soon forgotten, swept up by the political events of the coming years. No lasting monuments had been produced, no new museums opened, no ancient structures restored. It did not even yield a major publication. A *Geschichte Berlins*, finally published in 1943 after many war-induced delays, does not even mention the anniversary.[11] Today, there are few people left who can recall the events.

Fifty years after the Nazi celebration, a divided Berlin again decided to celebrate its anniversary. One is tempted to think that the authorities in both parts of the city wanted to seize the opportunity for a kind of historical restitution—that they planned the event to demonstrate that Berlin now is not what Berlin was then, that Berlin and Berliners had undergone a major change of heart since 1937. To some extent, that may indeed have been part of the agenda, although both East and West have maintained that there was no connection between the 1937 and 1987 celebrations. References to the antecedent of the 1987 jubilee are, indeed, sparse. Yet, when we survey the events in both parts of the city, much seemed to be a direct response to the spirit of 1937. Both East and West emphasized the role of the average citizen and the worker in the city's history, in direct contrast to the Nazi themes. Special commemorative celebrations took place in the old workers' districts in both parts of the city, in many instances acquainting a new generation with a past they had not known.

In West Berlin one was much concerned with giving proper emphasis to the Jews and their role in the development of Berlin's culture. The destruction of the Jewish community under the Nazis was shown as one of Berlin's great tragedies. Much was made of Moses Mendelssohn as a symbol of the enlightenment and of a German-Jewish symbiosis. Lessing's *Nathan der Weise* was performed in an open-air production in the Tiergarten. A special Alfred Döblin exhibition focused on the life and work of this great German-

Jewish writer, the author of the novel *Berlin Alexanderplatz*, whose books had been burned and who had been forced into exile by the Nazis. Jacob Steinhardt's works reminded Berliners of the gifted Jewish painters who once had been in their midst. The works of Jewish composers were extensively performed, and West Berlin's leading newspaper, *Der Tagesspiegel*, offered in installments Georg Hermann's novel, *Jettchen Gebert*, the story of a nineteenth-century Jewish family in Berlin, a loving portrayal of both the German and the Jewish cultural life of the time. Georg Hermann himself, who so much loved Berlin, perished at Auschwitz in 1943. A new generation of Berliners had to be made aware of what the Jews once meant to Berlin, and how greatly they had contributed to this city's culture.

In East Berlin, the image of the old city, destroyed first by the Nazis through their grandiose rebuilding plans, then by the war, was given a surrogate restoration in a somewhat stylized form more reminiscent of Rostock than Old Berlin. It is centered around the old Nicolai-Church, whose facade has been painstakingly preserved. The Ephraim Palace, razed by the Nazis in 1937, has now been rebuilt through a rare act of cooperation between the West Berlin Senate and the East German authorities. And, while in 1937 the celebration had a distinctly local, or at best regional character, in 1987 the emphasis in both sections of the city was on the international participation in the festivities.

The history of the 750th anniversary is in many ways a reflection of contemporary German history—emphases and accents in both parts of the city are quite different. When the West Berlin House of Representatives first discussed the jubilee, there was immediate consensus that this should be a common celebration, in which both parts of the city participate as partners. One representative even expressed hope that the same internationally recognized personality might present the keynote address both in East and West, as Thomas Mann had done in 1949 in Weimar and Frankfurt.[12] There was concern that a duplication of events would make Berlin the laughingstock of the world.

This cooperation, however, did not materialize. Instead, the Committee of the German Democratic Republic in Charge of Celebrating the 750th Anniversary of Berlin published nine theses, which traced the history of Berlin as seen by the GDR and emphasized the legitimacy of East Berlin as the capital of the republic. It refers to the West Berlin authorities as *Spalter*, "dividers," puppets of revisionists and imperialists. This pamphlet was one of the rare instances where actual cold-war rhetoric entered the celebration. It was, in any case, a flat rejection of any cooperation. From here on, the two parts proceeded in predictable fashion.

In West Berlin, the eyes remained open to the East. The official program contained information about events on either side of the wall, and visitors were urged to spend some time in East Berlin. East Berlin, on the other

hand, considered the West nonexistent and drew that part of the city as a
terra incognita, a white blot, usually marked "W. B." In a flyer published by
the Tourist Office of the GDR, we read: "In 1987, Berlin—the capital of the
German Democratic Republic (GDR)—celebrates the 750th anniversary of
the first documentation of the city with a year-long salute to its history and
culture." The other part of Berlin, beyond the wall, was totally ignored.
The West German postal service, on the other hand, issued a special commemorative stamp, showing the skyline of both West and East Berlin because, as the minister for postal affairs explained, "Berlin's horizon does not
end at the wall."[13]

It was the same birthday, but it was not the same celebration. What was
important to Berlin-GDR was the emphasis on its role as capital of the republic. The word *capital* was constantly used, as in 1937 the term *Reichshauptstadt* was employed. The new sense of history and tradition that permeates the GDR was reflected in many events. Thus the construction of a
city center in a pseudo-old-town style was an attempt to give the city a
much-needed heart and a focal point that had long been missing. It does indeed help to humanize Berlin.

The major event of East Berlin's festival was the historical pageant,
which, like the parade of 1937, combined images of the past with the
achievements of the present. There was a float commemorating the liberation of Berlin through the Red Army. Another showed the building of the
wall. As in 1937, several floats showed then-current productions of Berlin
theaters. In general, however, the pageant stressed precisely those elements
the Nazis had ignored: the role of the worker and the struggle of the labor
movement. In addition, representatives from the various districts of the
GDR greeted their capital with their own displays. The emphasis was again
on the capital motif. It is a truism that in earlier political constellations Berlin as capital had never won popularity contests. Therefore, this reiteration
of *unsere Hauptstadt* (our capital) was obviously designed to emphasize that
now Berlin had indeed been accepted as *volkseigen* (property of the people).
The preface to the *Thesen* states that "in the struggle for socialism and peace
in the heart of Europe the development of Berlin became simultaneously
more and more the concern of all citizens of our Republic."[14] The 750th
Anniversary in Berlin (East) was an extensive celebration of a state that had
gained self-confidence and that wanted to imbue its citizens with a feeling of
roots, legitimacy, and tradition.

While East Berlin emphasized its identity as capital, West Berlin stressed
its openness and international climate, its achievement of a degree of normalcy in an abnormal situation, its quality of life, especially in its ambitious
building programs (the International Building Exhibition took place in the
city in the midst of the festival), and its cultural significance as the traditional center of German enlightenment and tolerance. There was also the

hope that the festival would contribute to a deepening of the awareness of Berlin in the Federal Republic and the world, vital for the survival of the city. The anniversary was a convenient means to bring the city back into the limelight of world attention. Visits by the Queen of England, Charles and Princess Di, President Mitterand, and President Reagan to West Berlin were important aspects of this emphasis upon the close links to the West. "What would be these celebrations without the liberating nations" (Was wäre diese Feier ohne die Befreier") was the caustic comment of a *Spiegel* article reviewing success and failure of the two anniversaries.[15] This link with the outside world was an important aspect of West Berlin's celebration. It was no longer the *Insulaner* syndrome of the cold war. Rather, it was an emphasis on the many ties the city had and continues to have with the rest of Germany and with the world, a psychological denial of the borders that surround Berlin. This was reflected in the renewed interest in Berlin's old railyards. One of the major exhibitions, for example, was located in a restored nineteenth-century station and had as its theme the Journey to Berlin, a historic overview of travel to the city. Another, appropriately called *Mythos Berlin*, was staged on the territory of the old Anhalt Railway Station, once Berlin's main railroad hub. Serious discussions were afoot to restore this old station, not as a museum, but as the terminal for new fast trains to West Germany. *Mythos Berlin* displayed vintage railroad cars, and it also showed dream images of the city, of the total city, that has overcome the ugliness of the wall by building green embankments on either side. The exhibition was an attempt to break out of the confinement, but it also was a realization of what once had led to this confinement. Many artifacts, liberally spread over the exhibition grounds, constantly confronted the spectator with Germany's "undigested past," with that part of Berlin's recent history that lies at the roots of the city's present problems.

When the West Berlin parliament debated the 750th anniversary, strong voices were heard asking that the role of the immigrants from abroad should not be ignored and that the foreigners living in the city should experience the festival as their own celebration, to which they too would want to contribute as much as possible.[16] This was directed at the large Turkish population and other guest workers. They are so often considered the pariahs of West Berlin's society and live in near-slum conditions in some of the old tenement buildings. It was hoped that the festival might serve the educational and social goal of integrating the present-day outsiders. Obviously, in this the Berlin program planners did not succeed.

There were other voices, wanting to make the anniversary a memorial to the destruction of Berlin, begun by the Nazis, continued by the war, and completed by postwar city planners and modernizers. One representative of the Alternative Party exclaimed: "What kind of a city is this anyhow, in which tens of thousands can no longer find their birthplace today, because it has been torn down? What kind of a city is this in which one builds one museum after another, in order to show what one has lost . . . ?"[17]

The parliamentary debates offer a lively account of the planning process. The results have been very respectable. The goal of the festival, to reawaken an interest in and a consciousness of Berlin's history, seems to have been achieved. The activities of the 750th Anniversary Celebration in West Berlin offered a balanced picture of the city's past, its troubled present, and its hoped-for future. The very fact that the major exhibition hall, the Martin-Gropius-Bau, was located next to the wall, adjacent to the former Gestapo headquarters, within hailing distance of Göring's old Air Ministry and the ruin of the Anhalt Railway Station, places it squarely among the realities confronting Berlin. It is an environment not conducive to romantic escapism.

1937 and 1987 East—1987 West: three celebrations dedicated to the founding of the city of Berlin, three celebrations in which the historic event itself has been royally ignored. Three birthday parties, at which the guests celebrated themselves and brought the presents that pleased their own hearts. Three political events, for which each group wrote its own agenda. The Berlin anniversaries were political happenings in which systems and societies sought a reflection of themselves and tried to interpret their past to give meaning to their present. The culprit that started it all, Pastor Symeon of Cölln, whose name on a document in 1237 gave rise to the arbitrary birth date, was all but forgotten in the hoopla and activity connected with the celebrations. Forgotten? Not quite. A poster reproduction of the document sold briskly at the West Berlin Information Center.

NOTES

1. Heiner Kellig, "Jubiläum eines Jubiläumcoups," *Der Tagesspiegel*, 16 August 1987.
2. "Schlüterhaus fällt," *Berliner Lokal-Anzeiger*, 18 July 1937; see also various references in Thomas Ludewig, *Berlin, Geschichte einer deutschen Metropole* (Munich, 1986).
3. "Berlin gräbt Germanen-Siedlung aus," *Berliner Lokal-Anzeiger*, 8 August 1937. This and all subsequent translations by the author.
4. For a discussion of the 1937 celebration and contemporary pictures see also Gerhard Riecke, "Vom Dschungel zum Fahnenwald," in *Die Metropole. Industriekultur in Berlin im 20. Jahrhundert*, ed. Jochen Boberg, Tilman Fichter, Eckhart Gillen (Munich, 1986), 230–37.
5. "Ein Bahnhof erwachte," *Berliner Lokal-Anzeiger*, 20 August 1937.
6. "Glückwunsch des Führers," *Berliner Lokal-Anzeiger*, 16 August 1937: "Mit Stolz kann die Stadt Berlin auf ihren Aufstieg zurückblicken. Ich hoffe zuversichtlich, dass sie durch die gewaltige bauliche Neugestaltung, die im nächsten Jahre beginnen wird, immer mehr den Charakter einer wahrhaft würdigen Hauptstadt des Dritten und damit des Deutschen Reiches erhält."
7. *Berliner Lokal-Anzeiger*, 14 August 1937. "Der Reichshauptstadt Berlin wünsche ich für alle weitere Zukunft, dass sie so bleiben möge, wie sie ist: fleissig, fanatisch, grosszügig und lebensfreudig, mit einem Wort, nationalsozialistisch."

8. "Querschnitt durch 7 Jahrhunderte Berlin," *Berliner Lokal-Anzeiger*, 9 July 1937.

9. *Berliner Lokal-Anzeiger*, 17 August 1937. "Aber jene Bilder des Festzuges, die aufrüt-telten . . . —das waren die Bilder des dritten Teiles. Unsere Zeit! Unsere Leistung! Und unsere gestaltenden Kräfte! Die Fahnen des Dritten Reiches voran. Die gewaltigen Leistungen unserer Technik, unscres Verkehrs, Post, Reichsbahn, Industrie, Luftfahrt, Rundfunk. Und dann: Marschtritt. Und Jubel ohne Ende. Die Leibstandarte des Führers, und dahinter in einer prachtvollen Marschsäule die Männer des Spatens. Der Frontbann, die SA, die SS., die Jugend, das NSKK, Luftschutz. Der Reichsnährstand führt seine Symbole vorüber. . . . Wundervoll die Bilder von 'Kraft durch Freunde:' Figuren aus den Stücken, die in den KDF Theatern gespielt werden, hoch zu Ross, Götz reitet neben Frau Luna. . . . "

10. *Berliner Lokal-Anzeiger*, 19 August 1937. "Ein einzigartiges und herrliches Bild sol-datischer Zucht und militärischen Glanzes war der Einzug der Langen Kerls in das Stadion. Eine Sinfonie der Farben Blau, Rot und Weiss. Tausend Mann—ein Schritt, tausend Mann—eine Linie. Da brandete der Jubel der Hunderttausend auf bis der letzte Mann hinaus-marschierte."

11. E. F. Werner-Rades, *Reichshauptstadt Berlin* (Berlin, 1943).

12. Representative Kollat (SPD), *Abgeordnetenhaus von Berlin—9. Wahlperiode*, 41. Sitzung (10 March 1983).

13. *Das Parlament*, 24 January 1987: 24.

14. Komitee der Deutschen Demokratischen Republik zum 750 jährigen Bestehen von Berlin, *Thesen* (Berlin, 1986), 7. "Im Ringen um Sozialismus und Frieden im Herzen Europas wurde die Entwicklung Berlins zugleich immer mehr zur Sache aller Bürger unserer Repub-lik."

15. Karl Heinz Krüger, "Wat de kriegen kannst, det nimmste," *Der Spiegel*, 5 January 1987, 55–66.

16. Senator Volker Hassemer, "Senatsvorlage Nr. 1589/83," 30 June 1983, 7. (I am in-debted to Dietger Pforte, Cultural Section of the Senate of the City of Berlin, for making this material available to me.)

17. "Was ist denn das für eine Stadt, in der Zehntausende ihr Geburtshaus heute nicht wiederfinden, weil man es abgerissen hat?—Was ist denn das für eine Stadt, in der man ein Museum nach dem anderen baut, um zu zeigen, was man verloren hat . . . ?" Representative Jänicke (AL), *Abgeordnetenhaus von Berlin—9. Wahlperiode*, 44. Sitzung (5 May 1983), 2583.

Afterword: Writing about Berlin

Thomas Steinfeld

Berlin — the western half of the former imperial capital — is the only city that has been completely transformed into a monument without first having been exclusively the object of archaeology and history. Other cities have the status of monuments, of symbols, in addition to their function as domains of daily existence, as loci of industry, commerce, and politics. Berlin (West) is still different, different despite the fact that it has no fewer industrial parks, politicians, and brokers than other major cities. Yet only of Berlin can it be said — as it is in the introduction to this volume — that it "has become a city whose business is culture."

To be sure, the category "culture" must be understood very broadly — no, no, we are not talking of Las Vegas, although the toleration of gambling and prostitution also belongs to Berlin's cultural offerings. No, Berlin does not seek comparison with this city in the Nevada desert, but with the great capitals of the world, with London, Paris, New York. "We must wish for the future of the metropolis. We must wish for the future of Berlin as a metropolis," declares Karl Schwarz in his introduction to a three-volume exhibition catalog on just this topic.[1] And the expression of this wish provokes nothing so much as the antithetical conclusion that this very testimony of faith in Berlin as a metropolis itself exposes the lack of evidence to support it. To the extent that the metropolitan character of the city must be invoked, it is lacking in any basis. Urbanity becomes an artifact. And from Berlin's self-assurance of its status as a metropolis emerges — well, a demonstration of urbanity, a sort of metropolis-monument, in which even the daily functioning of a big city serves an apologetic aim.

"A city whose business is culture." Characteristic of this culture is the staging of business and political activities: Berlin (West) would not exist without the subventions from the federal budget of West Germany. Without the numerous tax incentives and generous financing programs, which eliminate most risks from investing in Berlin, industry and business would have

253

long ago departed for West Germany. This policy not only guarantees jobs and offsets the disadvantages of Berlin's geographical isolation: if these alone were the goals of federal subsidies, a planned economy and a generous social policy would be a more appropriate compensation. By support of investment, however, something else occurs: a free market as cultural project, a staging of private enterprise, which on the surface presents an image that could be mistaken for that of any Western metropolis. The splendid villas in Dahlem and the Grunewald, the misery of the tenements in Kreuzberg or in Wedding: they, too, belong to the monument that is Berlin, a demonstration of the principles of Western freedom.

For purely political reasons the situation of Berlin—as a city whose business is culture—has anticipated a trend now emergent in other cities for wholly other reasons. With the development of radically new communication and distribution techniques, the choice of location for business and industry has more and more been left open, thus threatening the economic raison d'être of many cities. Cities like Hamburg, Stuttgart, and Frankfurt have already responded to this phenomenon by investing in their attractiveness as places of cheerful consumption and higher education, of entertainment and culture, from which—as has become increasingly clear during the past decade—a new economic basis for these cities has emerged. "For reasons that are intimately connected to their superfluousness, their attractiveness grows in cultural, theoretical, and finally—for related motives—even economic respects."[2] On this basis a new rivalry between cities emerges, in which the small ones stand to lose, while the big ones find their limits only in the stature of their respective nations—like Paris, whose development works against all efforts at decentralization. Berlin is, to be sure, privileged in this competition—for political reasons. This city must be preserved as a metropolis, since its political function is based on this status. Berlin as a German Cleveland, Ohio—that would be a dismal "showcase of the West."

Berlin's status as a *Schaustadt*, a show city, as a staged metropolis, is not directed at compensating for the risk of economic atrophy, for its economy is itself a cultural project. It compensates, rather, for the city's loss of political function. President Kennedy's famous words, "Ich bin ein Berliner," were above all testimony to the desire to be as affected by Berlin's fate as if it were of direct national concern to the United States. To state it differently: in those days Berlin was the barometer of East-West relationships—there was the blockade and airlift of 1948–49, the workers' uprising in East Berlin in 1953, the construction of the wall in 1961. To the degree in which the relationship with the East bloc was normalized through treaties and tensions were lessened, the importance of the city in world politics diminished. In this new atmosphere, John le Carré's fictionalized exchange of spies on the Glienecke Bridge—complete with watchtower, wall, moving searchlights, and German shepherds—today appears almost like a gothic novel of the cold war. Now, the perspective might change again: the opening of the wall has not — at least not yet — reinstated Berlin as a capital, but it may open a new possibility of existence, which in fact was part of its former function: a gate to the East, much like Vienna.

Berlin (West) is a city whose existence depends on its being talked about. The Four Powers Agreement of 1971 dampened the discussion for a while. Berlin was relegated to the fringe of geopolitical discourse, and the decline of the student movement — however much wished for in the field of domestic politics — did little to reduce the threat of a growing provincialism.

Berlin's beginnings as a permanent cultural project are older than the fashionable urbanity that emerged in most of the major Western European cities as a feature of the political restoration of the late 1970s. In Berlin they date back to the era immediately after the Four Powers Agreement. Even then, there were festivals of world culture and theater, film festivals, and the famous performances of the Schaubühne, rock concerts, jazz concerts, and festivals of fools — much of this was intended as evidence of the universal validity of the discourse on Berlin, even before the city had become aestheticized, before those great celebrations of urban self-confidence had become a feature of the Berlin scene. Yet, these festivals, which hardly left a day that was not graced by some major cultural event, are to no small degree political projects; they are the embodiment of the principles for whose sake Berlin exists. Viewed from without, they are demonstrations of freedom as it can be consummately shown only by art; within Berlin they mark the transformation of politics into patronage. In the populism of such cultural policy there emerges the concept of a consensus between the governing powers and the city's inhabitants in which power seems to be relativized, as though something loftier were at stake than the furtherance of political interests. The proof of this consensus became the more manifest, the more freedom of culture encompassed those who previously had insisted on their distance from political power — on the one side the intellectuals, on the other Berlin's especially large alternative scene.

A string of cultural events filling every day of the year and attracting a more-or-less sizable audience constitutes a program, but it is qualitatively different from the transformation of the entire city into an aesthetic project, and the difference is not merely a matter of numbers. When Berlin celebrated its 750th anniversary in 1987, when in the following year it was designated the cultural capital of Europe, it attracted millions of visitors; hundreds of thousands witnessed some events. But this is only one side of this political success story. The other side was nowhere so apparent as in the cultural events in which there was little more to see than the city itself: the "city productions" of Marilyn Woods in the summer of 1986, for example, when mountain-climbers clambered down the facade of the Europa-Center on a rope and a crane swayed to music. Similarly, the outdoor exhibition *Mythos*

Berlin, held the following summer, linked a number of actual sites — some of them ruins — to constitute a chain of reflections on Berlin's history. That there was little to be experienced documents the final transition in Berlin's evolution from an aestheticized city to a *Gesamtkunstwerk*, a piece of art addressing every aspect of perception. Here urban self-confidence celebrates itself, and the mind rejoices in its unity with whatever it encounters. Here all critical intelligence ceases.

Since so much has been said about Berlin, it has become difficult to carry on the critical discourse about it with a free and unbiased spirit. The topic has become more or less corrupted, and the critical mind is faced with a fate that Walter Benjamin quite appropriately identified with an urban type: "In the *flâneur* the intelligentsia pays a visit to the market, ostensibly to look around, yet in reality to find a buyer."[3] On the other hand, it is by no means settled whether the talk about Berlin will retain its universal validity, not whether the culture of this metropolis, as it has been staged and distributed in the past several years, points beyond itself and will become a general culture.

Since this cannot be foreseen, precisely because of the variability of Berlin's political privileges, writing about Berlin, including scholarly writing, is pursued with conflicting feelings. One believes oneself to be writing for posterity and in reality is contributing to an apologetic. It is as with a biography of a living person: instead of a life being written about, it is being written.

A solution to the problem can only be expected if Berlin becomes "normal," if its existence and its meaning become separated. It is in this sense that the issue articulated in the introduction to this volume and addressed in its twelve essays — that uneasy relationship between Berlin and its culture — is to be understood.

NOTES

1. Karl Schwarz, "Die Metropolen wollen, Berlin als Metropole wollen," in *Die Zukunft der Metropolen: Paris, London, New York, Berlin*, ed. Karl Schwarz. (Berlin, 1984), vol. 1, 15.

2. Harald Jähner, "Tour in die Moderne," in *Die Unwirklichkeit der Städte: Großstadtdarstellungen zwischen Moderne und Postmoderne*, ed. Klaus R. Scherpe (Reinbek bei Hamburg, 1988), 227.

3. Walter Benjamin, "Paris, Capital of the Nineteenth Century," in *Reflections: Essays, Aphorisms, Autobiographical Writings*, ed. Peter Demetz, trans. Edmund Jephcott (New York, 1978), 156.

Contributors

John J. Czaplicka is an assistant professor of fine arts at Harvard University. Having published work on the pictorial image of the city, the German image of America (*Amerikabilder*), William Hogarth, and Edward Hopper, he is currently writing a book on the public monuments of Weimar Germany.

David Frisby is a reader in sociology at Glasgow University. Besides translating works by T. W. Adorno, G. Simmel, and K. O. Apel, he is the author of numerous books, including *Sociological Impressionism* (1981), *The Alienated Mind* (1983), and *Fragments of Modernity* (1986). Forthcoming works include *Simmel and Since* (1991) and *Detectives and Social Theory*.

Harald Hartung is a professor of literature at the Technische Universität in Berlin, where he has lived since 1967. He has published five books of poetry and two books of criticism, and is a regular contributor to the *Neue Rundschau, Merkur*, and the *Frankfurter Allgemeine Zeitung*. His study of contemporary German poetry, *Deutsche Lyrik seit 1965*, appeared in 1985.

Harald Jähner is currently director for press and public affairs at the House of World Cultures in Berlin. He has written extensively on urban culture and is the author of *Erzählter, montierter, soufflierter Text: Zur Konstruktion des Romans* Berlin Alexanderplatz *von Alfred Döblin* (1984), as well as coeditor of *Alfred Döblin zum Beispiel — Stadt und Literatur* (1987).

Peter Jelavich is an associate professor of history at the University of Texas, Austin, where he teaches modern European intellectual and cultural history. He is the author of *Munich and Theatrical Modernism: Politics, Playwriting, and Performance, 1890-1914* (1985), and is currently completing a study of cabarets in Berlin from 1901 to 1944.

Beth Irwin Lewis is an adjunct professor of art history at the College of Wooster. Lewis is currently coauthoring a social history of modern German art with Joan Weinstein, and her publications include *Georg Grosz: Art and Politics in the Weimar Republic* and *Grosz/Heartfield: The Artist as Social Critic*.

Her essay in this collection is part of an extended study of misogynist attitudes and images among German artists in the early decades of this century.

Lothar Müller is a member of the department of comparative literature at the Free University of Berlin. He is the author of *Die kranke Seele und das Licht der Erkenntnis: Karl Philipp Moritzs* Anton Reiser (1987), and has edited the writings of art critic Leo Popper in *Leo Popper, Schwere und Abstraktion* (1987).

Dorothy Rosenberg is a Five College Scholar at Smith College with extensive research experience in the German Democratic Republic. In addition to numerous articles, she is the author of *The Daughters of Eve: Women Writers of the German Democratic Republic* (1991).

Thomas Steinfeld is an editor. He received his Ph.D. from the Free University of Berlin in 1983 and has been a visiting professor at the University of Calgary and the University of Montreal. He has published on German and American literature, German as a second language, rhetoric, poststructuralism, and the history of academe.

Linda Schulte-Sasse is an assistant professor of German at Macalester College. She has published several articles on Weimar and Nazi cinema, is coeditor of *Film and Politics in the Weimar Republic* (1984), and has completed a book on Nazi cinema's appropriation of history as a mirror fortifying individual and collective identity.

Gerhard Weiss is a professor of German at the University of Minnesota, Minneapolis. In addition to research and publication in German literature of the seventeenth and late nineteenth and early twentieth centuries, he was founding editor of the *Minnesota Monographs in the Humanities* as well as editor of *Die Unterrichtspraxis*.

Index

Index

Page numbers in boldface indicate illustrations.

Vienna, 41, 102, 171, 254
Voss, Julius von, 96

Walden, Herwarth, 224
Waldoff, Claire, 100, 103, 104
Wall, Berlin. *See* Berlin
Weber, Max, 3, 42, 47

Westheim, Paul, 61, 132
Wolf, Christa, xx, 200, 211, 212
Wolzogen, Ernst von, 98, 100
Wunschkonzert, 178, 180, 181, 183, 184

Zille, Heinrich, xv, 16, **19**, 30, 46, 86, 104

Charles W. Haxthausen is associate professor of art history at the University of Minnesota, where he has taught since 1985. He has also taught at Indiana, Harvard, Columbia, and Duke universities. His publications include *Paul Klee: The Formative Years* (1981) and the exhibition catalog, *Modern German Masterpieces from the St. Louis Art Museum* (1986). His current projects include a collection of case studies on approaches to imagery in early twentieth-century German art.

Heidrun Suhr is deputy director of the New York office of the DAAD (German Academic Exchange Service) and teaches in the German department of New York University. From 1984 to 1989, she was a DAAD German studies visiting professor at the University of Minnesota. Suhr has also taught at the Universität Hamburg and the Université de Montréal. Her publications include *Englische Romanautorinnen im 18. Jahrhundert* (1983) and articles on contemporary literature and minority studies.